The People's England

The PEOPLE'S ENGLAND

Alan Ereira

Routledge & Kegan Paul

London, Boston and Henley

First published in 1981
by Routledge & Kegan Paul Ltd
39 Store Street, London WC1E 7DD
9 Park Street, Boston, Mass. 02108, USA and
Broadway House, Newtown Road,
Henley-on-Thames, Oxon RG9 1EN

Set in 10/12 Linoterm Baskerville
by Rowland Phototypesetting Ltd, Bury St Edmunds, Suffolk
and printed in Great Britain by
Redwood Burn Ltd, Trowbridge and Esher

British Library Cataloguing in Publication Data
Ereira, Alan
The people's England.
1. Great Britain – Social life and customs
2. Labor and laboring classes – Great Britain –
History
I. Title
941.07 DA470 80–41526

ISBN 0 7100 0596 2

TO MY FATHER

Contents

Illustrations

FIGURES

Preface

It is obviously impossible to write a book of this kind without the help of a great many people. Some of them are specifically acknowledged in my Note on sources. Some I would like to thank here by name: David Robins and Professor Peter Mathias, who read the draft and rescued me from some of my errors; Stella Hanson who typed it and who also proved a perceptive critic; and my wife Sarah who not only put up with me and was obliged to act as sounding-board for innumerable drafts, but who also undertook a major part of the picture research and the compilation of the index.

I would also like to thank the staff of the many institutions who helped me find the material on which the book is based – especially at the Middlesex Record Office, the Public Record Office, the British Library, the local studies sections of the public libraries in Birmingham, Manchester and Leeds, the Senate House Library, The Society of Antiquaries of London, the Hertfordshire Record Office, the Imperial War Museum, The National Army Museum and the National Maritime Museum, and the librarians of the BBC's Central Reference Library, whose eclectic knowledge and even more eclectic collection contributed some of the more curious insights.

Many people have helped me to tell the story truthfully. Where I have failed, the fault is entirely mine.

Alan Ereira

Acknowledgments

The author and publishers gratefully acknowledge the assistance of the following for the provision of illustrative material, and for allowing it to be reproduced: British Broadcasting Corporation (31, 91, 99); British Library (38, 51, 68, 69, 70, 92); Express and News Feature Services (81); Greater London Council, Middlesex Records (2, 3); Imperial War Museum (15, 16, 35); Kirklees Libraries and Museums Service (42); Leyland Historic Vehicles Ltd (52); Manchester Central Library (43, 44, 48, 73); Mansell Collection (1, 45, 57, 74, 75, 76); Mary Evans Picture Library (39); Museum of London (17, 18, 19, 20, 21, 82, 83, 84, 85, 86); Museum of Rural Life, Reading (6); National Army Museum (28, 29, 30, 33, 34, 36, 37, 50); National Coal Board (97, 98, 100, 101, 102, 104); The National Maritime Museum, London (54, 55, 56, 58, 59, 60, 62, 64, 65, 66, 67); Newcastle Literary and Philosophical Society (94); The North of England Institute of Mining and Mechanical Engineers (95, 103); Public Record Office (5, 47); The Science Museum (7, 8, 9); Tolson Memorial Museum (41); The Trades Union Congress Library (12); Trinity College, Cambridge (24); University of London Library (4); Victoria and Albert Museum (22, 26). Illustrations 10 and 49 are reproduced by courtesy of Birmingham Public Libraries, Local Studies Department; illustration 79, from a photograph in the Horace Warner Collection, is reproduced by permission of Hoxton Hall; illustration 93 is reproduced by kind permission of the *Guardian*; illustration 71 is reproduced by permission of Sir Edward Hulton, Hulton Publications Ltd.

Introduction

England, the first industrial nation, had its commercial history written in terms of entrepreneurs and empire-builders; its social history was about Lord Shaftesbury and Florence Nightingale; its political history was about Whigs and Tories.

The England that approaches 1984 is another country. Power has flowed away from the commercial classes, and the stubborn disputes which rack the life of the country are rooted in a past that was hardly recorded in their ascendancy.

When G. M. Trevelyan produced his *British Social History* in 1942, he described it as 'history with the politics left out'. Socialists and Marxists, as well as Whigs and Tories, shared that view. The great mass of people were portrayed as living their lives outside the political world, with their prospects of happiness or misery in the hands of their employers, their rulers, or impersonal economic and historical forces, according to the ideology of the historian. When they acted, it was in blind and helpless rage, as 'mobs'.

A new generation of historians has set out to explore the conscious participation of the poor in their own history. E. P. Thompson, in a work of central importance, *The Making of the English Working Class* (1963) depicted the traditions, experiences and political attitudes of workers during the forty years or so after the French Revolution. He introduced that book by saying 'I am seeking to rescue the poor stockinger, the Luddite cropper, the "obsolete" hand-loom weaver, the "utopian" artisan, and even the deluded follower of Joanna Southcott, from the enormous condescension of posterity.' At the same time, George Rudé and Eric Hobsbawm were producing (and are still producing) a series of works which showed that 'the mob' was not a mindless rabble, and developed the notion of 'collective bargaining by riot'.

In addition, the development of 'urban studies' and the work of the History Workshops, organised by the socialist historians of Ruskin College under the guidance of Raphael Samuel, has led to a more precise understanding of the 'common people'. The old image of an undifferentiated mass has given way to a picture of many sorts and conditions of people, with different kinds of experiences and aspirations. A new range of subjects – leisure, drink, housing – have been explored as economists and sociologists have widened the study of the past. Historians have tempered the emphasis of these disciplines on statistics with a growing understanding of the value of oral history and personal recollection, for people in different parts of our society have had very different kinds of experience which cannot be understood by 'objective' studies alone.

I have tried to draw some of these threads together into a general – though very incomplete – picture of how our society has been experienced and created by some of the ordinary people who lived and worked in it in the last two hundred years. I have generally avoided speaking of 'the working class', because I want to stress the wide variety of experience which was buried under that blanket expression. For the same reason, I have divided the chapters not by chronology but by kinds of life. The story is based, not on great economic or social forces, but on personal aspirations – on the struggle of a wide range of people to create decent living standards for themselves and their children, and, in more recent times, to 'improve' themselves.

A great deal of the material in this book is drawn from evidence at trials, from letters and articles in newspapers, union journals and pamphlets – campaigning material, pointing out causes of dissatisfaction and making a case against some aspect of the society of its time. Even where I have interviewed people about their personal histories, much of what I report has been shaped by them into a campaigning statement.

No one would suppose, I think, that protest and complaint are the main themes of most people's lives. But it is from moments of crisis and statements of protest that we are offered insights into how people have understood their world – what they valued, and what they feared.

Suffering and poverty are not inventions of industrial society. But the changing forms of poverty, the changing response to suffering, and changing visions of the future are necessary contours of the map of our past. It is a map that we need, to understand the new country we live in.

London, 1979

Chapter 1
LABOURERS

1

The fault is great in man or woman
Who steals a goose from off the common
But what can plead that man's excuse
Who steals a common from the goose?

In the winter of 1766, Sir William Gibbons, lord of the manor of Stanwell in the county of Middlesex, fenced off the village common and told the villagers they had no right to use it.

There were few remarkable events in the life of an eighteenth-century English village. There were occasional local surprises, such as the day in 1756 when Sir William's father, having newly purchased the manor, brought two Negro slaves called Reyn and Guilford to be baptised. The astonished rector made a note in the parish register – 'Both of 'em, men grown up'. Everyone knew that the old man's family were leading figures in Barbados, but it was a shock to have heathen savages presented in church.

If the villagers worried that their new lords would treat the manor as a slave plantation, young Sir William gave them good cause. When he inherited the estate, he left his uncle Robert to look after affairs in the West Indies, while he concentrated on improving Stanwell. A sudden *coup* which would deprive a hundred families of the right to seek fuel and pasture their animals on the common was a startling beginning.

Every household in Stanwell shared the same traditional rights on the common. It was open heathland, a waste of scrubby grass, and it supported sadly undernourished animals. The sheep on it were compared to greyhounds. But for villagers like the Ride family, these animals were an important source of food, and turves from the heath served as free fuel.

The Rides had once been farmers, as indeed had every old village family. Stanwell's houses still retain their original positions to this day. They do not butt up against each other, crowding

1 Cottagers (from Pyne's sketchbook, 1806).

for frontage on the road in the modern way. These were farmhouses, and they are tucked among one another in a way that leaves space for barns and farmyards.

In the seventeenth century, when a Ride girl married, her father (the village blacksmith) was able to give her a dowry that included orchard, pasture and farming land. But the Rides had gradually sold their land; the last eight acres were bought by Gibbons in 1765. Richard Ride would have to support his family on his earnings as a thatcher: supplemented by the pigs, geese, sheep and chickens he could keep in his little farmyard and on the common.

Gibbons was buying land for the same reason that he wanted to plough up the common. Stanwell had once grown food only for itself, but now it had a cash market for its crops. London, with a tenth of the population of the whole country, was only fifteen miles away, and the turnpike road to Hyde Park Corner ran along the bottom of the Town Field. Hay and corn, fruit and potatoes could be converted into gold, and Sir William wanted to rebuild his house and create a park.

The villagers had no intention of being treated as a parcel of slaves. They marched up to the common and tore down the fence. Sir William issued writs and, since it appeared that these people might actually have a legal right to their common, he also applied for a private Act of parliament to give him the authority to enclose it.

The villagers knew that the Act could be stopped by a petition, if parliament accepted that petition. They also knew that Sir

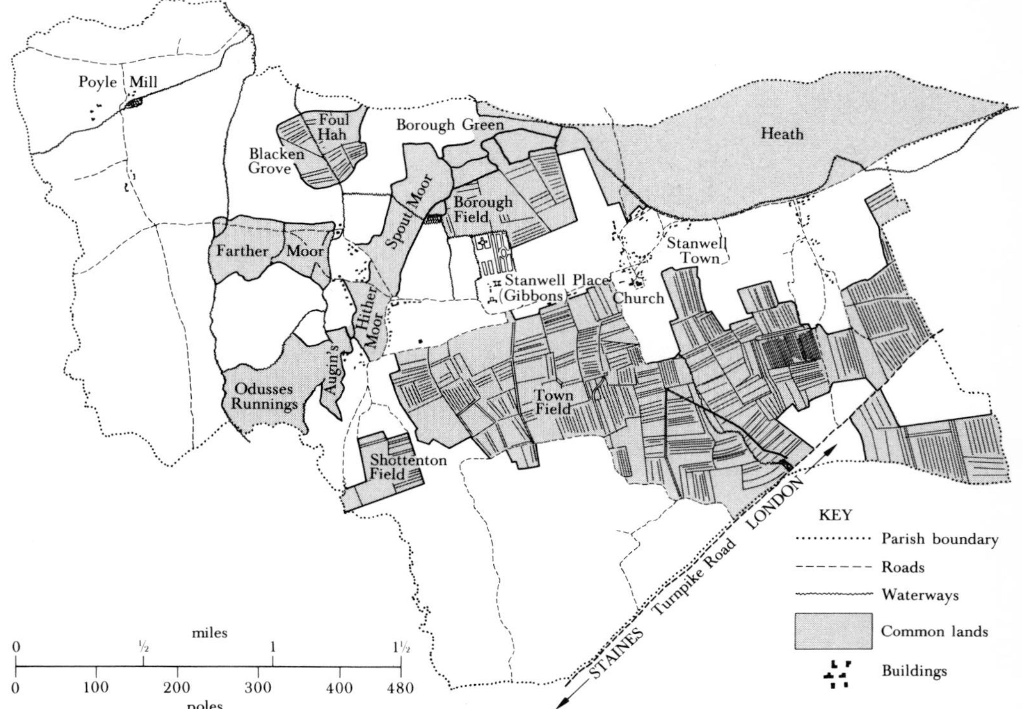

Figure 1 Stanwell village lands in 1748. Some land has already been enclosed and turned into private fields, but the large open fields are still divided into strips, and the heath in the north-east corner is used as common land.

William's father had been a Member of Parliament, and the House of Commons was not likely to listen to them unless their petition carried extraordinary weight.

They sent two: one from the cottagers, and one from the peasant farmers. They were, in effect, ignored, and Gibbons's enclosure bill was set down for a second reading on 26 February 1767. On that day the men of Stanwell arrived at Westminster in force, carrying a third and far more powerful petition.

Stanwell common was important to many people outside the parish. For Stanwell common was part of Hounslow Heath, and at least a dozen different parishes bordering the Heath made use of its 6,000 acres. The Stanwell men carried a petition from all of them, pointing out that they too had an interest in the Heath and that 'if the part of the Heath in Stanwell parish were enclosed it would be very injurious to all the owners and occupiers in the parish of Stanwell, except to the Lord of the Manor.'

> On Tuesday evening a great number of farmers were observed going along Pall Mall with cockades in their hats. On enquiring the reason, it appeared they all lived in or near the parish of Stanwell in

> the County of Middlesex, and they were returning to their wives and families to carry them the agreeable news of a Bill being rejected for inclosing the said common, which if being carried into execution might have been the ruin of a great number of families.[1]

They were fortunate in their timing. Parliament was in chaos. The opposition was defeating the government on major legislation, and delighting in demolishing a despotic administration which had given all the profitable jobs to its friends. The Gibbons family was known to be of the court party (their family motto was *Gratia est a rege pio* – 'Favours flow from a godly king') and the court party had lost its grip.

It was a sign of the times that John Wilkes, the government's old enemy, returned to England to stand again for parliament in 1768. He had been forced to flee to France after publishing violent attacks on the administration; now he felt the time had come to get back into the Commons in the name of the cause he had made his own: 'Whether English liberty shall be a reality or a shadow', especially for 'the middling and inferior set of people'. In March he stood as the candidate for Middlesex. John Ride owned the freehold of his house, and so had a vote. He cast it for 'Wilkes and liberty'.

Fifteen freeholders living in Stanwell travelled to the hustings in Brentford, where votes were cast in public amongst an excited crowd. Sir William was not one of them. Thirteen of them voted as John Ride did: they were peasant farmers. The two who voted against Wilkes were the rector, and an old man who had set his son up as a fruit wholesaler in London.

Sir William had lost the common, but he did not give up hope of trying to increase the value of his land. It was well known that modern farming methods could greatly increase the yield of farmland. Ditching and draining would make the land more productive; 'artificial' grasses would enrich the soil; winter feed crops such as turnips would enable animals to survive the winter in better condition; cross-ploughing the ground would break it up more effectively than traditional methods.

Unfortunately, all these improvements were impossible in Stanwell as it stood. Like thousands of other villages, its arable land was divided into narrow strips in vast open fields. The Town Field covered over 400 acres, but more than forty different farmers held strips in it. Any changes would require the co-operation of all of them, and they did not share Gibbons's enthusiasm for progress. They still used medieval ox-ploughs, and if they harnessed horses to the plough, it took six horses to drag it along, and three men to control it.

All farming in the open fields was governed by the jury of the manor court, a committee of villagers. It laid down the rules for everyone – which crops would be planted where, the first day of sowing and the last day of reaping, and the dates on which animals could be let into the fields to graze.

Sir William set about buying them out, as he had already bought out the Rides. It was an expensive business, but he was given substantial loans by one Edmund Hill, a wealthy man who wanted to invest heavily in Stanwell land. Between them, they reduced the number of farmers in the Town Field from forty to fourteen in twenty years. By purchase and sale the strips had been swapped around to form consolidated holdings, which were then fenced off and farmed in the new way. By 1789, 90 per cent of the Town Field had been enclosed.

Now Sir William made another attempt to obtain an enclosure Act. His object this time was not to seize the heath, but to force the remaining small farmers to accept the consolidation of their land, and complete the enclosure of the open fields. Everyone with rights on the common would be given a small plot of land in compensation, part of the heath would be farmed for the benefit of the poor, and another part would be sold at auction to pay the costs of the enclosure Act. The court jury would, of course, disappear, and statute law and rational agriculture would replace traditional rights and traditional inefficiency.

Many Middlesex parishes had already been enclosed in this way: more than 3,000 English parishes were enclosed by Act of parliament in the reign of George III, and probably the same number again were enclosed by private agreement, without Acts of parliament. Altogether some two to three million villagers were involved in a massive redistribution of land, and the constitutions of 6,000 village commonwealths were swept away.

The new proposal was tempting to families in the position of the Rides, and there were now many of them – cottagers dependent on cash earnings, who had sold their land and who just kept a few animals. The prospect of an acre or two of land, given free, was quite attractive. Richard Ride had two sons: he had bought a cottage for John, and Francis had taken out a £25 mortgage on another. Between them, with three homes, they would be given three allotments in compensation for their common rights.

The landowners in other parishes bordering the heath were less concerned to protect it than they had been twenty years before. The growing prosperity of trade to London had been accompanied by a growing crime rate. 'Our roads are so infested by highwaymen that it is dangerous stirring out almost by day', wrote Horace

Walpole in 1774; 'Lady Hertfordshire was attacked on Hounslow Heath at three in the afternoon.'

There were many who would agree with the writer of the *Report on the Agriculture of Middlesex* that the heath gave the worst sort of fuel to the poor, and was

> the constant rendezvous of gipsies, strolling players and other loose persons, living under tents which they carry with them from place to place, according to their convenience. . . . In short, the commons . . . are literally and proverbially a public nuisance.

There was no petition against the new enclosure bill, though some villagers refused to give their approval and others 'did not chuse to sign the Bill but made no Objection to the Inclosure'.

Francis and John Ride were given allotments of one and a quarter acres each on the heath. Between them lay the allotment of Ann Higgs. John bought Francis's allotment, and also the one next to it, which had been awarded to Thomas King. Thomas King lived in a hovel (an 'ancient cottage') on Stanwell Moor, and probably could not afford the compulsory fencing of his new land.

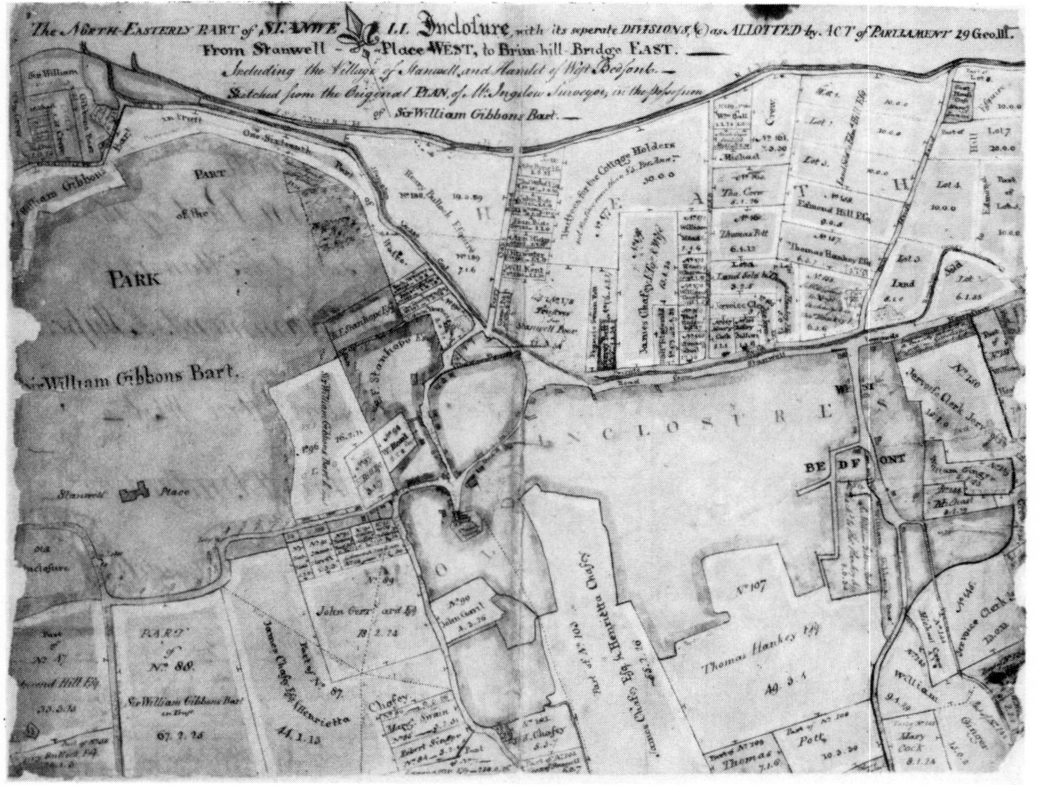

2 Part of the enclosure award of 1789. Richard Ride was given allotment 90, Francis was given 183 and John 185. 184 was given to Thomas King, 182 to Ann Higgs.

After about a year, Ann Higgs also sold her allotment to John. She lived in Reading, the widow of a grocer there, and needed the money to help raise her six children. Francis Ride, who had lost his common rights and sold his allotment, sank into debt as he struggled to live on his money earnings alone. John was unable to help; his new five-acre farm on the heath was swallowing money and giving nothing in return.

John Middleton, a reporter for the Board of Agriculture, visited Stanwell at this time, and described what he found. Most of the new smallholders on the heath had tried to plough it up for corn. They had made a large investment in seed-corn and fencing:

> They find that the dwarf-heath is of an imperishable nature, and that *it*, together with the remains of the *furze* and *bent*, is exceedingly troublesome to plough and harrow; it also keeps the ground too hollow and spongy, so that even rolling is no security, as immediately after the passing of the roll, the elasticity of the heath raises it to its former height. The crops come up well, and continue so till nearly half grown, at which time they die away, and produce not half a crop.

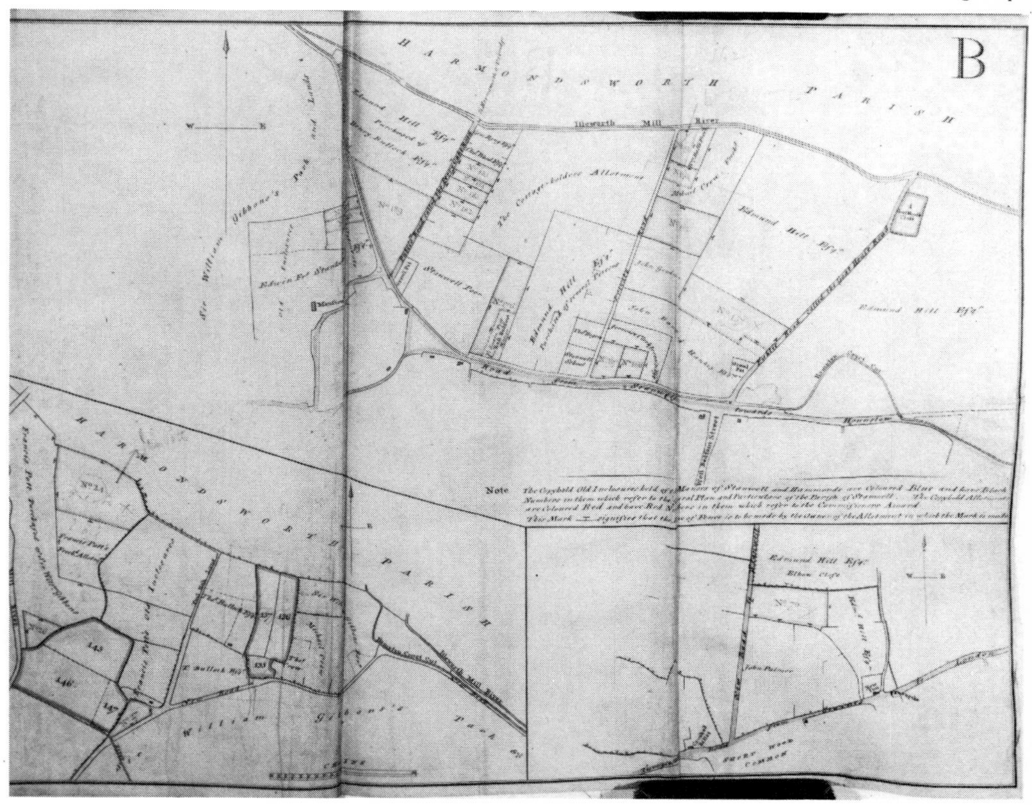

3 The land of Stanwell in 1796. Some of the old common land has been kept for the villagers, as tiny allotments and to raise crops on behalf of village charity, but the smallholdings on the heath have been bought up.

Edmund Hill, who had bought up the heathland sold at auction, had burnt off the furze to prepare the ground, and his crops were coming on well. But John Ride knew nothing about scientific farming. All he knew was the traditional wisdom.

John raised a loan of £70 to keep going, but he lost another crop and was obliged to sell out to Edmund Hill. He was ruined, and had to let his house. He seems to have gone to live with his aged father. Francis divided his cottage into two, letting half to a man known simply as Black. And in the Christmas of 1794 the charity for poor housekeepers paid three shillings to a Mrs Ride.

Two years later, John sold his house to a labourer from the nearby village of Feltham. The Rides were now members of a new class of villager created by the 'agricultural revolution'. They had neither land nor any hope of getting land: they had no right to enter the old common land, or to put animals on it. They were utterly dependent on what they could earn by their own labour through seasonal employment, on a daily basis, on other people's property. The village community had been cut off from the land.

The Rides had turned from small village farmers into day labourers in thirty years. The same process affected thousands of other families in a similar way. The land became more productive; rents rose sharply, and wealth was accumulated by some. But

Figure 2 The problem of trying to make ends meet on wages alone: average wages in Stanwell, compared to the price of bread.

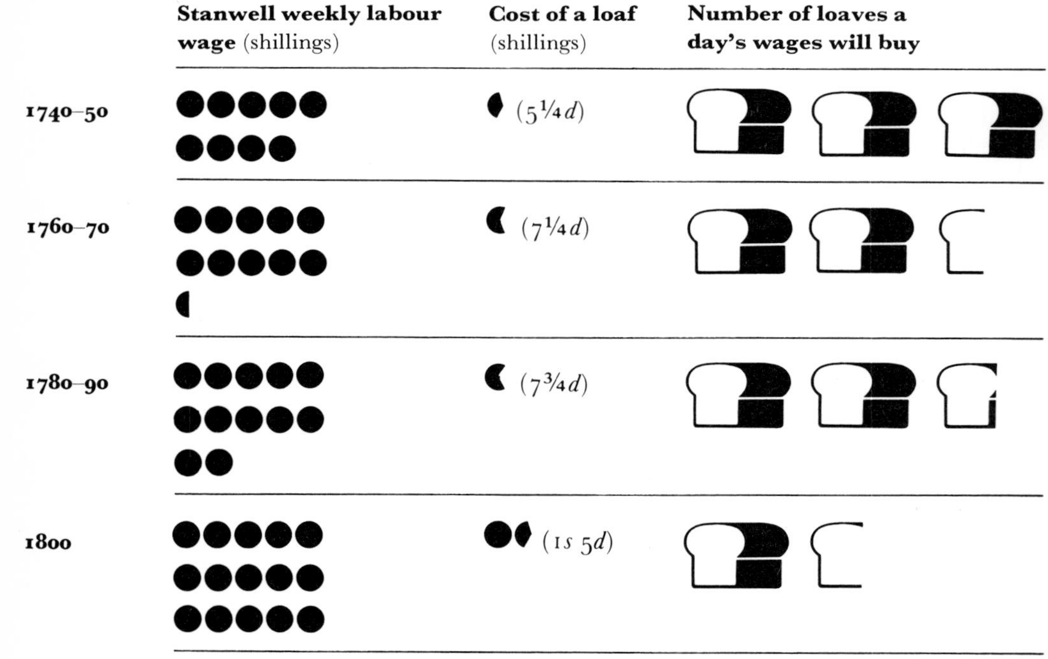

	Stanwell weekly labour wage (shillings)	**Cost of a loaf** (shillings)	**Number of loaves a day's wages will buy**
1740–50		(5¼*d*)	
1760–70		(7¼*d*)	
1780–90		(7¾*d*)	
1800		(1*s* 5*d*)	

Arthur Young, who had been one of the leading propagandists for modern farming, recognised that his own enthusiasm for enclosures had laid a curse on many. As he wrote, thousands could say, 'All I know is, I had a cow, and an Act of Parliament has taken it from me.'

David Davies, the rector of Cookham in Berkshire, put it even more bluntly:

> For a dubious economic benefit, an amazing number of people have been reduced from a comfortable state of partial independence to the precarious condition of mere hirelings, who when out of work immediately come on the parish.[2]

To which the *General Report on Enclosures* sternly replied, 'These little arable occupiers must give way to the general improvement of the kingdom and the burthens which accompany it.'

Tom Birt, of Tisbury in Wiltshire, was 23 years old in 1830. He was a sawyer. Although there was a saw-mill in the parish, on Linley Farm, Birt had not been employed at his trade for three years. By now he declared his profession as 'labourer', and was happy with whatever work he could find.

Birt was one among many. Ever since the end of the Napoleonic wars, when corn prices collapsed and a quarter of a million ex-soldiers were thrown onto the agricultural labour market, there had been widespread unemployment. The situation was worst in the corn growing counties of the south and east: the very counties which had been most subject to recent enclosures. The labourers there had lost the resources that would have helped them survive:

> The little farmhouses are falling into ruins, or are actually become cattle-sheds, or, at best, cottages, to contain a miserable labourer, who ought to have been a farmer, as his grandfather was.

This is William Cobbett, writing in 1800. Thirty years later, Cobbett described the condition of these labourers as he saw them on a tour through the eastern counties:

> The wages for those who are employed on the land are, through all the counties that I have come, 12 shillings a week for married men, and less for single ones; but a large part of them are not even at this season [spring] employed on the land. In walking out yesterday, I saw three poor fellows digging stone for the roads, who told me they never had anything but bread to eat, and water to wash it down.

The winter of 1830 was particularly hard for Birt, his wife and three small children. The only employment he could find during November was odd-jobbing, four miles from his home. He was paid seven shillings a week, out of which he had to pay a shilling a week for materials. No one could live on that wage; it would not buy two pounds of bread a day.

The old breed of farm labourers had been protected from extreme hardship by their contracts. Generally unmarried, they were hired at annual hiring fairs and were living-in servants, sharing a farmer's house and table. It was a system that offered food and shelter in season and out of it.

The disintegration of village farming created a new rural society, in which family men became day-labourers. Farmers began to prefer this arrangement, as they grew richer and built themselves new homes in the middle of their fields, away from the village. They became domesticated, with dinner services on their tables and piano lessons for their daughters; they did not want their labourers under the same roof. Besides, during the Napoleonic wars food became expensive – it was cheaper to pay a labourer than to feed him.

The logic of that argument led to the land being worked by starvelings, whose pay was too low to keep them alive. Tom Birt was a pauper, even when he was in work. The local magistrates supplemented his pay from the poor rate, in order to keep his family from actual starvation. Even so, if Birt's family ate anything more than bread they must have been given it – or else they stole it.

Until recently there had been winter work in Tisbury for anyone with the skill to use a flail. The parish was in the middle of rich corn lands, and threshing the corn was at least three months back-breaking work on every farm around. But that work had now disappeared, as the farmers had installed threshing machines. These machines were cumbersome and expensive, and by putting men out of work they led directly to increases in the poor rate. Threshing machines were invented in the 1780s, but for many years they were only used in large numbers in the north, where labour was scarcer. Eventually, however, southern farmers felt obliged to install the machines. By threshing the corn in days instead of weeks, a farmer could get his crop to market early, when prices were at their highest. By 1830, any Wiltshire farmer without a machine knew that his corn would come onto a market that was already glutted.

All over southern England, labourers were facing a winter of starvation, and the prospect that each year would be worse for them than the year before.

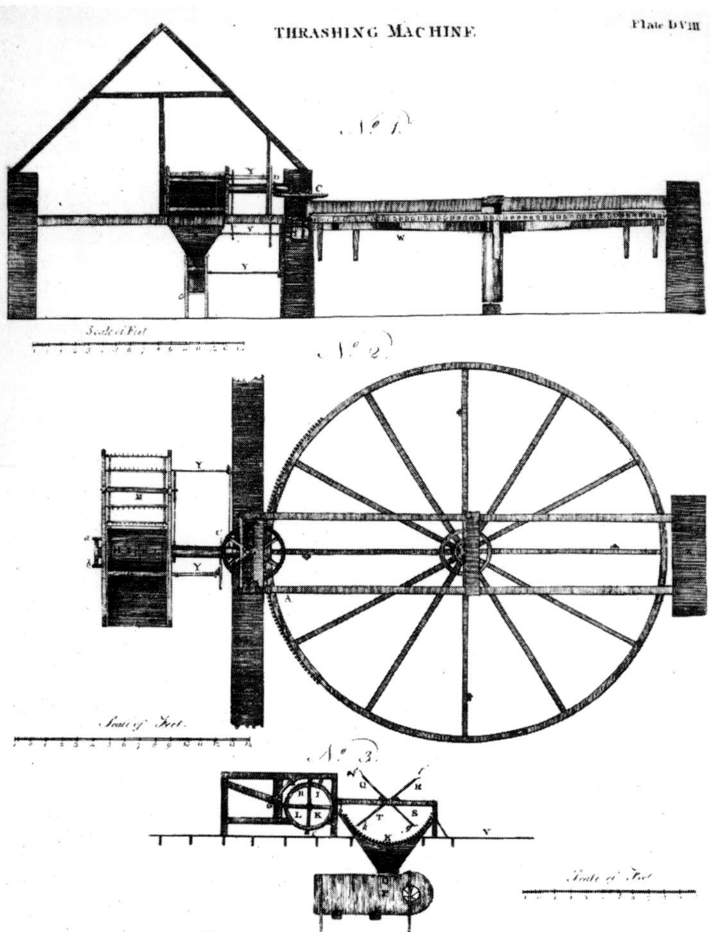

4 This illustration of a threshing machine appeared in the *Encyclopaedia Britannica*, 3rd edition, 1797: this one was powered by four horses. At that time machines were coming into use in northern England; they did not reach the south for another twenty years.

In the summer of 1830, villagers in Kent began setting fire to hayricks. By August, the same was happening in Surrey. Farmers and villagers were so cut off from each other that many farmers believed themselves to be victims of a widespread conspiracy. The fire-raisers encouraged the idea by claiming the credit for their work in the name of 'Captain Swing'. On 28 August, a threshing machine near Canterbury was smashed. Farmers were now receiving threatening letters, along such lines as:

> Sir,
> This is to acquaint you that if your thrashing machines are not destroyed by you directly we shall commence our labours.
>
> Signed on behalf
> of the whole
> Swing.

Barns burst into flames, mobs of labourers suddenly appeared and pulled the hated machines to pieces. In October the contagion spread into Sussex, and in November it came to Hampshire, Berkshire, Oxfordshire, Buckinghamshire, Dorset, Gloucestershire, Norfolk, Huntingdonshire, Lincolnshire and Wiltshire – including Tisbury.

Rumours abounded: 'gentlemen or strangers' were travelling round the country in 'green gigs', asking about wage rates and threshing machines, and using strange incendiary devices. Catholics and dissenters, it was said, were stirring up the people. It was hardly necessary to find plotters behind the unrest. Anyone who talked to the labourers could discover the true cause. Henry Hunt, a radical orator, travelling through the Wiltshire villages, was told, 'we don't want to do any mischief, but we want that poor children, when they go to bed, should have a belly full of tatoes instead of crying with half a belly full'.

It was in these circumstances that John Benett, Esquire, Justice of the Peace and Member of Parliament for the county, decided that it would be prudent to leave London and put in an appearance on his estate at Tisbury.

Benett was well-known and unpopular in the district:

> He's tall and he's thin and his legs are a twin,
> His visage the picture of grief, sir,
> He seems like a thing that's committed a sin,
> And less like a gent than a thief, sir.

His campaign for election had produced much scurrilous writing. He depended largely on intimidating voters with the help of a body of horsemen called the Wiltshire Cossacks, who travelled to the hustings to 'protect his voters'. It was said that the farmers and tradesmen who made up the Cossacks were members of the Wiltshire Yeomanry out of uniform.

Benett was an improving landlord. He had built himself a mansion at Tisbury, called Pyt House, and developed Pyt House Farm, and Linley Farm behind. He installed threshing machines on both. These were large machines. The one at Linley was water-driven, that on Pyt House Farm was powered by six horses, harnessed to a great horizontal wheel in a specially constructed wheel house. Machines of this kind were capable of driving all sorts of useful devices, as well as threshing corn: they could power turnip choppers, or pump water. The Linley machine could be used to power a circular saw in the saw-mill there, which may explain why Tom Birt was reduced to scraping around for odd jobs, instead of working at his trade of sawyer.

One writer on agricultural management described the threshing machine as 'The most valuable discovery, in machines of agriculture, which has been made for centuries past. Not merely as lessening human labour, but as relieving farm workmen from their most unhealthy employment.' It also relieved them of their livelihoods.

When a correspondent in *The Times* referred to the 'exceedingly low' wages in Benett's parish, and said that 'it is rarely that the poor are allowed more land than a very small slip of garden-ground', Benett riposted: 'The poor have . . . as much land as could be useful to them; and they can all rent land for potatoes.'

While Benett was preparing for the journey from London to his home, riots were breaking out all over the country; in three days sixty-one threshing machines were broken up by labourers. The magistrates of Devizes recommended an immediate increase in labourers wages to ten shillings a week. Benett, hurrying through the night, arrived at Pyt House at 4.0 a.m. and went to bed. A little later, Tom Birt rose. Birt left his house well before dawn and began walking the four miles to his work.

On the road, he met a crowd of labourers. They were led by two men, Charles Jerrard senior and his son, wearing particoloured sashes. Birt realised that this was a 'Swing' mob and dived into the hedge, but he had been seen. In evidence later he was to say, 'I wanted to get away, but they said that if I did not go with them they would kill me: so I was obliged to go. I tried to escape, but they would not let me.' And so Birt joined the crowd. They toured the early morning lanes, collecting men on their way to work on the turnpike road, or knocking them up in their houses. At eight o'clock Mr Benett was woken with the news that the men were assembling at Hindon, a small town about three miles north of his house. He set out with a party of men to meet them.

Years later, W. H. Hudson met an old man who recalled watching the labourers assemble:

> He was but a small boy, attending the Hindon school, when the rioters appeared on the scene, and he watched their entrance from the schoolhouse window. It was market-day, and the market was stopped by the invaders, and the agricultural machines brought for sale and exhibition were broken up. The picture that remains in his mind is of a great excited crowd in which men and cattle and sheep were mixed together in the wide street, which was the market place, and of shouting and noise of smashing machinery and finally of the mob pouring forth over the down on its way to the next village, he and other little boys following their march.[3]

The Squire met the labourers at Fonthill Gifford, on the road from Hindon to his farm. By now there were about 400 of them, forty or

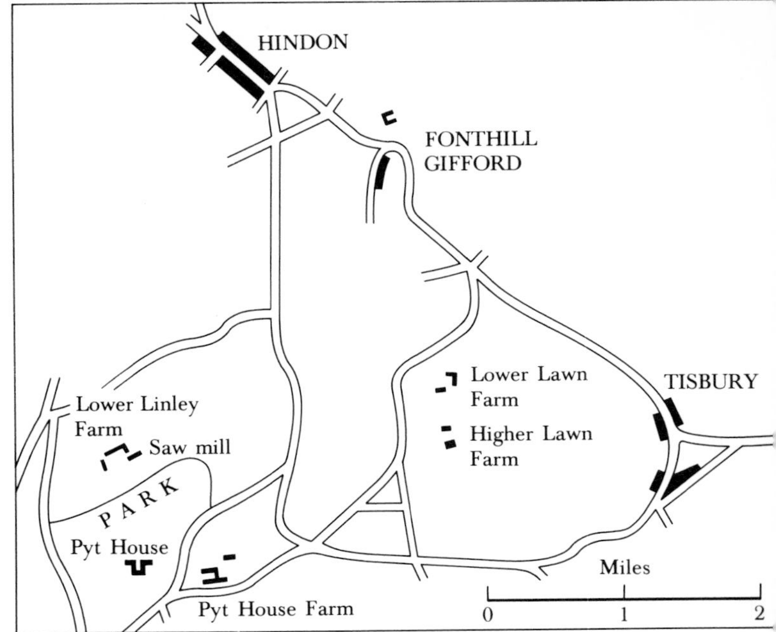

Figure 3 Tisbury, Hindon and Pyt House. The labourers presumably assembled in Hindon because it was a market day, and they could gather a crowd there; they then took a long way round to Pyt House in order to smash machines at Fonthill Gifford and Lawn Farm.

fifty carrying axes, the rest with sticks. Benett tried to adopt a paternal tone, speaking 'with firmness and good temper, and as loudly as I could speak'. He told the elder Jerrard, who had often appeared before him when he was a magistrate, that he was very sorry to see him at the head of such a riotous assembly; he was stern with Jerrard's son, saying, 'young man, that sash will hang you'. But the voice of authority no longer ruled. The young man carried a large stick; he walked up to Benett's horse and said, 'I don't care about hanging – I don't care'.

This was not a rioting mob: Benett claimed later that at one point they cheered him. He asked them whether they had any objection to him personally. 'They said they had not. They told me that they would not hurt a hair of my head; but they would break all the thrashing machines, and mine among the rest.' They also demanded two shillings a day in wages.

Benett produced a royal proclamation offering rewards of £50 for catching machine breakers, and £500 for catching fire-raisers. There was some indignation at the idea that they were fire-raisers, and he had to assure them that he had not supposed they were, 'and I really feel that conviction'. He tried to divide them by pointing out that 'any man, by informing against ten of you, will obtain at once £500', but they were not to be stopped, though some evidently needed to be encouraged by the rest to continue with their purpose.

By the King.

A

PROCLAMATION

Against lawless and disorderly persons assembled together to compel their Employers to raise wages, and committing various acts of outrage,

OFFERS A REWARD OF

FIFTY POUNDS

For apprehending each and every person so offending:

AND A REWARD OF

Five Hundred Pounds

FOR THE DISCOVERY OF EVERY INCENDIARY,

To be paid on Conviction by any County Magistrate.

NOVEMBER 25, 1830.

VARDY, PRINTER, WARMINSTER.

5 Posters announcing the royal proclamation were hurriedly printed.

They went to a nearby farm, and smashed the threshing machine there. They also raided a blacksmith's for tools. They went to a second farm, smashed the machine there, and then continued to Pyt House Farm.

Benett had arrived before them. He appeared on his horse and announced that they would open his barns and break his machines at their peril. Under his stern gaze they set about breaking up the great horse-wheel. Tom Birt was seen attacking a roof-beam of the wheelhouse with an axe.

Some of the labourers claimed that local farmers encouraged them in their work, and that one of the men appointed to guard the Pyt House machine shouted, 'That's it, my lads: down with it, my lads: I should like to see it down.' After about ten minutes the labourers put down their axes and hammers. Benett stared from his horse; the men stared back. One man, Thomas Topp, picked up a stone and threw it. It hit Benett in the face, covering his face with blood and knocking him unconscious. As his horse bolted, Benett's coachman, Tom Ball, pointed accusingly at Topp. Topp went for him with a sledgehammer.

Whatever bonds of hierarchy and duty had once held this community in balance were now broken, and when the men crossed Pyt House Park to get at the machine on Benett's other farm at Linley they had become a mob. And then Benett's Yeoman Cavalrymen arrived from Hindon.

WE the undersigned Magistrates acting in and for the Hundred of Gallow, in the County of Norfolk, do promise to use our utmost Endeavours and Influence we may possess, to prevail upon the Occupiers of Land in the said Hundred,

To discontinue the use of Thrashing Machines, and to take them to pieces.

Dated this 29th. day of November, 1830.

CHAS. TOWNSHEND.
ROBERT NORRIS.
EDW. MARSHAM.

6 Four days after the Pyt House affair, when machine-wrecking was at its height, magistrates in Norfolk issued this notice.

The labourers ran into the woods adjoining Pyt House, and there was a battle of sorts: trained gentry with muskets firing on labourers armed with sticks, stones and the tools they had used for breaking the machines. One labourer, John Harding was shot dead, many others were badly hurt. Twenty-five prisoners were taken. One of them was Tom Birt. They were carried off to Salisbury in carts.

Fifty years later, one of the drivers described how,

> the blood did trickle out of the wagons the whole way to Salisbury . . . they did cry out for summat to drink, poor fellows, but the cavalry wouldn't let them have nothing. They wouldn't. It were

> awful cold night and they were shramm'd with the frost and some on'em couldn' wag a bit. When we got to Salisbury we took one load to 'firmary and t'others to jail.[4]

When the senior officer in charge of keeping the peace, Lieutenant-Colonel Mair, visited the prisoners, they impressed him as reasonable men. They argued 'that their enemy was capital, and that if some should be allowed on bail to return to their families . . . (they) hoped they would evince by their loyal, industrious and peaceable conduct that they might be depended on'. Mair saw that this was done, and most of the men were allowed home. Mair also wrote to the Home Office on their behalf, saying that they did not receive a 'fair remuneration', and that something should be done to help them.

The Swing riots continued to spread for a few more weeks, but by the end of the year they had almost petered out. And then justice took its course.

The Tisbury men came up for trial on New Year's Day 1831, before a special commission in Salisbury. Altogether nearly 2,000 Swing cases were heard, over 300 of them in Salisbury. The farmers themselves were obliged to draw up the indictments: in this case, Benett was prosecutor and principal witness, and Tom Birt, having been seen to swing an axe, was sentenced to seven years transportation to Australia. Over 150 Wiltshire men went with him.

The labourers of Tisbury had been desperate. They had no right to land, no right to work, no right to a living wage. They were not revolutionaries out to overthrow the new order: they simply wanted the right to work again. But their actions made them outcasts. In court, in *The Times*, in parliament, they were held up as examples proving that the labouring poor were a rioting mob – and they must be crushed.

The King conferred special honour on the Wiltshire Yeomanry, as a tribute to their work. They were now to be styled the Royal Wiltshire Regiment of Yeomanry Cavalry, the first Yeomanry regiment to be so honoured.

On Wednesday 16 July 1835, the summer sun had set when Thomas Jordan and James Darvill left their homes in Rickmansworth and set out together through the lanes, with Darvill's dog at their heels. They would not return.

Setting out after dark they would normally have been taken for poachers. Darvill, aged 26, was a labourer: Jordan was five years older and had recently been widowed. He had three children to look after, one of whom was blind. But these men were not carrying snares or guns, and were not looking for game. They were on their way to work.

7 Watford tunnel face, by J. C. Bourne.

Four miles away, just outside Watford, the contractors for the London to Birmingham railway were tunnelling under Russell Wood. Men who could not earn their keep in the fields were only too pleased to have the chance to earn money labouring in the tunnel, even if it was a kind of work that they had never experienced before, demanding new skills and a new vocabulary. Jordan and Darvill had, for instance, learned what a 'night shift' meant, for that is where they were going:

> There was no day there and no peace: the shrill roar of escaping steam; the groans of mighty engines heaving ponderous loads of earth to the surface; the click-clack of lesser engines pumping dry the numerous springs by which the drift was intercepted; the reverberating thunder of the small blasts of powder fired upon the mining works; the rumble of trains, of trucks; the clatter of horses' feet; the clank of chains; the strain of cordage; and a myriad of other sounds,

accordant and discordant . . . with commands and countermands echoing about through air murky with the smoke and flame of burning tar-barrels, cressets and torches.

The London to Birmingham railway was the greatest earthwork that had been made. When it was completed, one of the engineers, Peter Lecount, calculated that four hundred million cubic feet of earth had been shifted, and that this put the Great Pyramid of Giza and the Great Wall of China wholly in the shade. His comparison made sense, because every cubic foot of soil moved in building the railway was excavated by men holding picks and shovels.

The track had to be dead level, with only the gentlest curves and only the most imperceptible gradients; it was reckoned that to climb a gradient of one in 300 needed twice the power of a level run, and the locomotives of the 1830s were hard pressed to manage that with a full load. To construct a suitable track meant filling in valleys with long embankments, slicing cuttings and building enormous tunnels, wide enough and high enough for trains to pass each other in safety. It required a great deal of manpower, and Peter Lecount made a virtue of that:

When the reader is informed, that for nearly three years, from 15,000 to 20,000 men were engaged on this work, taken almost invariably from the adjacent towns and villages, and that, in actual labour, nearly four millions have been expended (in earth-work, brick-work, brick-making etc.) among the local population, he will have some idea of how this would influence pauperism and the poor rates.[5]

There was indeed a great pool of pauperised labour to draw on. Despite a steady migration from country to town, the population of the agricultural counties doubled between 1750 and 1830. The problem of supporting the poor was so great that in 1834 the old Poor Law, which allowed magistrates to subsidise starvation wages, was swept away. From that date on, the only form of 'relief' available to an able-bodied man was the workhouse. Within three years, the amount being spent on the poor fell by more than two million pounds.

If Thomas Jordan and James Darvill were unable to find work, they would be stripped, searched and dressed in coarse workhouse costumes. Jordan's children would be taken from him and kept separately. They were fortunate that the railway passed their way, and that so much money was available to employ labourers. Between 1834 and 1836 about seventy million pounds was raised for railway building (ten times the poor rate of 1832). Railways were generally supposed to be profitable investments.

8 The interior of Kilsby tunnel, by J. C. Bourne.

The Watford tunnel was to be 1,700 yards long and twenty-five feet high. It was bored not only by digging in from either end, but also by drilling vertical shafts into the hill and working outwards from within. The shafts were dug with the help of a winding engine, or 'gin'. The gin was a large horizontal horse-wheel, on which was wound a rope, and it was used to lower men down the

9 The view from above Kilsby tunnel, on the London to Birmingham railway, by J. C. Bourne.

shaft, and to lift out the earth in great buckets. James Darvill was 'banksman', which is to say that he remained at the mouth of the shaft, looking after the gin.

Another worker in the tunnel, whose description of conditions was quoted earlier, was engaged at the age of 16 to steer the buckets away from the shaft sides:

> Placed upon the projecting edge of a scaffold some eighty feet above the level of the rails in the tunnel and one or two hundred feet below the surface of the earth, while brickworkers, masons and labourers were busy upon the brickwork of the shaft above, below and round me, while torches and huge fires in cressets were blazing everywhere . . . I was, in the midst of the din and smoke, to steer clear of the scaffold the descending earth-buckets . . . I was to clasp a pole with my left hand, hang over the abyss and steady the buckets with a stick held out in my right hand.

That particular job was vacant because the last boy, a runaway watchmaker's apprentice from Coventry, had worked three successive six-hour shifts and dropped down the shaft from exhaustion. The man in charge of the job warned his new employee of the dangers: 'Mind, if you fall, go clean down without doing any mischief. Last night I'd to pay for a new trowel that the little fool who was killed yesterday knocked out of a fellow's hand.'

The new boy, called Dick, survived, and soon he was taken out and offered slightly safer work. He joined a gang of 'navvies' working in the tunnel. Navvies (originally the 'navigators' who built the canals) were full-time railway builders, who travelled from one set of workings to another and had lost all connection with agricultural work. Lecount stressed the fact that his railway employed agricultural labour on a large scale, and was not wholly dependent on navvies, who

> are generally the terror of the surrounding country; they are as completely a class by themselves as the Gypsies. Possessed of all the daring recklessness of the Smuggler, without any of his redeeming qualities, their ferocious behaviour can only be equalled by the brutality of their language.

The gangs of workers were employed by small sub-contractors, and certainly included large numbers of navvies. The night shift that Jordan and Darvill were in consisted of five labourers and six bricklayers. The labourers were local men, but the bricklayers were navvies, from all over the country: Joseph Berker and William Byrd from Derbyshire, George Corrie from Somerset, Tomas Evans from Wales, Sylvanus Rubings from Leicestershire.

Navvies were distinguished from local labourers not only by the fact that they came from a great distance, but also by their dress and behaviour. Living in communal encampments, they developed a distinctive character. They wore moleskin trousers with rainbow waistcoats, and were generally violent, hard-drinking and ferociously hard working. According to report, it took a year to turn a man into a navvy: Dick had found that in practice the apprenticeship was not so rigorous.

> With my first fortnight's wages I had got me a suit of new moleskin and a pair of highlows [boots]; now, therefore, I had only to buy pick and shovel and my equipment was complete. My hands had become coarse, my face was sunburnt and my hair shaggy. What matter? I felt a hearty pride in myself and my prospects.

He had only to pay a fine of two gallons of beer to be accepted into a gang of navvies and given a navvy name – which, on account of his new gear, was Dandy Dick.

According to Dandy Dick, there were at least sixty gangs of navvies working in the tunnel. His own gang lived in a shanty near the tunnel mouth, and it was looked after by a crone named Old

Peg. On one side of the room were beer barrels, on the other, and at one end of the room, were berths fitted 'in a manner similar to the between-decks of an emigrant ship'. The room was full of dogs 'of the bull or lurcher breed; for a navvy's dog was, of course, either for fighting or poaching'. The far end of the room served as a kitchen.

> Over the fireplace, which was nearly central, there were also hung about a dozen guns. In the other corner was a large copper, beneath which a blazing fire was roaring: a volume of savoury steam was escaping from beneath the lid, and old Peg, muttering and spluttering ever and anon, threw on more coals and kept the copper boiling.

A shift lasted six hours, and was very heavy work. The shift that Jordan and Darvill shared was working ninety feet below ground. They were cutting through from the bottom of the shaft to the neighbouring working, and building tunnel walls in brick. Thomas Jordan had been given the job of superintending the brickwork.

When the two men arrived at Russell Wood on that Wednesday night they separated: Darvill went up with his dog to the horse and gin on the top of the shaft, while Jordan walked into the tunnel. The workings had already been connected with narrow tunnels that a man could walk through. Most of the excavation was complete, and Darvill had little to do.

Just what happened on that shift is unknown. But the story to emerge was that there was some uncertainty about the security of the roof in the narrow passage between the workings, and Jordan's team set about installing a cast-iron support. In order to fit it, Joseph Berker decided to cut away some of the chalk. According to Dandy Dick, Berker was drunk and was acting strictly against orders: anyway, the chalk came out, there was gravel beneath it and the roof collapsed.

At the top of the shaft, James Darvill was lying down, with his dog beside him, when he felt the ground shake. Slowly the whole mouth of the shaft, gin and all, began to slip down: a chasm was opening. He, his dog, the horse all slid into the pit: a stout timber landed across it and he was able to cling on. Darvill was the only member of the shift to escape destruction, though the horse, which fell nearly forty feet, was eventually dragged out unscathed. Darvill's survival was brief: he was crazed by the disaster, and died shortly afterwards, raving.

The shock of the deaths to the community around Watford was very great. Rubings' family came from Leicestershire to the funeral, as did Byrd's from Derbyshire. They were an affecting sight at church. So were Thomas Jordan's three children. It was a disaster on a scale which was quite new to the community. Fourteen men had died. Just as much of a shock was the behaviour of the navvies, as Henry Williams, a local historian, later recalled:

> Very great difficulty occurred in recovering the bodies of the unfortunate men, and the excitement that prevailed while the earth was being removed was very great. Thousands of people collected daily on the ground near the scene of the accident, which might be likened more to a fair than anything else; booths for the sale of beer and refreshments were erected, and a large trade was done, especially on the Sunday following the accident. The violin was an almost indispensable musical instrument at that time, and although the circumstance that called together so large a number of persons was of so solemn a nature, the fiddle was there nevertheless, and their hilarity could hardly be restrained when a mangled corpse was brought to the surface.[6]

One reason why it took a long time to recover the bodies was that, as the local paper put it, local labourers had 'betaken themselves to the labour of the harvest-field in preference to running the risk of life or limb in the work of excavating the tunnel'.

A year later, the line had moved on from Watford. The navvies' departure was very welcome. Henry Williams was 8 at the time, and the son of the beadle at Watford church:

> Although very young at the time the railway was made through Watford, I well remember the dreadful scenes frequently presented to the inhabitants. Scarcely a night passed without a drunken fight or a row at one of the public houses. The men were a terror to everybody, and respectable females were scarcely able to walk in the streets without meeting with some improper conduct from them. Black eyes and broken heads were the order of the day, and so daring were the navvies that the parish constables were really afraid of some of them . . . it was a great relief to them when the line was opened and they left the neighbourhood.

But the navvies had made a lasting impact on some families, for local labourers who had worked with them and survived had every reason to stay with their squalid, tough, cheerful gangs. The older, safer life of labouring in the fields could not support a family all the year round. Navvying was dangerous, but it paid well – Dandy Dick's very first job, guiding a tipping truck along the top of an embankment, paid twelve shillings a week.

Around the anniversary of the Watford disaster came a false rumour that there had been a tunnel collapse at Northchurch, about twelve miles further up the line. The local paper reported that 'females whose husbands and brothers were at work there' went over from St Albans to find out if the rumours were true. With the workhouse waiting behind, and the railway contractor beckoning ahead, the men were following the work. By 1848 there were nearly 200,000 men working on the railways.

A new kind of man was being created: the pick-and-shovel labourer, who worked on great public works. There was little future in tilling the land: perhaps there was a better one in tearing it apart.

4

Birmingham, at the northern end of Dandy Dick's railway line, was known as the 'toyshop of England'. The 'toys' were bits and pieces of brass and tinplate, the costume jewellery and bedsteads, buttons and screws, tin trays and gun-barrels that held Victorian England together and gave it its cheaper decorative flourishes.

Farm Street, Hoxton, was a working-class street about two miles from the city centre. In 1851, it housed 225 families, many of them in courts and back alleys. When the 'heads of the households' had to state their occupations in the census, nearly one in three said they were involved in metal work, hand-craft work, jewellery, button-making or gun-making. A further 25 per cent were engaged in the building trade, for Birmingham was spreading.

The city doubled in population every thirty years throughout the nineteenth century. Aston, the northern suburban district, more than doubled every twenty years while Victoria was queen.

> The richest crop for any field
> is a crop of bricks for it to yield.
> The richest crop that it can grow
> is a crop of houses in a row.

Will Thorne, who became a Labour MP and chairman of the Trades Union Congress, was born into a brick-making family in Farm Street in 1857, in a four-roomed house. 'Our house had no parlour', he wrote later. 'Perhaps it would have been superfluous, for as both my father and mother worked in and around the brickfields there was little time for using parlours. Twelve hours work was a short day then.' Looking back, he was struck by the inappropriate name of the street, 'I have no memories of the free air of a farm during those early far-off days, just the ugly houses and cobbly neglected streets that were my only playground.' In the 1851 census one householder in Farm Street did call himself an agricultural labourer – but he was 70 years old.

Life in Farm Street was nasty, brutish and often short: it figured high in the medical officer of health's annual statistics, sometimes

Farm Street in 1851: commonest occupations of the heads of households

Occupation	Number
'Toy making' (handcraft work, jewellery, button-making)	47
Building trades (building, painting, decorating, bricklaying, plumbing, brickmaking, glazing and slating)	39
Metalworking	19
Tradesmen, bookmakers, pawnbrokers	14
General labouring	12
Labouring servants (i.e. porters, packers, warehousemen, servants, gardeners, carters)	12
Coaches, waggons, carriages, horses	8
Gun work	7

taking the prize for the highest number of deaths from 'zymotic disease' of any street in Birmingham. 'Zymotic disease' was generally diarrhoea: the cause was polluted drinking water, and a sewage system more disgusting than a modern imagination can easily grasp.

Conditions were grim, but at least there was plenty of demand for bricks. The Birmingham Improvement Act had been passed in 1851, and so many streets were rebuilt in the 1860s that the *Birmingham Post* commented (on 12 June 1867):

> So rapidly are the landmarks of the town of Birmingham being changed that we may shortly be in a position to appreciate the story told of the Parisian, who, on returning at night to his lodgings, found that the house – and with it the whole street where he lived – had been demolished since the morning, and the lines of a new palatial block of buildings traced out amid the ruins.

There was thus every opportunity to find Will something useful to do once he could walk and talk and find his way about a little. Shortly after his sixth birthday he was put to work turning a wheel for a rope and twine spinner: 'I received 2*s.* 6*d.* per week, and worked from six in the morning until six at night, with a half hour for breakfast and one hour for dinner'. This was easier for a small child than heavy brickwork – it also avoided the seasonal nature of all work connected with the building trade. Will's father spent the summer on the tramp, working in brick works in different parts of Middlesex. In the winter he came back to Birmingham; he pro-

10 Court no. 1, Thomas Street, typical of inner-city Birmingham, about 1871.

bably did harvesting work on the way. Sometimes when he came back he would get work in the gasworks, which took on extra men for the winter. Many of these workers, who would be dismissed in the spring, were builder's labourers, navvies and men who went into the country for farming work in the summer.

It was not until he was 7 years old that Will Thorne got work on a brickfield. His father had been killed in a brawl, and his mother was sewing hooks and eyes onto cards for a penny-halfpenny per twelve gross (needles and cotton at her own expense). Will had to walk three miles each way to the brickfield where he carted 400–500 nine-pound bricks over a hot floor every day. It was a twelve hour day (not counting the walk to work) and eventually his pay rose to eight shillings a week.

Unfortunately, the child was then promoted to caring for one of the fires that baked the bricks. This involved fuelling the fire at night (and earned him an extra shilling). He was found to have fallen asleep one night and was sacked. He succeeded in finding work on another brickfield, but his mother grew increasingly worried about his health and the growing hunch to his back from stooping and carrying.

At 9 years of age, Will Thorne had to find a new profession. He moved to a succession of labouring jobs in the building trade – working for a plumber, sawing logs to make laths for lath-and-plaster work, collecting cow and human hair for mixing into plaster. He was growing up as a fully fledged member of the casual labouring class of a Victorian city, living on the very edge of starvation, with no education, no particular skill, no place in a wider community, and no reason to hope for any improvement. Surveys a few years later indicated that about 30 per cent of the urban population lived at this level or below it.

When Will was 14 the Franco-Prussian war broke out and he found work in a metal-rolling and ammunition factory. The work of the urban labourer was closely tied to economic and political events: perhaps that made urban labourers more politically conscious than rural workers. Certainly Will Thorne's fellow workers at Abraham's Metal-Rolling and Ammunition Works were well aware of the bargaining power the French and German demand for ammunition gave them, and so they struck for higher wages. They succeeded, but then the war ended, and Will was out of work again.

'There are few rosy patches, if any, in the fight for bread in the lives of the manual labourer with little skill or education. Just long years of drudging work in the past and in the future.' At 16 Will was labouring at a waggon works, then he was tapping nuts and bolts, and he worked his way through various jobs before finding his way back into the building trade. Or perhaps it is truer to say that the building trade found him, because in the mid-1870s it was a trade hungry for labour. There was a land boom: registered plans for houses and small shops in the borough soared from the 1867–74 average of 1,347 a year to 3,395 in 1875, falling only a little to 2,903 in 1876 and 2,700 in 1877. In 1875, too, the Artisans and Labourers Dwellings Act was passed, enabling local authorities to initiate slum clearance programmes. Joseph Chamberlain, the mayor of Birmingham, seized on this to reshape the centre of his city.

Central Birmingham had, by 1875, become an ungovernable warren of impoverished and hopeless 'scoundrels'. Things came to a head in March of that year, when some thieves robbed a room in the Bull's Head Inn in Fordrough Street, during a 'free and easy' – an early form of music hall promoted by pubs to attract business. 'They were seen by a young girl who gave the alarm. The thieves, however, contrived to get clear away, taking with them a vest, a pair of trousers and an empty cash box.' The whole proceeds of the robbery amounted to some seven shillings. On the next day, Sunday 7 March, one of the thieves was recognised in the Bull's Head. He was William Downs, a chandelier maker from the same street. The police were called, but as they were escorting Downs to the police station they had to pass through some of the roughest streets of the city – streets originally established by the labourers who built Birmingham's canal basin. As they passed down Navigation Street a crowd of thirty or forty young men collected. 'Can we see him go like that?' someone called. The answer was yelled back – 'No! Let's turn on the pigs'.

That was the evidence at the inquest on police constable Lines, who was fatally stabbed. Jeremiah Corkery, 'alias Corcoran,' a 20-year-old ironworker, was charged with murder. According to the police, he had confessed in a fine literary tradition: 'I done it: I chivied the copper'.

Birmingham policemen were notorious for their casual brutality, and the courts had been fairly hard on them, but Lines was the first to be killed. The popular reaction was striking. The *Birmingham Daily Mail* observed: 'A burglar is taken into custody, and forthwith a tribe of his kindred spirits pour out of the courts and alleys and make a determined attempt to release the prisoner. Their sympathies are with the man who has broken the law.' Lines lingered on the point of death for weeks: his funeral cortege brought 100,000 people onto the streets, and some £600 was raised for his widow.

Corcoran was sentenced to death. Will Thorne was working alongside Corcoran's brother, in a metal-rolling mill. In his later recollections, he offers no sympathy for the murderer and his gang:

> The action of the police resulted in the final clearing up of the neighbourhood. It was a relief, especially for the patrons of the Birmingham Theatre Royal, that was adjacent to Navigation Street. This was a favourite place for the gang to operate. One of their games was to come along when the people were lined up to go into the theatre. I was often in the crowd, and just as the doors were open they would leap-frog over the waiting crowd, run to the gallery and take charge of all the best centre seats. Later they would sell some of the seats, after keeping a number for themselves. Up to the time of the riots neither the police nor the theatre authorities were able to prevent these raids. Conditions were much better at the other music-halls, where the proprietors were very strict about their patrons, who had to be decently dressed, and where no man was allowed in if he was not wearing a collar.[7]

It is hardly surprising, in this atmosphere, that Chamberlain was able to get the council to agree to cut a swathe through the courts and alleys of central Birmingham, and to replace some of the infested warrens with a great new boulevard, to be called Corporation Street. Slum clearance was seen as an instrument of social reform – though it was a very blunt one.

Thorne found work with another brickmaker, but he still found the life too hard and went on the tramp. He was taken on as a navvy on the Burton and Derby railway. But he was soon back in

Birmingham again, working in brickfields in the summer and the gasworks in the winter.

In the building trade, the great employer was now the council, pushing through Chamberlain's plan for a new heart to the city. And the gasworks, too, was owned by the city as Chamberlain had taken over the gas supply, promising to make it pay.

Industrial disputes were now disputes with the council, and Thorne tried to organise his workmen to challenge the onerous working conditions.

> The ignorance of the Mayor and his committee of working conditions were shown when he visited the works, accompanied by the Chairman and members of the Gas Committee. When they passed through the retort house, we had just finished drawing and charging a set of retorts, and were having a breather. I heard Chamberlain ask the foreman why we were fooling about and sitting down. As a matter of fact the sweat was rolling off us at the time, and our muscles were aching from the hot fast work of drawing and recharging the retorts.

Thorne succeeded in getting compulsory Sunday work abolished at the gasworks but he found his fellow-workers hard to organise, complaining that they did not have the brains of a rabbit, and lacked courage. 'The long hours of tiring work, and the home lives they endured, robbed their brains and bodies alike of any chance to develop the natural characteristics of a normal man.'

He ascribed his own fiercely independent character to his period of navvying away from Birmingham. He had already learned the navvy's skills – 'the shovel and I were old friends' – but he had learned them in the cramped narrow world of the city. Release into the free air of the railway builders, out in the countryside, encouraged a new way of thinking: 'I am sure that the days that I spent in the open air working as a navvy, living with these big-hearted, carefree men, and absorbing their conversation, had much to do with my future. They were an independent type, with the spark of rebellion glowing bright within them.' Thorne carried this spark of rebellion back into the city, but it took a lot of blowing to keep it alive. Urban labourers, shifting from place to place and from job to job were not easily persuaded to act together in their own interests.

11 Will Thorne aged 25, when he was working at the Beckton gasworks.

In 1879, Will married the daughter of a self-educated man, and learned much from him about political economy. Jack Hallam, like Thorne, spent his summers labouring in the brickfields, and the winters in the gasworks. He introduced Thorne to a broad-based political outlook, so that he began to think of himself as a cog in a great machine. 'We were poor, ignorant victims of the growing machine of industrialisation'.

1879 was a particularly grim year for Birmingham labourers. There was a 'depression in trade': the land boom collapsed, and private building contracts all but disappeared. It was a hard winter. There were sixteen weeks of frost, and the workhouse population rose to an intolerable peak of over 4,000. There were many more on outdoor relief. The local papers began reporting that labourers were being caught poaching, and the *Birmingham Gazette* urged that workhouses should be given enough land to make them self-supporting.

The most important building work still going on was, of course, the council's urban improvement plan, and as a charitable gesture the borough surveyor was instructed to give employment to not more than 500 of the able-bodied poor of the borough. It was a double-edged charity: the new employees were not to receive poor relief, and they were to be paid a miserly two shillings a day.

The work on which they were engaged was, to some extent, actually making their living conditions worse. The splendid new boulevard of Corporation Street was indeed destroying 'narrow streets, houses without back doors or windows, confined yards – housing and shopping so dilapidated as to be in imminent danger of falling, and incapable of proper repair.' But what was happening to the people who lived there?

The *St James Gazette* gave the answer in 1885:

> It is little to the credit of the men who have managed the municipal affairs of Birmingham that not one artisan's dwelling has been built out of the £1,800,000 which has been spent on the new street, and therefore, that wretched and unwholesome dwellings, which still remain standing, are over-crowded to a fearful extent.

But Will Thorne had made his escape. In 1885 he was in London, working with Karl Marx's daughter and her husband for the overthrow of the economic system that he blamed for having robbed him of a childhood. And four years later he founded the National Union of Gas Workers and General Labourers of Great Britain and Ireland. It was the first successful organisation of its kind: a national union of unskilled urban labourers.

Thorne saw his union as an instrument of social revolution. 'By your labour power you create useful things for the community, you create wealth and dividends,' he told his audience when launching the union, 'but you have no say, no voice, in any of these matters. All this can be altered.'

Organised labour was on the march and its banner proclaimed the coming of socialism. In June 1890, gasworkers at Leeds struck for an eight-hour day. Will Thorne organised a full-scale battle against blacklegs imported under guard by the council. He massed

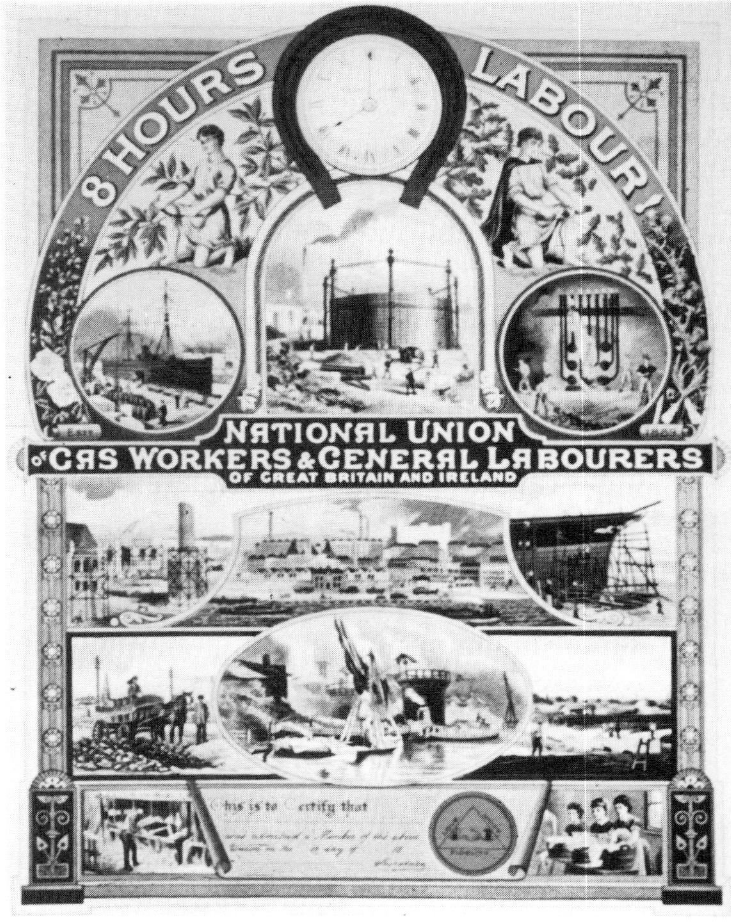

12 Membership certificate of the National Union of Gas Workers and General Labourers.

his forces on a railway bridge: 'coal, sleepers, bricks, bottles and assorted missiles were hurled down by pickets and sympathisers upon the civic procession.'

Later, Friedrich Engels presented him with a copy of Marx's *Capital*, dedicated to 'the victor of the Leeds battle'. *The Times*, like Engels, believed that labourers had been ignorant of their power, and now they were discovering it England would never be the same: on 5 July 1890 it stated that

> The teaching of the strike has been most mischievous . . . the gas men have not only been made aware of the commanding position which they occupy – but they have also been brought to commit themselves to an armed struggle with the authorities, and they have been victorious in the end, and have gained what they have been

13 'An impression of the battle of Wortley Bridge during the big Leeds gas strike', from Will Thorne's autobiography.

> fighting for. The affair has been unfortunate at every point, troublesome while it lasted, discreditable in its conclusion, and worse perhaps of all, in the permanent lessons which it will enforce.

5

Although there was a growing scale of urban violence in the 1890s and there were long and bitter strikes, *The Times*'s fears proved false. Trade unions failed to grow out of their narrow sectional interests into great national organisations of the unskilled.

Will Thorne had been a gasworker and general labourer, but his gasworkers' and general labourers' union was principally for workers in the gas industry alone. By 1900 there were over two million trade union members, but over 1,300 unions. Each proclaimed that 'union is strength', and was prepared to fight endless disputes with other unions to protect its own members from competition with others.

The pick-and-shovel labourers remained ill-organised. They were, in any case, beginning to vanish as steam-powered excavators appeared which could do the work of a hundred men. In 1895 Mrs Garnett, a missionary who ran a *Quarterly Letter to Navvies*, met what she called 'a real old navvy' who had come to Nottingham looking for work on a new railway line. He was 68, and had walked 186 miles in the week. She felt he was a member of a dying race.

But there was still one great effort of human muscle-power required before the shovel lost its place as the prime mover of earth. This new earthwork was for neither the railway industry nor the building industry: it was for the war industry – the western front.

> War is really an industry, organised for a single, definite purpose. A peace-time industry accomplishes its purpose by using: technical labour; specialised labour; unskilled labour. Likewise the war industry.

Those words, from a lecture at the School of Military Administration in 1923, represent hindsight. In the heady, early days of war in 1914, warfare was a matter of infantry, cavalry, and a little artillery. Britain's small professional army was used to service in Africa and India, where it found the general labour it needed from among the native population. When it landed in France, it employed large numbers of healthy young Frenchmen for its baggage trains. The General Staff was irritated and surprised when the French insisted on taking these men back for their own army.

By 1915 the pattern of the war was beginning to emerge. A wry account of how to simulate it was written for readers at home.

> Select a flat ten-acre ploughed field, so sited that the surface water of the surrounding country drains into it. Now cut a zig-zag slot about four feet deep and three feet wide diagonally across, dam off as much water as you can so as to leave about a hundred yards of squelchy mud; delve out a hole at one side of the slot, then endeavour to live there for a month on bully beef and damp biscuits, whilst a friend has instructions to fire at you with his Winchester every time you surface.

A forward battalion would have to build the trench. Then it would have to allocate two-thirds of its men every night to the job of carrying up rations, stores and ammunition, and repairing and maintaining the barbed wire that ran along the trench top. When these dropped back into reserve for a rest, they would be expected to provide working parties to dig reserve and communication trenches, construct dug-outs, repair roads and prepare artillery emplacements. They would also, of course, rehearse attacks. Actual fighting was the last of their duties, and by the time they came to do it they were often already exhausted.

When Lord Kitchener appealed for able-bodied men aged between 17 and 35 to join the Army, his appeal was headed 'A call to arms'. Hundreds of thousands joined up for adventure and excitement, and no one was going to tell them that they were needed as labourers. They wanted to be fighting soldiers, and fighting soldiers were certainly needed, so heavy labouring simply became part of a soldier's job.

The first group of men to be taken to France purely for labouring were the men who were laying sewers under Manchester. They did

14 A clay kicker at work.

this lying on their backs on sloping boards, excavating horizontal tunnels three feet high and two feet wide. They pushed the spade forward between their legs and kicked away the loose clay – they were known as 'clay kickers'. As they inched their way forward under the city streets, their mates crawled behind moving the clay.

They turned up for work as usual on Wednesday 17 February 1915. One of the assistant engineers on the work, a man called Leeming, was waiting for them. Leeming had gone to London at the end of the previous week. Now he was back, and dressed in an officer's uniform. He had experienced the most hectic five days anyone could ask for. The contractor, Norton Griffiths, had whisked him off to London on Saturday and taken him to Lord Kitchener's office. They crossed the Channel the same night, in a rough sea, and began a tour of Army headquarters, ending up examining the soil at Givenchy, on the front line. Now Leeming was back with important news for the clay kickers. They were sacked.

Leeming was able to offer them a proposition. They could work on a new set of tunnels the contractor was planning in northern France. They would, of course, have to join the Army, but as specialists, not ordinary soldiers. Ordinary volunteers received a shilling a day: they would get six times that.

Probably not one of the clay kickers was eligible to volunteer in the ordinary way. They were too short, too narrow in the chest, and some of them had too many white hairs to convince anyone they were under 35. The country was in a fever of volunteering, and this offer was hard to refuse. Leeming had twenty volunteers.

They were brought to London the next day, and Norton Griffiths explained that they were to tunnel out from British positions and lay explosives under the German trenches.

Two of the men were found to be so unfit that they could not go. The rest were sent straight down to Chatham, where they were given uniforms and kit. Norton Griffiths followed them, and just two days after being sacked in Manchester they were marched onto a ship at Chatham carrying a rifle and 150 rounds of ammunition each. Of course, they had no idea how to use their weapons, but regulations insisted that they have them for the crossing. Griffiths disarmed them as soon as they arrived in France. The men were rushed to Givenchy and by 21 February, with no military training of any kind, they were working in the front line.

Norton Griffiths was a man of dash and influence. He was a Member of Parliament and a major in the 2nd King Edward's Horse, which he was instrumental in raising. He had not only transferred his civilian undertaking directly onto the western front; he had even persuaded the War Office to buy his Rolls Royce, so that he could continue to ride around in it. His initiative led to the creation of specialist tunnelling companies, manned largely by miners from northern England and south Wales.

Tunnelling was not a job the ordinary soldier could do. All the labouring work required for the normal conduct of the war stayed in the hands of fighting soldiers until 1916. There were simply not enough volunteers available to create battalions of labourers. The situation changed with the coming of conscription in March 1916. Those who were fit became soldiers. Those who were not were turned into labourers. 'May 1916 saw the birth at Chadderton of the 19th Labour Battalion of the Cheshire Regiment. The men . . . included cotton spinners and factory hands from the Midlands, farmers from the country towns and miners from south Wales.' These words are from the war diary of the 58th Labour Company, by Captain T. C. Thomas. He prefaced it with the words, 'I am but a plain Labour Officer, and more used to wielding a pick and shovel.' Inevitably these conscripts were unskilled and unfit. Skilled men would generally be kept out by their employer's refusal to certify that they could be spared. Fit men would be snapped up for the fighting forces.

Thomas's battalion arrived on the Somme on 18 July. Seventeen days earlier, the 'big push' that was to break through the German trenches had collapsed in a sea of blood. It was clear that the war of trenches would endure, and the battalion was put to work building a railway.

15 An army of labourers, with shovels instead of rifles.

The war industry was under way, and its labour force was under constraints that civilian labourers had never known. It had to learn a new discipline:

> Pte. C. was brought before me, and just to show him what he was up against in the Army, I entered his crimes in full and a little over, and read them out, with the punishment that could be given. The list was as follows:
>
> Refusing to assist in making a military work in the field when on active service. Maximum sentence fourteen years penal servitude.
>
> Insolence to his superior officer when on active service. Maximum sentence fourteen years penal servitude.
>
> Disobeying the lawful commands of his NCO when on active service. Maximum sentence death.
>
> Disobeying the lawful command of his officer when on active service. Maximum sentence death.[8]

It is not too hard to imagine the act of rebellion which led to this – a manifestation of that 'independent spirit' which Will Thorne was so eager to foster in labouring men. It would not have been sheer fear, for that was usually handled more brusquely in the British Army; Brigadier-General F. P. Crozier, describing 1 July 1916, recalled:

> I hear a rumour about riflemen retiring on the left and go out to 'stop the rot'. . . . They mean business. They are damned if they are going to stay, it's all up. A young sprinting subaltern heads them off. They push by him. He draws a revolver and threatens them. They take no notice. He fires. Down drops a British soldier at his feet. The effect is instantaneous. They turn back . . .[9]

The labour battalions were not officially required to display military valour, and the House of Commons was told in 1916 that none of them worked within twenty miles of the front line. But the 19th were at that time less than three thousand yards from the line, working in the open without gas masks, steel helmets or trenches to protect them. Their work was often 'shelled off':

> A small party of from 6 to 12 men working alone, busy repairing breaks in the line, amid that awful waste, with, as a rule, not another living soul in sight. Suddenly comes a shriek of a shell, perhaps a salvo of four, pitching close to the party. Like one man they drop instantly to the ground, taking what cover they can. If they are lucky and the first shells fall clear, as soon as the salvo is finished and the pieces cease flying, they are up and off, racing away at right angles to the direction the shell travelled and taking refuge in any convenient trench or dugout.[10]

In the worst months, labour battalions suffered more than a thousand casualties a month. Ever more men were drafted into them, so that by the end of 1917 the Army's Directorate of Labour controlled a force of 387,000 unskilled labourers, including 90,000 Chinese coolies who had been brought in as indentured labour. The coolies were kept further back, because their indentures included complex details of the way they were to be buried should they be killed. They were, after all, there of their own free will, at least in theory. The British labourers were not.

> They it is who tidy up behind the men whose business is destruction, straightening things out so that the destroyers may be fed. They clear away torn wire, tear down barricades, bury dead, build camps for their comrades. Forever they are working – working on the greatest battlefield the world has ever seen.

These lines are from a propaganda pamphlet, *The Men Who Tidy Up* 'by one who has served in a British Labour Battalion'. It ends:

> And more than once, when tired Divisions have come marching down from duty in the trenches, some lad, trudging in the ranks, rifle on shoulder, has seen a figure he knows working by the roadside. And at his gay shouted greeting a father has looked up from his unaccustomed toil and learned that his son still lives.

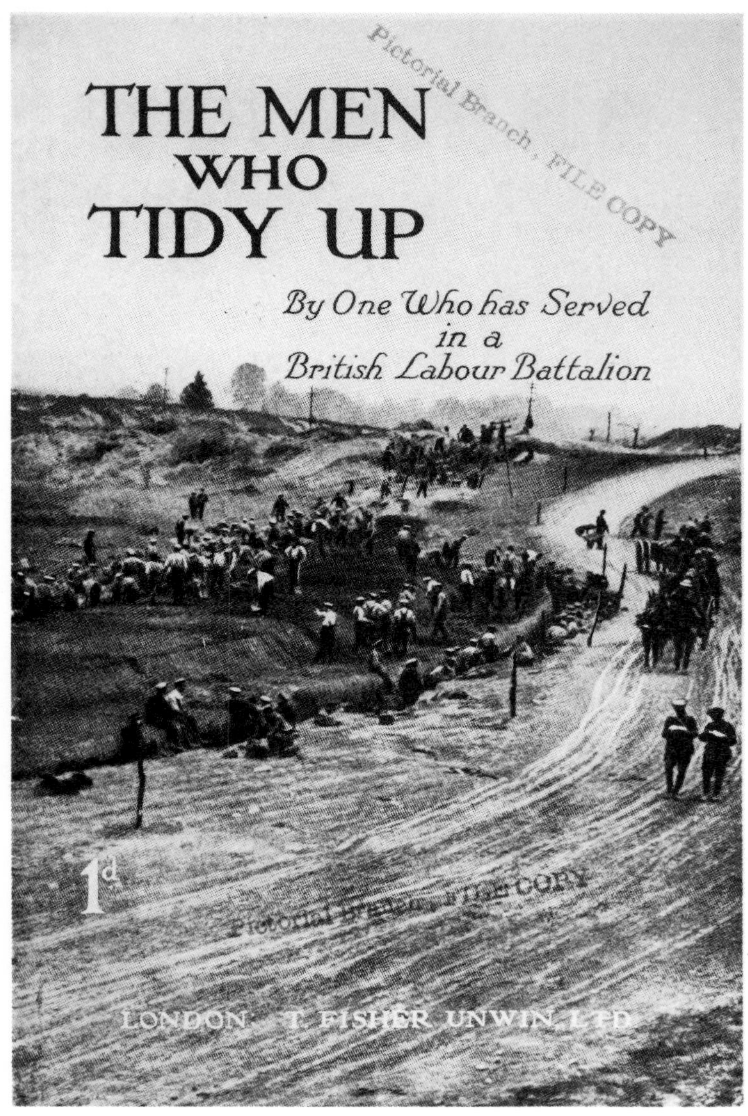

16 *The Men Who Tidy Up.*

Chapter 2
SERVANTS

1

> About five and twenty years ago, very few even of the most opulent citizens of London kept any equipage, or even any servants in livery. . . . At present, every trader in any degree of credit, every broker and attorney, maintains a couple of footmen, a coachman, and a postillion. (Matt Bramble in *Humphrey Clinker*, by Smollett, 1771)

One of that new class of liveried London servants – one of the very few to leave an account of his life – was John Macdonald. Macdonald was a Highlander: 'My father, who had no estate of his own, rented near 1,000 acres of the Laird of Grant. He reared cattle, and drove them to the south of Scotland, and into England, where he sold them.'[1]

Farmers' children were the most popular source of servants, as a letter in the *London Packet* explained in 1772: 'In the remoter parts of the kingdom, which have little connection with the capital, servants are tractable and industrious; at least they are infinitely more so than those to be met with in London and its environs.'

The same changes which were creating great prosperous estates and stimulating trade were drawing people in desperate poverty away from the land. Macdonald's family was ruined by the Jacobite uprising of 1745. His father fought as captain of the Macdonald clan, and fell at Culloden. The children were left homeless, landless and fatherless. At the age of 4, John Macdonald became a beggar child in the streets of Edinburgh, creeping from one shelter to another with his 6-year-old brother Daniel:

> In town we lay in the stairs; for about Edinburgh, as in Paris and Madrid, many large families live upon one staircase. They shut their own door, but the street door is always open. There was an opinion at that time very prevalent among us poor children, of whom, after the Rebellion there were a great many, that the doctor came at night to find poor children asleep, and put sticking plasters to their mouth, that they might not call out, and then to carry them away to be dissected; and indeed I believe it very true, for what everyone says must be true, and the poor Highlanders were more despised at that

> time by the Scots in general, of the other party, than the devils in hell. So when we passed the night in a stair, or at a door, one slept and the other kept watch.

Hanging around a hackney coach-yard, the small child was taken on by the yard's owner as a postillion, riding one of the horses that drew the coach and helping to guide it from that position. Roads were bad and the less a postillion weighed the better. 'He put me in livery and looked upon me as an apprentice. I was fitted out with a green jacket with a red cape, a red waistcoat, and a leather cap with the forepart lined with red morocco.' Then, when he was 9, the young postillion was hired by a great landowner, Mr Hamilton.

To be more accurate, he was hired by Mr Hamilton's coachman. For in a substantial household, the servants themselves ran the house and its affairs. In theory, a house and its servants were an extension of the householder's family; in practice, the householder and his family were proprietors of a great hotel, employing a staff of perhaps eighteen or twenty (and far more in a really important house). Half of the staff would be men. The term *maitre d'hotel* at this time meant the house steward, who managed the household.

The servants were formed into an elaborate hierarchy, with administrative and supervisory staff, such as the clerk of the stables and clerk of the kitchen, man-cook, bailiff, valet and butler all dressed in ordinary clothes. The woman servants too would wear normal dresses. The lower grades of manservant, though, wore uniform livery, splendidly coloured and decorated. At the head of the liveried servants came the coachman. Under him were the footmen, the groom, the porter at the gate, the park keeper and the gamekeeper. At the bottom of the list was the postillion.

Macdonald was given his livery – a scarlet jacket trimmed with gold – and £2 a year. He was also entitled to one third of all tips he received. He stayed in this post for five years, and was never paid a penny of his wages until he left. All his essential needs were met by living in the household: a large house at this time was almost a self-contained world. Any out-of-pocket expenses had to be met out of his tips.

Tips were called 'vails' – a vaguely feudal term referring to a vaguely feudal custom. By the mid eighteenth century they had become a vital part of the income of domestic servants: all servants were expected to live on tips from their master's guests. In 1760 a letter in the *London Chronicle* explained the importance of vails. For there was a campaign to wipe them out.

> I have been fifteen years a servant; the last nine I have lived with a Gentleman in the middling station of life; and having made a

memorandum of my gain and expences, I am able to give a true estimate of the same. My wages for the first four years were £6 *per* year, the other five at £7 *per* year;

the whole nine years wages amounts to the sum of	£59	0	0
My vails and perquisites in the said term amounts to the sum and no more than	£25	7	6
Which being added together makes my nine years gain to be	£84	7	6
My expences, one year with another, viz.			
For four pair of shoes, at 6*s*. *per* pair	£ 1	4	0
For mending ditto, at 2*s*. *per* pair		8	0
For three shirts, the making, mending, etc.		15	9
For three neckcloths, at 2*s*. each		6	0
For two pair of stockings, at 4*s*. *per* pair		8	0
For washing the whole year	£ 1	10	0
For one wig in two years, is *per* year		10	6
For spending money, when out late at nights, etc.		5	0
The real expences in one year is	£ 5	7	3
Which in nine years amounts to the sum of	£48	5	3
Which being deducted from the sum above, there will remain, clear gains, in nine years	£36	2	3

And now, sir, if I had no *vails*. . . . I should have had no more to shew for my *nine* years service than £10. 14*s*. 9*d*., a great sum indeed, to keep me when out of place, in sickness or other casualties.

For servants of richer men, vails were even more important, probably worth more than their wages. The word 'servant' had a very wide meaning – any employee was a 'servant', and domestic servants were still as independent as any other class of employee. Many of Hamilton's servants were married men, and these were installed in cottages on his estate and actually paid him rent for them. Vails were the most obvious example of the independence of domestic servants. The ever-growing class of servant-keepers wanted to diminish that independence:

> It is the true wisdom of a State, to encourage *Virtue* and Industry, by making the *Servant* depend solely on the *Master for his pay*. We might then naturally expect to see that *discipline* restored amongst us, which is essential to the good order of society.[2]

Thus wrote Jonas Hanaway, in 1760, in support of the crusade against vails-giving. He described the way in which servants lined up at the door to receive their vails from departing visitors, so that it was more expensive to dine with a rich household than to eat at an inn:

> Perhaps your Guest has not consumed the value of a *Shilling*, and he gives six Servants half a Crown each, in return for it. . . . In some

> places, in the country, there is so much paid for a *breakfast*; in others, *for drinking tea in an afternoon; for holding a horse*, and for opening a *Coach-door*.

Macdonald received his vails for acts such as these, and the coachman who hired him suspected, correctly, that he was keeping more than his allotted third of them: 'When he was out with the coach-and-four horses, he thought I did not give him all the vails I got when I gave gentlemen their horses.' The result was that Macdonald found himself frequently beaten, and he took to hiding his tips in such secret crannies that he could not always reach them himself, and lost them completely.

'If we enquire into common-life,' said Hanaway, 'the case is just the same, except that the Servants receive *Shillings* instead of *half Crowns*; and there is but *one* or *two* attend instead of *five* or *six*.' He went on to give examples of the 'absurdity and inconvenience' which followed – for instance, when one gentleman had dined with his friend, servants brought him his hat, sword, cane and cloak, and he tipped a shilling for each,

> but as he was going away without taking his *Gloves*, one of the Servants reminded him of it, to which he answered, *No matter friend, you may keep the Gloves, they are not worth a Shilling* . . . I can assure you, that there have been actually some Servants, who expostulate with their Master, *for not ringing the bell, to call them up to collect their dues, and remonstrate against it as an unfair practice, that any Guest should depart* WITHOUT PAYING. . . . One would be tempted to think the whole order and Economy of Life *reversed*, and that people kept Coaches for the benefit of their *Coachmen*; and *Tables*, for the *Emolument* of their Footmen.

By 1760, when this was written, John Macdonald was rising in the servant hierarchy: having studied hairdressing, he became Mr Hamilton's personal servant, in effect a valet, travelling with him to parliament at Westminster. His predecessor in the post had saved £600 in twelve years, after which he had taken a farm and married the lady's maid. A play had appeared the previous year which claimed to show how servants could divert such large sums into their own pocket. It was called *High Life Below Stairs*, and it first appeared at Drury Lane: 'The whole race of domestic gentry . . . were in a ferment of rage at what they conceived would be their ruin; and from the upper gallery . . . came hisses and groans, and even many a handful of half-pence was flung at the stage.'[3] The play was a moralising satire, showing servants extravagantly entertaining when their master was away, stealing from him while aping the manners of high society. It included extracts from '*The Servant's Guide to Wealth*, by Timothy Shoulderknot, formerly

17 'The Old Beau in an Ecstasy': a valet was the flatterer of his master's vanity, and hairdressing was a vital accomplishment.

Servant to Several Noblemen, and now an officer in the Customs: Necessary for all Servants'.

Advice to the Footman:
Let it ever be your Plan
To be the Master, not the Man,
And do as little as you can . . .
Advice to the Coachman:
If your good Master on you doats,
Ne'er leave his House to serve a stranger,
But pocket Hay, and Straw, and Oats,
And let the Horses eat the Manger.

High Life Below Stairs came to Edinburgh, where Macdonald was living, in January 1760, and some seventy footmen, evidently members of a secret combination, threatened to burn the theatre down if the play went on.

> Soon after it began, a great noise was heard from the footmens' gallery. The gentlemen in the pit called out to them to be silent; or that otherwise they should be turned out, and never permitted to enter the playhouse again. [The footmen were granted free access to the gallery while their employers sat in the pit.] The disturbance still continuing, the footmen were all turned out, and the managers were desired not to admit any footmen into the gallery for the future. Several more letters were, however, sent to the managers.[4]

On the same day, according to the *Gentleman's Magazine*, 'at a meeting of the nobility and gentry of *Scotland* at *Edinburgh*, it was unanimously agreed to abolish the inhospitable custom of giving vails to servants.' The spirit of independence had to be crushed, by making servants more dependent on their masters.

Macdonald himself was no angel; in his later years he wrote 'I did not know the value of good luck, nor of money . . . I thought the whole world was the Garden of Eden. . . . My master saw that I had no conduct, and did not know the value of a good place.' He was sacked. After working for a couple more years in Scotland, he went to London by ship. Many Scottish servants had made the same trip, hoping to find work that would still allow them the vails they were denied in their homeland. But the old system was ending everywhere.

Some servants grew desperate about this attack on their independence and their hopes of saving for old age. In 1761 one of the leading opponents of vails, Sir Francis Dashwood, was threatened with death:

> for when you go to dine You go hout hand neare leaves won farthing nor wont let Your Sarvants tak One farthen . . . if Sarvants has but nine Pounds tha cannot Ceep a Wife and Female. For You must bild Work Houses and Cep them but You will not live to see them bilt for I wod have Yout be all wase prepared for Deth for You do se thare is nothing but robin upon the hi Way and that is o caisened by no thing Else but by Starven the Poore Sarvants.[5]

The situation was made more tense by the obvious and growing gulf between the opulence of society life and the desperate poverty into which a servant might fall if he lost his place. Opulent display was the mark of gentility in the second half of the eighteenth century, and men displayed their wealth by the number of liveried footmen who followed them about. One sign of the new extravagance was that when Macdonald came to London he stopped referring to coaches and wrote instead of carriages. These light, elegant vehicles had only just come into use, but already the mark of being in polite society was that a family had 'set up a carriage'.

The old coach was a cumbersome vehicle, intended for rough rural roads: footmen were originally running-footmen, whose job

18 The old fashioned coach, with a postillion on the front; this example is drawing into Burlington House around 1700. Slow, ponderous and uncomfortable. Footmen could ride over the back axle when it picked up speed, but were expected to jump down and run on country journeys.

19 'The Return from a Masquerade': the sedan chair of the eighteenth century.

was to run alongside the coach to support it over difficult ground, and run ahead of it to arrange accommodation. Persons of rank travelling alone in London might find a six-horse coach rather cumbersome, but they could hardly walk in the dirt of the street, so they travelled by sedan chair. The footmen acted as bodyguards.

In the eighteenth century roads became smoother, with the new turnpikes: London streets in the new districts were splendidly wide, with large squares. In these conditions, there was room for a new kind of vehicle, fast and well-sprung. Since the footmen could not keep up with it, they clung to the outside, making a splendid display. Their main job, apart from looking impressive, became acting as messengers and waiters.

Setting up a carriage involved not only arranging for the whole establishment of large stables, coachmen and grooms, but also making up an impressive train of footmen, carefully matched for height and appearance. When a family moved up to carriage status, they could expect their spending on servants to rise by 250 per cent. Since it was important for the whole affair to be seen, carriage society travelled to places of public entertainment. These had to be set in large grounds, so that there would be room for all the carriages and servants. The most popular was Ranelagh, a large circular building (the Rotunda) in the middle of large gardens about two miles west of London, in the village of Chelsea. The Rotunda was the scene of magnificent fancy-dress masquerades, attended by the finest London society. It was also, in 1764, the scene of a pitched battle between liveried servants and their masters:

> A great disturbance was created at Ranelagh-house by the coachmen, footmen, etc., belonging to such of the nobility and gentry as will not suffer their servants to take vails. They began by hissing their masters, they then broke all the lamps and outside

20 A dress coach or formal landau – the 'carriage' of the 1790s. Light, fast, elegant – the footmen who will ride on the back serve no useful purpose, and would find it very hard to jump down in a hurry.

windows with stones; and afterwards putting out their flambeaux, pelted the company in a most audacious manner, with brick-bats, etc., whereby several were greatly hurt, so as to render the use of swords necessary. In the scuffle one of the servants was run through his thigh, another through his arm, and several more otherwise wounded.[6]

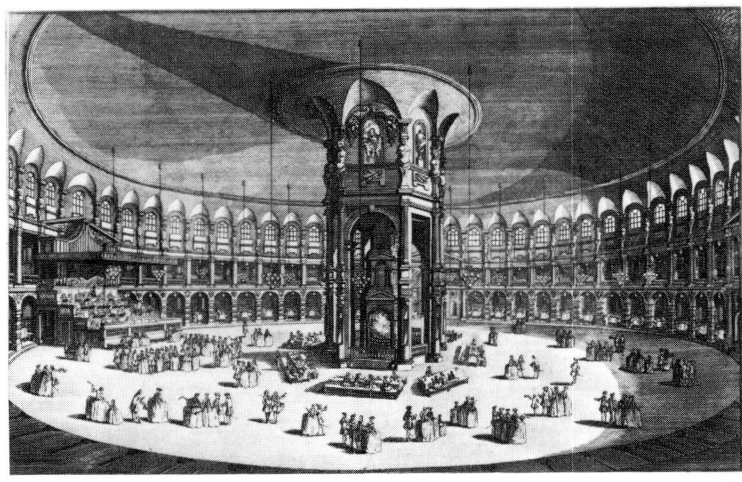

21 A masquerade at Ranelagh.

It was a battle which could achieve nothing. By 1767 it was said that vails were virtually extinct – though middle-class families, who might have found it harder to keep servants, allowed tipping to continue for a while longer than the leaders of society. As some compensation for the servants, wages generally rose by about a third. This was certainly equivalent to a wage cut for servants to the upper members of society, where vails were very substantial. But more significant than the change in a servant's income was the change in status. Servants had been made wholly dependent on their masters.

Footmen's annual wages (excluding vails)

1700–35	£ 5
1745–55	£ 7
1755–75	£12
1755–95	£16

Around 1766 Macdonald was a liveried attendant on John Crauford of Errol, who moved between London and Bath, and then set off for a German spa. On the way, they stopped near Liege, and Macdonald saw the difference between his own position and that of a servant in a different kind of society.

Macdonald and a fellow-servant were put into the kitchen of the inn to eat, while John Crauford sat in the parlour and ordered his dinner. Shortly after they had arrived, a Dutch family came in. Macdonald was struck by their servant's dress: the man had 'a coarse livery and a large Dutch hat'. Instead of staying in the kitchen, the Dutch servant made himself a sandwich and took it into the parlour,

> and kept speaking to his master and the ladies, with his large hat on his head, about the roads, and postilions and the country. . . . Henry and I laughed till we were like to split our sides, to think our master was dining with the footmen; for Mr. Crauford was so proud that he would not let a servant ride in the chaise with him, but would rather be at the expense of a horse.

To waste money by hiring an unnecessary horse for your servant was the mark of wealth and status: in Britain, you showed what a great man you were by making the gap between master and servant as wide as possible.

John Macdonald was a man of his time: he regarded the Dutch family as rather comical, and had no objection to the role he was educated into. 'I did not want to be fine. I wanted to be like a servant.' But in that sentiment, he shows how the meaning of 'servant' had changed. A word which, when he was born, meant simply 'one who works for another', had begun to represent a particular kind of worker, one who wore his master's clothes, slept in his master's house, and waited on his master's needs. A man who had no independent being.

> It is the privilege of women of the superior order to be provided for, served and protected by others; and any labour, therefore, which they undertake is chiefly voluntary.[7]

To maintain the ever growing class of genteel mistresses in the idleness to which they were entitled, there had to be a huge number of domestic servants. By 1851 the second largest occupational group in England and Wales was servants; only agriculture employed more people. Nine out of ten of the servants were women.

Men had become rarer 'below stairs' because they were expensive. A capable manservant in London in 1800 could expect to earn £15 or £20 a year: on top of that, his employer would have to pay a special tax on male servants (by 1808 large households had to pay £7 a head), provide a livery and even pay a tax on the man's hair powder. A raw girl from the country would be prepared to accept six guineas a year, and did not need special clothes. By 1800 there were probably already seven or eight women to every man in service; eighty years later there were twenty-two.

The social distinction between servant and employer was carefully emphasised: maids were expected to wear distinctive dress (at their own expense) in order to make their position clear. The maid's working dress for the morning in the 1820s was 'black stockings, a stuff gown, a cap, and a neck-handkerchief pinned corner-wise behind'. On Sundays and holidays, and perhaps in the afternoon (when housework was over and she was able to get on with her sewing) 'she changes her black stockings for white, puts on a gown of better texture and finer pattern, sets her cap and her curls jauntily, and lays aside the neck-handkerchief for a high body which, by the way, is not half so pretty.'[8] Within a few years her clothes had developed into a standard uniform of a print dress white cap and apron for the morning, and a black dress for the afternoon.

Servants had to know their place: in larger households, this was extended into a hierarchy 'below stairs' dominated by the housekeeper, who engaged all the female staff except for the lady's maid and the nurse, and by the butler, who emerged from the wine cellar, and grew steadily in status until he became everything from valet to house steward. The servants in such a household lived in a very close world; they hardly ever went out except to go to church or run errands, and their lives revolved around household gossip and their own relationships with each other. These were based on a class tyranny that was in a way as severe among servants as between servants and masters. The junior servants were often very frightened of upper servants, who could, if they chose, make life very unpleasant.

Hannah Culliwick left her charity school in 1841, when she was 8, to go into service. She entered a large household in 1855, when she was engaged as a kitchen-maid in Lord Stradbroke's residence near Ipswich, and was terrified by the housekeeper.

> I'd made her a curtsey and when she made no answer I thought I was sure she was unkind and my heart began to fail me. . . . I made haste and put on my cotton frock and cap and apron on to be in the kitchen by 6. Mrs Smith the housekeeper was most unkind to me in ordering, and I was ready to say I'd go back in the morning, and I told Bill the groom I would but he said 'never mind *her* – she's drunk and doesn't know what she's about – you stop and you'll get on all right.'

The symbol of the housekeeper's authority was the bunch of eys she carried, to open the storeroom, the linen cupboard, the hina closet and the still-room. The rattle of those keys, as she talked the house, represented order, discipline and the secure vorld of the substantial Victorian household. The majority of auntings in Victorian ancestral homes were believed to be the hosts of housekeepers.

Domestic service was the natural refuge of girls from poor omes; it offered food, shelter and some security. It is interesting to ompare two accounts of desperate poverty a hundred years apart: he first, by Rose Allen, describing her girlhood in Liverpool in the 820s, when perhaps a quarter of all girls expected to spend at least few years as servants; and the second by Helen Forrester, describing girlhood in the same city in the 1930s, when servant-eeping was in steep decline.

Both girls came from servant-keeping families themselves, and vere suddenly pitched into poverty. Rose Allen was born in 1809 nto a farming family in south Lancashire; although they were rosperous, there was no sense of idle luxury in her upbringing. My mother . . . took care to make us good housekeepers, and imple in our tastes and feelings.' In 1824 the harvest failed. 'The pening of 1825 saw us with only one servant in the house, most of ur cattle dying, and our father's strong health failing.' When Rose's father died, her two elder sisters went straight into service, nd one of her brothers was apprenticed to a farmer.

> I was then sixteen, and the rest of the family consisted of four little ones. It was decided that we should go to Liverpool, where we should be near cheap schools, and should have more chance of obtaining such light work as my poor mother was capable of undertaking.

Her mother was in constant poor health.

They found accommodation in Frederick Street, a decaying ighteenth-century street in the south of the town, near the original Pool. They had three rooms on a third floor. 'A thick yellow fog ung over the town; carts and carriages rolled by incessantly; and uarrelsome children were crowded on the steps of the lodging-ouse.'

Having sold up, and investing the small sum they received, the amily was left with an income of £30 a year 'for the support of six ndividuals'. Their rent was 5*s*. 6*d*. a week. In 1834 James Lucock ublished his *Hints for Practical Economy*, showing how to manage n a small budget. It indicates the problems that faced the Allen amily:

Estimate of Household Expences, for a Man, his Wife, and two Children – Income, One Guinea per Week.

	£	*s.*	*d.*
Rent, per week	0	2	0
Eatables, 4*d.* per day each	0	9	4
Beer	0	1	2
Clothing, Man, inc. shoes	0	1	9
Ditto, Woman, ditto	0	1	3
Ditto, Children, 9*d.* each	0	1	6
Coals	0	1	9
Washing	0	1	0
Wear and Tear	0	1	3
	£1	1	0

It would appear a very ungracious task to attempt to exhibit a lower scale; for, though every reader must be conscious that thousands or millions are compelled to live on a very much reduced rate, yet he will be utterly at a loss to know how it is accomplished.

Rose found some sewing to bring home for her mother to work at.

The next morning I got up in the dark, and going into the parlour, was astonished to see her at work, wrapped up in her cloak, without a fire, and pale with cold. 'Oh, mother, you will be ill – I know you will; and you will die; and what shall we do without father or mother?' 'My dear Rose, remember that when our rent is paid we have only 6*s.* a week to look to, and that will scarcely find us in bread; the schooling [for the small children] will be 6*d.* weekly; and the chief part of our food, fire and clothing, where are they to come from?'

Her mother did indeed fall ill, and the doctor who came arranged for a district visitor to call, 'as he thought we wanted some better instructions for managing in a large town'. Miss Evelyn, the district visitor, was one of those 'women of the superior order' who were liberated by money and servants to perform voluntary work. She came from a wealthy radical family, and devoted her time to helping the poor to help themselves.

Miss Evelyn staid at least a couple of hours, showing us the best mode of ventilating our rooms, telling us the shops where we should find good and cheap materials, and giving me receipts for cheap and nourishing food . . . and then she spoke to me of the absolute necessity for the poor to try to save.

Miss Evelyn also suggested that Rose should ease the family's burdens by going into service, and found a place for her with a Quaker family. 'My wages were to be £10 . . . and besides sending something home, I regularly put by 5*s.* every quarter.'

Rose Allen had come to Liverpool when England was still suffering from the depression that followed the Napoleonic wars: in

1824 the real value of wages was probably about 6 per cent less than in 1816, and although people were drinking more tea and using more sugar, life was not generally very easy; on average, men smoked 20 per cent less than they had done in the closing years of the war, when there was more money about. There was a definite improvement in 1825, but with the next year came a depression, with heavy unemployment.

It is hard to compare the conditions in Rose Allen's Liverpool with the slump of 1931, when Helen Forrester came to the city. Real wages in 1931 were actually over 17 per cent up on 1923, but unemployment had more than doubled. One of the few widespread luxuries, smoking, had increased by about 14 per cent since 1923, but with shipping freights having fallen by over a quarter, and more than half of all men in the ship-building and repair trades out of work, Liverpool was in a desperate state.

Helen, like Rose, came from a comfortable family that had been ruined by bad luck in difficult times, but her family was even less well able to adapt. She had been brought up by parents who expected their servants to look after them in every way, and when they brought their seven children to the city in search of work and shelter they had no idea how to cope. Raised in a world of rigid social distinctions, Helen's mother looked down on the charitable priest who tried to help them, and spurned him. Her father had to learn the principles of domestic economy from the other men in the dole queue. He was given 43 shillings a week, 27 shillings of which went on rent. The family lived on the very edge of starvation. Their baby was kept alive by the anonymous gift of a daily pint of milk, provided by the local policeman.

Helen was about 13. Although there were still domestic servants, it was no longer the normal course for a poor girl to go into service. There were very few families who could afford living-in help, and anyway, at 12 or 13, Helen was supposed to be kept at school. She had to be secretly hidden at home, looking after the younger children.

> I tried to think constructively, to devise ways in which the family might get out of the morass in which it was floundering, but my experience was too limited and my mind too dulled by lack of use, my body by lack of food, to be able to come up with a possible solution.

Rose Allen was really much better off; domestic service saved many families like hers from total destitution. The worst suffering that she faced was the sensation of being adrift in a strange and lonely world. The Quaker family was solemn, their other servants were elderly. 'My greatest want was some one to speak to of the past, of my home, and the hopes and wishes which fill a young person's imagination.' When she moved from that post to another, she spent one precious day with her family: 'This interchange of thoughts and feelings . . . was like drinking from a cool well "in a dry and thirsty land".'

The contrast between Rose Allen's fortunes and those of Helen Forrester shows the importance of domestic service to the respectable poor: there is also a contrast in the purpose of their writing. Helen Forrester's publishers described her autobiography as a 'reminder of the dark days before the welfare state': Rose Allen's story was edited by 'A Lady', who wrote in her preface that 'It is hoped . . . that the story may help to induce a more generous recognition of the reciprocal dependence of Master and Servant, and a more conscious appreciation of the responsibilities of their respective stations.'

As the number of servants and servant keepers grew, it was necessary to train both into their positions. Ladies were offered works such as Mrs Beeton's *Book of Household Management*, which explained the duties of different servants. In 1861, when it first appeared, the number of servants was growing twice as fast as the population: one of the tasks of the book was to set out the generally recognised scale of servant-keeping.

Income	*Staff*
About £250 or £150 p.a.	A maid of all work.
About £300 p.a.	A maid of all work and a nursemaid.
About £500 p.a.	A cook, housemaid and a nursemaid.
About £750 p.a.	The same, with a footboy.
About £1,000 p.a.	A cook, upper- and under-housemaids, a nursemaid and a male servant.

This was a scale which stretched from the country curate or skilled London artisan at the bottom to the reasonably successful shopkeeper or tradesman at the top. To run a large household, which would include such luxuries as a lady's maid, required an income of at least £2,000 a year.

Rose Allen, being well-bred and none too strong, was engaged as a lady's maid or a nursery governess, comfortable positions which did not involve heavy work. Her most difficult time was spent in a family which was desperately struggling to preserve an appearance of ancestral dignity: maintaining a coachman, and footmen in livery, but going without fires in winter.

> It makes me almost shudder to think back to that period of my life: besides plain work, mending undergarments until they would no longer hang together, repairing household linen, making caps,

> gowns and bonnets, there was endless trouble and time expended in perpetually re-making and altering, to keep up with the rapid changes in the fashion!

The governess in that household almost died of malnutrition; the example is one of a series which 'A Lady' hoped would show how servants should not be treated. The whole book stresses that

22 *The Poor Teacher* by Richard Redgrave. Nineteenth-century governesses were in a pathetic position; poor but from good families, they were trapped by their own sense of station in a shadow-life.

servants are human beings, not workhorses. 'Remember that kindness and consideration are as much due to their feelings as is attention to their bodily comforts, or the punctual payment of their wages.'

The need for such advice was alarming, but real. It was typified by a middle-class lady who interviewed Rose for a post as maid. Mrs Bennett sat in her suburban drawing room with a fat poodle on her lap: opposite, with his gouty leg propped in front of the fire, reclined her husband. The first time Rose had called, Mrs Bennett had not been in the mood to see her, and sent her on the long walk home again. Now she outlined the duties of the post.

> 'There's my old china in this room, in my bedroom and the closet, which must be dusted every day: there's breakfast for the dog, cat and parrot; indeed, all the meals you have to prepare; and my dear poodle can't eat meat unless it's nicely minced. They must be washed every other day and combed every day; and the poodle must go for a walk when it's sunshiney, only you must never let him wet his feet, but carry him across the street. They must sleep in your room, as I should not feel easy for them to be left alone. Then there's my caps, you would wash and make them, and I always change

> them three times a week. Of course, you would have to attend my toilet; but that would not take long, as I am never more than an hour morning and evening, and two hours before dinner.'

Rose would also have to act as the target for Mr Bennett's abuse. When she declined the post, Mrs Bennett observed; 'Really girls are so saucy these days, there's no bearing it.'

23 Fear of the unknown world below stairs, and guilt at its neglect, combine in Leech's paranoid fantasy.

Rose Allen's ideal household was one in which servants and those they served were united in common respect and even family affection. In fact the trend was in a quite different direction: households became increasingly divided into two camps, 'above stairs' and 'below stairs'. The *British Weekly* recorded a conversation with a group of ladies in 1888, in which they discussed the difficulties they had with their servants. The central feature of their discussion was this division of the home into two distinct households:

> Once a day all the inhabitants of the house meet at prayers, and then they go their separate ways for the day. One family lives upstairs, and the other downstairs: there is no place where they come together except the nursery.

Servants were expected to do their work quite unseen: cleaning was done while the family were still in bed in the early morning, and if a maid was seen by a member of the family, she was commonly expected to turn her back and make herself as invisible as possible. Of course, there was always the possibility of the master or his son seducing a maid – and she was likely to give in for fear of being sacked without a 'character' to show to another employer – but this was a major argument for keeping the barriers between 'above' and 'below' stairs as rigid as a mistress could make them. One of the ladies in the conversation, though, claimed to have overcome the barriers of the divided household:

> My servants always come upstairs on Christmas Day (unless it is Sunday) to play games with the children, and on New Year's Day my children go downstairs to tea in the kitchen. But it is always done by written invitation: the children write to the servants and the servants write to the children.

This domestic rigidity ('all are equal when they die, but there must be social distinctions', as one of the ladies put it) went together with a certain amount of mutual hostility. Mistresses feared, generally rightly, that their servants were robbing them one way or another, while servants regarded many of their 'betters' as petty tyrants. 'When one remembers the double life which is led by most servants,' commented the *British Weekly*, 'one is inclined to think that the whole race had better be abolished. Day after day they discuss "Old——" in the pantry and the servant's hall, they laugh at his weaknesses and make fun of his guests.'

In exchange for the privilege of having servants to wait on them, freeing their women from the need to do any practical work, the middle classes of nineteenth-century England surrendered their domestic privacy. They felt constantly watched and spied upon by servants whose loyalty was always in doubt. They spent their whole lives on their guard, creating that stuffy, pompous, self-righteous image which dominated the latter part of the century. The standard warning, 'Not in front of the servants', created habits of speech which eventually became habits of thought, valuing propriety over frankness.

The servants, objects of constant suspicion, were allowed as little freedom as possible. Servants found it easiest to get work in districts where they were (or pretended to be) strangers: they were less likely to spread gossip, and would be more dependent on their employers. 'Followers' – sweethearts – were not allowed; since most servants were young single girls, who intended to marry and raise their own families, this led to constant difficulties. Time off was severely limited – often just one half-day a week or fortnight. And every opportunity was taken to teach servant girls how to know their place.

Most of this training was done in the home; not only through casual remarks ('Attend to your work, Rose; you'll please not to mind what your betters think right to say; a pretty piece of presumption in you to suppose you have any right to think about such matters,') but also by formal lectures on Sunday mornings and from religious visitors. They particularly resented being obliged to go to church on Sundays, and even being told which church to go to. Preachers might subject them to those fragments of Christian doctrine which stress submission by servants to their masters:

> Servants, be obedient to them that are your masters according to the flesh, with fear and trembling in singleness of your heart, as unto Christ; not with eye-service, as men-pleasers, but, as the servants of Christ, doing the will of God, from the heart.

Attempts were also made to train girls before going into service. One of the most elaborate systems was set up in the North London suburban village of Finchley.

> The general inefficiency of young female servants, and not infrequently of elder ones, has long been a subject of complaint in families of the middle class of society. 'Pretending to everything,' observes a mistress, 'they can do nothing – literally nothing – as it ought to be done.' What are the consequences of all this? Perpetual discomfort and annoyance in families, with incessant changes of servants. What is the radical cause? Ignorance – want of practical training, i.e. a want of education on the right principle.

To remedy this, the Holy Trinity National and Industrial Schools, Finchley, were opened in 1848. The object was 'to turn out really *useful* members of society; that is, boys and girls already *used to*, and *handy at*, some definite work.'

The girls were taught their duties as servants by catechism:

> Q. Are you aware that it is part of your business *immediately* to answer the bell, or the knocker at the hall door – never to *keep any person waiting*?
> A. Yes, ma'am. . . .
> Q. On the call of a stranger, or even a friend, what do you do?
> A. I request the card of the party, and immediately apprise my mistress, or my master, if at home.
> Q. If your master or mistress be at home, what do you do then?
> A. I open the parlour or drawing room door, distinctly mention the name, and allow the party to walk in.
> Q. I hope you never show strangers into the parlour or drawing room, and leave them there alone?
> A. No, ma'am.[9]

Other catechisms covered such tasks as cleaning and blacking stoves, and doing the washing; everything, in fact, which covered 'The Duties of Female Servants, in Tradesmen's and other Respectable Middle-Class Families'. The girls were being trained as maids-of-all-work, the only servants in hundreds of thousands of suburban Victorian villas. Here, with the assistance of an occasional help, they acted as unregarded drudges. Hannah Culliwick recorded one day in her life – 14 July 1860 – as a maid-of-all-work for an upholsterer in Kilburn, North London.

> Opened the shutters and lighted the kitchen fire – shook my sooty things in the dusthole and emptied the soot there, swept and dusted the rooms and the hall, laid the cloth and got breakfast up –cleaned two pairs of boots – made the beds and emptied the slops, cleared and washed the breakfast things up – cleaned the plate –cleaned the knives and got dinner up – cleared away, cleaned the kitchen up – unpacked a hamper – took two chickens to Mrs Brewer's and brought the message back – made a tart and picked and gutted two ducks and roasted them – cleaned the steps and flags on my knees – blackleaded the scraper in front of the house – cleaned the street flags too on my knees – had tea – cleared away –washed up in the scullery – cleaned the pantry on my knees and scoured the tables – scrubbed the flags round the house and cleaned the window sills – got tea at 9 for the master and Mrs Warwick in my dirt but Ann (*a fellow-servant*) carried it up – cleaned the privy and passage and scullery floor on my knees – washed the door and cleaned the sink down – put the supper ready for Ann to take up, for I was too dirty and tired to go up stairs.

There were over 900,000 female servants in England and Wales in 1860; 600,000 of them were maids-of-all-work. The numbers continued to rise: by 1888, when the *British Weekly* investigated the situation, some one and a-half million women were in domestic service: 'It is impossible to say how many of these working women are "slaveys". By a "slavey" we mean a child-servant . . . who drudges from morning till night in some house where "only one servant is kept".' Girls from poor homes may have needed to go into service – it may have held out the best hope of shelter and food – but they were desperately reluctant to go. Their mothers might try to keep them at home for a few years 'to get the benefit', but they could not afford to keep them long, and anyway they soon lost control over their daughters. At this point they commonly recognised:

> that good food is necessary for a girl while she is growing, and that street life is very pernicious. But the girls prefer to live at home, even if it means drudgery that keeps them occupied from morning till night, blows, and drunken parents . . . they complain of 'lonesomeness'.

The newspaper sent lady reporters, whom it called 'commissioners', to find out how such girls lived: they returned with case after case of girls who had been brought up in a large family, crowded into one or two rooms, sharing beds and warmth, and who could not bear the loneliness of an empty kitchen, while the family they served sat apart in the parlour.

> Well, missus always sat in the parlour, and I always sat in the kitchen, and I felt lonesome. Then missus used to go out at night,

> and leave me all alone in the house, and I got scared, and runned away. I won't go back, no, not for nobody.

It was possible for a slavey to run away back to her family, and get a factory job, if she had a family to run to. But many of them were, like Hannah Culliwick, paupers with nowhere to run. 'Pauper girls make, as a rule, very good servants. Their spirit is broken by long and severe discipline before they leave the workhouse.'

24 The kitchen range dominated the life of the maid-of-all-work. This pair of posed photographs by Hannah Culliwick's husband were taken in 1872, and titled '7 a.m.' and '7 p.m.'

These girls were the subject of much charitable attention. Ladies who worked for the Metropolitan Association for Befriending Young Servants were urged to read *The Work of Lady Visitors*, which told them:

> It is not a difficult task this, to win a girl's heart – in the case of the pauper girls a touchingly easy one. The girl, brought up in an enormous school, with teachers to teach, nurses to nurse, mistresses to order, no one to love . . . it is this girl, whose character comes to us as 'sullen, obstinate and sly', whose eyes at the first word of kindness fill with tears.

These girls were trapped into servitude. Those that wrote to the *British Weekly* were far from typical – very few would have read the paper or had the courage to write – but their complaints stand for hundreds of thousands of lonely, impoverished young women slaving under the domestic tyranny of strangers.

Madam,
What is worse than the work is the whims of my mistress. I am a Dissenter, but I am supposed to go to the Established Church as they do. I can scarcely ever get out for myself, but I must go wherever they choose to send me; if I am busy or ill it makes no difference. She is neither willing for me to see my friends nor for them to come to see me. Servants are treated more as slaves than as free persons. If my mistress knew I wrote this I should be discharged at once, so, madam, I trust you will keep my name secret.

MISTRESS AND MAID.

"WHERE HAVE YOU BEEN, JANE?"
"I'VE BEEN TO A MEETING OF THE GIRLS' FRIENDLY SOCIETY, MA'AM."
"WELL, AND WHAT DID THE LADY SAY TO YOU?"
"PLEASE, MA'AM, SHE SAID I WASN'T TO GIVE YOU WARNING, AS I MEANT TO. SHE SAID I WAS TO LOOK UPON YOU AS MY THORN—AND BEAR IT!"

25 'Mistress and maid', *Punch* 1886.

Even the introduction of modern household appliances could make the slavey's lot worse. The gas-stove replaced the warm and friendly kitchen range and left the poor girl in the cold dark on winter evenings.

> Dear Commissioner,
> Will you tell the servants to ask if a gas-stove is kept before they take a situation, for them stoves is the cruellest things in the winter. My mistress makes me turn off the gas after 7 o'clock, and I sit shivering till prayer-time, when I go to bed with cold feet, and I cry sometimes becos I can't well help myself . . . them is the cruellest things for us poor servants.

At the end of its investigation of London slaveys, the *British Weekly* quoted Ruskin: 'A nation is in a bad way when its girls and young women are sad.' It went on to say that 'if he could glance into the many suburban villas in which slaveys sit alone in the kitchen, he would think the case of London hopeless.' The paper intended to study other classes of servants in the capital, but was side-tracked into investigating girl factory workers, sweatshops and home workers. There, its readers could feel indignation without guilt; the exercise was so popular that the servant investigation was dropped.

Servant girls in big cities may have escaped starvation, but they paid a heavy price for their board and lodging and £5–£7 a year. They were made to surrender their claim on the common humanity they shared with their employers. The most startling and grotesque example of what this could mean was revealed in the life of Hannah Culliwick. She was courted by Arthur Mundy, a barrister, for eighteen years. Eventually he summoned the courage to tell his father that he was in love with a servant, but begged that his mother should not be told. Their marriage, in 1873, remained secret for their whole lives: Hannah Culliwick continued to live as Arthur Mundy's servant, waiting on his guests.

Hannah Culliwick accepted her sub-human status. The next generation of girls did not.

> The young girl goes into service today [1925] with a sense of resentment against the mistress she has never seen, not because she herself is being badly treated, but because her mother, and her mother's sisters and girl friends were over-worked, underpaid, badly housed, badly fed and often seduced without redress: they were powerless to resist this treatment, but they resented, and by their example their children learnt to look upon the employer caste as enemies.[10]

In 1873, when Hannah Culliwick had married, there were more women in domestic service than there were men in any single occupation. It had taken over from agriculture as the nation's largest employer. By 1925 domestic service was slipping down the league; the largest employer was the manufacturing industry. Between 1911 and 1931 the number of houses with servants fell by nearly 40 per cent. Middle-class families complained that they could not get servants 'for love or money'.

The rebellion began to appear in the later years of the nineteenth century. As jobs appeared in shops and offices, girls chose that kind of work rather than the indignity of 'service'. At first the situation was masked by the fact that girls who had taken up the work in earlier years could be employed until they were old maids, as shown by the table below.

Changing age distribution among domestic servants 1871–1911

under 15	*15–19*	*20–24*	*25–44*	*45–64*	*over 64*
fall 19%	fall 17%	fall 15%	fall 6%	fall 4%	fall 9%

Some of the change was caused by the introduction of compulsory education. But there were plenty of other reasons why young women servants were becoming hard to find. Unhappily, middle-class ladies had been brought up to regard housework as beneath them, and could not imagine life without servants: 'A woman may sit in a dirty drawing-room which the slip-shod maid has not had time to clean, but she must not take a duster in her hands and polish the legs of the chairs; there is no disgrace in the dust, only in the duster.'[11]

If servants were actually impossible to find, then the domestic civilisation of nineteenth-century England would collapse. Edwardian mistresses were constantly complaining that they could not get the right sort of servants: in place of docile girls born in the country and prepared to spend many years with one family, they were increasingly having to make do with middle-aged worldly-wise women, who changed employer as often as it suited them, or town-bred girls who felt forced into servitude and hated it.

The First World War gave girls opportunities they were ready to seize. They were needed in munitions factories and service trades in large numbers: it was reckoned that half of all bus and tram conductresses had been domestic servants before the war. When other jobs were available which offered limited hours and some personal independence, why should girls go into service?

The shortage of servants after the war was so acute that the Ministry of Reconstruction asked a Women's Advisory Committee to produce a report on the domestic service problem. The report, in 1919, urged that there should be fixed hours of work,

26 It was reckoned that half the bus conductresses in the First World War had been domestic servants.

with definite breaks. It also observed that 'Much of the dissatisfaction and discomfort felt by workers and employers arises from preventable waste of labour and bad general conditions, which could be remedied.' By 'waste of labour' the ladies of the committee were thinking of wasteful fetching and carrying, but the truth was that domestic service was far less necessary anyway than it had been fifty years earlier. The married women of mid-Victorian England were constantly giving birth. In the 1870s there were five and a half million women of childbearing age, and eight and a half million live births. A girl marrying at nineteen in 1871 could expect to have at least seven children over the next twenty-five years, and she would have a one in four chance of dying in those years. If women were expected to maintain a reasonably elegant home, with entertainment for visitors, they had to have help with the children, the cooking and the cleaning.

A girl marrying at the same age in the post-war years faced a very different prospect. In 1919 there were two million more married women of childbearing age than in 1870, but only 115,000 more legitimate births. By 1931 the average family would expect only three or four children, and their mother's chances of surviving her childbearing years had trebled. But middle-class ladies had grown up in houses where servants had taken over all the work, and they could not easily imagine a different kind of life. That very attitude made girls resist going into service if they possibly could.

27 Typing classes, Blackheath Road, 1914.

'The servile attitude of thirty years ago does not exist today,' wrote the owner of a domestic employment agency in 1922. 'In its place is a demeanour of "I'm as good as you".' He went on to say that this was shown in ways which were 'certainly not polite' and which he put down to 'a smattering of education and the democratic times in which we live'.

A second government inquiry into the problem, in 1923, pointed again and again to the hateful sense of class which poisoned relationships between mistresses and maids: the housekeeper who asked, 'What's the use of preaching about it being a dignified calling if they are treated as undignified beings? A domestic servant is made to feel that she is inferior to anyone else'; and the housemaid who complained, 'Some of them make the maids so much lower than themselves – when there is not such a big difference after all.'

There were persistent complaints in the newspapers that unemployed girls were not under enough pressure to take the living-in jobs that were available; this letter from a reader in Worthing to the *Daily Mail* in 1923 is typical:

> Sir,
> It is almost impossible to get a domestic servant in this town and it is high time this dole business ceased. The streets are full of girls dressed to death, who frankly say that as long as they are paid to do nothing they will continue as they are.

In fact, domestic servants were specifically excluded from unemployment benefit until 1938. If they had a choice, girls preferred to work in factories, shops and offices rather than as living-in maids, but if there was no choice then they still went into service.

Winifred Foley was in that position. Born in 1914 in a mining community in the Forest of Dean, she knew that, for her, there was no avoiding the humiliation of domestic service when she was fourteen.

> Now I was to be parted from my family, my friends, my home, the school, the village – all that I loved most dearly. To them too I was a person; but I knew from hearsay that once I had donned that maid's cap and apron I would become a menial, a nobody, mindful of my place, on the bottom shelf.

Her first job was in Islington, at 6*s*. 8*d*. a week: then she went to work for an old lady in the Cotswolds for 5*s*. a week. While visitors were staying, she 'was up at 6.30 pronto and on at the double until nearly 11 o'clock every night'. The visitors included two daughters who took pleasure in sly kicks and throwing stones at her:

> Worse than that was their toffee-nosed attitude of looking me slowly up and down as though I was dirt. I detested them, but, poor kids, it was the way they had been brought up. Their mother was quite aware of most of their antics, but as it was only the maid she turned a blind eye. If they soiled the fronts of their dresses, that was a different matter.

Her mistress refused to accept her notice, and Winifred ran away. Her next job was working for a Cheltenham family who could not afford a maid and she nearly starved.

Although there were certainly families which could afford to feed and house their servants properly, and who treated them as part of the family, such households were becoming comparatively rare. Servant-keeping had been central to a way of life which was disappearing: by 1930 the only families which could afford to keep up servants were in comfortable residential areas. Manufacturing and mining areas had never had many servants (less than one family in a hundred in Lancashire kept servants in 1881) and while the outcry over the 'servant problem' became louder and louder, places that offered anything better than starvation wages were increasingly hard to find. Middle-class families found that they were having to spend far more on their children's education in an increasingly competitive world, and they simply could not afford to offer proper wages. During the depression the number of domestic servants rose, but about 40 per cent of these 'servants' were 'dailies', living in their own homes. It was cheaper to pay a servant than to keep one.

In the late 1930s Celia Fremlin attempted to explore the life of domestic service. She had been brought up in a wealthy Mayfair home, and was just down from Oxford. She was fascinated by the gulf which divided maids and mistresses. 'In this society,' she wrote, 'people who rub shoulders every day can ask such questions about each other as one would expect to be asked about the inhabitants of the Cannibal Isles'.

Like an anthropologist, then, she plunged into the life of the natives, seeking work herself. She found, to her surprise that there was no work available, except on derisory terms. 'If you are prepared to sleep in, and work an average of 14 hours a day for 10*s*. a week, job-hunting can become really pleasant, and will certainly do much to raise your self-esteem.' Since these were terms which neither she nor anyone else would accept, she sought work as a 'daily'. Her background gave her the experience to draw a precise chart of the eddies and currents of social awkwardness involved. Her description of an interview for a job in a suburban semi-detached house gives a clear insight into what makes England different from Germany, France or the United States: clearer by far than comparisons of industrial production or days lost in strikes. The door

> was opened by a mouse-coloured, rather depressed-looking woman who had evidently just taken off her apron.
>
> 'Good afternoon', she said, with a sort of defensiveness which I have learned to be characteristic of the lower-middle-class housewife in dealing with her servants.
>
> 'Please I've come about your advertisement for a general.'

> 'Advertisement for a general?' she said in tones of nervous surprise. 'Come inside. My maid is out this afternoon.' This apparently irrelevant statement was evidently meant as an explanation of the fact that she, the lady of the house, had answered the back door. I followed her to the sitting room. There a fearful doubt assailed her. Was I a visitor still, so that she should show me in? Or was I already a servant, so that she should go in first herself? A few seconds agony on both our parts, and then she solved the problem by going in first herself, making an agonised but sufficiently indeterminate noise in her throat, which could have been interpreted as 'Excuse me' if I wished, and not if I didn't.
>
> That ordeal being over we drew breath once more, feeling rather like convicts who have just crossed some frontier into temporary safety. The interview followed the usual line, though somewhat interspersed with nervous laughs. While I was making up my mind whether the wages she offered would be enough, she showed me into the kitchen, and explained to me how you had to turn the gas on with a jerk, to prevent it burning back. There was a cat on the rug with two kittens. Mrs X stopped and stroked them.
>
> 'These are my babies; aren't they sweet?' she asked, and then stopped nervously. Evidently this was a little bit too familiar. So I stood in painful indecision as to whether to follow her first lead and stoop and stroke them, or her second and say 'Aren't they madam?' with a slight laugh. I chose the latter course, perhaps wrongly. Then we returned to the sitting-room and I decided that the wages were not enough. So we parted, after once more navigating the perilous class-haunted journey through two doors, and ending up with her painful indecision between 'Good afternoon' (servant) and 'Good-bye' (friend). I could almost hear her sigh of relief as I turned my back for good and all.

Celia Fremlin was evidently not able to disguise her background as well as she thought. For her, this was not a serious problem. For Helen Forrester's mother it was a disaster: when she tried to get daily work, and could not hide her accent, she found that employers were so uncomfortable they would not take her on at all.

The Second World War more or less finished off the servant-keeping way of life except for the very rich. Suburban housewives became their own 'general helps'; they had vacuum cleaners, and, eventually, washing machines and central heating to help them, but they were condemned to working in the small, isolated kitchen which had been designed for the servant, while the rest of the family remained sitting in the sitting-room, and ate in the dining-room. Many of these women found that their husbands had inherited the attitudes their own grandmothers had taken to housework. To parody *Fine Ladies and Good Housewives*:

> A man may sit in a dirty drawing-room which the slipshod wife has not had time to clean, but he must not take a duster in his hands and

polish the legs of the chairs, there is no disgrace in the dust, only in the duster.

After the generation of unwilling servants comes the generation of unwilling housewives.

Chapter 3
SOLDIERS

1

The year is 1804: the place, a beer tent at Winchester fair. A party of local men are being entertained in the tent by two strangers. One of the strangers, called Andrews, mentions that he is considering enlisting in the Army, when a recruiting sergeant happens to drop in. Andrews offers him a drink, and finally volunteers to join up. The other stranger, named Peters, declares that he might as well go with his friend. Each is given a shilling in the king's name, and the company give three cheers.

The sergeant then pulls out a handful of coins and a couple of watches, presents the watches to the new recruits and gives them the first part of their bounty money. A number of the locals, impressed, say that they too will volunteer, take the shillings and get a cheer. One man throws down a challenge.

'Oi tell you what, Mr Sergeant! You'll not have me unless you makes me the same as yourself now. So if you loiks to do that, why here's your man.' The sergeant solemnly cuts three v-shaped tapes and pins them on the man's sleeves. He tells the yokel to kneel, and then proclaims: 'Rise, Sergeant Turner, in the name of St George and the Dragon.' 'We had done the trick,' wrote Andrews later, 'and brought in eighteen as able-bodied boobies as any in Hampshire.'

Britain's volunteer army needed all it could find to fight the French. Of course, there were men who joined up freely, many because they were moved by the martial stir of music, uniforms and tales of glory. John Shipp had never been the same since he heard a recruiting sergeant speak of 'gentlemen soldiers, merry life, muskets rattling, cannon roaring, drums beating, colours flying, regiments charging and shouts of victory! victory!' His one desire was to be a part of that spectacle. In 1797 he was working in a field when he was approached by a man with enlistment papers.

> 'Shipp, I have frequently heard of, and observed, your great wish to go for a soldier.' He then read me what was on the paper, and asked

> if I was willing to go. . . . My heart leapt into my mouth. Willing to go! . . . The affair was soon settled and off I marched whistling 'See the conquering hero comes' as I went.

John Shipp was 10 years old. He was an orphan living on the parish, and his benefactor was one of the parish officers. The government wanted to recruit 3,000 pauper children to replace regiments wiped out by disease in the West Indies. John Shipp was no longer a charge on the rates of his native Suffolk village: he had signed up for life.

The Army he had joined went up and down in size according to need. Britain was traditionally hostile to the idea of a standing army: that was seen as an instrument of royal despotism. The real

L^t COL. HOLROYD'S LIGHT DRAGOONS

ALL thoſe who prefer the Glory of bearing Arms to any ſervile mean Employ, and have Spirit to ſtand forth in Defence of their King and Country, againſt the treacherous Deſigns of *France* and *Spain*, in the

Suſſex Light Dragoons,

Commanded by

Lt. Col. John Baker Holroyd,

Let them repair to

Where they ſhall be handſomely Cloathed, moſt compleatly Accoutred, mounted on noble Hunters, and treated with Kindneſs and Generoſity.

28 This recruiting poster of about 1780 neatly presents the appeal of a soldier's life to the simple-minded.

defence of these islands lay in the wooden walls of the Royal Navy. It was recognised that colonial garrisons were needed, and that there had to be a strong force in Ireland, but when there were wars on the Continent regiments were hurriedly raised and even more hurriedly disbanded.

Nobody tried to make the Army attractive for recruits: pay was kept as low as possible (a shilling a day from 1793) and discipline was harsh. The theory was that it had to be harsh, because the recruits were scum, who had to be brutally held in check. They were officered by gentlemen, who purchased their commissions, and between the officers and men there was an absolute gulf. The men had simply to obey. They were drilled in rigid formations for the battlefield, so that they would form up, stay in position and fire when told to do so. A foot soldier in battle was an automaton, and he dressed like one, as Shipp discovered:

> A large pad, a bag filled with sand, was poked into the back of my head, round which the hair was gathered tight, and the whole tied round with a leather thong. When I was dressed for parade, I could scarcely get my eyelids to perform their office; the skin of my eyes and face was drawn so tight by the plug that was stuck in the back of my head, that I could not possibly shut my eyes; add to this, an enormous high stock was poked under my chin; so that, altogether, I felt as stiff as if I had swallowed a ramrod.

This method of tying hair was officially dropped in 1804, but in practice it survived until 1814.

The boy soldiers were marched down to Portsmouth, and were billeted at inns on the way. Some of them stole a goose from one inn and hid it in the drum. When the landlord discovered his loss, he pursued the soldiers and complained to the colonel. A search was ordered, and unfortunately the goose was not yet dead:

> We were all enjoying the fun when the poor goose now near her end gave a heavy groan. The landlord, who was standing near the drum, burst out in surprise 'Dang my buttons my old goose is in that there drum!'. . . . The bird was given up to the publican and we were ordered a flogging, but luckily for us the landlord was a kindly man. Taking a closer look at the bird he pretended not to recognise it as his. 'Mine was pure white Sir,' and he marched off muttering 'Get a child flogged for a tarnation old goose, no no . . .'

The two principal forms of punishment were flogging and the 'black hole'. John Shipp was sentenced to the black hole when he exchanged his shoes for a piece of plum pudding: seven days in solitary confinement in total darkness. Because he was a child, he was released after twenty-four hours.

He benefited from the same indulgence after he had been

transferred to the Cape of Good Hope. He fell in love there, and tried to escape from the Army. A court martial sentenced him to 999 lashes, but 'my commanding Officer was a kind and compassionate man, who had known me from the day I joined the regiment, and he would not consent to my receiving a single stroke'. Men were flogged in public, lashed to a tripod of halberds, to the beat of a drum. After a few strokes there would be blood: after fifty a man's back would usually be a jelly. One hundred lashes would be considered a light punishment. It took four hours to give 1,000 lashes, and it was a sentence of death.

John Shipp went from South Africa to India. He became a fine soldier, brave and resourceful, and when he was 19 he was commissioned as an ensign. 'From the day of my appointment I was

29 John Shipp in action.

metamorphised into a gentleman. I had a new coat, my hair was cut and curled and I was invited to dine with the Commander in Chief.' Under the stress of continuous warfare, the Army was becoming professional enough to give a commission to a pauper, but it required him to change his class. He was now a gentleman, and had to live like one. This needed money, and Shipp could not have been commissioned without senior officers becoming his patrons and supplying his needs.

The Army did not normally offer such career prospects to young men: if they enlisted with full knowledge of what they were doing it was usually because they were starving. Many were Scottish and Irish peasants escaping from abject poverty, or starvelings from the manufacturing towns. Those who wanted a bounty and a uniform, rather than a new life, preferred to join the Militia. This was a local defence force which was greatly enlarged during the French war. Eligible men were called up by lottery, but they could pay substitutes to stand in for them. Most of the men who served were substitutes: few of the balloted men could afford extended periods of duty, and there were insurance schemes to find and pay for substitutes. The Militia could not be obliged to serve overseas.

Thomas Jackson joined the Staffordshire Militia in 1803, as a substitute. His father was a buckle-maker ruined by the wars. 'Nothing but starvation was looked for by the working classes. I used to see my mother always weeping, and my father always grieving.' A man might collect up to £60 for acting as a substitute, as well as a £6 bounty. Jackson knew that his parents needed the money, but he joined secretly, knowing they would forbid him if they could.

The regular Army looked to the Militia as a potential source of recruits: in the later years of the war with France, it was the main source.

> The Militia would be drawn up in line, and the officers, or non-commissioned officers, from the regiments requiring volunteers, would give a glowing description of their several regiments, describing the victories they had gained, and the honours they had acquired, and concluded by offering, as a bounty, to volunteers for life £14, to volunteers for the limited period of seven years £11. If these inducements were not effectual in getting men, then coercive measures were adopted; heavy and long field exercises were forced on them, which were so oppressive that to escape them men would embrace the alternative and join the colours.

The Army also collected a harvest of men when the Militia was stood down after a long period of service: where else could these half-soldiers go?

Eventually Jackson joined the Coldstream Guards, living the tidy life of a British barrack soldier. Poor John Shipp had also come back to England, where he soon got into debt trying to live as a gentleman; he sold his commission and left the Army, but he was adrift, and 'in six months I found myself without a home, without a friend, and without a penny'. He returned to the familiar world of military life, happily re-enlisting as a private and being sent back to India.

Of course, there were boys who were filled with patriotic fervour and who wanted to serve their king: but if they could not afford a commission they might well prefer to join a local volunteer force, to

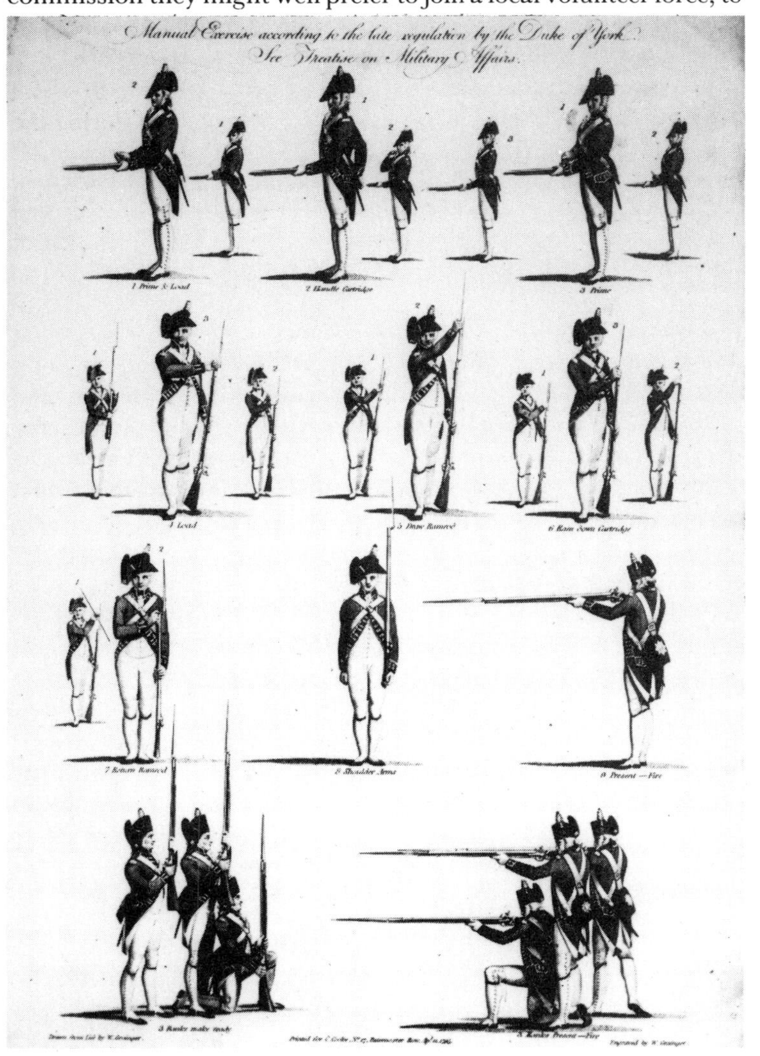

30 Formal infantry drill was intended to turn men into automatons, who could be trusted to hold their position and respond to simple orders in a precise way.

defend their community against invasion, rather than become a regular soldier on a shilling a day in some God-forsaken spot abroad. Thomas Morris joined the Loyal Volunteers of St George's, Middlesex, when he was 16; this was in 1812, when there were stirring victories in Spain, and it would be dashing to wear a uniform. He was rather disillusioned by his comrades, who saw the force as a device to evade conscription in the militia without having to pay for a substitute. Earnestly wishing to be among fighting men, he transferred to the 73rd (Highlanders) Regiment. Under 18 he would be classed as a boy, with lower pay, so he lied about his age.

The regiment sailed to Denmark. On the way, a soldier who stole a couple of carrots was given 150 lashes, to Morris's dismay. When they arrived, their first task was to repair fortifications destroyed by the French.

> There being a defiency of labourers, about 1,000 young women of the lower classes were engaged, and, dressed in male attire, were set to work, and were found very efficient, the women in that country being inured to field labour. Several ludicrous mistakes took place with some of our men, who in carrying on affairs of gallantry were not always able to distinguish the women from the men.

From there they went to the Low Countries, which were now the main theatre of war. Thomas Jackson, too, had gone there with the Coldstream Guards: by now he was married, and although some soldiers were able to take their wives with them, the number was restricted to six per company. Jackson's wife was not one of the six.

Jackson was wounded at Bergen-op-Zoom, and he had to have his leg cut off:

> When the saw was applied I found it extremely painful; it was worn out; it stuck in the way, as a bad saw would when sawing a green stick. I said, 'Oh, sir, have you not a better saw?' He said he was sorry he had not, as they were all worn out.

The operation lasted half an hour.

Morris was luckier, and was still in one piece at the battle of Waterloo, in June 1815. The French army had once been made of aristocratic officers and parade-ground soldiers like the British, but the revolution had changed all that. Napoleon had developed a conscript army of citizen patriots, who formed great columns to charge and sweep all before them. Morris was in the front of the line that faced them:

> My comrade was on my right hand, in the front face of the square in the front rank, kneeling; he had a trifling defect in his speech, and at every charge the cavalry made, he would say 'Tom, Tom; here comes the *calvary*.'

First the lines were swept by French artillery:

> It came as thick as hail upon us. On looking round, I saw my left-hand man falling backwards, the blood gushing from his left eye; my poor comrade on my right, by the same discharge, got a ball through his right thigh, of which he died a few days afterwards.

Then came the charges, but all day the lines held. At the end of the day, when Napoleon's reinforcements failed to arrive, he launched his Old Guard in a final massive assault. They had never yet failed in an attack.

As the accelerating storm of horsemen thundered forward, the British line remained still and silent. When they were only a few feet away, the signal came, and the volley crashed out. Three hundred horsemen fell, the attack faltered. The 52nd Foot wheeled and poured a volley into the French flank. Wellington waved his hat, and the whole of his line charged. The column was destroyed, and the revolutionary war was over.

Tom Morris received the Waterloo medal, the first campaign medal issued. Thomas Jackson, of course, did not. He had already returned to England. Two months after Waterloo, he appeared before a board at the Royal Hospital, Chelsea, where he was awarded a pension of a shilling a day.

> a mighty poor recompense, I thought, for having spent twelve years of the prime of my manhood in the service of my country; lost the benefit of my trade during that period; and, worst of all, crippled for life by the loss of a limb.

He was also awarded a wooden leg, 'free of cost – without money – without price; a free, gratuitous national gift. Ought I not have been very grateful? Somehow or other, at that time, I was not grateful.'

As for Tom Morris, he had one more service to perform for his country. With the war over he was needed for peacekeeping duties at home. Barracks had been set up near the large manufacturing towns in 1792, so that large forces would be on hand in the event of trouble. Morris was stationed in Birmingham. There was a strong radical movement in the town, urging the reform of parliament, and this, combined with high prices and unemployment, led the authorities to expect trouble.

On 28 October 1816, there was a rioting mob in the Birmingham streets.

> The two troops of the 15th Hussars were in the barracks, and my company was scattered over the town in quarters. As soon as I heard of the riot I went round, collected our men, and took them to the captain's quarters, who complimented me for my alacrity in getting the men together. The idea of having an opportunity of contending

> with a mob seemed most congenial to his sentiments. . . . The high constable went with us, and proceeded to read the riot act. On some brickbats and stones being thrown at us, our brave captain gave orders to load, and he then gave direction that we should fire among the mob, when the high constable interposed and said 'There was no necessity for that yet.' 'Then,' said the officer, 'if I am not allowed to fire, I shall take my men back!' The constable's patriotic answer deserves to be recorded: 'Sir,' said he, 'you are called upon to aid and assist the civil powers, and if you fire upon the people without my permission, and death ensues, you will be guilty of murder; and if you go away without my leave, it will be at your peril.'

Morris knew that 'the male population of Birmingham contains a greater number of old soldiers than any other town in the kingdom, and in war time they furnish double the number of recruits of any town in the kingdom'; he was afraid of the consequences of 'an uncalled-for and wanton attack on the lives of their townsmen.'

The disturbance ended without shooting. In Morris's account of the affair, there is one point worth noting. He says that 'the riot was produced by a tradesman who had the superintendence of some relief fund, saying that seven shillings a week was enough for a man and his family to subsist on.' According to *The Times*, the sum in question was actually nine shillings a week. Not even the hardest heart was credited with expecting a pauper to keep a family on a shilling a day. That was, though, the pension on which Thomas Jackson was expected to keep his wife. And it is not hard to guess why it was the figure Tom Morris remembered. It was the pay of a soldier.

2

The age of heroism ended in 1815. In the long peace that followed Waterloo, the Army was seen as a burden, and the soldier was regarded with contempt.

> A man one degree removed from idiocy, with brains sufficient to direct his powers of mischief and endurance, may make a distinguished soldier. As to the men, they get the word of command to advance or fall back, and they do it; they are told to strip and be flogged, and they do it, or to flog, and they do it; to murder or be murdered, and they obey; for their food and clothing and twopence a day for their tobacco.

The force at home was as small as possible: when there were war scares in the 1840s, only 5,000–10,000 men were available to form a field army, after garrisoning forts and ports. Soldiers were kept in barracks where they were allowed 300–400 cubic feet each; convicts were allowed 1,000 cubic feet.

A Sergeant MacMullen analysed the reasons for men joining up in the 1840s: he concluded that two in three were driven to it by unemployment, and the rest were almost all 'idle – bad characters – criminals – perverse sons – discontented and restless'. He reckoned that in a batch of 120 recruits, one joined out of ambition, and a further two could be described as 'respectable persons induced by misfortune or imprudence.'

The Army had to be maintained at some strength, however, because Britain had to garrison a world-wide empire. Up to three-quarters of the infantry were kept abroad, in Canada, Gibraltar, The Cape, and, above all, in India. Half forgotten at home, they fought small wars against natives. Grand strategy was not needed; what counted were the regimental qualities of discipline, order, pride and courage.

The short-service enlistments of the Napoleonic wars were ended: men signed on for life or, after 1847, for twenty-one years. Their whole existence was the army, and inevitably Britain was developing a military caste, with officers brought up to the service of the empire. A man looking back on his career at the end of the century was able to write:

> I am a soldier's son, born in an Indian garrison (December 9th 1838), a soldier's grandson, with a host of relatives, near and distant, and as I write this I gaze at family portraits and miniatures in uniforms of a bygone day. My earliest associations were with soldiers; a soldier's wife was my nurse, my father's orderly carried me on his shoulders at the immature age of three to the dame school where I learned my A.B.C.; my favourite toys were a wooden sword and the buttons off an old regimental coat.

These words are from the reminiscences of Arthur Griffiths (called *Fifty Years of Public Service*). He was brought up in the Isle of Man, where his family lived with other army families, and he was sent to a public school that specialised in such boys,

> a rough and ready Spartan institution, run on bare, economical lines. . . . There was a so-called English side specially designed for the preparation of candidates for the army commissions to meet the newly devised tests of examination, curiously imperfect and inadequate as they were.

The examinations were so imperfect as to be irrelevant. The British public, and especially parliament, feared a standing Army run by professional soldiers; commissions were awarded to gentlemen who could buy them, rather than soldiers who trained for them. In 1856, Palmerston defended the system by saying that

> I think it extremely desirable that the British Army should be officered by gentlemen as a rule . . . I think, speaking plainly, that in all armies it is the higher classes who lead the lower classes, and it seldom happens that the persons belonging to the lower classes can rise, with comfort to themselves, to a position for which they were not originally destined.

The result was a military force commanded by men who did not know what they were doing. Having purchased their commissions, many barely served at all, but carried on their normal lives on half pay, waiting for their country's call. Those officers who were the working soldiers of the empire were generally called 'Indian' officers, and, since they were plainly not gentlemen, could not expect to be left in charge should a real war take place.

Arthur Griffiths would obviously not fit into the Army as an enlisted man – he was not a starving Irish peasant or a child from an industrial slum – but his father could not afford a commission for him. He was therefore considering possible civilian careers in 1854, when he was 15 and coming to the end of his schooling. And then the Crimean war began.

> The whole countryside was eager to send help, and, returning home for the Christmas holidays, I tumbled upon a family party intent on knitting mufflers and cardigans for the men at the front. Within a few minutes of my arrival home the war came still closer to me. I caught a meaning look on my father's face as he asked my mother, 'Shall I tell him?' and a sad look on hers as she answered, 'I would rather you did not accept it.' 'It' was the offer of a commission at once, provided I could pass the necessary examination.

The war had broken out in a fever of public excitement. The Army had been occupied for forty years with colonial wars: Britain, the world's only great industrial power, still basked in the glory of Waterloo. The British had forgotten what war meant, and the popular press turned foreign policy into a moral crusade: 'We are sure that there is not an honest British bosom, within the wide range of Her Majesty's Dominions, which will not heave with indignation at the intelligence which we this day publish from Constantinople,' – thus wrote the *Morning Advertiser* in January 1854. The news concerned the fighting between Russians and Turks which had been going on for more than two months, and might ultimately give 'the Autocrat' (i.e. the Czar – also known as 'this fiend in human form') mastery of part of the collapsing Turkish empire. 'Has the British bosom ceased to throb in response to the claim of humanity?' demanded the *Advertiser*. 'Has justice ceased to occupy her throne in the English heart? Has the national honour – that which used to be the glory of every Englishman in every part of the world – lost its hold on the minds of the people of these realms? It is impossible.'

The *Advertiser* was right. There was a new Britain, with a population of concerned town-dwellers; they responded to just such language. The government was swept unwillingly, but irresistibly, into a war which was to be fought for the highest motives.

> We had been blessed with peace for 40 years. The soldiers had degenerated in the eyes of the public; they were looked upon as useless and expensive ornaments. But suddenly a change came over the people, and every sight of the Queen's uniform called forth emotions of enthusiasm from all conditions of men. Our highest mortal interest – 'Honour' – was now at stake, and the pulse of the whole country beat high for her soldier sons.

Those are the words of a volunteer soldier called Timothy Gowing, the 19-year-old son of a Baptist minister from Norwich. In the early days of the war there were plenty of volunteers like himself, neither destitute nor fools. For soldiers were the darlings of the nation. When Gowing's regiment set off from the barracks at Manchester 'one could have walked over the heads of the people, wrought up to such a state of excitement as almost amounted to madness'.

31 As the soldiers went away to war, the *Illustrated London News* published a song-sheet, so that families could demonstrate their feelings round the piano.

The industrial age had produced a new political force – 'public opinion'. For the first time, there was an informed audience in England who would follow the day-to-day conduct of a war with concern not only for the grand questions of victory and defeat, but with a hunger for details, including details about the soldiers themselves. The steam ship, the railway train, and the electric telegraph enabled such news to come quickly: 40,000 copies of *The Times* were sold every day, and the paper sent a special correspondent to the war. Gowing's letters to his parents normally began, 'Long before this reaches you, you will have seen . . .'

The Army was in no condition to withstand the spotlight of public attention. The soldiers were first sent to Varna, on the Bulgarian shore of the Black Sea. Cholera broke out among them. The dead were laid to rest in the harbour, with weights round their ankles. The weights were too light, and as the decomposing bodies filled with gas they bobbed up, and, weighed down at the feet, they floated head and shoulders above the waves. With relief, the Army left Varna and sailed out past the corpses of their comrades to the Crimea, where they came to Calamita Bay. It took five days to complete disembarkation. As the soldiers in the tail end of the fleet climbed down into the small boats that would take them ashore, they looked across the water, and saw, to their horror, the same sightless eyes watching them, the same death's head grins welcoming them, as Balaclava's first fever victims lifted their rotting heads from the sea.

The war degenerated into a long siege of the Russian naval fortress at Sebastopol, and the men who were responsible for keeping the British troops supplied and fed and healthy had no idea how to cope. Timothy Gowing had become a sergeant in a doomed Army.

> October 29
> My dear Parents . . .
> Well, I've got back to camp again. We have had a rough 24 hours. The enemy kept pitching shell into us nearly all night, and it took us all our time to dodge their Whistling Dick, as our men have named them. We are standing up to our ankles in mud and water, like a lot of drowned rats, nearly all night; the cold, bleak wind cutting through our thin clothing (that is now getting very thin and full of holes, and nothing to mend them with). This is ten times worse than the fighting. We have not an ounce too much to eat . . . we cannot move without sinking to our ankles in mud. The tents we have to sleep in, are full of holes and there is nothing but mud to lie down in . . .

The British public, alarmed by reports of the lack of food, clothing and shelter, began to send everything they could. But the army was unable to do anything about it. There was not even the elementary organisation to unpack the supplies that were delivered, let alone get them to the men – and all the world knew about it. 'The England of European history is now in the Crimea', said *The Times* in its 'Christmas Message' for 1854. 'At this moment it would be rash even to conjecture the fate of those 54,000 men. Do they still maintain the unequal fight – chilled, drenched, famished, utterly neglected?' By February, less than 5,000 of those men were still fit: about 9,000 more unfit men were with them. Of the rest, 7,000 had been killed or wounded by the enemy. The bulk of the Army, over 30,000 men, had fallen victim to disease and starvation. Those who had not died in the field had endured the journey across the Black Sea to the hospital at Scutari. Gowing, bayonetted in hand-to-hand fighting, made the journey in a crowded steamship:

> We were packed on board anyhow, live or die; and away we went at once. . . . We had not enough medical officers with us to look after 50 men, much less three or four hundred. . . . We lost a very great number of men, I must say, for the want of sufficient medical men.

32 Leech's cartoon in *Punch* indicated the sympathy of the public for the plight of the soldiers, and the contempt for the men who ran the Army.

THE BRITISH FORCES AND THE CRIMEAN WAR.

PATIENT HEROES.

"WELL, JACK! HERE'S GOOD NEWS FROM HOME. WE'RE TO HAVE A MEDAL."
"THAT'S VERY KIND. MAYBE ONE OF THESE DAYS WE'LL HAVE A COAT TO STICK IT ON!"

When the ship reached Scutari, the hospital was too full to receive them. *Times* readers were given a full account of the place, with corridors lined with trestles bearing the sick and wounded: 'For some weeks there were men lying in bed, with dysentry or with open sores, who had not had a change of linen for months.' Gowing was obliged to endure a continuation of the voyage, on to Malta. Between decks were 'men shrinking with pain, others lying in a state of putrefaction, others in a morbid state, others being carried up on deck, to be consigned, wrapped in a blanket, to a watery grave'.

As the Army perished, the French took over most of the British line before Sebastopol. It was hard to find enough recruits to man even the small British force remaining: the horrors had been too well reported. Raw lads like Arthur Griffiths were pushed into uniform. He passed his examination readily enough, and was appointed as a subaltern to the 63rd West Suffolks. When he went to the regimental agent for his uniform,

> dear old Mr. Codd came to me himself, saying, 'And who might you be, young sir?' Then when I declared my name and quality Mr Codd laughed aloud and, calling to his head clerk within, cried, 'Alfred! Sebastopol will soon fall! Come and look at the last reinforcement!'

Griffiths was first sent to Ireland, where recruiting was in full swing, and new recruits were running wild, drunk on their bounty money. Even this perennial source of men was drying up: too many Irishmen had perished of starvation or escaped abroad. By the time Arthur Griffiths arrived before Sebastopol, in July 1855, conditions had much improved: supplies were properly organised, and Florence Nightingale had reduced the hospital death rate from 44 to 2.2 per cent. But Britain's surviving Army was now so small that it had to be supplemented by foreign mercenaries. Griffiths himself was still only 16, and found that 'It was delightful, a source of endless and absorbing joy, to be doing the work of a full-grown man, as I thought, to give orders and to be obeyed, not without condescension, by the war-worn veterans I was supposed to command.' Those veterans had, by now, considerable contempt for their leaders in the field: Gowing observed that '*Punch*, in 1855, might well have it that the Crimean army was an army of lions led by donkeys.' And the new drafts were raw boys. Some had not even learned to fire their rifles when they were sent into battle.

On 8 September 1855 there was a massive Allied attack on Sebastopol. The French assault captured major sections of the defences. The small British force achieved nothing so splendid: it was routed, losing 2,500 men. Britain's soldiers had no more stomach for the fight. But neither had the Russians. That night, and the next day, the Russians evacuated their citadel. And the allies marched in. A British captain wrote:

> I looked towards the Malakov, there was the French flag, the Tricolour, planted on its Parapet . . . no flag floated on the Parapet on which I stood and if it had, I could have seized it and dashed it into the ditch we could not pass, or hid it in the bosom of the young officer dead at my feet.

For every British soldier who had died on a battlefield, eight more had died off it. But they had not died in vain. The whole nation had, for the first time, been deeply concerned for its soldiers. From the Crimean war dates a series of investigations and reforms which eventually led to the Army being recreated as a centrally-organised and professional body, with efficient officers in charge of short-enlistment volunteers. Even the lynch-pin of the old system, the purchase of commissions, was discarded.

The depth of national feeling for the soldiers was shown when they came home. Gowing was deeply moved by it.

> The whole nation appeared determined to do honour to the Crimean Army . . . a very great number had lost their limbs, but were looked after by the nation at large. Her Most Gracious Majesty showed a kind motherly feeling, for that kind loving creature shed many a tear over her maimed soldiers.

The country was taking new interest in its soldiers – and the soldiers felt a new concern for their country. Literate soldiers like Gowing were themselves part of the patriotic public that read *Punch* and the *Morning Advertiser*. No longer could it be said that soldiers obeyed their orders simply to receive 'their food and clothing and twopence a day for tobacco'. Gowing ended his account of the return:

> A rough old loyal soldier of the Emerald Isle called out in Aldershot after Her Majesty had said a few kind words to the Troops, and thanked us for doing our duty, 'Where is the man that would not fight for such a Queen?' I would re-echo it, 'Where is the Briton that would not do or die to uphold our glorious old flag?'

The reform of the Army after the Crimean was thorough, but it was very slow. William Robertson was the son of a Lincolnshire village tailor and postmaster, and he joined up in 1877. He was ambitious to make a career as a professional soldier, but the Army he joined was still cast in the mould of Waterloo: 'Pipe-clay, antiquated and useless forms of drill, blind obedience to orders, ramrod-like rigidity on parade, and similar time-honoured practices were the chief qualification by which a regiment was judged.'

Robertson was an unusual recruit: at least 90 per cent of enlisted men came from ordinary working families, and two-thirds of those were from the poorest slums. His mother was aghast. 'There are plenty of things Steady Young Men can do when they can read and write as you can . . . [the Army] is a refuge for all Idle People . . . I shall name it to no one for I am ashamed to think of it. I would rather Bury you than see you in a red coat.' Army pay was still based on the shilling a day of the Napoleonic wars, and Jack Frost was still the best recruiting sergeant the Army knew.

The conditions were slowly improving. In 1857, the death rate in Army barracks was higher than in the worst civilian slums, or the most dangerous occupations. By 1877, better sanitation and medical knowledge had done some good. One man in three still had venereal disease, but at least Army education tried to ensure that soldiers could read the awful warnings issued to them. And in 1870 the term of service had been cut from twenty-one years to twelve, with at least half spent as a Reserve. This meant that the 'old soldier', hard drinking, hard swearing, past his prime and with nothing to look forward to, gradually disappeared.

At the same time, increasing emphasis was placed on the education and training of officers. An officer was still a gentleman, and although the purchase of commissions was ended in 1870 it did not become any easier to commission a poor boy from the ranks. 'Wullie' Robertson happened to be blessed with probably the best administrative brain in the whole Army, and worked hard for a commission, but when he was eventually offered one he turned it down because 'I had no private means, and without some £300 a year it was impossible to live as an officer in a cavalry regiment at home.'

He was eventually persuaded that he could manage, but only by being posted to India, where pay was higher and the expenses of officers were lower. India had now become the Army's true home, and as the empire expanded, the garrison forces everywhere were based on the Indian model.

> The army carried its own life with it wherever it went, and you lived pretty much the same, whether you were in India, China, or any other place. You lived between the barrack-room and the wet canteen, without any social life at all. . . . There was a ritual every evening. The men would make themselves absolutely spotless – uniform pressed, boots polished, hair plastered down – as if every

> one of them had a girl-friend waiting at the gate. But they had no girl-friends, and they never went out of the gate. They went straight down to the wet canteen and got drunk. That was what they got dressed up for.

It was unattractive, but better than a life of misery and want. Almost every minute of the day, from 6 a.m. Reveille to 10 p.m. Lights Out, was ruled by ritual and bugle calls, but it was a life that transformed weak and ignorant boys into a well-drilled and capable body of men. Discipline was severe; the lash was reluctantly abandoned in 1881, and prison sentences were common for minor offences. Soldiers were not encouraged to think, and certainly not to criticise. Regimental loyalty and courage in battle were their highest values. Such changes as took place were always the result of discussion outside the Army, not in it.

Their duties were mainly concerned with maintaining order: no longer in England, where the police had taken over, but in far-flung lands and, depressingly, in Ireland. Robertson was in Ireland in the 1880s.

> Evictions for non-payment of rent were the most common source of trouble, and some of them would be attended by thousands of sympathisers from the countryside, necessitating, in the opinion of the authorities, the presence of a considerable military force. I have known as much as a brigade of all arms employed on this duty, the evicted tenant being an old woman occupying a dilapidated hovel, and the unpaid rent amounting to a few shillings.

The wars they fought were struggles with natives, requiring heroic qualities of courage and determination. Up to the Boer war it was regarded as cowardice to fire rifles from cover, but humiliating defeats at the hands of the South African farmers taught the Army that modern rifles were best fired lying down. Khaki was accepted as a practical fighting uniform. Junior officers were expected to act with dash and initiative. By 1914 the regiments of the British Army were a highly professional fighting force. But they were in no way prepared for war with another industrial power.

When war came with Germany, Britain was able to muster a force of 160,000 men, including reserves: only 100,000 could be put into the field at once. Germany and France had conscript armies which, on paper, amounted to some four million men each. The British Army was efficiently organised, but it was overwhelmed by the sheer weight of numbers. The British and French finally held a line against the German advance, and dug in. The great trench war had begun.

Industrial Europe had created defensive weapons far more powerful than the means of assault. Barbed wire, machine guns and rapid-fire rifles created walls which neither side could cross. But the British Army, trained for rapid movement and skirmishing in open country, did not suppose that it would stay in the trenches. The trenches themselves were left as crude ditches – they were, after all, soon to be abandoned, in theory. As winter drew on, they filled with cold water.

> Paddling about by day, sometimes with water above the knees, standing at night, hour after hour on sentry duty, while the drenched boots, puttees and breeches became stiff like cardboard with ice from the freezing cold air. Rain, snow, sleet, wind, mud and general discomfort all added their bit to the misery of trench life.

The British Army had lost about half its strength meeting the initial German impact. The First Battalion of the Queen's Royal Regiment, for instance, was reduced from 998 men to 29 in ten weeks, in the autumn of 1914. Attempts to break through the German trenches in the weeks that followed reduced the man-power still further. In March 1915, the 2nd Scottish Rifles were sent 'over the top' at Neuve Chapelle, and ninety minutes later 400 casualties were lying between the trenches or hanging on the barbed wire in a space 200 yards by 100. That battalion was down to less than 150 men by the following morning.

By the spring of 1915 the Army that had garrisoned the empire was virtually wiped out. Only its General Staff remained intact. The war, so far as Britain was concerned, passed into the hands of a new and utterly different kind of soldier. The soldier of Kitchener's Army – the New Army Man.

The war minister, Lord Kitchener, set about creating an entire new Army at the end of August 1914. His appeal went out to a population that was enthusiastic for the war, and the results staggered everyone. In three weeks, half a million men enlisted.

These were men of a different stamp from the Regular Army recruits of earlier years. Most of them still came from the great industrial cities, but they were far from starving. Frank Burn, for instance, worked for his father in Bradford market: 'I was about 17 year old and I weighed 17 stone, you can tell what I was like, y'know, Fatty Arbuckle . . . I got to know my pal had joined up, so I went to try and join them.'

He was under age, but that was no problem. They turned him down simply because Bradford had already raised an entire battalion and there was no room for him. But in February a second local battalion was raised, and he was in. Officially known as the 16th and 18th West Yorkshire, the men preferred to call themselves the 1st and 2nd Bradford Pals. Similar bodies were formed all over the country: 'The atmosphere was wonderful: a gang of lads all

33 The recruiting posters for Kitchener's Army bore a stark message: the Army was no longer a separate world, but laid claim to everyone.

together and more or less of the same age, with the same ideas – they all wanted to travel and to see life and adventure, you know, just something different.' They had the encouragement of their friends and families, and the promise of release as soon as the war was over – which most thought would not be long. The act of joining up was no longer a sudden step into a different world. This Army was being formed before it had officers or weapons or uniforms or even accommodation for many of its soldiers. Frank Burn was billeted in his own home: 'I was doing guards with dummy guns and me dad was coming along at night and bringing us fish and chips and bottles of beer.'

Officers, where possible, were supposed to be public school men, but even that touch of the old order was hard to maintain. It did not take long to produce weapons and uniforms, and after an enjoyable period of open-air training, the New Army was put into the trenches. George Coppard, another of Kitchener's volunteers, wrote a detailed account of the routine there:

> The danger period for attack was at dawn and dusk. . . . Sleepers were roused, and the front trenches were speedily manned ready for any move by the enemy. Sentries stood on raised fire-steps, peering over the parapet, let rip a devilish traverse, which skims the topmost sandbags. Dirt is flung into faces and foul language seethes through everyone's lips – the bastard. Not far off a Vickers gun returns the hate at an appreciably faster tempo as it shoots a hundred rounds or so across No Man's Land. Although there is no special cause for alarm, intermittent rifle fire develops . . . it is the morning hate.

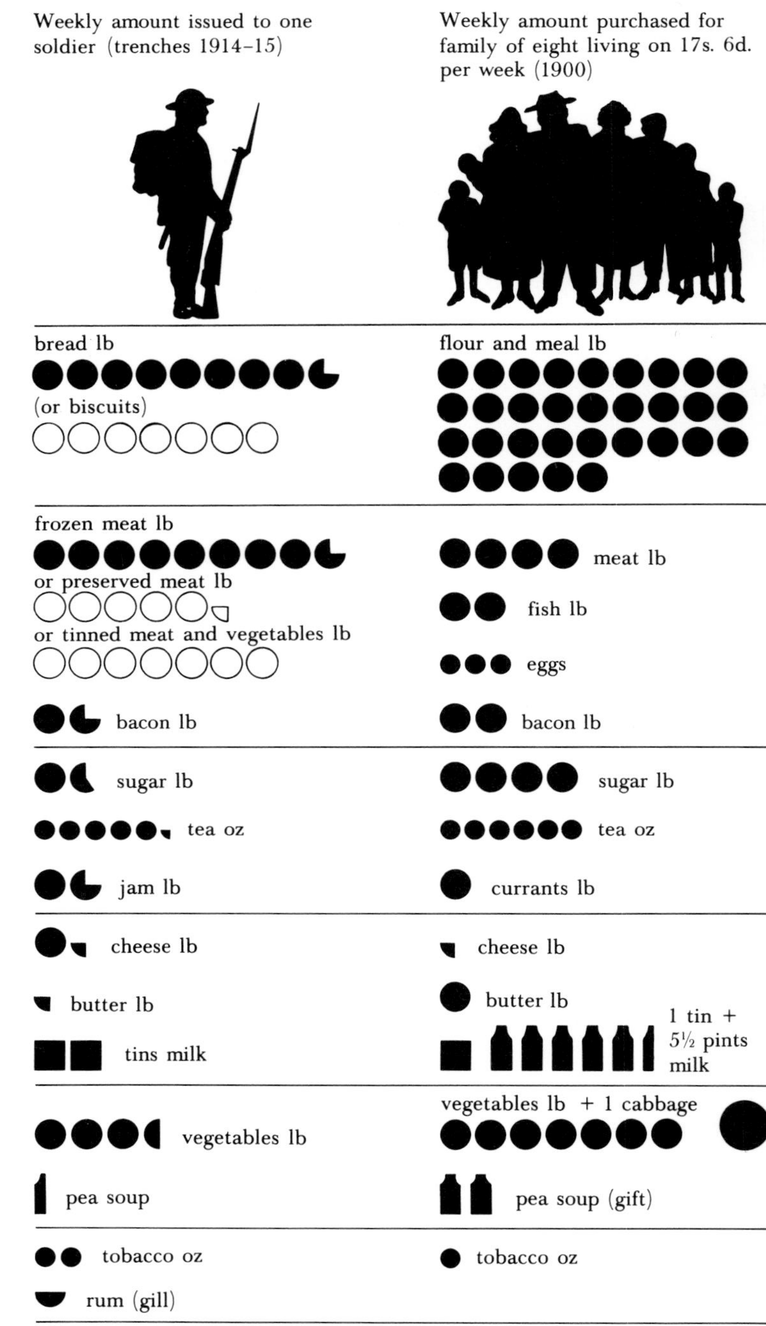

Figure 4 Food in the trenches.

Hate was important. No-man's-land was sometimes so narrow that soldiers of the opposing armies could speak to each other across it – they were often further from their own officers. Officers were trained in the importance of an offensive attitude: a pamphlet, allegedly produced by the General Staff, was entitled *Am I being Offensive Enough: Notes for Junior Officers*. The frequent shooting that was encouraged was particularly dangerous for tall men. The Regular Army soldiers, from the poorest homes, were generally under-sized and the trenches were not deep enough for six-footers. The New Army was not only younger than the old but also taller – but the trenches were no deeper.

The Regular Army regiments still existed in name, of course, but by the spring of 1916 few of their officers or men had served in the pre-war Army. Most were new volunteers, like the New Army men. The main inheritance from the original Army was its language, full of Hindustani words like 'Blighty' and 'Napoo'.

This Army could not be expected to act with dash and initiative and so, when a breakthrough was planned across the River Somme, the main work was given to the artillery. A massive bombardment was designed to destroy all life in the German trenches and cut the barbed wire: then the troops would simply rise from their trenches and advance in waves to occupy the German lines.

Unfortunately, the German trenches were strongly reinforced and the artillery barrage did not even destroy the wire. There had been 24,000 British soldiers at Waterloo; 54,000 had been sent to the Crimea. British casualities on 1 July 1916, as battalion after battalion walked through concentrated machine gun and rifle fire onto the wire, exceeded 60,000. The 2nd Bradford Pals were roughly halved in number. Many battalions fared far worse than that: 'You changed completely over, after July 1st, your mind changed completely over.'

34 Field Marshal Sir W. R. ('Wullie') Robertson.

Frank Burn, like thousands of others, resented what he saw as the uncaring remorselessness of the General Staff. For instead of stopping the attack, the men were told to continue it. The battle of the Somme officially ended on 20 November, when total casualties exceeded one million.

'Wullie' Robertson had made his career in the General Staff, and by 1916 had risen to become its chief. Trained in the old regular Army, and never having been in battle himself, he never understood the men he now controlled. Years later he wrote that this battle was a step towards victory

> But the far-reaching effects . . . were not in all cases appreciated by ministers, some of whom asserted that the Battle of the Somme was a

> ghastly failure, and one persisted in measuring the amount of our success by the kilometres of ground gained, with little or no regard to the moral ascendancy our troops had established.

Frank Burn did not feel morally ascendant. 'I'm very bitter. Always have been and always will be. And so was everyone else.'

There was resentment at the sheer physical distance between commanders like Field Marshal Haig and the trenches, and there was increasing resentment at the different treatment of officers and men when they came out of the trenches. George Coppard wrote:

> On my frequent visits to company HQ I saw the kind of life the officers led when not in the front line or on patrol. Their greatest comfort was sleeping bags and blankets, and room to stretch out for sleep. Batmen were handy to fetch and carry. Meals and drinks were prepared and set before them. . . . Such things, and many other small trifles, demonstrated the great differences between the creature comforts of the officers, and the almost complete absence of them for the men. That's what the war was like.

Individual officers were respected. But the emphasis on 'offensiveness', the idea of fighting the war by attrition, without concern for the lives of the men, created a dull despair that led men to hope for a wound that would send them home, 'a blighty one'.

Although little of this was revealed in the press, volunteers no longer came forward in great numbers: to continue the war of attrition, conscription had to be introduced. The whole available manhood of the country was put into uniform: even the unfit could be used in labour battalions. Only the needs of the factories, or the limits of age, were allowed to keep men at home. War on this scale was quite new; many began to think that it would last for ever. By the time Germany finally collapsed in exhaustion, over five million men had put on British Army uniforms. Nearly one million of them were dead. And then came demobilisation.

George Coppard's story of his return to civilian life will stand for many.

> Lloyd George and company had been full of big talk about making the country fit for heroes to live in, but it was just so much hot air. No practical steps were taken to rehabilitate the broad mass of demobbed men, and I joined the queues for jobs as messengers, window cleaners and scullions. . . . Single men picked up twenty-nine shillings per week unemployment pay as a special concession, but there were no jobs for the 'heroes' who haunted the billiard halls as I did. The government never kept their promises. It is a sad story.

The experience of life in Kitchener's Army had cemented life-long bonds between men who served together, but it had also destroyed their trust in the men who ran the affairs of the country. Above all, there was anger at the contrast between the condition of so many ex-soldiers, and the handsome awards given to the leaders of the Army. I met Frank Burn at a reunion dinner of the Bradford Pals, on Remembrance Day, 1977. When we talked the next day, he was still wearing his Earl Haig Fund poppy, but he had no love for the memory of his commander-in-chief: 'They made him an Earl, and gave him an hundred thousand quid. I know what I'd have given him.'

THE EX-SERVICE MAN.

The Independent Paper for Those Who have Served.

VOL. 1. No. 51. SATURDAY, NOV. 1, 1919. (Registered at G.P.O. as a Newspaper.) Price 2d. Weekly.

"Damn Your Charity!"

See Page ONE

35 *The ex-service man.*

4

In 1918 people thought their sacrifice had brought an end to war. The Army was a bad memory. But soldiers had still to cope with the Irish troubles, and the General Strike, and difficulties in distant parts of the empire. As usual, recruits came from the desperately poor: 'Every Monday morning there would be a queue a couple of hundred yards long outside the pawnshop.' Gerry was one of the

36 Recruiting poster, 1920.

desperately poor. His family had come to London from Ireland when he was a child; his father found occasional casual work as a docker. In 1928, Gerry was 20 years old, and unemployed.

> My brothers and I, we often slept out in the parks so that we wouldn't go home, because we knew that at that time there wouldn't be enough food for everybody. That was the sole reason I joined up. I think that was the reason the average chap went in the Army.

And once he was in, the average chap received the old-fashioned treatment of tough discipline based on drill and smartness, teaching pride in the regiment and the flag.

Some things were changing: in place of the old 'wet canteen', where soldiers sat on long benches drinking beer from gallon cans, new cafeterias were being opened by the Navy, Army and Air Force Institutes – the Naafi. Sport and entertainments were now part of Army life. But in other ways, things were still the same as they had been. There was still virtually no chance of a private soldier being commissioned. In 1939 a soldier's basic pay was still no more than pocket money – fourteen shillings a week – and he was not allowed to marry 'on the strength' until he was 26.

Small wonder, then, that the Army found it hard to recruit even the few men it needed. But the catastrophe of total war had not yet run its course and in 1939, when this truth became inescapable, National Service was introduced. Once more the whole available manhood of the country would have to go into uniform. In September 1939, Hitler had 105 divisions available to fight in Europe, France had over 90. Britain had four.

Conscripts joined up without any of the enthusiasm of 1914: they understood what war meant, and they had no illusions about the Army. The 'Pals battalions' of 1914 had sung cheerful ditties such as:

> Ere we are, ere we are, ere we are again,
> Pat and Mack and Tommy and Jack and Joe.
> Never mind the weather,
> Now we're all together
> Are we downhearted? No! ('av a banana!)

In 1939, conscripts were more likely to be heard chanting:

> We had to join, we had to join, we had to join Belisha's army.
> Fourteen bob a week,
> F—-all to eat,
> Marching round the square with bloody great blisters on our feet;
> We had to join, we had to join, we had to join Belisha's army.
> If it wasn't for the war,
> We'd have f—d off long before,
> Hore-Belisha – you're barmy.

Hore-Belisha was the minister of war, the latter-day Kitchener. Kitchener is remembered for his call to arms, Hore-Belisha for his beacon. Men had heard from their fathers and grandfathers what it meant to be in the 'poor bloody infantry'; simple patriotism had been killed by it.

> In the 1914 war they was loading mules and horses at Southampton to go to France, and they wouldn't go up the gang-plank, and a soldier was hitting them. So Lord Roberts said, 'Leave those mules alone; a mule and horse costs me £40 and I can buy a man for sixpence a day.' He definitely said that, my grandfather heard him.

The man who recalled that story, Mr Jarvis, had been taught as a young man that the Army treated men as cannon-fodder, and National Service did not change his mind. He was himself given the job of persuading soldiers to volunteer for especially dangerous duty in the Special Air Service. Men were not eager to volunteer: he did not expect them to be. He drove up in a coach, hid it, and had the men lined up:

> Someone would say, 'All those that want to join, one pace forward.' Nobody would move. So then the sergeants and corporals used to get about those blokes and they'd say 'You're all right, you're a flash bastard, pushing lance-corporals about and you won't do this and you won't do that, why don't you go and join a man's lot? What, are you frightened or something?'

Eventually thirty men would be pushed into agreeing to join, sure that they could wriggle their way out later if necessary. And then, to their great surprise, they would be immediately bundled on to the coach and away to their new life.

Those who had avoided volunteering for dangerous duties might even dodge the fighting altogether; the administration, feeding and supplying of fighting soldiers was a complicated business. The petrol engine, radio and armour plating had transformed warfare since 1918. The actual fighting forces in battles were much smaller now: only a minority of soldiers fired at the enemy (and the British Army only lost a sixth of the men it had lost in 1914–18, though this war was two years longer).

It was hard for a soldier to control his fate in the Army: if there was a logic that gave some men 'cushy' jobs and sent others into the jungle, few privates could see it. There were exceptions: some strove to exercise a degree of control over their lives. Filed under 'malingerers', the Imperial War Museum keeps a solitary document. It is the memoir of Private Bratton of the Royal Army Medical Corps. His father was a sergeant-major in the Guards, and Private Bratton had inherited a deep understanding of the Army. When he was given a mechancial aptitude test, he perceived the silken thread that led from success in the test, by way of training, to handling something mechanical at the sharp end of the war. He demonstrated no aptitude at all. In desperation, the sergeant in charge of the test brought him a dismantled bicycle pump.

> 'I've tried fixing the pump, sergeant, but I can't make head or tail of this little rubber tube lying beside it. I wonder if it belongs to another article?' The sergeant's face and neck went a vivid red. I really believed he thought I was taking the wee-wee out of him.

Bratton was an extravagantly limp-wristed soldier, with crushed strawberry underwear which was a sensation in his barracks.

> He snatched the pump and tube from my hand saying, 'Stick it up, stick it up, you silly bugger.' I was a little offended, and may have shown it, for I was thinking there's no need to bring sex into it. 'Stick it up', the sergeant repeated, then in a very quiet voice he said 'The rubber tube goes up the hole at the bottom of the pump.' I was dumbfounded.

The Army's traditional view of the soldier demanded unquestioning obedience, instilled by the discipline of the drill. But when that traditional view had formed, men came into the army already 'knowing their place'. Society had changed since those days. The new conscripts were not necessarily highly educated (a quarter of them failed the Army's elementary education test) but they lived in an increasingly democratic and questioning society.

In some ways the Army itself prompted the men to be questioning. Conscripts did not fight because they were paid to do so, or because they had the habit of obedience: they had to know what they were fighting for. Lectures were laid on to explain that they were fighting against tyranny for democracy and freedom. The lecturers were themselves conscripts, usually fresh from university, often inspired by socialist ideals. When in 1945, the troops in Cairo set up a soviet, the blame was laid at the door of Army education.

These soldiers were likely, then, to be suspicious of their senior commanders, and resentful if they were pushed around. R. M. Wingfield, in *The Only Way Out*, described his embarkation for France shortly after the D-Day landings.

> Same wag in the first file let out a quavering 'b-a-a-a'. Soon the noise spread throughout the ship and on to the waiting lines on the quay. A Brigadier, purple and frothing, stormed up and down the line screaming at us. The sheep stopped in his immediate vicinity and resumed their frenzied bleating when he passed.

The Brigadier had good reason to froth. This was exactly how the great French Army mutiny began in 1917, when the lambs refused to go to the slaughter. Plainly there were soldiers here who thought they were going to a new western front. They were finally loaded on to the ship, but threatened not to get off: 'We shambled up on to the deck, wandered up to the bows and settled there, stubbornly refusing to move. "You can fetch Monty! We won't even move for him! So — off!"'

They were eventually 'pacified' and Wingfield joined a division that was pushing through Belgium. To his surprise, the rigid hierarchy of the Army in England had changed completely in the field. 'In the division our wants were the law. Until we received our supplies no one else did.' When these soldiers felt they were recognised as human beings, their rebelliousness vanished:

> We were proud to belong to a formation where a Major did not mind showing nine replacements (the lowest form of life) where they could get their food. This was the rare unit where the men who had to do the dirty work were considered the most important.

Wingfield's platoon had an exceptionally dangerous job – acting as infantry support for tanks, carrying out reconnaissance and attacking anti-tank guns. The platoon carried democracy to new lengths: officers were called by their first names, wore no distinguishing marks, and 'the orders come from the man in the best position, not the man with the biggest number of stripes or pips'.

When it came to fighting, the old regimental structure had broken down: men operated in specialist groups. They were not fighting a 'regimental war', and they had no particular attachment to regimental tradition: they were usually much more comfortable and effective in a small 'mob' where officers and men lived together and relied on each other. In India, when Orde Wingate prepared a daring penetration into Japanese-held Burma, his conscript force regarded the regimental Indian army types as creatures from another world: 'The ordinary military inhabitants of the place, in whose lives spit-and-polish still played its part, were known to us with indulgent contempt as "starch soldiers".' In Wingate's force, anyone who wanted to drop out could do so. When he needed volunteers for particularly dangerous acts, he had an embarrassment of choice.

When Robert Graves became an officer in 1914, he found 'my greatest difficulty was talking to the men of my platoon with the proper air of authority'. That 'air of authority' was exactly what was not required thirty years on.

The crew of a landing craft, for instance, recall a visit by Mountbatten. The division between soldiers and sailors had broken down: they were in Combined Operations, landing assault troops on enemy beaches: they wore sailors' trousers, but their blouses were Army battledress. They formed a self-contained crew of twenty-one, officers and men living together, sharing everything. They were self-catering, which meant, in effect, living off the land: buying food if they had to, stealing it if they could, trading with the Yanks and drinking the profits.

> Mountbatten came on board us one time, weren't on board ten minutes and the lights went out; generator packed up. Stoker's trying to get ruddy generator going, so Mountbatten says 'Have you got any f—ing spanners down there?' Now I'm not joking this is how he spoke. And in five minutes he got the generator going.

The crew were shell-shocked and exhausted after landing troops under heavy fire at Anzio. They were due to go on leave; Mountbatten had come to ask them to forgo their leave and go back there. They responded to his personality, and agreed to do it. The survivor who tells this story regards those days as the best of his life.

37 A page from a national serviceman's photo album captures the spirit of 'the mob'.

After the war, 'demob' came slowly. The landing craft crew were stuck for months up a river in Indonesia, waiting for a pilot to lead them out. 'Terrorists' slit each pilot's throat as he arrived. Jarvis, of the Special Air Service, had to stay on in the Palestine police. Private Bratton slipped £10 in the right direction and was discharged as a homosexual.

Soldiers who had been told they were fighting for freedom were themselves deprived of it: they described themselves as 'browned-off' – bored and dispirited. The 'soldiers vote' in the 1945 election was solidly anti-Churchill. Men had received a political education in the Army, and now demanded a fairer society. They would run the mines and the railways and the steel industry themselves.

The Army itself recovered from wartime soldiers, and became regimented again. National Service continued until 1960. Unwilling recruits faced tougher drills and harsher discipline than in wartime. In place of the self-reliance that had flourished in 'theatres of action' came the old philosophy, expressed in *Drill (All Arms) 1951* 'that the foundation of discipline in battle is based on drill has been proved again and again'. That handbook contained four advertisements: one for the Naafi, and three for boot polish. Spit-and-polish was once more the order of the day. In the official history, Wingate was condemned for his 'unorthodox views' – 'there was a risk . . . that a form of private army would result'. Central military authority was re-asserted: the old imperial army was back. A generation of National Servicemen learned that the Army was a dinosaur that had somehow survived into the new age – an age that had itself been forged out of the experiences of Army life.

Chapter 4
FACTORY HANDS

1

The great difference between our civilisation and any other is the machine. We measure in horsepower, but no horse ever worked with the unchanging rhythm of a machine. The inflexible discipline of its beat demanded that people learn a new way to live.

> Whilst the engine runs the people must work – men, women and children are yoked together with iron and steam. The animal-machine – breakable in the best case, subject to a thousand sources of suffering – is chained fast to the iron machine, which knows no suffering![1]

Factory work, where large numbers of hands tended giant machines, powered by inanimate force, was a novelty which fascinated, horrified and ultimately overthrew a community in which work was domestic and gave its own rhythm to life.

Because the life was so new and different, very few people were prepared to work in the earliest factories. Few working families had clocks at the end of the eighteenth century; they timed their day by the sun and their stomachs. An employee was not a wage labourer but a member of the family: apprentices were treated as extra sons or daughters. The agreement between a master and an apprentice imposed obligations on both sides which went far beyond 'a fair day's work for a fair day's pay':

> Taverns and alehouses he shall not haunt, dice, cards or any other unlawful games he shall not use, fornication with any woman he shall not commit, matrimony he shall not contract. He shall not absent himself by night or by day without his master's leave, but be a true and faithful servant.

For a fixed term he was to live with his master and keep his secrets. The master was obliged, in return, to teach a trade to the child,

> Finding and allowing unto his said servant meat, drink, apparel, washing, lodging and all other things during the said term

> of . . . years, and to give unto his apprentice . . . double apparel, to wit, one suit for holydays and one suit for worken days.

When Robert Blincoe was apprenticed in 1799, at the age of seven, he was bound by just such an indenture. That was, after all, the normal way to put a child into regular employment. But Blincoe did not go to live as a member of a family, in a domestic workshop. The master to whom he was bound for fourteen years was a company, the premises from which he must not absent himself were factory premises, Lowdham Cotton Mill, in Nottinghamshire.

Cotton mills were built because they could meet the apparently limitless demand for yarn in a country that was dressing less in wool and more in cotton. The cloth was woven in domestic workshops.

> The workshop of the weaver was a rural cottage, from which when he was tired of sedentary labour he could sally forth into his little garden, and with the spade or hoe tend its culinary productions. The cotton wool which was to form his weft was picked clean by the fingers of his younger children, and was carded and spun by the older girls assisted by his wife, and the yarn was woven by himself assisted by his sons. When he could not procure within his family a supply of yarn adequate to the demands of his loom, he had recourse to the spinsters of his neighbourhood. One good weaver could keep three active women at work upon the wheel, spinning weft. . . . He was often obliged to treat the females with presents, in order to quicken their diligence at the wheel.[2]

The spinsters weft was often lumpy and irregularly twisted, as well as being spun so much more slowly than it was woven: they could not spin warp at all, and linen or wool was used for this.

In 1771 Richard Arkwright built his first water-powered spinning factory and broke this bottleneck. Not only did the machines produce yarn in great quantities, but the cotton was well spun and could be made into warp as well as weft. Arkwright had to overcome local difficulties: a mill he built near Chorley was attacked and destroyed during a trade depression in 1779, and he installed a battery of cannon to defend his spinning mills at Cromford. He succeeded: 'Within the small space of ten years, from being a poor man not worth £5, now keeps his carriage and servants, is become a Lord of the Manor, and has purchased an estate of £20,000.'[3]

Others were naturally eager to share in the bounty, and built mills of their own. They were very expensive to build and to run: by 1790 Arkwright was employing 800 at Cromford. But the work could be learned in weeks, and did not require much strength, and so the mill owners could employ large numbers of children and keep their costs down.

But the weavers would not send their children into the mills. The buildings themselves looked like workhouses or prisons, and the regimes within were more disciplined than either. Advertisements were made to sound enticing: at Arnold Mill, boys and girls might be 'well clothed, lodged and boarded; they will attend church every Sabbath and have proper masters appointed for their instruction'; but the children were not volunteered in any numbers. If a man with several children did bring them to the mill, he was unlikely to get work there himself: only about one in ten mill workers was the father of a family. Few men wanted to be unemployed and dependent on their children.

Some mill owners tried to solve the problem by offering fringe benefits:

> DARLEY COTTON MILL. *Wanted*, Families, particularly women and children to work at the said mill. They may be provided with comfortable houses and every necessary convenience either at Darley or Allestry: particularly a milking-cow to each family. It is a very good neighbourhood for the men getting work who are not employed in the manufactory.

Factory owners created whole communities to attract workers. Arkwright built a market square and public house for his workforce; Robert Owen set out to create an entire model society. More pragmatic community-builders, such as Samuel Oldknow, found themselves engaged in building operations largely to provide employment for the fathers of families working in the mill.

The inducements were not enough. The records of one mill, Cuckney, between 1786 and 1805 show that only one-tenth of the children employed there were placed by their families or private individuals. The other nine-tenths were placed, as Robert Blincoe was placed, by the workhouses and charitable institutions which cared for foundlings, orphans and the children of the desperately poor.

Blincoe was an orphan in the care of the St Pancras poor house in Mary-le-bone, near London. In 1822, when he was 30, he told his story to a campaigning journalist called Robert Brown who wrote it up as a public scandal. Brown described how, at the age of seven, Blincoe longed to escape from the poor house:

> He was cooped up in a gloomy, though liberal sort of a prison house. . . . He wistfully measured the height of the wall, and found it too lofty for him to scale, and too well guarded were the gates to admit of his egress unnoticed.

The chance to escape was offered by Messrs Lamberts of Lowdham Mill, who like a number of other mill owners scoured the

A

MEMOIR

OF

ROBERT BLINCOE,

An Orphan Boy;

SENT FROM THE WORKHOUSE OF ST. PANCRAS, LONDON,

AT SEVEN YEARS OF AGE,

TO ENDURE THE

Horrors of a Cotton-Mill,

THROUGH HIS INFANCY AND YOUTH,

WITH A MINUTE DETAIL OF HIS SUFFERINGS,

BEING

THE FIRST MEMOIR OF THE KIND PUBLISHED.

BY JOHN BROWN.

MANCHESTER:

PRINTED FOR AND PUBLISHED BY J. DOHERTY, 37, WITHY-GROVE.

1832.

38 The title page of Blincoe's *Memoir*.

London parishes for pauper children. The traditional device for engaging children was an indenture of apprenticeship, and the poor house children were allowed to expect that at Lowdham they would go into something like the domestic life of a normal, if rather idealised, apprenticeship – 'that they would be fed on roast beef and plum pudding . . . [and] be allowed to ride their masters' horses.'

Eighty children from the poor house were taken on by Lamberts. They were shipped to Nottingham in locked wagons. The journey took four days. Lamberts themselves made some effort to operate as traditional masters: they bound themselves to teach the children a trade (stocking weaving for the boys and lace making for the girls) and supplied the children with working clothes and 'holyday dress' before they set out, as well as giving each one a shilling, a handkerchief and a large piece of gingerbread. When they arrived at Nottingham, the children were taken to see the sights, including the castle and Sherwood Forest.

But when they arrived at the mill, ten miles from the city, it became clear that there was nothing very domestic about the life of a factory hand. They were shaken by the noise of the machines, and the constant smell of oil. They were taken into a dining hall just like the one at the poor house, and given unfamiliar food – oatmeal porridge and black bread.

> Some of the girls began making faces, and one flung a dab of bread against the wall, where it stuck fast, as if it had been plaster. This caught the eye of the governor – a huge, raw boned man, who had served in the army, and had been a drill sergeant. Unexpectedly, he produced a large horse-whip, which he clanged in such a sonorous manner that it made the house re-echo. In a moment the face-makers and bread throwers were reduced to solemn silence and abject submission.

Discipline was the essence of factory work: discipline, and the communal life. 'The bed places were a sort of crib, built in a double tier, all round the chamber. The apprentices slept two in a bed'. Everything stank of oil and cotton waste. Each newcomer was allocated a bed, each sharing with an older child:

> The boy with whom Blincoe was to chum, sprang nimbly into his berth, and without saying a prayer, or anything else, fell asleep before Blincoe could undress himself. So completely was he cowed, he could not restrain his tears.

The work itself was not so much hard as unrelenting. These 7-year-old children were expected to work from 5.30 a.m. until 9.30 p.m. – an 83-hour week, with an hour for dinner. There were no seats; they were not allowed to sit down in working hours. The remorseless discipline of the machines had taken over their lives: 'The overlooker, who had charge of him, had a certain quantity of work to perform in a given time. If every child did not perform his allotted task, the fault was imputed to his overlooker, and he was discharged.' The inevitable result was that the overlooker would use kicks and blows to keep the children going when they faltered through tiredness. The overseers were unlikely to be the gentlest of men: the general prejudice against factory work meant that they were usually 'restless and migratory workers' rather than solid citizens.

Children did not flourish in mills. Cuckney Mill lost over a third of its 780 'apprentices' between 1786 and 1805: sixty-five died, ninety-six were thrown out, and 119 ran away. Robert Blincoe tried to run away from Lowdham Mill, but he was recognised by a tailor in the village and taken back. Doubtless the tailor meant well: his wife gave Robert a meal, and the tailor gave him a lecture on the obligations of an apprentice to God and man. What, after

39 Children working in a mill.

all, would become of a 7-year-old on the run? But Blincoe's *Memoir* rages against the man, and hints darkly at the five shillings reward offered for captured runaways.

The fate in 1815 of 1,977 children from London parishes bound between 1802 and 1811 to masters in the country

Still serving under indenture	644
Transferred to other tradesmen	246
Served their time and still in the same employ	108
Served their time and settled elsewhere	99
Sent back to their friends	57
Quitted their service (chiefly run away)	166
Dead	80
Enlisted in the Army or Navy	86
Not bound to person listed in records	58
Not satisfactorily accounted for	433

When he got back to the mill, 'the manager gave me a severe but not cruel chastisement'. There was no malice in what was done to Blincoe. When his fingers were severed in a machine, and the bloody stump was quickly dressed, it was not out of cruelty that he was sent straight back to work. It was simply the discipline of the machine.

In 1802 Robert Peel, a mill-owning home secretary, was responsible for an Act of parliament which restricted the working week for mill children to seventy-two hours (not counting meal breaks), and insisted that they were to receive religious and secular instruction. They were not to sleep more than two in a bed. A magistrate and a clergyman were to check that the Act was observed, and that the premises were clean and airy.

Peel's own mills had been criticised by magistrates in 1784 and 1796. He later wrote: 'Having other pursuits it was not often in my power to visit the factories, but whenever such visits were made, I was struck with the uniform appearance of bad health, and in many cases stunted growth of the children.'

At about the time the Act was passed, the committee of St Pancras poor house came to see what had become of their charges. The overall result was that Lowdham Mill built a new and more spacious dormitory house, started providing a more satisfying diet and sacked the harshest overseers. Shortly after these improvements the mill went bankrupt. Because large loans were needed to build mills, bankruptcies were common. When a mill folded, its 'apprentices' were often carted off to the parish boundary and dumped there.

The owners of Lowdham Mill apparently tried to do better. Those children who had nowhere to go were transferred to Mr Ellice Needham of Highgate Wall, Derbyshire, the owner of Litton Mill, near Tideswell. Litton Mill turned out to be a nightmare. To the rigour of machine discipline was added inhuman neglect and brutality. Peel's Act was apparently unknown to the children and ignored by their masters. The working day lasted sixteen hours.

> Blincoe, in common with his fellow sufferers has often dropped down at the frames, and been so weary, when, at last he left work, he has given a stronger boy a halfpenny, or a part of his supper, to allow him to lean upon him on his way back to the 'prentice house.

The children were half starved, and envied the pigs their rations: 'As soon as he saw the swineherd withdraw, he used to slip downstairs and, stealing slyly towards the trough, plunge his hand in at the loop holes, and steal as many dumplings as he could grasp.' The pigs soon stopped this trick by rolling all their dumplings in thick mud the moment they received them.

Blincoe recounts casual and systematic brutality, virtually torture: his overlooker

> used, when Blincoe could not or did not keep pace with the machinery, to tie him up by the wrists to a cross beam and keep him suspended over the machinery till his agony was extreme. To avoid the machinery, he had to draw up his legs every time it came out or returned. If he did not lift them up, he was cruelly beaten over the shins, which were bare; nor was he released, till growing black in the face, and his head falling over his shoulder, the wretch thought the victim was near expiring.

In 1807 an inspector for the 1802 Act reported that apprentices at Litton were 'worked successively in the night, though this is expressly prohibited by the Act'. He could not discover the hours of work, but they were plainly receiving no instruction at all. The apprentice lodging house was so overcrowded that 'it appears almost impossible to contain so many persons consistently with health and anything approaching comfort'. Any pretence at 'apprenticeship' had been abandoned by the mill owners: they accepted no responsibility for their labour force, beyond the basic commercial need to keep them alive and working.

Needham's Mill, on this account, appears to have been a real pioneer of the totalitarian factory economy: as the *Memoir* puts it, 'the *parish children* were considered, treated and *consumed as a part of the raw materials*; their strength, their marrow, their lives were converted into money.'

Blincoe's story was published as a shocking exposé: it showed a life wholly bent to the factory machine. The factory hand 'chained fast to the iron machine' produced wealth for himself and the world, but his human reality was denied, his human possibilities unfulfilled. The ghost of Robert Blincoe, the pauper child, stalks through British industrial history. But his story has a happy ending. One day, he had his own mill.

2

On the night of Saturday, 12 April 1812, about 150 men, generally masked or with their faces blackened, surrounded a woollen mill at Rawfolds, halfway between Huddersfield and Leeds. The men were drawn up in companies; musketmen first, then men with pistols, and finally men with hatchets and mauls to destroy the machinery within.

William Cartwright, who leased the mill, had been expecting an attack. He had enlisted the aid of five soldiers of the Cumberland Militia; they and four of his workmen were sleeping in the mill. Guards were posted outside, and the building was fortified. There were revolving spikes set into the stairs, and the flagstones of the first floor could be raised so that the defenders could fire down on intruders or pour carboys of acid onto them.

Most of the attackers were croppers, skilled craftsmen who gave a high-quality finish to cloth. Newly-woven cloth is rough and hairy. They used teazles to raise the surface 'nap' and shears to shave it off. The surface of good cloth would be raised and sheared perhaps seven times. It required skill to draw the wet cloth taut and 'tazzle' it without straining it: it took years of practice to manage the shears, four feet long and weighing 40 lb. You could tell a cropper from the 'hoof' on his right wrist, a deformity caused by years of shearing.

Cartwright had once employed croppers. But for three years now he had used the mill instead. He raised the nap with mechanical rollers in a device called a 'gig-mill': his shears were set floating in frames, and could be worked by an unskilled hand.

The force outside his mill included men from Huddersfield and Halifax, as well as more local croppers. A further contingent was on its way from Leeds. There were men like Samuel Hartley, who had once worked for Cartwright, and whose skills were now apparently worthless. A lifetime's training, as apprentice and journeyman, was meaningless in a factory mill.

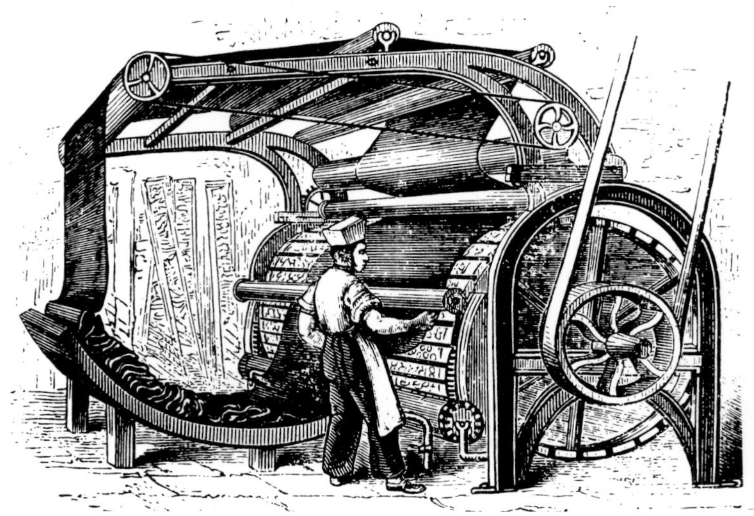

40 A gig-mill.

41 A shearing frame.

There had been legal restrictions on factory work until 1809. The state had an obvious interest in the good of the trades that flourished in the country, and there was a system of laws that enforced apprenticeship for entry to them, and controlled the pattern of work. Factory owners pressed to have these laws rescinded, and a great campaign was waged against these restrictive practices in the woollen trade.

A parliamentary committee investigated the trade in 1806, to see if the restrictions could safely be withdrawn. The committee was mainly concerned about the survival of the cloth makers, or clothiers, who were organised in Yorkshire on the 'domestic system'. Their report described the system:

> The greater part of the Domestic Clothiers live in Villages and detached houses, covering the whole face of a district of from 20 to 30

> miles in length and from 12 to 15 in breadth. Coal abounds through the whole of it; and a great proportion of the manufacturers occupy a little land, from 3 to 12 or 15 acres each. They often likewise keep a Horse, to carry their Cloth to the Fulling Mill and the Market.

The committee heartily approved the system, and 'the facilities it affords men of steadiness and industry to establish themselves as little Master Manufacturers, and maintain their families in comfort by their own industry and frugality'.

They decided that the factories would never destroy the domestic system, and so, despite the opposition of the little master manufacturers themselves, recommended repeal of the controls. The problems of the croppers were treated rather differently by the committee.

The croppers waiting in the dark, silently rounding up the sentries outside Cartwright's mill, did not work on the domestic system. John Tate, who had been a cropper for Cartwright, had testified to the 1806 committee that these workers were 'a body of men who generally work in large numbers together, 40, 50, or 60', and one establishment at least had employed eighty. Although they served apprenticeships, they seldom lived as members of the masters' families. John Wood described his training to the committee. He had been apprenticed in a shop that employed more than twenty-five men.

> For the first year of my apprenticeship my parents received so much yearly for my washing and lodging: I eat with my master, and slept at my father's, that was the first part of my apprenticeship: the latter part I received 7*s*. a week and eat at my father's.

The seven shillings were to pay for his lodging. A large finishing shop would have many apprentices, who lived 'perfectly at liberty', just like the workmen, and who came in for a regular day's work – commonly from five in the morning to eight at night in summer.

These shops were, in fact, factories, but factories without machines. The rhythm of the cropper's life was not dictated by a mill wheel, and his value to the shop lay in his skill: 'The Cropper strictly speaking is not a servant. He does not feel, or call himself as such, but a cloth-worker, and partakes much more of the nature of a shoe-maker, joiner, taylor etc.'[4]

The croppers came before the 1806 committee to defend their skills and argue against the machines that would turn them into 'servants'. Because they were independent men, they despised mechanical work; because they were craftsmen, they could see the flaws in machine-finished cloth; because they worked in large shops, they could organise to resist machines; because they earned

42 The interior of John Wood's workshop.

twenty-five or thirty shillings a week, they could afford a fund to support strikes against workshops which used machines.

Their organisation – 'the Institution' – succeeded in holding down the number of gig-mills and shearing frames in Yorkshire up to 1806. But the government did not like workers' associations. Revolution had succeeded in France because of independent-minded workmen like these: the conspiracy laws and Combination Acts existed to prevent workmen trying to act as masters of their own (and their employers') destiny.

The cropper delegates who appeared before the committee were funded by the Institution. They found themselves being brow-beaten to reveal the source of their funds and the names of the collectors. Their books were seized and they were treated as criminal conspirators.

> Your Committee need scarcely remark, that such Institutions are, in their ultimate tendencies, still more alarming in a political, than in a commercial view. Their baneful as well as powerful effects, have been fatally exemplified not long since in a Sister Kingdom.

The restrictive laws were scrapped. The survival of the craft factory depended, from then, on the ability of the croppers to hold back machinery by their own illicit organisations. Around Leeds they were very successful, but in areas of scattered hamlets like the Spey Valley it was not so easy.

The machine owners were prepared to help each other, too. Cartwright's mill would have gone bankrupt in 1811, but for the assistance of other mill owners. Thus Cartwright was able to keep undercutting the finishing-shops, and they were laying men off. Now the croppers had come to put him out of business. Their leader was George Mellor, the stepson of a master finisher called John Wood. Other men from the same shop were with him – two of them, Benjamin Walker and William Hall, were later to give evidence against Mellor.

Mellor ordered the hatchetmen to break down the mill gates. They smashed them down, and the men poured into the yard. Then they began breaking the ground floor windows.

The men had been given shots of rum before they attacked: they needed it all the more because many of them were half-starved. Britain's export trade had collapsed as Napoleon controlled Europe and war with America was imminent. There had been three years of bad harvests, and bread was now a luxury. The poor had been parading through the towns of Yorkshire carrying bloody loaves on spears, demanding bread. Conditions seemed ripe for revolution, and the wave of food riots and machine breaking which had begun in 1811 created much alarm. In Nottinghamshire, Derbyshire and Leicestershire starving cotton and lace weavers had been smashing wide looms, which some hosiers were using to produce cheap shoddy goods to corner what was left of the market. The wreckers sheltered behind the fictional leadership of General Ned Ludd.

Repression was severe: troops were brought in, and a bill rushed through parliament to make frame-breaking punishable by death. But just as Nottinghamshire came under control, the Yorkshiremen declared themselves to be fellow-members of General Ludd's army.

> We will never lay down Arms [until] The House of Commons passes an Act to put down all Machinery hurtful to Commonalty, and repeal that to hang Frame Breakers. But We – We petition no more – that won't do – fighting must.
>
> Signed by the General of the Army of Redressers
>
> *Ned Ludd* Clerk

They drilled at midnight: they seized arms and ammunition. Later, Benjamin Walker described their training to an examining magistrate:

> We were all masked with different sorts of masks . . . and we were all ordered . . . to put pieces of white paper in our hats to see that no stranger or spy came among us . . . when we had done we were all called over by numbers to know if all were come out but no man's name was to be mentioned.

They swept all before them. Until they came to Cartwright's.

> The guard within the mill flew to arms, and discharged a heavy fire of musketry upon the assailants; this fire was returned and repeated without intermission during the conflct . . . a number of voices crying continually 'Bang Up', 'Murder them!' 'Pull down the door!' . . . every renewed attempt ended in disappointment.

By the time the Luddites had run out of ammunition, they had some forty men wounded, two of them, as it turned out, fatally. These two were left when the rest fled. One was Samuel Hartley. The other was John Booth, whose father, a clergyman, had once been a cropper. Cartwright tried to extract information from the dying men, and Booth eventually whispered 'Can you keep a secret?' 'I can' came the hopeful reply. 'So can I', said Booth, and died.

Up to now the croppers had hurt no one, but the bloodshed and deaths at Rawfolds Mill made them vengeful. Popular sympathy was with them, and the scale of their operations gave conviction to the reports that were coming to the Home Office that 'it is not the cropping shears only which they aim at but a general *revolution* which you may rest assured is near at hand'. And now a new violence appeared.

'I think if no one had been shot we should never have thought of taking anybody's life', said Benjamin Walker later. It was part of his confession for taking part in the murder of a manufacturer called Horsfall on 28 April 1812. It was an act of desperation, which marked the degeneration of the Luddites into banditry. They had failed, though it took an army larger than the force being used in the Peninsular war and months of remorseless investigation to break the solidarity of the community and discover the culprits.

Local popular sympathy was not much diminished by the murder. The *Leeds Mercury* reflected a widespread conviction that the Luddites were driven by hunger and desperation. A week after Horsfall's murder it wrote:

> A facetious correspondent from Barnsley observes that, the army of General Ludd was the other day completely put to rout in the neighbourhood by the discharge of a substance called a *potatoe* into the stomachs of the refractory. A boat load of this kind of ammunition it seems arrived very opportunely, and being distributed to the labouring classes at 10*d*. a peck, an instantaneous impression was produced, and the whole army dispersed. Our Correspondent

> recommends that funds should be formed in all the large Manufacturing towns to purchase ammunition of this kind, and that it should be distributed in a similar way.

But at the same time, rumours abounded in the governing class that Luddism was part of a great revolutionary conspiracy through the whole kingdom: as Walter Scott put it, 'the whole country is mined beneath our feet'.

Mellor, who organised the murder, may indeed have had revolutionary aspirations. When he swore the rest of his workmates to secrecy, a passage from Ezekiel was read to each of them: 'Iniquity shall have an end: thus saith the Lord God. . . . Exalt him that is low, and abase him that is high. I will overturn, overturn, overturn it: and it shall be no more, until he come whose right it is; and I will give it him.'

But there was no overturning: the Luddites were hunted down. The underground movement to defend the craft factory was finally crushed at York special assizes in January 1813, when eight croppers were sentenced to death – three for the murder of Horsfall, and the rest for the attack on Cartwright's Mill.

One man, John Hirst, was acquitted – no one would give evidence against him. He went back to his home in Liversedge, but 'finding himself pestered with questions' he moved to a nearby village, and stood by his oath of secrecy. In his dotage, however, he was heard 'constantly muttering mysterious pass words, administering secret oaths; or going through imaginary drills'. Frank Peel, the local historian, wrote down the lullaby the old man sang to his grandchildren.

> Come all you croppers stout and bold
> Let your faith grow stronger still
> These cropping lads in the County of York
> Broke the shears at Horsfall's Mill.
> They broke the shears and the windows too
> Set fire to the tazzling mill;
> They formed themselves all in a line
> Like soldiers at the drill.
>
> The wind it blew, and the sparks they flew
> And awoke the town full soon
> People got up in the middle of the night
> And they ran by the light of the moon:
> When these lads around the mill did stand,
> And they all did vow and swear,
> Neither bucket, nor can, nor any such thing
> Should be of service there.

But the mills stood, and the croppers were extinguished as a class of men.

An account in 1881 explained how:

> Since the introduction of machinery, the whole of the cloth . . . is dressed by a comparatively small number, chiefly boys at from 5*s*. to 8*s*. . . . and a few men at from 10*s*. to 14*s*. per week. The old croppers have turned themselves to anything they can get to do, some acting as bailiffs, water-carriers, scavengers, or selling oranges, cakes, tapes and laces, gingerbread, blacking etc. etc.

They survive, however, in song and story in their own communities. The tale is still told in Liversedge. When I went there looking for Rawfolds Mill (now a wire-drawing mill), everyone I met, in the street, at factory gates, by the church, all knew the story of the siege of Rawfolds Mill.

3

Ancoats, a working-class district of Manchester in the 1840s, was made of mill hands and steam engines.

> A wide-lying labyrinth of small dingy streets, narrow, unsunned courts terminating in gloomy culs-de-sac, and adorned with a central sloppy gutter. Every score or so yards you catch sight of one of the second- and third-class mills, with its cinder-paved courtyard and its steaming engine-house. Shabby-looking chapels, here and there, rise with infinitesimal Gothic arches and ornaments, amid the grimy nakedness of the factories.

This description was written by a reporter on the *Morning Chronicle* in 1849. His name was Reach, and he was one of a number (another was Charles Booth) commissioned to investigate the condition of life in some of the great cities of England.

43 View of Manchester (about 1840). A forest of chimneys pour smoke over a dense undergrowth of narrow alleys and back-to- back houses. Industrial cities were fascinating, alarming and mysterious to the world outside. Along with the cloth, they produced statistics that were consumed almost as eagerly: a death rate of one in twenty-seven in the poorer streets, 22,950 dwelling houses without access to a tap, 5,070 cellar dwellings.

Manchester, like the other towns of the textile districts, had grown enormously in a few years: at the start of the century there were around 90,000 souls in the borough but by now there were some quarter-million. This growth was entirely due to the need for the mills to have their workforce living around them.

Although the textile factories were still called mills, few of them had mill wheels: their driving force was the steam engine. This meant that they could be put up anywhere convenient, and grow to any size. For example, Birley's mill at Chorlton-upon-Medlock consisted of

> Several huge buildings, separated from each other by streets, but connected by subterranean tunnels, in which iron tramways are laid down for the speedier and easier conveyance from ware-room to ware-room of the raw material. Nearly 2,000 hands are regularly employed in this vast industrial colony.

Most of the steam engines at work in England (apart from pumping and railway engines, and in iron works) were being used in the mills. The typical machine factory was a textile factory, and the typical factory worker was a woman.

The original resistance to working in factories had been broken down by sheer hunger. Many families had become dependent on hand weaving in their own homes, as they lost access to the land. The great output of the spinning mills encouraged them, and handloom weaving became a refuge from starvation. Soon, however, a golden age for handloom weavers turned to nightmare, as the sheer weight of numbers depressed the industry. Things were made worse by the growth of power-loom weaving in factories. By 1838, journeymen weavers on handlooms were earning about six shillings a week. They could make twice that in a factory.

The depression of wages meant that handloom weavers worked ever longer hours, leaving cooking and housekeeping to their children. If the whole family moved into a town and worked in a mill, they would actually work shorter hours. The very fact that a mill was highly organised meant that working hours and conditions could be defined and controlled in a way that was impossible for home-workers.

In 1833 a Factory Act was passed which took advantage of the fact that factory work could be easily supervised. It was meant to protect children, and it was to be enforced by a regular system of inspection. Children under the age of 9 were not allowed to work in any mills except silk mills. Children aged between 9 and 13 could only work eight hours a day. And young people under 18 could not work more than a twelve-hour day, or do night work (except in lace mills).

Some people are afraid that the use of such wonderous Machines as Throstles, Mules, Jennies, and Steam-Looms, will do harm, by throwing many workmen out of employment; but let us not forget that whilst the steam-power is performing the hardest part of the work, many hands are needed to make the engines; and, as the goods are made better, quicker, and cheaper, the demand for them is much increased. It seems, too, that where machines increase, the working people increase faster, for Manchester, which is the chief seat of the cotton trade, is three or four times as large now as it was before the steam factories were built.

44 This instructional print shows how carded cotton was mechanically prepared for spinning in a cotton factory. On the left is the drawing frame, where strips of cotton are drawn out and combined in fours to produce longer strips with the fibres stretched out. These strips then pass to the bobbin frame, where they are twisted into a soft string, and then on to a jack frame, where the process is repeated.

This is one of a series of coloured prints published by J. R. Barfoot in the 1840s, and would have been used as a visual aid at lectures in Mechanics' Institutes and other institutions of self-improvement. The accompanying text (there is an extract above) was intended to be read aloud by the lecturer, and included a little light relief: after seeing a print of a cotton plantation, for instance, it was suggested that the audience should sing a verse from Isaac Watts' hymn, 'There's not a plant or flower below/ but makes Thy glory known'.

The text for this picture ends, 'I wonder what the girl has done amiss who is being rebuked by the overlooker!'

Mills now stopped employing large numbers of children, and recruited women instead. 'Their labour is cheaper, and they are more easily induced to undergo severe bodily fatigue than men, either for the praise-worthy motive of gaining additional support for their families, or from the folly of satisfying a love of dress', observed one of the inspectors. By 1839 there were nearly 300,000 cotton mill hands, and some 60 per cent of these were women. They formed an even higher proportion of the hands in woollen, silk and flax spinning mills.

The presence of so many women at work on the machines worried many people. The *Examiner*, in 1832, proposed that women should be barred from factory work. The female operatives of Todmorden replied:

> In this neighbourhood, hand-loom has been almost totally superseded by power-loom weaving, and no inconsiderable number of females, who must depend on their own exertions, or their parishes for support, have been forced, of necessity, into the manufactories, from their total inability to earn a livelihood at home. . . . [If we are barred from factory work] we see no way of escape from starvation, but to accept the very tempting offer of the newspapers, held out as bait to us, fairly to ship ourselves off to Van Dieman's Land, on the very delicate errand of husband hunting, and having safely arrived at the 'Land of Goshen', jump ashore with a 'Who Wants Me?'[5]

That was the case for single women being in the factories, but what about wives and mothers? One factory worker described how 'I have seen in the factory in which I worked wives and mothers working from morning to night with only one meal: and a child brought to suck at them thrice a day.' He was a member of a short-time committee, one of many formed by the operatives to petition parliament for a legally enforced ten-hour day.

About a quarter of the women in the mills were married. Small babies would commonly be handed over to home-working neighbours (often laundresses) for the day. These would keep their charges quiet with 'Godfrey's Mixture' or 'Infant's Quietness' – laudanum or opium mixture. A druggist told Reach 'I believe that women frequently drug their children through pure ignorance of the effects of the practice, and because, having been brought up in the mills, they know nothing about the first duties of mothers.' Drugged babies became thin and listless, their fingernails turned blue, their bellies swelled. Often they grew up weak, stunted and with damaged brains. Often they did not grow up. In the grimmer parts of Manchester the death rate was one in twenty-seven. And about half of the deaths were of children under the age of 5.

The sanitary conditions did not help. Mill hands in Ancoats lived in terraces of two-roomed back-to-back houses. Downstairs was a room about ten feet by eight feet, with a street door and shutters and a big doorstep for cleaning and sitting on. Furniture would be a deal table, a small sofa and the clock that was so essential to the life of a factory hand. Five minutes late at the mill and you were fined. Ten minutes late and you were locked out.

The houses, of course, had no taps: only a quarter of the dwellings in the borough had piped water, and only another quarter had access to a tap in the street. The rest depended on wells, rainwater ('unfit even for washing in until it has stood some time to purify and settle') and canal water. The rivers on which the town had been built were dead and deadly; Reach referred to the 'black foetid water' of the Medlock with 'wreaths and patches of green foam'. Stealing water from a tap was a common offence.

> In the houses of Ancoats a conspicuous object is very frequently a painted and highly glazed tea-tray, upon which the firelight glistens cheerily, and which, by its superior lustre and artistic boldness of design, throws into the shade the couple of prints, in narrow black frames, which are suspended above it.

45 'To the mill', is the awful prospect before children in this melodramatic illustration of 1839 (when children under 9 were already barred from mill work). The bare interior, dominated by the clock and the oven, is probably fairly accurate.

Of course, the cheeriness of this picture depends on there being a fire. In a household of 1840, where the whole family worked in the mill, when they got home some time after eight at night they would be greeted by a cold grate. Having to rise again at five, they would be too tired to do much except sleep. If there were children, they might have tended the fire, or they might have just wandered the streets. More than 4,000 children were lost each year in Manchester.

Conditions in the mill towns were grim enough, then, when trade collapsed in the early 1840s. Unemployment rose in some towns to 60 per cent. In Leeds, in October 1841, there were nearly 20,000 people living on less than a shilling a week. In Stockport 3,000 houses stood empty, and on a door was chalked 'Stockport to let'. Wages were cut as the poor rate rose: by the summer of 1842 they had fallen by as much as a third. There was an eruption: strikers called for a return to the wages of 1840, and toured the textile districts closing all the mills and turning out the hands.

46 In Stockport, the starving hands stormed the workhouse for bread.

Frank Peel was ten when he saw the strikers on the march.

> The sight was just one of those which it is impossible to forget. They came pouring down the wide road in thousands, taking up its whole breadth – a gaunt, famished-looking desperate multitude, armed with huge bludgeons, flails, pitchforks and pikes, many without coats and hats, and hundreds upon thousands with their clothes in rags and tatters. . . . As they marched they thundered out to a grand old tune a stirring melody . . .
>
> 'Men of England, ye are slaves,
> Though ye rule the roaring waves,
> Though ye shout from sea to sea,
> "Britons everywhere are free".'

As workers were turned out of their factories they became emboldened to present their demands to their masters. When the hands of a mill in Chorlton-upon-Medlock wrote demanding higher wages, the women added their own note:

> Sir,
> Also the Feameals Wishes that yous will comply And give them the same wages the had in the year 1839 we remain yours
> Feameals Hands

From factory to factory they went, knocking the plugs out of the boilers to bring the machinery to a halt. The strike quickly closed down the whole manufacturing district. Nothing on this scale had happened before. The Chartists had called for such a strike in 1839. They wanted the whole working population to take a holiday – a 'sacred month' in support of their National Charter, that would give the vote to all men. The sacred month had not had much popular support, but now the Chartists saw the strike they had wanted happening, without them. They rushed to take the credit for the strike, promoting their Charter as the strikers' demand. The government found it easy to believe that a mass movement on this scale was organised by politically motivated men, and the strike was soon known as the 'Plug Plot'. But there was no plot, and for the great majority of strikers there was no political goal.

Special constables were sworn in and troops rushed to the stricken counties. After a few weeks the hands sullenly returned to work, having achieved nothing. The alarm and concern created by the strike did, however, have longer-term results. The short-time committees found that parliament was more sympathetic, and in 1844, when trade had recovered, a ten hours bill was passed.

The Act did not become effective at once: loopholes had to be plugged with successive Acts. But the shorter working day for women gave them a chance to create something more like a home.

AT A

MEETING

OF THE

OPERATIVE COTTON SPINNERS

OF BOLTON AND ITS VICINITY,

HELD IN THE LARGE ROOM,

AT THE CROWN INN, DEANSCATE,

AT SIX O'CLOCK THIS MORNING,

The following Resolutions where unanimously agreed to:

First Resolution.—That this Meeting pledges itself not to encourage or sanction any illegal proceedings.

Second.—That this Meeting views vith disgust and abhorrence those principles of injustice and tyranny that we, as operatives, have so long laboured under:—namely, in the reduction of ou' wages, and in unjust and unreasonable abatements, and in forcing upon us unhealthy and disagreeable houses, and charging us unreasonably exorbitant rents, and in meanly and disgracefully employing apprentices to supersede the regular journeyman, and in various ways of curtailing our wages by not paying up to the list that the masters have unanimously agreed to, thus proving their unprincipled meanness and trickery.

Third.—That this Meeting is of opinion that great deal of the distress in the Manufacturing districts is owing to the improvements of Machinery, thus superseding manual labour, and creating a redundant and burthensome populatin. And this Meeting is further of opinion, that the best means to be adopted, would be to establish an efficient TEN HOURS' BILL, with restrictions on all moving power; and to immediaely colonize the Crown Lands, which would thus employ the redundant population and at the sam time improve and augment the home trade.

Fourth.—That it is the opinion of this Meeing that the above evils ariseth from Class legislation, and we are further of opinion that misery, ignorance, poverty and crime, will continue to exist, until the peoples Charter become the law of the land.

Fifth.—Resolved that this Meeting ceases fron labour aud calls upon all trades to meet and dedevise the best means to be adopted under presen circumstances.

Sixth.—That Delegates be appointed to mee those from other Trades; and that this Meeting request all other trades to APPOINT DELEGATES to meet at the CROWN INN, Deansgate, at Two o'Clock in the Afternoon and at Six o'Clock in the Evening.

BY ORDER OF THE GENERAL MEETING.

Bolton, August 15th, 1842.

HARGREAVES, PRINTER AND STATIONER, FOLDS-STREET, BOLTON.

47 The resolutions proclaimed here, after a meeting of Bolton mill workers, express the spirit of the 'Plug Plot'. First, in bold type, a denunciation of any illegality; second, and more to the point, a demand for higher wages (but coupled with a demand for the employment of 'regular journeymen' instead of apprentices); third, an attack on the way machinery is replacing manual labour, and the demand for 'an efficient TEN HOURS BILL'; and fourth, well down the list, the meeting adopted a Chartist resolution that 'the above evils ariseth from Class legislation' and that the Charter should become the law of the land.

'"I have time now to clean my house, and I do it, too, every evening", is the phrase I have heard repeated a hundred times by the tenters and female weavers', reported Reach.

'"Before, I was so tired that I could do nothing but just eat my supper and go to bed"'.

The working day now ran from six in the morning to five in the afternoon. At around 5.30 a.m.

> the streets in the neighbourhood of the mills are thronged with men, women and children flocking to their labour. The girls generally

> keep in groups with their shawls twisted round their heads, and, every few steps, in the immediate vicinity of the mill, parties are formed round the peripatetic establishments of hot coffee and cocoa vendors.

The streets would be empty at six o'clock, when the factory machinery started up, and not fill again until half past eight, when everything stopped for breakfast. Not everyone went home: 'many bring food in – generally tea and coffee, bread and butter, sometimes a slice of bacon'. At five minutes to nine a bell rang, and at nine everyone was back at work. The next break came at one o'clock. 'From every workshop, from every industrial establish-

48 A court in Hulme.

ment, the hungry crowd swarms out: the most popular meal is "flesh meat" in good times, and more commonly potatoe pie, eaten at home or in a cook-shop, or brought in to the heat, oil and dust of the mill itself.' The bell brought everyone back to work by two, and they were released again at five. And now began a new life. With regular and limited hours, it was possible to have entertainment – music halls began to compete for audiences. It was possible for adults to study after work: evening classes began, and a great age of self-improvement was launched. And it was possible for dwellings to become homes, and streets to become neighbourhoods. 'The women, in particular, are fond of sitting in groups upon their thresholds sewing and knitting; the children sprawl about beside them,' wrote Reach in 1849.

> Certainly the setting of the picture is ugly and grim enough. A black, mean-looking street, with a black unadorned mill rising over the houses, and a black chimney pouring out volumes of black smoke upon all – these do not form very picturesque accessories to the scene, but still you are glad to see that, amid all the grime and dinginess of the place, there is no lack of homely comforts, good health and good spirits.

There was still no piped water or sewer; life expectancy was still short and life was still, especially in bad years, hard and hungry. But these people were more than mere hands. They had their own lives to lead, as well as their masters.

4

The factory system introduced a revolution that spread far beyond the textile mills. Although Britain invented the system, other countries developed it faster.

> In consequence of the scarcity and high price of labour in the United States and the extreme desire manifested by masters and workmen to adopt all labour-saving appliances, from the conviction of such being for their mutual interest, a considerable number of trades are carried on in the same way as in the cotton manufacture of England, viz: in large factories, with machinery applied to every process.

These words are from the report of a mission to North America in 1854. The mission was to buy machinery for the Army to make rifles. Its report led to the first engineering factory being set up in England, the Royal Small Arms factory in Enfield.

Sam Page was one of the men who worked in a Victorian gun factory. He was a gunmaker in the Black Country town of Darlaston, which specialised in making locks for muskets. A musket was made in many parts – the barrel, the stock, the lock and so on – and each part was made by a specialist. The crafts were centred on Birmingham, and the gunmakers of that town collected parts from the various craftsmen and 'set up' the gun. The men of Darlaston worked in small workshops behind their houses, forging the locks on their own anvils. It was a trade restricted to a few men 'whose wonderful skill became proverbial'. They were artisans, small masters, independent men.

When the British Army decided to adopt and improve the rifle, it made a cautious decision to make its own. In 1854 Britain went to war in the Crimea, and suddenly the advantages of a large factory at Enfield became obvious. It was hard to guarantee delivery dates when guns were assembled from many sources. The parts of hand-made guns were unique, and could not be interchanged.

The factory was still not ready when the Crimean war ended in 1856. The Birmingham gunmakers had made a fortune out of the war. One set up his own saw-mills in Turin to produce walnut for stocks, and 'left but few sound trees standing in the district in which he carried on his operations'.

49 Sam Page.

The Enfield factory began production in 1858, and in the next six years produced over 500,000 handguns and pistols. But the Birmingham workshops still flourished, as the American Civil War had started in 1861, and there was a booming trade with the southern states. Men as skilled as Sam Page's father were making £5 or £6 a week, and there were stories of the local 'gunnifins' eating £5 notes in sandwiches. The craftsmen and manufacturers became natty dressers, and Birmingham tailors reserved certain cloths as exclusive patterns for gunmakers.

The Civil War ended in 1865, and suddenly the craftsmen found their trade had collapsed. To sell in large numbers, hand-made guns had to be dirt cheap. There were such guns. They were reputed to be made out of gas pipes. They were flintlocks with a barrel five or six feet long; the lock was stamped out, not made on an anvil; the stock was beech, painted red to appeal to the customer – the customer being a native of West Africa. They sold for 6 shillings or seven shillings and sixpence. A few years later it was said that

> the men who made them considered themselves public benefactors. They supported the 'survival of the fittest' theory, and looked upon the natives of West Africa . . . as the unfit, proudly boasting that one

of their weapons, when fired, would kill the man who held it and probably the one next to him.

Many craftsmen were faced with a choice between the gas-pipe trade and the factory. The Birmingham gun merchants, recognising what was happening, set up a joint stock company to build an arms factory of their own at Small Heath. They carved out a twenty-six acre site on the heath, six acres for the factory and the rest for other buildings and wharves.

Sam Page's father was being put out of business, so he left Darlaston and went to Enfield. In place of the anvil, he found steam hammers and stamping machines. Milling machines, drilling machines and setting-up rooms enabled guns to be completed from scratch in a single building.

When Sam was 2, the family moved back to Birmingham, where the Birmingham Small Arms factory was in full swing. There were other factories starting up in the town, too; Will Thorne worked in an ammunition factory at Adderley Park in 1871, when he was 14: 'The roar and the rattle, the steam and the heat of that inferno remains vivid in my memory, and many times I have dreamt of the place, waking up in a cold sweat of fear.'

50 The Enfield factory in 1861.

The Army mission to America had been impressed by working conditions in transatlantic factories: they were struck by 'the care almost universally bestowed on the comfort of the work-people . . . clean places for washing being provided, presses to contain their change of clothes and an abundant supply of good drinking water, in many cases cooled with ice'. Things were different in Adderley Park, as Will Thorne remembered in his old age:

> My hands today still show the scars I received . . . taking the annealed bars to the pickling tubs, where a strong vitriol solution was being used for cleaning and pickling the metal. This biting acid would splash my hands and eat the flesh to the very bone, and only by washing my hands in milk was the excruciating pain eased and the effect of the vitriol killed.

Will Thorne was a labourer, and unskilled labouring work in an engineering factory was difficult and dangerous. But Sam Page's father would not have been an unskilled labourer. It took skill and knowledge to assemble and work engineering machines, and craftsmen were rewarded with piecework rates that enabled them to earn up to fifty shillings a week. There was no 'production line': a workman took his work from machine to machine, and saw it through a sequence of processes. A man who had gone into a factory had ceased to be his own master, but he worked the machines at his own pace and his earnings were according to his skill.

Sam was apprenticed when he was 12, first in a sewing-machine and bicycle factory, and then in the Birmingham Small Arms factory, which had also turned to making bicycles. Bicycles first appeared in the 1860s, and were very suitable for mass factory

IN EVERY HOME A USE IS FOUND FOR **ELLIMAN'S.**

USEFUL TO FIREMEN.

FOOTBALL.

STRENGTHENS the MUSCLES.

RUNNING.

SORE THROAT FROM COLD.

CRAMP.

ADVANTAGES OF PLE[N]TY OF FRICTION.

ACHES, SPRAINS AND STIFFNESS.

ACCIDENT.

CYCLING.

LUMBAGO.

RHEUMATISM.

"And it I will have, or I will have none."

A STITCH IN TIME. CYCLISTS SWEAR BY ELLIMAN'S.

FOR ACHES AND PAINS.

ELLIMAN'S UNIVERSAL EMBROCATION.

" AN EXCELLENT GOOD THING."

One Shilling and Three-Halfpence. Prepared only by ELLIMAN, SONS & Co., Slough, England.

51 By the time this advertisement appeared, in the 1890s, bicycles were commonplace as cheap if unstable transport.

production. Millions were to be sold before the end of the century, and although new bicycles might cost £12 there was a flourishing second-hand market, so that even labourers would ride them.

The success of the Small Heath factory transformed the district. The scattered hamlet grew in a single generation into a town as large as the Oxford or Worcester of its day. It was linked to Birmingham by a frequent steam tram service, and was soon absorbed into the city.

In the 1880s the government opened the Royal Small Arms factory in Sparkbrook, and Sam moved there to become a fitter. Sparkbrook, like Small Heath, was turning into a suburb of Birmingham: 'rows and rows of anaemic-looking houses, depressingly uniform in pattern effacing the picturesque delights of lane and meadow'. The pattern was terraces of two-bedroomed houses, with bow windows in alternate houses and sometimes a tiny front garden. Each house had a sitting room, kitchen and small scullery; some had attics and cellars. None had bathrooms: all shared the outside toilet with at least one neighbour. A well-paid man like Sam could afford to rent such a house and, if he was prepared to make the sacrifice of hard saving, even buy one.

In material terms, Sam was not badly off. The value of his wage was much higher by the end of the century than his father's had been at Enfield – though he could not hope to make £5 a week in a boom year, or become his own master, he was part of a comfortable class of men. He went by tram or bicycle to football matches on Saturday afternoons (he was a referee) and he could afford to visit the music hall. He believed in self-improvement and was involved with an early morning school (better than evening classes, because it did not interfere with overtime).

Self-improvement had become a popular movement among serious-minded workmen. Samuel Smiles, in *Self-Help* (1859) had pointed out that the working man who had nothing but his wages was a wage slave, but thrift and education could give him back the independence of an earlier life.

> The healthy spirit of self-help created amongst working people would more than any other measure serve to raise them as a class and this, not by pulling others down, but by levelling them up to a higher and still advancing standard of religion, intelligence and virtue.

By 1904, *Self-Help* had sold a quarter of a million copies, and its philosophy was evidently accepted by the committees of public libraries, workmen's libraries and craft institutions, for the books they bought were more likely to encourage personal improvement than social reform. But self-improvement actually made Sam Page more dissatisfied with society. He became an inspector of other men's work, and was acutely aware that as factory machines became more sophisticated, the satisfaction of work declined. Piecework was replaced with flat-rate payment: production lines were introduced: men no longer worked at their own pace, but at the rate of the line – they no longer moved from one machine to another with a piece of work, but waited by one machine as the work came to them.

An article in Sam's union journal in 1914 reflected on the way in which workers were no longer required to be 'practical mechanics', but were reduced to being operators

> who, year in and year out, will watch and control a machine, will have to maintain a certain output week by week for a given wage. . . . From daily intercourse with men who have become victims of this system of sectionalism, who today and for ever must remain a Driller, Miller, Turner, Capstan Hand, Machine-Moulder, Automatic Attendance, &c., &c., we know that the monotony of life is detrimental to the interests of the individual from a physical or mental standpoint.

Neither labourers nor artisans, these men belonged to a new order. In 1898 the Workers' Union was born. As the name implied, it was not a craft union, aiming at helping specific groups improve their lot, but a union with universal pretensions. Sam Page joined it for exactly that reason: he did not think of himself as a skilled artisan but as a worker, whose interests lay in collective action with semi-skilled and unskilled men, to change society.

The Workers' Union, in Sam's view, was 'an organisation in which the strong were expected to help the weak', which meant that skilled men like himself would be prepared to strike to raise the wages of labourers earning about a pound a week. In return, the politically-literate aristocrats of labour expected mass support for their own programme, which was set out by Tom Mann: 'it is nothing less than the workers themselves becoming the controllers of the industries in which they are occupied'.

The change from workshop to factory had created a new civilisation – the average Englishman was no longer a countryman, but lived in a heavily built-up suburb and worked in industry. The transformation had brought him material goods, though no security – it was a disaster to lose a job – and a feeling that he had less control over his life. Every aspect of his life was becoming, like his home, 'depressingly uniform in pattern'.

This sense of dissatisfaction was increased by the fact that in the early twentieth century, industry was failing to deliver the goods. The advance in incomes which had taken place began to go into

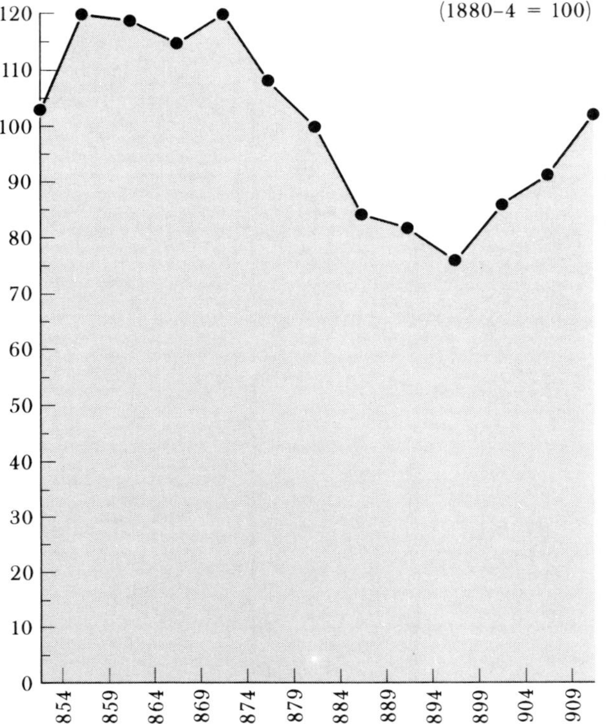

Figure 5 Real prices 1850–1913.

reverse. Prices began to rise much faster than wages. England was no longer the 'workshop of the world' and competition from Germany and America was driving real wages down again. The years immediately before the First World War were marked by long and bitter strikes.

Industrial society seemed to have taken away men's control over their own lives, without guaranteeing them growing wealth after all. The riches being produced were evidently going to the wealthy. Sam Page, like many others, concluded that the only remedy was for the workers to take control of society for themselves. The fine gradations of his father's society had no meaning in the factory world. The only distinction there was between the workers and their bosses, and Sam knew where he stood. 'If I had my way' he said in the union journal of 1916, 'the people who do not perform useful work would not be allowed to take any part in political or citizen affairs, or have a voice on any question which affects the community.'

It was a crude doctrine: his unconscious rejection of the unemployed as well as bloated capitalists and effete aristocrats expressed a genuine prejudice of respectable working people. But the point was clear enough. Having turned men into 'hands', their employers found themselves confronted by raised fists.

5

Many of the workers in the engineering factories of Edwardian England were discontented, but their work offered better opportunities than anything else open to them. Mark Stokes was born into a craftsman's family in Earlsdon, a suburb of Coventry, in 1898, but neither he nor his five brothers became watchmakers like their father. They did what most boys did in Coventry, and went into factories.

Mark's father was a highly skilled artisan, working in a trade for which Coventry was famous. He had a watchmaker's habits, smoking tiny spills of tobacco with the lighted end inside his mouth, so that ash would not fall on his work. He had the personal position that went with his craft: he had served seven years as an apprentice, and was enrolled as a freeman of the city, with a freeman's rights: he was entitled, for instance, to graze cattle on the common.

These rights did not mean much in practice. The hard reality was that he worked for a large manufacturer and had to support his wife and children on twenty-eight shillings a week, plus occasional half-crowns from private repair work in the evenings. Since the law obliged him to keep his children at school until they were 14, the family was poor. There was a special dispensation which allowed a child to leave a year early by passing an examination, and the oldest child, William, did just that. Once he had started work, he was soon earning more than his father. The family was now a little better off, and Mark could stay at school until he was 14; once he started earning, it was possible to consider technical college for his younger brothers.

Even the old age pension, introduced in 1908, turned out to be more of a problem than a benefit. Men expected to carry on earning until they were too weak to work. But as soon as old Mr Stokes reached 70 and became eligible for his ten-shilling pension, his employers told him they would knock it off his pay. Furious, he left his job.

Mark's first job was in a motor-cycle factory, making valves. The working day, as usual, started at six in the morning, with breaks for breakfast and lunch, and finished at half past five, unless there was overtime to be worked. Saturday was a half day. There were about a hundred workers in the factory, organised in gangs under a chargehand. Each gang worked as a unit, and was paid for the amount of work it did. Mark had the simplest kind of work, operating a single machine which was set up for each job by someone more experienced. At the end of the week the chargehand collected the gang's money in gold, and divided it up among them.

This was the standard pattern. Engineering factories were male preserves; women stayed home having babies and running the house. With ten or more in the family, this was a major task: Mark's household was run like a small hotel, with potatoes by the sackful and beer by the barrel.

For the boys, progress meant learning more about the machines; becoming a skilled operator meant knowing how to set the machine up for each new batch of work to be done on it. Mark left the motor-cycle factory to work at Alfred Herbert's machine-tool factory, which was the heart of England's engineering enterprise. Here were built the machines which made the factories work, and here Mark could gain experience that was recognised throughout industry.

The Great War gave the industrial Midlands all the work it could handle. Many factories were turned over to producing guns and ammunition. Instead of having to stop and re-set machines for small batches of work, they were producing millions of identical objects. Mark's working day was fourteen hours long; everyone was on overtime.

Mark was too young to see much of the war in uniform: he came back to a city that was pulsing with optimism. Many demobbed soldiers were finding it hard to get work, but that was seen as a temporary problem. The positive side of unemployment was seen in a shorter working week, with two day weekends and work starting at eight in the morning. Money had lost its value, and wages were paid in paper instead of gold, but wages were going up. Germany was going to pay for the war, and British industry would surely reap the benefit. The war had given manufacturers the experience of continuous mass production. Now they hoped to switch their wartime methods to new products. The favourite hope was making cars.

William Morris was one of the men who had been building cars before the war, and discovered the joys of mass production when his factory produced munitions for the war. In America, Henry Ford had already succeeded with mass production of the model T. Morris like others (including Ford himself) hoped to do the same in England.

English car factories did not manufacture anything: they

assembled components made in other places. The problem with a mass-production line was not how to enforce industrial discipline, but how to arrange for the right numbers of parts of the right types to be made and transported to the right places at the right times.

For a small company it was headache enough. William Stanley worked for Calcott, in Gosford Street, Coventry, and he is quoted as remembering 'how he once had to take a wheelbarrow to the Coventry Radiator Factory nearby in order to bring back a couple of mudguards'. Calcott cars were built on chassis which were made outside the city, and which arrived from the railway station on horse-drawn drays. The bodies were made by the firm of Thomas Pass, a little way up the road. The 120–150 men in the factory were almost all employed assembling parts made elsewhere. It was unsteady work, highly seasonal. When demand for the cars was slack, the workmen would assemble spares. When company funds were too low to carry large stocks of spares, the men were sent home. About 2,500 Calcott cars were produced before the company was bought by Singer and ceased production in 1926.

Morris set up a 'production line' in his suburban factory at Cowley, near Oxford. Trying to keep a regular flow of production

52 The Morris assembly line.

made the difficulties of supply even greater than they were for Calcott. The factory next to Calcott was that of Hotchkiss, which supplied Morris with engines, and when Hotchkiss refused to expand production to meet Morris's needs, the company found itself taken over. Production was increased from 300 engines a week in 1923 to 1,200 a week two years later. The Gosport Road workshops were converted into a six-storey factory; the workmen found themselves inside a single great machine. A grid lift carried cylinder block castings to the top of the building, where they were stored. They went down a spiral chute into a pickling bath, and were then moved through a production-line process in which fifty-three different operations were performed in 224 minutes and a complete cylinder block came off the line every four minutes.

As the work was widely spread, so were the benefits: workers in many factories expected to make double their basic wage by fast work and overtime. The key to a good pay-packet lay in the work done by the rate-fixers. They were supposed to set a time for the job in such a way that a man of average ability could expect to earn an agreed sum per hour. In the optimistic years of 1919 and 1920, rate-fixers were able to be generous. By 1921, the situation was changing. Unemployment was not falling. The government intended to restore sterling to the gold standard, and that meant driving prices and wages to a lower level. Car makers were short of customers, and began to fail. Rate-fixers were lowering the times allowed for jobs, and earnings were falling.

At Siddeley's car factory in Coventry, there was a story of a youth who had been at work for a few days when he told his foreman, 'I'm packing up.' The foreman asked him why, and he said, 'I'm not earning enough money.' 'Oh my lad,' replied the foreman, 'there's no need to worry about that. Give it a fair trial. Rome wasn't built in a day.' 'No,' said the youth, 'but it would have been if you had been the rate-fixer'.

Matters came to a head in the spring of 1922. In the boom years trade union membership had risen; it was nearly eight and a half million by 1920, more than double the 1914 membership. But as wages were cut around the country, the unions were too weakly organised to fight back. As men lost confidence in the unions they dropped out. Now the Amalgamated Engineering Union decided to make a stand. It had been created in 1920, and was the richest union in the world. When the engineering employers demanded a cut in wages, the AEU and forty-seven other engineering unions called a strike. The employers responded with a lockout. Mark Stokes, like thousands of others, found he had no job.

Throughout the Midlands, soup kitchens were set up in the

streets. The lockout lasted until the union funds were exhausted. Then the beaten men agreed to go back, and accepted the cuts.

When Mark got married, times were hard. He was better off than a textile worker, or a shipbuilder, who probably had no work at all, but it was a struggle to make ends meet. Every Thursday he went into the Co-op to put down money to buy a bed. If that left him two shillings at the end of the week, he considered himself lucky. Still, he had been able to save a lot from the good years – he had £100 put away, and that represented half the cost of a small house. His father too, was a frugal man, and was able to lend him the other half. In this respect Mark was unusual; most of his workmates rented their houses. He was also able to boost his income by turning the front room into a general store, which was run by his wife.

And things did get better. Since costs – including wages – had fallen, it was possible to cut the price of cars. Morris did this, and found customers. By 1926, when Morris was already a millionaire, the Society of Motor Manufacturers and Traders reckoned that a car could be run on an income of £450 a year. That was about three times the average industrial wage, but three-quarters of a million households did have this level of income. About 150,000 cars were made that year: over 40 per cent of them were 'bull-nosed' Morrises. Mark went to work at the Hotchkiss factory.

Now the benefits of mass production began to show. As production went up, prices went down: between 1924 and 1935 Morris's cars were halved in price. By 1935 production had doubled, and there were over two million vehicles on the roads.

Production on this scale was changing the face of England. The car needed roads, and it took up space: it created new hazards, new crimes and new possibilities. It brought government into the regulation of daily life, with speed limits and driving tests and rules about lighting systems. It brought a new class of citizen into the courts, as they knocked people down and drove through red lights. It created a new attitude to adult death: just as new standards of housing and sanitation made infant life more secure, the casual slaughter of the slow and elderly on the roads got under way. Not everyone agreed with the West Middlesex coroner who was reported as commenting on the fate of a lady of 86 killed by a car: 'Old ladies who go about like this may cause any amount of danger to other people. In trying to avoid them motorists and cyclists may find themselves in other difficulties.' But once speed limits had been introduced in built-up areas it seems to have been tacitly accepted that death on the roads was somehow unavoidable bad luck. Killing someone with a car was so far removed from manslaughter in the popular mind that juries refused to convict for it, and a new crime had to be invented – motor manslaughter – with lighter penalties.

With the production lines so vast and fast-moving, and the product itself being built by the combined efforts of so many different industries, the motor car production line was a miracle of social co-operation. At Austin's plant at Longbridge, for instance, 20,000 men were employed on a hundred-acre site, with six miles of conveyor belts and 6,000 productive machines. Mark Stokes moved on to work at Rootes Number 1 plant, and was astonished by the sheer beauty of it. Each section of the engine was being assembled on a tributary line, and arriving on the main stream of the conveyor at the precise moment when it was needed to fit into the whole. The factory was a single-storey open space, in which thousands of people were operating as components in a single machine that ran day and night without a hitch.

Outside, the component firms scattered around the city, and around the country, were also acting as tributaries to the same flow. They were making parts specifically designed for this car, in a way that was exactly prescribed, at a rate that was precisely determined.

The work on the line itself was, of course, extremely boring. It had become recognised that the most repetitive work was best given to women: when a study was made of 'fatigue and boredom in repetitive work', every one of the situations studied dealt only with women. The women were usually unmarried: surveys showed that they were more concerned with the company they met than with the prospects of the job, or even with what they were paid.

As the factories had grown, life-styles had become more alike. Although there were about 140,000 factories in England in 1935, just 519 of them employed 21 per cent of all workers. The new factory suburbs like Luton, Slough, Dagenham, and Reading became single-class communities.

The life of the factory depended on the co-operation of the men on the 'shop floor'. Central union organisations were hardly relevant: some manufacturers, like Morris, were able to keep the unions out of their factories altogether. Where the men were unionised, power lay mainly with the shop-stewards, the men who represented the workers on the spot. For as the production lines grew larger and faster they became more vulnerable. The entire financial edifice depended on keeping the lines moving.

In November 1936 the rate-fixers at Longbridge had bad news for the night shift in the west works. The shift had been doing a finishing job faster than the time allotted, and now that time was to be cut. It meant that it would be harder to earn a bonus for working faster than the stated rate. The forty painters, polishers and trimmers on the shift walked out.

The fatal weakness of the production line was immediately obvious. With those forty men out, everything began to grind to a halt. Soon 5,000 men had been laid off.

The dispute was quickly settled. It had to be. The factory system itself was transferring power to the men who worked in it. But this was an exceptional situation; the mood of the factories was not usually militant. Any feeling of class warfare between 'bosses' and 'workers' was generally outweighed by the need to stay in work, and for some, the hope of promotion.

When Mark Stokes was offered the chance to give up his job as a machine operator at Rootes and become an inspector, he took it. It meant a cut in pay, because he would no longer be on piecework, but he was getting older and the work would be less heavy. It also meant that he would take off his blue overall and put on a white coat: 'I thought it would be cleaner.'

He did well as an inspector. The collar of his coat was changed from an inspector's red to a chargehand's yellow, and then to blue when he became a foreman of inspectors. But real progress come when he was made assistant chief inspector. 'Then you didn't have to wear a white coat at all. You wore a suit. That's when you knew you were somebody.'

53 Mark Stokes.

This was the big jump. Mark was now a member of staff, paid monthly instead of weekly, eating in the executive canteen. He paid for the privilege of promotion, because he was paid a flat salary, without overtime. By the late 1930s he was earning only £16 a week, while some of the men who were still in overalls could make three times that.

Earlsdon, where Mark still lived when I met him, used to be called 'the village of brown boots and no breakfasts'. The way factory work was organised, with promotion from overalls to suits being loaded with status and penalised in pay, suggests that Earlsdon folk were not alone in their readiness to make sacrifices for a dignified and respectable appearance.

Mass production was helping to make a middle-class way of life possible for people who had never had servants. A national electricity grid powered lights and vacuum cleaners; bathrooms and toilets were standard fittings on the new housing estates. And as hire purchase schemes became widespread, even motor cars could be bought by factory workers.

Earlsdon was built in the 1850s, as Coventry shared in the explosive growth of Midlands cities. Its central cross-roads was known as 'Ation Corner', because it offered the four choices of Victorian life – co-operation (the 'Co-op'), salvation (the church), education (the public library) and damnation (the pub). Mark Stokes, though, hardly ever used those facilities in the 1920s. He had a shop in his front room, he was a Methodist, he listened to the radio and he drank in the Albany Club, which was cheaper and more cheerful than the pub. Choices were more varied than a generation earlier.

There was a visible improvement in the quality of life for families in work during the 1920s and '30s, despite the problems of unemployment. The greatest problems for the factory economy, however, still lay in the future.

Mark Stokes worked for many of the major industrial names of the time – Alfred Herbert, Morris, Daimler, Rootes and others. I asked him what had changed in factory work, as he saw it, over his working life, from 1912 to 1952. He puzzled for a moment and then said, 'Nothing, really.'

Of course, that was an immediate response – many things had changed. But not, as he saw it, anything very fundamental. Which goes part of the way to explaining why not a single one of the companies he had worked for still remained solvent when we met.

Chapter 5
SEAMEN

1

The signal for 'battle' in the Royal Navy was a blood-red flag. On 21 April 1797, the flagship of the Channel fleet was seen to hoist a red flag. But the *Royal George*, like the rest of the fleet, was at anchor at Spithead, between Portsmouth and the Isle of Wight. The signal represented mutiny – not on that ship alone, but throughout the entire fleet.

Well over a hundred ships were to come under the command of the red flag in the next six weeks. The mutiny was to spread until London itself was blockaded by British warships: Napoleon's invasion force was held at bay by a phantom fleet of just two ships. The British Navy had gone on strike.

The sailing ships of the Napoleonic wars were part machine, part prison and part floating state. The great mutiny was compounded of grievances against all three.

As a machine, a warship belonged to the pre-industrial age. For nothing moved unless it was powered by muscles. Even in 1844 a sailor could write: 'A ship contains a set of *human* machinery in which every man is a wheel, a band or a crank, all moving with wonderful regularity and precision to the *will* of its machinist, the all-powerful Captain.'[1]

It took 280 men to turn the main capstan on a first-class ship of the line: without them the anchor could not be raised. There were 159 fore-top, main-top and mizzen-top men: without them, the sails could not be set on the three great masts. The ship itself was a lumbering platform for a hundred cannon; it took between ten and fourteen men to manage a pair of guns. Each of the largest guns weighed three tons: the mainmast was 175 feet tall from the deck, and the lowest yard-arm on that mast was a hundred feet from end to end. Everything was on a massive scale, but nothing worked without enslaved muscle-power. The commonest injury on such a ship was a rupture.

It is hard to imagine the conditions under which men lived on a great ship. A first-class ship of the line held 839 officers and men, in a space less than 200 feet long. The ordinary sailors – called 'the people' – lived among the guns, where they were given fourteen inches each to swing a hammock. In the damp, dank, crowded filth, where smells and rats rose from the bilges, fever was endemic.

The only refuge from the cramped space below was the great sky above, and many sailors spent a lot of time there – up masts, out on yards, controlling heavy canvas and stiff hemp ropes. In good weather, it was a spectacle: in bad weather, with the ship rolling and pitching, the canvas catching in the strong wind, in the dark, when a man was cold and wet and tired and his fingers were raw with salt sores, it was easy to slip.

54 Cruikshank's 'Saturday Night at Sea' shows how seamen lived among the guns. The men were grouped in 'messes', with a hanging board for each mess. Here two messes have come together for a Saturday night drink.

Over 100,000 British seamen died in the French revolutionary wars, but only one in sixteen of them was killed by the enemy. Another two were killed when their ships were lost by accident. Thirteen out of every sixteen deaths – at least 80,000 – were due to disease or personal mishap as men fell victims of their service to the ship-machine.

Britain fought the war by controlling the seas, blockading the continental ports. The ships were in constant danger of being overwhelmed by wind and sea. In the twenty-two years of the war, 354 British ships were lost – but only ten of them were sunk by the enemy. The rest were wrecked, foundered, or caught fire or exploded of their own accord. Without fresh food, the blockading ships were prey to scurvy, despite the issue of lemon juice to prevent it.

> If you only made a dent with your finger on the flesh it would remain a considerable time before it filled up again. From a small pimple that broke out on a man's thigh (and which the doctor could not stop) it increased until all the flesh on the thigh was consumed.[2]

The sailors themselves were literally prisoners; they were not said to be part of a crew, but to belong to the ship. There was no fixed term of service. Men remained with their ship until it was taken out of commission, when the masts were cut down, the cannons taken out and everything else movable was disposed of.

55 Rowlandson went on board the man-of-war *Hector* in Portsmouth harbour, to make sketches. The seamen were not allowed ashore; women were brought out from the town to share the communal life on the middle deck.

The Navy treated its recruits as prisoners, because it assumed that most of them would desert if they were ever allowed ashore. In a sample period from May 1803 to June 1805 there were in fact 500 desertions a month – four times as many men as it was losing in other ways – so perhaps the Navy was right. The more experienced seamen were leaving in the largest numbers. There were certainly not many inducements to stay. The food was old salt meat, from which men carved buttons and models, and maggot-ridden biscuits ('cold . . . like blancmange'), with rum to keep the men quiet. There was every opportunity to get drunk, but that was an offence punishable, like most offences, by lashing with a cat-o'-nine-tails four times heavier than that used by the Army. The sailors were guarded by Marines. The Navy wanted one Marine to every six sailors before the 1797 mutiny. It asked for one to every four sailors after it.

The pattern of authority on a naval ship was almost a model of the autocratic state. At its head was the Captain, who governed from the relative luxury of his day-cabin, with its sweep of windows in the stern, or from the weather-side of the quarter-deck, the safest part of the deck in a heavy sea. On the downhill side of the quarter-deck his officers might stand. The quarter-deck was the territory of rank and breeding: very few men rose from a common background to share it. Commoners belonged 'before the mast', on the lower deck, which ran forward from the mainmast. The Captain did not rule by Divine Right, but the next best thing, the Articles of War. These gave him almost absolute power over his officers and men. If the men were unhappy, they could put up with it or mutiny. The penalty for mutiny was death.

In 1792, before the war started, there had been 16,000 men in the Navy: by 1797 there were six times as many. Some were volunteers, but only a minority. The standard form of recruitment was the press gang.

56 Gillray's cartoon, 'Liberty of the Subject', reflects popular outrage at the press gang. In this case the point is emphasised by the fact that the man seized is plainly a tailor.

The press gang was a form of conscription: seamen, with some exceptions, were obliged to serve the Crown in times of war, and the press gang saw to it that they did. It was a ruthless and virtually lawless system, which encouraged violence. In previous wars, Captains had been obliged to mount their own press gangs, which meant that the gangs themselves would sometimes battle each other for a seaman, but for the revolutionary wars the system was put on a proper footing. An Impress Service was officially established, clubbing men wholesale and throwing them into tenders, which carried them off to Receiving Ships. Charles Pemberton was caught by a press gang in Liverpool in 1806, when he was 17. Once at the tender, he was shown:

> a hole . . . called the Steerage . . . I looked down . . . through a heavy wooden grating . . . I saw a crowded mass of disgusting and fearful heads, with eyes all glaring upwards from that terrible den: and heaps of filthy limbs, trunks and heads, bundled and scattered, scrambling, laughing, cursing, screaming and fighting at one moment.

Seamen who had been away for years in the merchant service might be seized in the act of returning home. One journal records the death of William Skill, seaman, who fell overboard:

> We had pressed him out of the India fleet, just on his return from a three-year voyage, pleasing himself with the idea of beholding those he held most dear (a mother and sister) for whom he had brought presents many a long mile: and although in his spare time aboard us he had made away with most of his apparel for grog, which he was fond of, yet the presents remained untouched, hoping one day to take them home himself.[3]

The press gangs were efficient, but could not supply all the men the Navy needed without paralysing the merchant fleet: coastal areas were soon stripped of eligible men.

In 1795, to solve the problem, counties, cities and towns were made liable to find an additional quota of men for the fleet, in much the same way as they had to find a quota for the Militia. As with the Militia, a bounty was paid, and substitutes could be bought. Since the terms of service in the Navy were far nastier than the Militia, the quota men were generally found in the gaols and in front of local justices: vagrants, debtors, petty criminals and seditious nuisances.

Men who had joined the Navy as volunteers joined it on its own terms, and accepted it. Men who were pressed out of the traditional seaports also accepted the naval autocracy: they were used to merchant ships in which the Captain was a lonely figure of authority, just as he was on a man-of-war. But the quota men found it particularly hard to accept the way they were treated. So did the east coast collier sailors.

The quota men included many who were well-educated and truculent. The sailor whose voice was most clearly heard in the mutinous fleet at Spithead was Valentine Joyce, who had served a sentence for sedition. The nominal 'president' of the fleet that blockaded the Thames was Richard Parker, who had been an

57 Richard Parker.

officer, was demoted by a court-martial for disobeying a superior, and was found in a debtor's prison. Both men were brought in on the quota.

The quota men were likely to be rebellious: some of them were well-educated, and there were even a few like Parker who knew something of ships. But it was the east coast collier sailors who knew how to organise a mutiny. W. S. Lindsay argued that this breed of men were the best seamen that England produced:

> During her great naval engagements England looked to that trade

> more than to any other for the best, or at least the hardiest and most daring seamen for her navy. Indeed, it afforded a supply of men who could go aloft in any weather and fight the guns, with the green sea frequently rolling through the port-holes. They never saw danger.[4]

These men were a product of the new industrial society: the steam age demanded coal, and it came from Northumberland and Durham mines in ever-greater numbers of vessels. Sailing a deep-sea ship out of some Devon harbour was a clean and relatively attractive occupation: the seaman and his family probably lived in the harbour town where their ancestors had lived before them, and the seaman's skills were in splicing and seizing rigging lines, and decorative ropework. Sailing a collier out of the Tyne was a filthy business. The seaman and his family probably lived in a growing industrial centre like South Shields, which by 1792 had grown from almost nothing to 14,000 inhabitants in thirty years 'without a single magistrate to control it. None of its inhabitants are of a description to qualify for that office.'

This seaman's ancestors were more likely to have been down a mine or on the land than in a ship; South Shield's fleet quadrupled in those thirty years. Deep-sea, long-haul sailors moved from port to port, with long months at sea, but the men on collier brigs had their own shore-based community, with its own clubs and customs. The Tyneside seaman was likely to be engaged on a contract that demanded that he unload the vessel himself, and supply his own food: his skills ranged from finding his way safely in and out of ever-shifting channels between sandbanks, to jumping off a platform in time with three of his fellows, holding ropes, so that the sudden jerk would capsize a great basket of coal over the side when they were unloading.

> Accustomed to work their way amongst shoals and sandbanks, and along iron-bound coasts in their frail craft, and during the most tempestuous weather, the shelter of a man-of-war was like a haven of rest to them. But though they frequently faced dangers without a thought that would have made the regular man-of-war's man tremble, they stood sadly in want of discipline, and were with great difficulty trained to order, so that the comparatively easy life of a man-of-war's man had few attractions for them.

Although they resented discipline imposed from above, they were capable of acting in an ordered and disciplined way among themselves. They had frequent strikes. When they struck in 1792, demanding a share in the rising price of coal, *The Times* reported that 'This riot has the order and energy of a system.' The sailors had waited until there was a long period of easterly winds, and the Tyne had become clogged with shipping from other ports unable

58 Unloading a collier, about 1800, by Atkinson.

to get away. By the time the wind turned there were some 400 vessels packed in the river: the whole trade was in their grasp.

They went from ship to ship in boats, calling the men out: they delegated some men to form an organising committee, setting up a blockade of the river and imposing a firm discipline on the strikers themselves: 'Watches are kept with regularity, pass-words are established; the streets paraded, *traitors* punished, and not a ship suffered to leave the harbour, before notes for four guineas per run are given to the established crews.'

Vessels which had accepted their terms were distinguished by a Union Jack being nailed to the mainmast. The strike was a total victory for the seamen: negotiations with the owners were completed on a naval sloop stationed in the river.

The mutiny at Spithead was organised in a remarkably similar manner. It began with petitions for higher pay. Able Seamen were paid twenty-four shillings a month, a rate fixed in 1653; more than half the money was taken in compulsory deductions, and in any case the Admiralty did not pay up for years at a time. At the end of 1796 seamen were owed nearly one and a half million pounds in back pay.

The sailors of the north-east had been protesting for years about naval pay. In 1793 they had given the local Impress Officer a copy of a handbill they were circulating: 'Why should our situation in Time of War be rendered so much worse than in Time of Peace . . . Our children and Dependents are neglected; they are exposed to all the miseries of Poverty, and hindered in their Course of Life.'

They petitioned parliament that year for higher naval wages, without success. The Impress Service continued its work through the next three years in the teeth of vigorous local opposition and some hard physical battling. And in 1797, petitions for higher pay were flooding into the Lords of the Admiralty from the pressed men.

The red flag was raised when the petitions had been ignored too long. Sailors went from ship to ship in boats, collecting delegates to an organising committee. As ships joined the strike, they nailed the red flag to the mainmast and hung a noose from the yard-arm, as a symbol of the committee's own discipline. They drew up a fuller list of demands, asking for better provisions and fair measures (a 'Purser's Eight' was seven: a pound of naval food weighed fourteen ounces), demanding better care of the sick, 'and that we may be looked upon as a number of men standing in defence of our country; and that we may in somewise have grant and opportunity to taste the sweets of liberty on shore, when in any harbour.'

The mutineers also demanded the removal of tyrannical officers; one petition to the Admiralty read:

> It is our unanimous desire that Lieut. Fitzpatrick and Lieut. Hicks be dismissed out of HMS *Glory*, as the former has every means behaved tyrannically to the people with ordering them to be beat in a most crule manner . . . beating, blacking, tarring and putting the people's heads in bags.

Altogether fifty-nine officers and warrant officers were dismissed by the Admiralty on the insistence of the mutineers, as part of the price for putting an end to the action. For, faced with a well-organised strike and reasonable demands which had public sympathy, they were obliged to give in.

Raising pay, guaranteeing proper weights of food, dismissing quarter-deck tyrants and granting a royal pardon brought an end

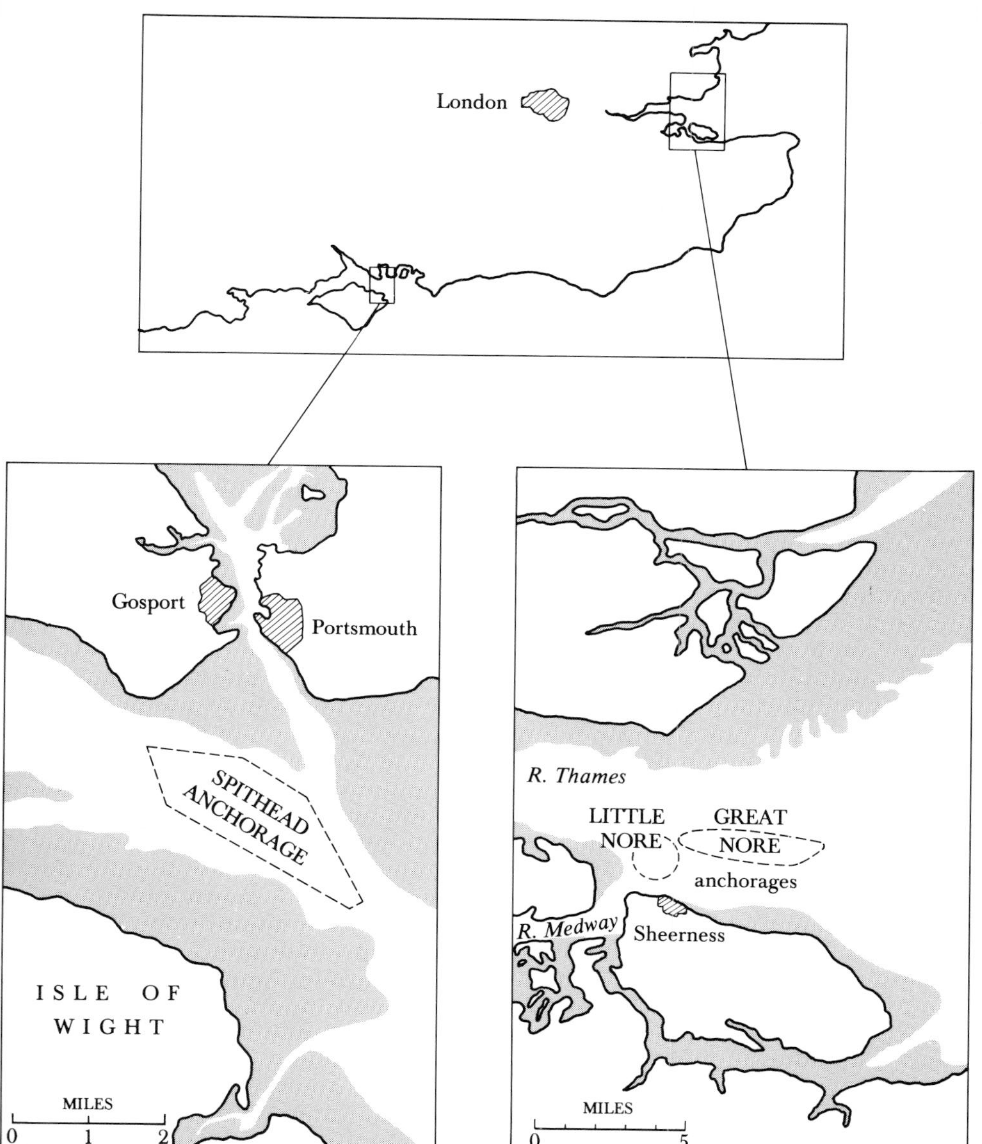

Figure 6 Spithead and the Nore.

to the Spithead mutiny. But as it was ending, a similar mutiny was erupting in the ships anchored at the Nore, in the Thames estuary. The same organisation was established: officers were sent ashore, and a committee of delegates was set up to enforce discipline and negotiate with the Admiralty. They were joined by most of the fleet that was supposed to blockade the Dutch coast. But now the Admiralty would not negotiate.

There had always been strong voices opposed to negotiating with organised strikers. During the Tyne strike of 1792 one ship-owner had written to the prime minister:

> When I look around and see this country covered with thousands of pitmen, keelmen, waggonmen and other labouring men, hardy fellows strongly impressed with the new doctrine of equality, and at present composed of such combustible material that the least spark will set them in a blaze, I cannot help thinking the supineness of the magistrates very reprehensible.

The king himself had told parliament that the French had a hand in the strike, 'to attempt the destruction of the Constitution, and the subversion of all order and government in these kingdoms.' Now that the Spithead mutiny had been settled, those voices were louder than ever. Why should more sailors mutiny, if their object was not subversive?

The sailors themselves had simpler demands. The Spithead delegates had accepted terms which did not mention details such as granting seamen leave. And the pardon which they had been granted did not cover other mutineers. But as the authorities now refused to come to terms with the men at the Nore, where did striking end and rebellion begin? Where did the rights of men become the Rights of Man, and revolution start?

> The Age of Reason has at length revolved. Long have we been endeavouring to find ourselves men. We now find ourselves so. We will be treated as such. For, very far from us is the idea of subverting the government of our beloved country. We have the highest opinion of our Most Gracious Sovereign, and we hope none of those measures that have been taken to deprive us of the common rights of men have been instigated by him.

That appeal to the people of England was written when the Nore ships, isolated and desperate, were blockading the Thames to capture food and water for themselves, in the dwindling hope of 'redress of grievances'.

> Hitherto we have laboured for our sovereign and you. We are now obliged to think for ourselves, for there are many (nay, most of us) in the Fleet who have been prisoners since the commencement of the War, without receiving a single farthing, have we not a right to complain?

It did not take very long to starve the Nore ships out, and divide the men among themselves. Of the 400 sailors arrested, fifty-nine were condemned to death; no one is quite sure how many were actually executed.

The great mutiny at Spithead was a successful industrial action based on principles that had already been developed on the Tyne.

At the Nore, where the same kind of action was met with a flat refusal to compromise, 'the new doctrine of equality' began to sound like a political threat. The spectre of a 'floating republic' that might set off a general revolution had much to do with the repressive ruthlessness of the early nineteenth century.

After the French wars, some 100,000 men were discharged from the Navy, to find work or starve. Merchant shipping revived, but not quickly enough to absorb so many men. The seamen of the north-east attempted to force shipowners to take on larger crews, and organised another strike along the lines they had already learned so well, but this time they were defeated utterly. After seven weeks, the strike was broken with armed force, and its nominal leader, 'Admiral' Nicholas Greener, was caught and imprisoned.

Men were now obliged to go to sea – if they could get work at all – on the shipowner's terms. Often this meant going out in overloaded, undermanned and unseaworthy vessels. If they made port safely, the shipowners made large profits: if they did not, then the insurance underwriters made up the loss. As the *Westminster Gazette* put it in 1836, the shipowners and insurers were growing rich on the sacrifice of 'brave seamen who are sent out in crazy ships to be drowned with as little ceremony as rats. Annihilate wrecks, and the underwriters' occupation is gone. By wrecks and drownings they live and move in splendid houses and equipages.'

The number of wrecks had become so scandalous that a parliamentary select committee was set up in 1836 to examine the problem. They were told of ships like the *Princess Victoria*, which was so badly built that when it was laden with grain it simply fell to pieces on its first voyage, in fine weather; and the *Nathaniel Graham*, which was so rotten that it was impossible to plug the gaps between its planks, and which disintegrated when it hit a rock, drowning forty-one men. They were told of the 'coffin-ships', built to cheat the tonnage laws. Charges on ships were levied according to the 'registered tonnage' which was, in theory, the ship's capacity for cargo: since the depth of the hold was always assumed to be half the width, shipowners built deep, narrow ships with large holds but low 'registered tonnage'. Heavily insured and weak at sea, these ships deserved their gruesome title. In the spring of 1834 alone, 700 lives were lost in the North Atlantic, when eighteen emigrant ships went down. No enquiries were held.

The committee, disturbed by the evidence of unseaworthy ships and incompetent masters, recommended that ships and officers should have to be approved by a Mercantile Marine Board. Parliament, however, decided that nothing should be done apart from changing the way ships were measured.

One of the seamen crossing the Atlantic in 1834 was W. S. Lindsay, who had just signed on as an apprentice in a three-masted ship sailing out of Liverpool. He was 16, and had run away from work in a Manchester draper's shop. He entered a strange, tough world: 'Anyone who went to sea in a merchant ship in those days required to make up his mind to very hard work and harder fare.'

There was a crew of twenty and the master. Lindsay's berth was with two other apprentices, ten seamen and the cook, all jammed into a forecastle twenty feet long and five feet high. Entry was by a scuttle from the deck: there was no other light or ventilation, and the scuttle was closed in bad weather. The only furniture was their hammocks and sea-chests: 'the staple articles of our food were beef and biscuit and biscuit and beef'.

As an apprentice, he had signed indentures like those of any apprentice on land. He had hoped to learn seamanship and to enjoy the adventure, and he did both. 'The few hours recreation allowed to us in the "dog watches" from 4 to 6 and from 6 to 8 p.m., were amongst the happiest in my life.'

The rest of the seamen had signed articles of agreement which bound them to stay with the ship for the return voyage. This was supposed to be a free contract, but in reality the long-distance seamen rarely had much choice about which ship to join, and on what terms. When a ship came in to port like Liverpool, lodging-house keepers known as 'crimps' swarmed aboard. Havelock Wilson experienced the crimps of San Francisco in the 1870s, when his ship was coming to anchor:

> Some carried ladders in their boats, and others hooks to go over the rail of the ship. During this time the crew were aloft stowing sails and making them fast.
>
> The runners swarmed up the rigging after the men, with bottles of whisky in their pockets, helping the crew to stow the sails, and making their acquaintance. They were wonderfully ingenious in this . . . . Whilst this was going on the rest of the gang were in the forecastle packing the men's bags; they were not particular as to whose bag or which clothes they put in. Sometimes they would mix up the clothes deliberately. The bags would then be passed out of the forecastle over the side of the boats.

The crimps gave the men whores and drink and lodging on credit: the security was that they were already signing them up willy-nilly for another voyage. On signing articles, a seaman received an advance note against a month or more of his wages. The crimp took this. To get it, he might have to forge the sailor's signature. A few days after coming ashore, the seaman would probably be knocked unconscious with drugs or drink and taken to his ship.

The masters of the vessels accepted the system. If they refused to take crews from the crimps they would get no crews at all. It was true that crimps often induced men to desert their ships half way through a round trip, but as the sailor lost his wages, masters did not necessarily mind too much.

In 1851 there were some 7,000 desertions from British ships – nearly half of them in Quebec alone. Thomas Moore, in a pamphlet published the following year, explained why seamen were so reluctant to sail home from Quebec. If they could escape from their ship and the crimps, they could get work dragging timber for up to a dollar a day, or cross the border into the United States, where seamen expected to be given better treatment on better ships. If they could not, they were trapped in the 'worst of all craft'. Vessels used in the Quebec timber trade were often so rotten that they were kept afloat by day and night pumping as they crossed the ocean. The bottoms of the ships were not sheathed in any way, so that by the time they came to make the return trip they were partly eaten through by worms, 'and all sorts of expedients are resorted to on the return voyage, to keep them from falling to pieces'. The *Venus* brig had no less than seven chains passed under her, to bind her frame, so as not to break up at sea. The ships were so slow that almost all of them ran out of provisions before completing the voyage, and the men might starve or die of thirst before sighting land.

Moore's pamphlet was necessary because parliament had at last decided to take some action over the state of merchant shipping; it had, however, decided that problems were caused less by bad ships than by bad seamen. The answer, in their view, was to make the merchant sailor more like a Navy man, and to that end they passed the Merchant Marine Act of 1850. This Act made no demands that ships should be seaworthy, and did nothing to prevent overloading: the only important demand it made so far as living conditions were concerned was to insist that each seaman should be provided with lighted and ventilated living space equivalent to six feet by eighteen inches, in the forecastle or a deck-house. Enough space to lie down in, but that was all.

To improve discipline on board, owners and masters were empowered to arrest men who were guilty of dangerous misconduct or wilful breach of duty through drink. As in the Navy, such misconduct became a crime. Naval courts, held by naval officers, were to be set up abroad to hear complaints of masters, mates and seamen. To improve the standard of officers, compulsory examinations were introduced. To reduce the power of crimps, shipping offices were set up, where seamen were engaged and advance notes issued. The shipping masters there were empowered to oversee the articles of agreement, which were to include the duration of service, the man's capacity (the equivalent of his naval rating), the scale of pay and provisions and conditions of conduct on board.

There was a 'recommended' form of articles, which laid down compulsory deductions of pay for minor breaches of discipline. These ran to twenty-two articles, including the following, all of which incurred the loss of one day's pay: swearing or using improper language; smoking below; not attending divine service on Sundays, unless prevented by sickness or duty of the ship; not being cleaned, shaved and washed on Sundays; washing clothes on Sundays. Payment at the end of the voyage was to be at the shipping office, where the seamen would be given a discharge document including a report on their character, conduct and ability. There was uproar.

The ever-growing number of coasting and short-voyage men on the Tyne and Wear resented being obliged to use shipping offices, being told which vessel to sail in and being charged for the use of the offices. The object was to stamp out crimping, but it would fail (it did) and anyway, crimping was only a problem in long-distance shipping. Above all, the men detested the twenty-two disciplinary clauses – the Act, they said, 'treated the seamen as a parcel of Mexican slaves'.

W. S. Lindsay described the collier ships of the north-east as little democracies: 'master, mate and men smoked their pipes together . . . creating an equality and freedom'. They knew who they wanted to sail with, and on what terms. The owners fully supported them; the regulations were an interference with the freedom of trade and contract. The *North and South Shields Gazette* reflected the shared views of owners and seamen in its editorials:

> We are tired of this bungling work of law-making . . . let us have Free Trade, full, fair and unrestricted. . . . By the Merchant Marine Act, and still more by the subsequent regulations of the Board of Trade, they are deprived of the commonest rights of British Citizens and of men. . . . These rubbishy regulations must be rescinded at once.

The ports of the north-east were squalid havens of free enterprise. The banks of the Tyne were lined with heavy industry – gasworks, potteries, steam flour-mills, engineering works, chemi-

59 A collier unloading, about 1800, by Cooke.

cal and glass works, chain and anchor factories, and collieries. The fishermen, seamen, pitmen, lightermen and factory workers lived jammed into terraces of back-to-back houses in enclosed courts, often linked to main streets by covered passages. An investigation of South Shields in 1843 found up to seventeen people sharing each house, with only one house in three having access to a tap or a pump. The lack of sewers 'had led to the formation among the poorer classes of habits not only disgusting and unwholesome but inconsistent with a high tone of morals'.

The largest alkali works in the world belched poisonous fumes over the river, so that on the other side, in North Shields, all the trees in High Town had died, and the birds had gone – the insects on which they fed had been destroyed. Drinking water came from a small polluted reservoir or from the river itself; the area was prey to cholera epidemics. It was far safer to drink beer, and the Shields men were famous for their drunken excesses. Though there was suffering, the people were sturdy and vigorous, living with the booming prosperity of the frontier of the industrial revolution.

60 Shields, about 1840, by J. W. Carmichael.

The Merchant Marine Act came into force in January 1851. On 19 January, 2,000 seamen demonstrated against it in Sunderland. They also took the opportunity of denouncing the identity cards which had been forced on them five years earlier – 'Register Tickets' – which they believed were to make it easier to impress them into the Navy, and which 'are regarded as a badge of slavery and degradation to Seamen, to which no other class of Englishman is subject'. They resolved there and then to form a Seaman's Friendly Association, each member to pay one penny a week, to support a strike.

They marched to South Shields, and then to North Shields, and were enthusiastically received. On the 23rd a procession a mile long and three or four abreast, led by a brass band playing 'Hearts of Oak', marched to Sunderland Moor to make the strike general throughout the north-east. The Seaman's Friendly Association spread, and was determined to maintain the strike until the obnoxious Act was withdrawn. This was a remarkable event: the first attempt to change a law by going on strike. And it was organised by a union of men earning around £1 a week. The law they were fighting was designed for their own protection: they shared the shipowner's belief in freedom of trade and contract.

It was important for the seamen to impress upon parliament that they were sober and responsible citizens who knew how best to regulate their own affairs, and the *Gazette* helped them by its reporting: 'at least 2,000 well-dressed and tidy seamen assembled . . . . Mr James Shepherd, a mate, a smart intelligent-looking sailor, presided . . . the day's proceedings were characterised by the most orderly conduct.'

On 27 January, Kilberd, the blind bellman of North Shields, was sent along the river in a boat to announce a meeting of strikers: by mistake he announced it for New Quay instead of the Assembly Rooms. Sixty policemen came by train from Newcastle, and went to the quay. The strikers had been re-directed to the Assembly Rooms, but the policemen were so intent on their plan that they apparently did not notice. The *Gazette* saw it all:

> The policemen formed themselves into two lines at the North end of the Quay, with their cutlasses brandished in all positions, some with their points over their shoulders, threatening to poke out the eyes of those behind, others holding them straight up like a musket, and others with their points stuck out right before them. . . . The first division charged across the quay, which they did in admirable confusion, sweeping all the small children before them. They then right-about-faced, and, taking a sweep round, they cleared away all the people that were looking on.

The authorities were in confusion: the seamen were not. The whole coastal and foreign trade of the north was paralysed for a month: the Seamen's Friendly Association established itself in every important port, and elected Thomas Moore as its president.

Moore came from a naval family in Whitehaven, Cumberland, and had started on a naval career himself. He was surprised and troubled by the arbitrary bullying which went on, and did his career no good by composing a popular shanty about his own Captain; he ended up in the General Steam Navigation Company. He campaigned in the press against abuses in both the merchant service and the Navy, and was just the kind of educated, knowledgeable reformer the Friendly Association needed at its head.

The Board of Trade could not remove an Act of parliament, but with trade paralysed it offered what it could. The form of articles with the twenty-two clauses in it would not be used in northern ports, and the Board would review the working of the Act. The *Gazette* trumpeted:

> The 22 'claws' of the Board of Trade are pared off already. The register ticket system – the compulsory shipping offices – the muster roll – likewise must go. But, for this end, let the seamen continue united! Let them keep up standing committees in each port! Let them finally organise and finally adhere to their Friendly Association! They now know their own strength. It consists in sobriety, order and union!

It could have been written by Moore himself: it certainly expressed his own view of the situation. The victory was celebrated with great processions in the northern ports. On Tyneside an effigy of the president of the Board of Trade was burned while a dirge was recited:

> To darkest shades of everlasting night
> May tyranny and tyrants take their flight . . .
> Avaunt! The soil, the birthplace of the free
> Was ne'er designed to harbour snakes like thee,
> Who seek to bind the bravest of the brave
> With ticket, number, mark and badge of slave.

The dummy's head was packed with gunpowder. 'The combined attraction of bands, colours and effigies completely stole away the senses of the youngsters, who hurrahed, shouted and danced until they were both hoarse and weary.'

The Friendly Association, otherwise known as the Penny Union, not only maintained committees in the ports to oversee the working of the shipping offices – virtually taking over from them – but also petitioned parliament for various improvements, and raised money to buy and maintain lifeboats. So long as they concentrated on keeping the Board of Trade at bay, the shipowners were with them. Moore believed that there was a deliberate plan to assimilate the merchant marine to the Navy, and he fought that as hard as he could:

> The merchant marine service cannot be treated like the naval. In the navy, scrubbing, scouring, drilling and dressing, is the chief employment, but on board merchant vessels dress and frivolity must always be discarded for hard work and few to do it. The naval system will only turn the heads of masters, breed discontent, and make dockyard horses of our merchant seamen.

The Penny Union was successful in this battle. The Navy gave up the idea of manning itself by seizing seamen as and when they were needed. In 1853 a system of continuous service was introduced, in which boys signed into the Navy for ten years' service when they were 18, and when their service was ended passed into a Naval Reserve. Pressure to impose 'the naval system' on merchant ships was removed.

But as the union scotched 'the naval system', it turned to the real problems of merchant seamen: undermanned, unseaworthy ships. Undermanning was the obvious problem for them to attack, especially since so many seamen blamed the high rate of wrecking on a gruesome economy in men. Moore wrote a pamphlet which argued that 'Vessels are positively lost by being driven on shore before their crews can shorten sail, and on the English coast our colliers, principally sailed by boys, will fly away with crews some distance before they can be got under management.' Emigrant ships could even be manned by passengers working their passage for £5: they counted as crew members.

Until now, owners and union had been at one, but on this issue they were not. In August 1853 a meeting of seamen was told that the owners were forming a combination to fight them. One speaker pointed out the difficulty of getting parliamentary support; he was quoted as saying:

> The House of Commons, as at present constituted, represented the shipowner rather than the shipping interest, and consequently 'Poor Jack' was not represented, but most grossly misrepresented. . . . Unless they were possessed of a certain amount of bricks and mortar, they could not have a voice in the legislature of the country.

At the end of September, to demonstrate the strength of the union, pitmen and seamen together held a great meeting in South Shields. It was necessary to show that they stood together. For the Penny Union was weakening.

From 1 October 1853, shipowners would be allowed by law to carry foreign crew in place of British: seamen were afraid for their jobs. At the same time, they suspected that the union was squandering their money. Thirty years later, when Havelock Wilson was thinking of reviving the idea of a national union, he heard tales of the way the Penny Union dissipated its funds in great banners and expensive funerals, and by the system of manning the lifeboats it maintained:

> There were four or five crews who, according to regulations, were to assemble whenever a north east gale was blowing. Each man was to be paid 10*s*. for a watch of 8 hours and . . . those watches were appointed very often when there was no semblance of a gale . . . the crews would assemble at a 'pub' and have a good time until about 11 p.m. When matters were not too prosperous with them, they would decide, on some pretext or another, that the lifeboat crew should be mustered.

The confrontation between union and shipowners came at the end of March 1854. The attempt at a strike collapsed quickly. The owners could bring foreign seamen in as they needed. The ships themselves were no longer the only way of moving the coal south: it could go by rail. If the pitmen came out in sympathy, London could take its coal from other fields, thanks again to the railway. The union was broken.

Perhaps the final nail in its coffin came from the fact that the old skills of its members were no longer needed, as sail gave way to

61 This wreck chart was published in *Our Seamen*. Every dot represents a coastal wreck in 1869.

steam. Shipping itself was constantly expanding. Between 1846 and 1854 two and a half million emigrants left British ports. Merchant tonnage rose by 40 per cent in the 1840s, and by a further 30 per cent in the next decade. But there was no comparable increase in the number of seamen. By 1875, 60 per cent of the vessels leaving Newcastle were steamers. When the seamen were as powerful a force as the shipowners, they had spurned parliamentary protection. Now they were weak, and sought it in vain.

The union's last important act was to introduce before parliament the idea that a seaman might be allowed to leave his ship, if it was unseaworthy. Parliament would have none of it. In April 1854, three-quarters of the prisoners in jails in the southern and western district were seamen, serving twelve-week sentences for desertion or refusing to sail. In the first week of that month alone, the newspapers mentioned that the *Sea Nymph*, bound for New York from Liverpool with over fifty on board, had broken up at sea, that the *Julie* from Newcastle was lost and two hands drowned, that the *Russel Sturges* had been found in a sinking state, and that two other ships from Liverpool to New York were missing. Those were the transatlantic ships, and they made the news: no one even reported the sinkings of the collier ships, which were going down at the incredible rate of 1,000 a year. With the constant and growing threat of railway competition, there was nothing the seamen could do.

In 1873, Samuel Plimsoll, MP, spelt out what this meant in lost ships and lost lives. His book, *Our Seamen*, was one of the most powerful works of propaganda of the century. He explained how it was profitable for masters to send out overloaded, unseaworthy ships and for underwriters to over-insure them. The book created uproar, for who could resist the simple appeal, 'Whoever you are that read this, help the poor sailors, for the love of God'?

Samuel Plimsoll was not a shipping man. His fortune was made in the railways, carrying coal to London.

Wooden walls are obsolete, long and long ago,
All their fighting sailormen are dead and gone below.
Fortresses of steel and steam now command the sea
Bearing men of different stamp from those that used to be.

Thus wrote a naval poet around the turn of this century. The change was a long time coming. In 1858 the Surveyor of the Navy had explained that:

> It is not in the interest of Great Britain to adopt any important change in the construction of ships which might have the effect of rendering necessary the introduction of a new class of very costly vessels until such a course is forced upon her by the adoption of Foreign Powers of formidable ships of a novel character requiring similar ships to cope with them.

The British Navy was in an odd position. In 1858 Britain was the world's only industrial nation. Over 500,000 people were employed in the cotton industry, where 'by iron fingers, teeth and wheels moving with exhaustless energy and devouring speed', some 200,000 horsepower of steam-driven machinery was manufacturing cloth for the world. More than 60,000 men worked on the 9,000 miles of railways. Nearly 80,000 men worked in the great blast furnaces, iron mills and foundries.

In 1859 HMS *Victoria* was launched. Her sailors were to be dressed in cotton duck made by the great machines of Lancashire. They would probably travel to join her by train. And the great blast furnaces of industrial Britain would make her anchor. But HMS *Victoria* was a wooden, three-masted man-of-war. Britain was

DY'E MIND THE ROLL SHE GAVE.
DINNER TIME AT SEA.

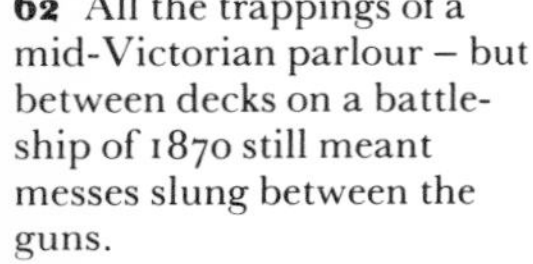

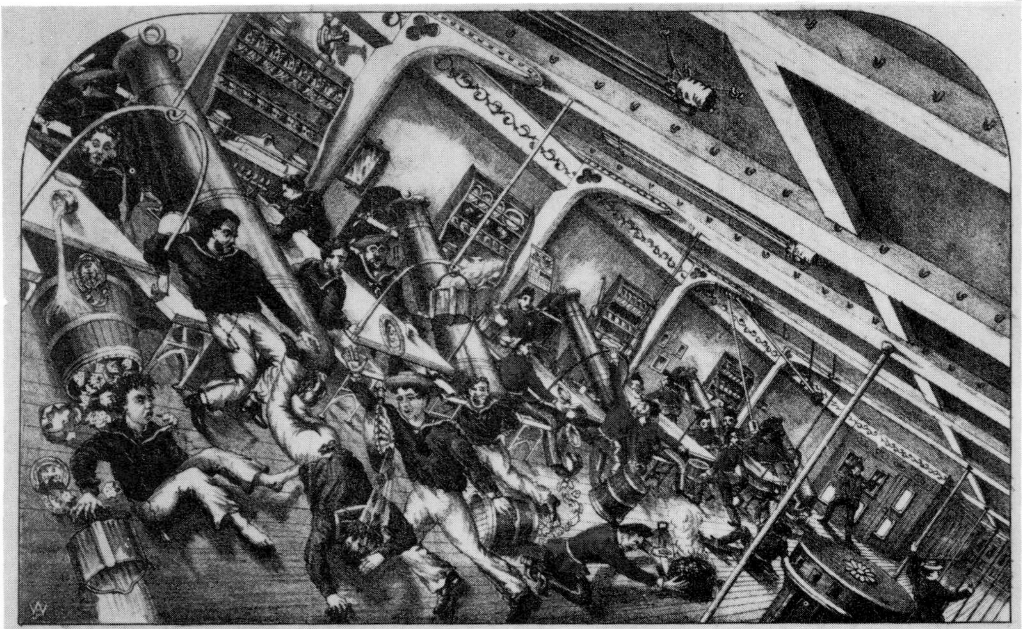

62 All the trappings of a mid-Victorian parlour – but between decks on a battleship of 1870 still meant messes slung between the guns.

the first industrial nation, yet the Navy preferred to progress at the rate of her closest competitor.

Gradually, the Navy was obliged to build iron ships and to give up sail. The Crimean war began with the Russian destruction of the Turkish fleet, and Britain took note of the power of explosive shells when used against wooden sailing ships. In 1872 the first 'mastless' British battleship was built – HMS *Devastation*. But in the great days when the might of Britain was expressed in the call 'Send a gunboat', that gunboat was made of wood, with canvas sails.

James Wood served on a gunboat in the Persian Gulf around 1879. He wrote about it under the name of Lionel Yexley, in *The Inner Life of the Navy*. The seamen had nothing to do except 'show the flag' – the flag being backed up by two 64 lb muzzle-loading cannons and a light gun. The guns were never fired in anger; indeed, they were hardly fired at all. Such gunnery practice as they had to carry out was considered complete if they dropped the ammunition over the side. One gun could in any case only be fired by dismantling the Captain's cabin.

The deadly monotony of our lives, with day after day spent cleaning

63 The question is plainly whether it is easier to put the shell in the gun, or drop it over the side.

paintwork that needed no cleaning, or polishing brasswork that already glittered like gold, resulted in a kind of mental atrophy, while the ennervating climate killed whatever physical energy one might have originally possessed, so that each evening after the day's work was done, the hands simply lolled about the forecastle or hurricane deck in various stages of lassitude.

The forecastle, where most of the 126 men slung their hammocks, was 'a wedge-shaped compartment extending from the bows to a bulkhead, which divided it from the stokehold and engine room . . . about fifty feet long: twenty-six feet at its widest part, tapering to a point.' There was indeed a steam engine and propellor, but this was still a sailing ship. Even under power it was necessary to put up some sails when the wind got up, to prevent her rolling dangerously. For she was unstable at sea, rolling wildly and taking water below in bad weather, so that everything in the forecastle became a sodden, jumbled mess and the galley fire could not be lit.

From here, Yexley transferred to the *Euryalus*, a much larger ship, where 'The days . . . passed rapidly and pleasantly enough. The *Euryalus* being a full-rigged ship there was always plenty of work to be done. . . . Sail drill was *the* thing of that period . . . steam only meant a beastly mess both aloft and on deck.'

The ships had changed little since Napoleonic times, but the men had changed a great deal. The food was still hard tack and pea

64 The crew of a gun-boat at prayers, while at war with China, 1858.

soup – even in the Persian Gulf – and disease, was still a constant killer below decks; but the old 'people' who lived a life of near-slavery had begun to disappear. One man on the gunboat was found stealing from the others, and Yexley commented 'He was one of the old-time ordinary seamen, a type that is not found on the lower-deck today, a big, hefty fellow . . . one of the Queen's "Hard Bargains", as they were called.'

These men were being replaced by boys who had chosen the Navy as a useful way of spending their years from 18 to 28; Yexley was one of them. The Navy was no longer in a position to send out press gangs and hold men for as long as it liked: it had to offer a definite term of service to young men looking for work.

Few of the boys who accepted the naval shilling came from comfortable homes; Yexley was an exception: 'Here was I, a town-bred lad, the pet of a widowed mother, my every wish gratified, a comfortable home, good friends to push me along, no knowledge of the sea (I had never seen it), when suddenly the sea fever seized me.'

He was put onto the training ship *Impregnable*, where boys under 18 were drilled into the naval life – up at 5.30 to scrub the decks, breakfast at 6.30, then sail drill or mast and yard drill, followed by divisions for inspection or prayers, then instructions by classes for the rest of the day. At 11.40 everyone fell in to watch offending lads being flogged with a cane for minor offences, or, for major ones,

65 Boys on the training ship *Wellesley*, at South Shields.

with a birch that drew blood at every stroke. 'No day passed without some caning – generally from six to a dozen boys.'

It was a training system designed for boys from the poorest backgrounds. Vagabond children had been put into the Navy for many years: in 1756 the Marine Society had been founded for just that purpose, and the Industrial Schools Act allowed boys to be committed to training vessels in circumstances which would today have them committed to the care of a local council. 'Character' and obedience were instilled into them by casual beating:

> Notwithstanding the free use of canes and rope ends, the corporals and instructors were anything but brutally inclined. That was a custom of the service and they carried it out. . . . It was thought at the time that the proper way to bring up a boy for the Navy was on a rope's end.

The career that these boys were offered was strictly confined to the lower deck: the officer class remained quite separate. Henry Capper was one of the few to progress from a training ship (in 1869) to a commission as Lieutenant-Commander, but on the way one naval wife explained to him: 'I have the greatest sympathy with you personally in your desire to rise, but you have chosen the wrong service. The Navy belongs to us, and if you were to win the commissions you ask for it would be at the expense of our sons and nephews whose birthright it is.'

On the lower deck, the men were indeed of a different stamp from those who lived behind wooden walls. On the upper deck, and in the Admiralty, the change was not so striking.

4

Nineteenth-century Britain lived in the shadow of Nelson. Wellington may have broken Napoleon at Waterloo, but it is Nelson who stands high over London, with great lions flanking the base of his column. In the popular mind, what happened on the Continent mattered little, so long as Britannia ruled the waves. Paul Fontin, head of department at the French Admiralty, explained early this century that

> For England . . . the sea is not to be looked upon as a means of transport between the different Continents, but as a territory: a British territory of course. The English fleet which owns the empire of the seas, places its frontiers at the enemy's coasts, and will dispose of all commerce behind that frontier, just as an army disposes of the resources of a conquered province.

That was how Britain fought Napoleon, and how she fought the Kaiser, obliging the German fleet to spend almost the whole of the First World War sheltering in harbour. When it suddenly appeared that Britain could no longer rely on her Navy, the shock was critical.

In September 1931 mutiny broke out in the lonely seclusion of the Cromarty Firth, in the eastern highlands. A number of great fighting ships had been brought there to take part in the fleet's autumn manoeuvres (the smaller ships were at Rosyth). The largest was the battle cruiser *Hood*, almost 300 yards long, with eight fifteen-inch guns and over thirty others. There was another battle cruiser, the *Repulse*, just sixty feet shorter, a number of battleships of similar size and just as massively armed, and some cruisers, much lighter ships but still carrying 1,000 men each; the *Hood* carried 1,300.

One of the men of the cruiser *Norfolk*, who was regarded as a ringleader of the mutiny, later wrote his own account of what happened. He was Fred Copeman.

Copeman had come into the Navy as a pauper child. He was born in a workhouse in Suffolk in 1907. When he was 40 he wrote 'I can still remember the cold uncharitableness of the place and its inhuman poverty.' He described it in terms which are reminiscent of Robert Blincoe's childhood over a hundred years earlier:

> The building itself looked like a prison, being of red brick, three stories high, very solid and drab. . . . The whole place was walled in. . . . All the ground floors, with the exception of the Master's quarters, were of stone. . . . The dining hall was to me a huge place. It had lines of well-scrubbed tables and stools on the stone floor.

He was the only child there.

> My mother was a little old lady, thin and frail and practically deaf. . . . Mother's way of practically shouting was embarrassing . . . I would often meet mother, scrubbing the stone passages, which, to me, were miles long. It seemed that she did all the work. Often I saw her crying, but I did not get to know the reason.

He was deeply shamed by his first appearance at the village school, where he arrived in his workhouse clothes to be greeted by a roar of laughter. 'I was the only boy in the school with long trousers and with his hair shaved off. I must have looked like a funny little old man.'

For a boy in this situation, the Navy had much to offer. Fred Copeman was offered a chance to go to Watt's Naval Training School, a Barnardo's Home in Norfolk. 'I was really surprised – no Workhouse this!' He made friends, and enjoyed a regime based on naval life.

> The whole of the staff were ex-Navy. A manliness existed. Every one of the instructors was a hero to at least one section of the lads . . . I shall always be grateful to Dr Barnardo's for those two years . . . Watt's was a wonderful place and I was proud to belong to it.

From there he transferred, with thirty-one other lads, to the Navy's shore training establishment in Suffolk, HMS *Ganges*, where the mornings were devoted to drill, instruction in seamanship and general education and the afternoons to sport. This was in 1920, when the age of sail was a dim memory for the Navy, but the centre of HMS *Ganges* was still a great mast with standing rigging. 'All the boys had to climb the mast at least once a week, and this became quite an ordeal for me . . . It was some 100 feet high.'

After about fifteen months, Fred Copeman sailed to Malta as part of the crew of a battleship. It was there that he saw the great central ritual of the steam-powered navy: loading thousands of tons of coal. He had just transferred to the *Iron Duke*, the flagship of the Mediterranean fleet, and was nearly 15 years old.

> The whole of the ship's company, including the Padre, fell in on the upper deck at 7 a.m., the crew dressed for coaling, which meant in most cases almost naked, with the officers in their overalls . . . the Commander with a stop watch ready to give the order. I stood beside him dressed in my brand new duck suit . . . and attracted a

66 Coaling in progress on an ironclad.

> lot of attention from the men. . . . Every new intake of boys is eagerly looked at by so many of the old sailors, and the attractive ones carefully picked out. . . . A sharp order from the Commander, a pennant broken at the yard-arm, and immediately din and activity commenced. The winches were started. . . . In twenty minutes the ship was smothered in coal-dust from stem to stern, and the ship's company as black as niggers, including me in my white duck suit. The marine band played incessantly.

Three or four thousand tons of coal were being shovelled into sacks on barges, and carried aboard, while tugs chugged back and forth towing empty barges away and bringing out full ones. The whole fleet coaled at once, and it was a race, with marine bands thundering out on every ship, while everything gradually disappeared in swirling clouds of black dust. It took a week to clean up afterwards.

Normal life on board was more relaxed, with the main emphasis on keeping everyone busy with games and cleaning: everything was polished, including the edges of watertight doors and hatches, so that they no longer served their purpose.

Pay was low – four shillings a day for an Able Seaman. It had been raised from 1*s.* 10*d.* in 1919, to avert a general mutiny. The Admiralty would not have known how desperate the men were then, if they had not been told by Lionel Yexley. The men who

67 Officers of the *Trafalgar* after coaling. The board indicated the rate at which they worked.

were such willing workers when it came to loading coal could hardly help comparing their lot with other working men, particularly if they had families at home. Shipbuilding labourers and engineering labourers earned about £2 a week, and stevedores made more than eleven shillings a day. Merchant seamen made fifty shillings a week – and that was for a limited working day with overtime on top, in theory at least. When the crew of a naval ship was allowed free time, the family men ran little businesses to bring in some extra money: 'Every six-inch gun emplacement would be used for some sort of work. . . . In one would be a barber's shop, in another cigarette-making firms, in a third an old stager would be making or ironing clothes, while in a fourth a sewing-machine would be going.'

Sailors were themselves increasingly conscious of comparisons with life ashore. In 1921 there was an attempt to use a battalion of the Royal Fleet Reserve stationed at Newport, Monmouthshire, to break a coal strike. The men flatly refused to co-operate, pointing out that almost all of them were trade unionists themselves. Sailors' families expected to live at the level of the community around them, and by 1930 were often heavily involved in hire purchase.

At the same time, they knew that things were going to get worse. The nation was in financial trouble: unemployment had risen from just over one million in 1929 to 2,700,000 in July 1931. New recruits (since 1925) were already on pay 25 per cent lower than men who had joined earlier. In the summer of 1931, as Ramsay MacDonald struggled to form a government that would accept brutal cuts, sailors steeled themselves for a general drop of about ten per cent; Copeman wrote

> Naval pay had never been high, but in spite of this, every man was prepared to answer the call for economy. It came, therefore, as a complete surprise when newspapers were read throughout the ships, indicating that in most cases the lower ranks would lose more than the senior ranks. The actual reductions were – Admiral, 7 per cent, Lieutenant-Commander 3.7 per, Chief Petty Officer, 11.8 per cent and Able Seaman 23 per cent.

The men in Cromarty Firth were stunned. It was perfectly obvious that the Admiralty did not understand what such a cut would mean to men who were already tightly squeezed. It was also obvious that the Admiralty placed their problems very low in its own priorities, since there was no move to curtail the massive expense of the autumn manoeuvres. Worst of all, the Admiralty was lazy and ill-organised about informing the fleet; the newspapers arrived first.

DAILY HERALD, September 11, 1931

WANTED 100 Persons (either sex) who have the ambition to earn a nice sum in their spare time.

Would you like some crisp £1 notes to spend just as you please? Then if you are enterprising, you can have the thing you so much want this very Christmas by selling Private Christmas Cards to your friends and acquaintances. This is the way. Address a postcard to us asking for one of the beautiful Sample Books. This book and full particulars will be sent you by return of post, quite free of charge. Remuneration most generous, and many valuable prizes in addition. Apply FIRTH GRAHAM AND CO. Ltd., Dept. F 71, Corporation St., Accrington.

Daily Herald

No. 4859 • FRIDAY, SEPTEMBER 11, 1931 ONE PENNY

STOP THAT HEADACHE WITH GENASPRIN *The SAFE brand of Aspirin*

MORE AXES & TAXES BUDGET

MAJOR WALTER ELLIOT, Financial Secretary to the Treasury.

MORE TO PAY ON JANUARY 1

ALLOWANCES CUT BESIDES EXTRA SIXPENCE

YOUR first instalment of higher income tax will be that which falls due on January 1 next.

The standard rate is now 5s. in the pound instead of 4s. 6d., but instead of the first £250 of taxable income being charged at 2s. in the pound, the first £175 is **now charged** at 2s. 6d.

Furthermore, while under the [illegible] Budget the rate of 4s. 6d. was not charged until the taxable income reached £250, the new rate of 5s. is to be charged after the taxable income has reached £175.

If you are single your personal allowance is reduced to £100, against £135, and if you are married, to £150 against £225.

The allowance in respect of children is reduced from £60 to £50 for the first child and from £50 to £40 for other children.

THE ONLY RELIEF

The only relief afforded to the taxpayer to counterbalance the extra bur-

SIXPENCE ON INCOME TAX AND ANOTHER TEN PER CENT. ON SURTAX

New Imposts On Petrol and Entertainments: Extensive Wage Reductions

'Dole' Cut by Two Shillings In the Pound & Needs Test Imposed

HIGHER DUTIES ON BEER AND TOBACCO

SEVENTY-SIX MILLION POUNDS WILL BE RAISED OR SAVED BY TAXES AND ECONOMIES THIS YEAR, AND £171,000,000 NEXT YEAR UNDER THE EMERGENCY BUDGET INTRODUCED YESTERDAY BY MR. SNOWDEN.

BEER, TOBACCO, PETROL, AND ENTERTAINMENT TAXES ARE TO BE INCREASED. THERE IS TO BE AN EXTRA 6d. IN THE POUND ON THE INCOME TAX, AND TEN PER CENT. ON THE AMOUNT OF THE SURTAX.

CUTS ARE TO BE MADE IN THE PAY OF MINISTERS, M.P.S, JUDGES, TEACHERS, POLICE, HEALTH INSURANCE DOCTORS, AND PUBLIC SERVANTS GENERALLY.

GRANTS FOR EDUCATION, HEALTH, AGRICULTURE, EMPIRE MARKETING, ROADS AND OTHER PUBLIC SERVICES ARE TO BE LOWERED.

APPLICANTS, AFTER RECEIVING SIX MONTHS' BENEFIT IN A YEAR, ARE TO BE PUT THROUGH A "NEEDS TEST" ON A POOR LAW BASIS. THE TOTAL "DOLE" ECONOMIES ARE £35,800,000.

THE SINKING FUND FOR REDUCTION OF THE NATIONAL DEBT IS TO BE REDUCED BY £13,700,000 THIS YEAR AND £20,000,000 NEXT YEAR. AN OPERATION FOR CONVERTING WAR LOAN FROM 5 PER CENT. TO A LOWER RATE OF INTEREST IS TO BE LAUNCHED AT THE FIRST SUITABLE MOMENT.

"INTRODUCING THIS BUDGET IS ONE OF THE MOST DISAGREEABLE TASKS THAT HAS EVER FALLEN TO MY LOT," SAID MR. SNOWDEN. "WE HAVE FOR SOME TIME BEEN LIVING BEYOND OUR MEANS, AND TO A CONSIDERABLE EXTENT ON OUR CAPITAL."

HE ESTIMATES THAT HIS ECONOMIES AND TAXES WILL BALANCE THIS YEAR'S AND NEXT YEAR'S BUDGETS, AND LEAVE A SURPLUS OF APPROXIMATELY

Mr. W. GRAHAM, who will lead the attack on the Budget.

MR. HENDERSON AND A TARIFF

BETTER THAN CUT IN UNEMPLOYED PAY

Conditions on which he would support a 10 per cent. revenue tariff were stated by Mr. Arthur Henderson in his speech to the Trades Union Congress at Bristol yesterday.

"I am going to make a little confession to you," he said.

"If I am faced—and I claim to be as strong a Free Trader as any who were there—if I am faced with a large cut in the payments given to the unemployed or a 20 per cent. revenue tariff as an emergency expedient, the revenue accruing therefrom to be assigned to unemployment purposes, I am going to try the value of that experiment."

It was afterwards explained that Mr. Henderson really meant 10 per cent., the reference to 20 being a slip of the tongue.

Mr. Henderson said also that the proposal for a suspension of the Sinking Fund was never seriously discussed when he made it during the conversations on balancing the Budget before the late Government fell.

[Report on Page 11.]

TOBACCO NOT TO COST MORE

But Dearer Beer, Theatres and Cinemas

TWO famous tobacco firms announced last night that they would not pass on the new tobacco taxes to the public.

The Imperial Tobacco Company will bear a tax of halfpenny on packets of 20 cigarettes and on each ounce of tobacco, a total estimated at nearly £1,000,000.

Carreras, Ltd., state that the Budget will not involve any change in the price, size or quality of their cigarettes.

The consumer will have to pay other imposts. The situation summarised, is:

PETROL.—Extra price of 2d. per gallon was charged to motorists at all leading London garages last night.

BEER.—Expected that beer will cost a penny a pint more to-day, although some brewers are still undecided.

ENTERTAINMENTS. — Theatre and cinema prices will be increased to cover taxes. The effect on the poorer patrons is revealed on Page Six.

Mr. Walter Payne, chairman of Syndicate Variety Theatres, and president of the West End Theatre Managers, said last night:

"The entertainment tax increases will certainly be passed on to the public."

Mr. A. M. Wall, secretary of the British Actors' Equity Association, said "the increased entertainments duty is nothing less than a disaster. . . . The tax on the cheaper cinema seats will hit the working classes, whose only weekly recreation is a visit to the pictures."

The petrol companies responsible for "nationally distributed petrol"—the Combine—announce that from to-day the consumer will have to pay 1s. 4½d. for Pratts, Shell, B.P., and National Benzole.

Lord Ashfield, asked last night if bus fares in London would be increased, said, "We shall have to see."

In regard to income-tax, Lord Decies, President of the Income Tax Payers' Society, said: "The period of stress will be next January. The burden must be temporary. If not, money will leave the country."

68 The *Daily Herald* 11 September 1931. The details of the cuts appeared in the newspapers on Sunday 13th, which should have given the Admiralty time to inform the men first. But the Admiralty did not get around to it.

The sailors held meetings ashore, in the town of Invergordon, and in their desperation determined to strike. They would refuse to allow their ships to take part in the manoeuvres. Strike committees were formed on each ship, and Copeman, who had spoken at the largest meeting, was elected to the committee on the *Norfolk*. A manifesto was drawn up: 'Unless we can be guaranteed a written agreement from Admiralty confirmed by Parliament stating that our pay will be revised we are resolved to remain as one unit refusing to serve under the new rates of pay.' Preparations were made for the sailors to go to London by train, to besiege the Admiralty in Whitehall, if the agreement did not come.

The Cabinet took fright. Only three weeks earlier, Britain had been rescued from financial crisis by a Franco-American loan of £80 million. Now sterling was collapsing again. News of the mutiny came on Wednesday 16 September. By lunchtime on Saturday half the loan had been used up as people exchanged their pounds for gold. On Sunday the government announced that it would no longer make the exchange. The financial crisis was bad enough but they feared something worse. After all, the country was full of people who must be feeling equally desperate. Means tests

DAILY HERALD September 16 1931

WANTED 100 Persons (either sex) who have the ambition to earn a nice sum in their spare time.

Daily Herald

No. 4863 · WEDNESDAY, SEPTEMBER 16, 1931 · ONE PENNY.

ATLANTIC FLEET RECALLED—*Official*

CLEANING THE DECKS under the guns of H.M.S. Warspite, one of the big ships now lying at Invergordon.

UNREST FOLLOWS PAY CUTS AMONG LOWER RATINGS

Exercises Suspended Pending Admiralty Inquiry

REAR ADMIRAL TOMKINSON

Premier's Talks With Crew of Warship at Portsmouth

SAILORS HOLD MASS MEETING ON SHORE

THE Admiralty issued the following statement last evening:

"*The Senior Officer, Atlantic Fleet, has reported that the promulgation of the reduced rates of naval pay has led to unrest amongst a proportion of the lower ratings.*

"*In consequence of this he has deemed it desirable to suspend the programme of exercises of the Fleet, and to recall the ships to harbour while certain representations of hardship under new rates of pay are being investigated for the consideration of their lordships.*"

Rear-Admiral Wilfred Tomkinson, C.B., M.V.O., is the senior officer mentioned. He commands in the absence on sick leave of Admiral Sir Michael Hodges, K.C.B., C.M.G., M.V.O.

AIR DASH TO LONDON

At Invergordon, where ten ships of the

SNOWDEN HINTS AT ELECTION

SUGGESTS IT MAY COME ABOUT IN FEW WEEKS

MR. SNOWDEN, in the House of Commons last night, hinted at the possibility of a General Election within the next few weeks.

"During the last few days," he said, "I have been able for the first time to study in the House the faces of my late associates. I have admired the way they have cheered to keep their spirits up.

"I have admired those who have done that, knowing that only a few weeks possibly remain before the place which now knows them will know them no more."

MISS SLADE

£500 A WEEK FILM ACTOR

RECORD SALARY FOR MR. LESLIE HOWARD

From Our Film Correspondent

Mr Leslie Howard the young English actor, who played here in Tallulah Bankhead's "Her Cardboard Lover," has come over from Hollywood to play in a British film at a salary of £500 per week.

This is a record salary for a film actor in this country.

Mr Howard has the leading part in the Paramount Company's new picture, The Head Waiter, now starting at their Elstree studios under the Austrian director Mr Alexander Korda.

Another American company, Warner Brothers, have engaged Mr John Longden, Mr Ben Field, Miss Florence Desmond and Miss Pat Paterson, for "Murder on the Second Floor," their first British film, now started at the Teddington studios.

Two leading young West-End actresses, Miss Gillian Lind and Miss Jane Welsh, will play with Mr Edmund Gwenn, Mr Gordon Harker and Mr Arthur Wontner in "Jack o Lantern" at the Twickenham studios. P. L. M.

TRUTH ABOUT MISS SLADE

LIFE DEVOTED TO INDIA

LUXURY RENOUNCED

"I have come to London to strive my utmost to find points of agreement," declared Mr. Gandhi yesterday in putting before the Round-Table delegates the claims of the All-India Congress (as reported on Page Four).

Congress, he said, was intent on complete independence. He contemplated a partnership of two absolute peoples "held, not by force, but by the silken cord of love."

Mr. Gandhi (says the Central News) will visit Manchester on Friday week.

By Our Special Representative

A TALL, slight woman, wearing Indian costume but unmistakably British, who is now to be seen sometimes moving among the costermongers' barrows and entering the little shops in the streets of Bow, is the centre of as much interest and curiosity, almost, as Mahatma Gandhi himself.

She is Miss Madeleine Slade, daughter of the late Admiral Sir Edmond Slade.

She renounced a life of ease and elegance in London to become a disciple of the Mahatma, and she has followed him through good and evil report for the past six years.

Women write to her, begging for advice.

Poor people send her their blessings.

American journalists besiege the doors of Kingsley Hall asking for a message from her to the United States.

She meanwhile, has probably slipped out by a side door to buy a cabbage or

69 The *Daily Herald* was regarded as a dangerously left-wing newspaper by the Admiralty, but in giving news of the events at Invergordon, the paper avoided using the word 'mutiny'.

had been introduced for welfare payments, national insurance contributions had been raised, millions were unemployed and state wages generally had been cut by between 10 and 20 per cent. According to the official Admiralty narrative

> It was realised that if some thousands of ratings broke out of their ships simultaneously on Tuesday morning 22nd September at 0800 and marched into the Towns very serious rioting would result and the revolt might induce other classes of the community to join in.

There is no evidence that the sailors themselves had any such revolutionary goals. They called it a strike, and Copeman's own verdict was that it 'sprang from the spontaneous reactions of the men of the fleet against injustice. . . . The Navy at that time was manned by volunteers with few if any political opinions.'

But some of them certainly acquired political opinions as a result of what happened next. The pay cuts were indeed revised, there was a promise that there would be no victimisation, and the ships were returned to their home ports. But Copeman, with twenty-three others who were identified as having played a significant role in the mutiny, was isolated from his ship and soon summarily discharged with thirteen shillings. Eventually over 400 sailors were thrown out of the Navy as a consequence of the

Daily Herald

No. 4867 MONDAY, SEPTEMBER 21, 1931 ONE PENNY

BRITAIN OFF GOLD STANDARD—*Official*

LORD READING, arriving for yesterday's Cabinet meeting.

STATEMENT FROM TREASURY ON SITUATION

The following official statement was issued by the Treasury last night:—

HIS MAJESTY'S Government have decided, after consultation with the Bank of England, that it has become necessary to suspend for the time being the operation of Subsection (2) of Section 1 of the Gold Standard Act of 1925 which requires the Bank to sell gold at a fixed price.

A Bill for this purpose will be introduced immediately, and it is the intention of His Majesty's Government to ask Parliament to pass it through all its stages on Monday, September 21.

In the meantime, the Bank of England have been authorised to

ONE-DAY CLOSING FOR STOCK EXCHANGES

Bill to Stop Export of Bullion: But Banks to Carry on Business As Usual

Bank Rate Raised to 6 Per Cent.: Sudden End of General Election Intrigues

NO NEED FOR ALARM

TO-DAY A SHORT BILL PROHIBITING THE EXPORT OF GOLD FOR A PERIOD OF SIX MONTHS WILL BE PASSED THROUGH BOTH HOUSES OF PARLIAMENT IN ALL ITS STAGES.

Stock Exchanges in London and the Provinces are to be closed, but they will resume business to-morrow.

The Bank Rate is to be raised this morning by 1½ points, to 6 per cent.

For the rest of the community, including joint stock banks, the motto is " Business as usual." There is not the slightest reason for alarm.

in the Cabinet throughout Saturday, return- to Chequers at night.

The Prince of Wales lunched there yesterday, and learned the full position from him.

In the afternoon the Premier returned to No. 10, and a Cabinet meeting was held.

For the drain of gold and credit there were three prime causes:—

Difficulties in which foreign countries, including Holland and Switzerland, found themselves.

Uneasiness in the United States and France due to grossly exaggerated reports published there of the unrest in the Fleet at Invergordon.

Loss of confidence abroad owing to the imperative Tory demands for an early General Election.

The departure from the gold standard, which

Mr. J. H. THOMAS entering No. 10, Downing-street yesterday.

HITLER'S LOVER DEAD IN HIS FLAT

JEALOUS OF RICH WIDOW

From Our Own Correspondent

MUNICH, Sunday.

A BEAUTIFUL dark-haired girl, Geli Raula, the sweetheart of Herr Adolf Hitler, has been found shot dead in the Nazi leader's flat here.

She had lived there for the past two years and was frequently seen with Hitler at theatres and cinemas.

It is believed she committed suicide in a jealous rage because she thought Hitler had fallen in love with the widow of an industrial millionaire.

The Nazi leader, who is on a political motor tour, has been recalled to Munich by telegram.

This is stated to be the second time that a girl in love with Hitler has com-

ARMED MENACE TO FREE STATE

ILLEGAL BODY WITH MACHINE GUNS & EXPLOSIVES

A WELL-DRILLED, illegal organisation, with " hundreds of machine guns," rifles and explosives, is training in the Irish Free State.

This statement was made by Mr. E. Duggan, one of the signatories of the Anglo-Irish Treaty, in a speech near Navan, County Meath, yesterday.

He said that the organisation was in opposition to the Government.

"These fellows," he added, "have hundreds of machine guns." One of the first things the Government would be asked to do when the Dail reassembled would be to enact a law to destroy that organisation.

Membership of it would involve drastic penalties, and he would advise any young man who had been foolish enough to get into that organisation to get out of it at once.

Mr Duggan added that there would be a General Election soon, but he did not know how soon.

MISS BONDFIELD ILL

BREAKDOWN FOLLOWS HER POLITICAL WORK

Miss Margaret Bondfield, who was Minister of Labour in the last Cabinet, is suffering from a severe nervous breakdown in a nursing home at Tunbridge Wells.

A "Daily Herald" representative was informed at her home last night that there was no danger, but that the doctors had stressed the importance of complete rest.

70 The *Daily Herald*, 21 September 1931 – and national humiliation.

mutiny. Many of them, like Copeman, were picked up by the Communist Party. But the mutiny itself was not the product of political agitation. It had much more to do with the fact that Able Seamen thought of themselves as men with the rights and family obligations of other working men, and the Admiralty did not.

Fred Copeman was disillusioned by Russian Communism; his autobiography is called *Reason in Revolt*, and traces the political education which followed his discharge. He earned an OBE for his work in the Second World War. By then the gulf between upper and lower decks had become a little shallower. On 29 March 1939 the cat-o'-nine-tails had been finally and officially abolished.

5

The mutiny of 1931 was not, as many thought, a sign that the Navy no longer commanded the sea. Nevertheless, in the Second World War Britain could no longer regard the oceans as her own territory. German submarines had been a serious threat in the First World War; in the Second, they came close to taking possession of the sea lanes.

At every stage of Britain's growth, shipping was increasingly important to survival. By 1939 half of all the nation's food, and most of its industrial raw materials, came from abroad. There had also been a new industrial revolution, as steam gave way to petrol and diesel engines. Without oil ships could not move, tanks and lorries could not move, aircraft could not move. Every drop of Britain's oil came by sea. If the merchant ships could not be protected, there was no way Britain could avoid defeat.

Britain began the war under the happy illusion that Britannia did, indeed, rule the waves. She had the world's largest merchant marine, with 3,000 ships – nearly 18,000,000 tons of shipping, as much as the next three nations combined (USA, Japan and Norway), over four times as much as Germany. To protect it, she had the world's most powerful navy. But there was no appreciation of the need to control the space under and above the waves.

Without mastery of the air, great battleships were terribly vulnerable. In the grim days of 1940, when a German invasion armada was massing in the Channel ports, Britain could not keep large fighting ships in the Dover Strait – they were defenceless against bombers. The facts were plainly spelt out by the Japanese, first by their air attack on Pearl Harbor, on 7 December 1941, when they crippled the American Pacific fleet, and then three days later by their destruction of the battleship *Prince of Wales* and the battle cruiser *Repulse* near Singapore. The task was performed by the Japanese Navy's First Air Group, and marked the first sinking of major warships while steaming at sea.

The submarine threat, too, was not properly understood until almost too late. It was generally assumed that submarines needed to surface to operate most effectively, and that they would not fight at night: in pre-war anti-submarine exercises, everything stopped at dusk. A week after war broke out, Churchill, First Lord of the Admiralty, announced that he intended to arm 'a thousand merchant ships' in order to force the Germans to use submarines under water: he told shipowners

> They will not be successful with underwater attacks: there is nothing like the free play on the surface. So although the war will become more brutal, nevertheless it will be to our advantage . . . they will have the ignominy of adopting a weapon of warfare which is condemned by the whole world of opinion.

By the end of 1940, more than a fifth of Britain's tonnage had been sunk, most of it in the north Atlantic, more than half of it sunk by German submarines, U-boats. By the end of 1942 more than 70 per cent had gone to the bottom, and less than half of the ships lost had been replaced. Britain's seamen were victims in a war of attrition; and, remarkably, they stuck it out. It is remarkable not only because they suffered so terribly and helplessly – a quarter of them were killed – but because they had been among the most neglected and deprived of working men. The nature of their deprivation emerged in a parliamentary debate, and was recorded in a *Times* report of Commons proceedings on 8 July 1938:

> Mr B. Smith (Rotherhithe, Lab.) said that . . . Mr Amery had painted a dreadful picture of the position of the British shipping industry. . . . The conditions under which the men lived and fed were very unsatisfactory. He had a very vivid recollection of his first coasting ship. He was paid 15*s*. a month, and there was one bunk for a crew of three. When they had a cup of coffee they would throw weevilly biscuits into it and bet how high the weevils would jump in the heat. . . . He had a list of 20 companies . . . showing that the weekly periods of work ranged from 92 hours to, at the lowest, 81 hours a week.

These reminiscences were prompted by two articles in *The Times* on conditions in the merchant marine, articles that created wide concern. For they showed that the ships on which Britain would depend in time of war were miserable floating hovels:

> The worst ship I saw was a mean and disreputable coasting vessel. . . . As I arrived the new crew arrived. One, after going below, refused to sail; he took the risk of breaking his articles of agreement. But, indeed, the forecastle was not a fit place in which to require any man to live for a single day. It was a dismal and delapidated forepeak, without a vestige of paint on its narrowing iron sides . . . In two miserable bunks there were fragments of old matresses; the other bunks were so broken as to be unusable. The lower bunks were on the level of the deck. There was no table, no seat, no locker; and this forecastle was the only space for mess room and sleeping quarters.

The articles in *The Times* were written because new regulations were coming into effect to impose minimum standards of accommodation in new ships; but those standards would not apply to the small vessels that made up the bulk of Britain's merchant fleet – or, indeed, to any ships that had already been constructed.

'A ship', *The Times* observed, 'as much as a factory is a unit of industry and, like a factory, it must pay its way'. Merchant ships had, in fact, become the last bastion of the totalitarian factory economy. The hands were wholly subject to the demands of their 'unit of industry' – they even had to live in it. The communal life still survived, with crews living in an undivided dormitory space. They often had their accommodation in the stern, but it was still called the forecastle and the men in it were still regarded as half-human. They signed articles for a single round voyage, and could never be sure of re-employment, especially in the depression years. One sailor recalled how

> You had to put your fiver in your discharge book when you showed it to an Officer. If you got the job you were provided with a bunk and a straw-filled mattress – we called it the 'donkey's breakfast' – but you had to provide the rest of the bedding and your cutlery. I was a cabin boy and often worked fourteen hours a day and Sunday was like a Monday, in fact Sunday was worse because it was Captain's inspection day, 9.0 a.m. sharp. If everything was not in order you were 'logged' five shillings loss of pay. Then there were the 'field days' that we hated, when all hands were ordered out to work extra to their normal watch, usually chipping and painting.

The working week had in theory been limited, and overtime agreed, as a result of a strike in 1911, but the system of signing on for single voyages defeated all other controls. As the same seaman pointed out 'it was very rarely that there was any overtime pay and if you complained you were never employed by that company again'.

The ships were hidden worlds, away from public view, and those who did see within were often intimidated from speaking out. When *The Times*'s reports finally brought things out into the open, letters came from a pilot and a minister at a seaman's mission, saying that they had been threatened by shipping companies not to reveal what they knew.

The same system of signing-on undermined the official minimum diet (which in any case offered little more than bread, biscuits, preserved meat and potatoes) – some British shipping companies were generally known as 'starvation lines', but little was done about this.

Not all British ships were floating slums: the best were as good as the ships of any other nations, and a good line might have a regular 'following' of seamen, perhaps a quarter of the crews, who were automatically signed up for each successive voyage on their ships. But the majority of men were unqualified casual labourers, who might spend their summers rigging scaffolding or navvying and their winters on tramping steamers. For the ships themselves inevitably created the seamen – men who had a dismal reputation for a slovenly, uncaring attitude to their own accommodation and to their work.

The men usually came from the great ports – London, Liverpool, Cardiff, Glasgow, Hull and Southampton. They had generally been trained as boys and most of them left the sea within ten years; if they were lucky they had learned a skill, such as that of engineer or steward, which had a better-paid and more comfort-

The official weekly diet of a seaman in 1939

Bread and biscuit	7 lb
Salt or preserved meat	7¼ lb
Flour	2 lb
Potatoes	6 lb
Tea	1¾ oz
Coffee	4 oz
Sugar	1¼ oz
Jam, marmalade, syrup	1½ lb
Butter	½ lb
Dried veg	½ lb
Peas & beans	1⅓ pint
Condensed milk	5 oz
Currants, sultanas etc	5 oz
Onions	3 oz
Rice	½ lb
Oatmeal	½ lb
Pickles	½ pint

able equivalent ashore. But there was a small group of seamen who were so desperately poor that they never came ashore at all, but lived out their working lives on board ship. These were generally Lascars, the coloured seamen who made up between a quarter and a third of Britain's sailors, and who worked on the ships that traded with East Africa, India and the Far East. Three-quarters of the Lascars were Indians; the Africans usually had the most unpleasant jobs of all, working in the engine rooms. Speaking little English, they were often 'christened' by the chief engineer, with names that seem to come from another century – Mickey Finn, Jawbone, Ben Coffee, John Trybest, Tom Everyday. The work of firemen – the filthy work of tending the coal furnace of a steam ship – was gradually being eliminated as diesel engines were introduced, but it was certainly not dead yet.

The system of casual employment was ended by the demands of war. In 1941 a central register of seamen was begun, and seamen were guaranteed continuous pay, afloat or ashore, with continuous payments of allotments to their families. They had to register at local merchant navy pool offices, where they were offered a new ship. They could refuse two; if they turned down the third, they were liable for instant call-up into the armed forces. The following year identity cards were introduced. The whole system which the seamen of 1850 had rejected was re-created – and with the same purpose, of drawing the royal and merchant navies closer together. For there was no escaping the fact that merchant seamen were in the front line of the war. They sailed armed, in convoy, with naval and army gunners aboard.

Many young men joined the merchant marine as an alternative to national service; many older men who had left it returned to serve in the barely seaworthy ships that were kept going by sheer desperate need for every ton of shipping. And Lascar seamen were, for the first time, allowed to serve in ships that were not trading with African, Indian and Far Eastern ports. They became the

71 *Picture Post*, 1947.

IS THERE A BRITISH COLOUR BAR?

Photographed by BERT HARDY

Britain stages Colonial Month—a campaign to stimulate popular interest in the life and people of the Colonies. The King attends the opening ceremony. But there are more than 20,000 Colonial people who live among us. What do we know of them—of their work, of their living conditions, their hopes and grievances? Picture Post conducts a survey into this dangerous and important question.

IT is not possible to find out the exact number of colonial coloured people in Great Britain. There is no registry of people with black skin, any more than there is a registry of people with black hair. And there you discover the first important fact about the colour bar in Britain: officially it does not exist. For the purpose of the law and the administration of Britain there is no distinction whatsoever made between white and coloured British subjects—they are all just British subjects. And the same official lack of discrimination is echoed categorically by all government departments, professional organisations and trade unions. But offices and organisations are run by human beings, and inside the minds of human beings, both in and outside offices, strange fogs of ignorance and prejudice can be at work.

Although there are no official figures, the coloured population of Great Britain is estimated by both the Colonial Office and the League of Coloured People at about 25,000, including students. This total is distributed over the whole of Britain, but there are two large concentrated communities: one of about 7,000 in the dock area of Cardiff round Loudoun Square, popularly known as 'Tiger Bay', and the other of about 8,000 in the shabby mid-nineteenth century residential South End of Liverpool. These came into existence largely as a result of the immigration of colonial coloured people to work as seamen, soldiers and factory hands in the First World War. They were supplemented during the Second. Smaller coloured communities are found in all the main ports including London (there is one of about 2,000 in North and South Shields), in Manchester and the industrial areas of the Midlands. The prosperity of these different communities varies.

The term 'colonial coloured people' is, of course,

Continued overleaf

On the Curb of a Liverpool Pavement a Coloured British Subject Expresses the Indignation of His People

Officially there is no colour bar in Britain. But from restaurant-keepers and landladies, employers and employees, even from the man in the street, says Nathaniel Ajayi, he and his people meet with considerable colour prejudice. Ajayi has lived in five European countries, was a British Prisoner-of-War in Germany, but says he knows of no European country where the coloured man is treated with more unofficial contempt than in Britain.

backbone of the difficult, dangerous northern routes: in the words of the Merchant Navy Official History 'they were always plentiful, almost invariably docile and they gave no trouble'. In 1949, when Britain was safely through the war, there was a new journalistic investigation to stir the public conscience. It included a study of unestablished seamen, unable to get work, living in squalid and overcrowded conditions. This was published not in *The Times* but in *Picture Post*: 'In the war, when voyages were dangerous and Britain needed men, they could always get a ship. Now they need a job, but Britain has no job for them.'

They were Lascars. The article was headed 'Is there a British colour bar?' Around the dock areas of Cardiff and Liverpool, in North and South Shields and in the East End of London, Britain's neglect of her seamen was giving birth to a new generation of hidden outcasts.

Chapter 6

IMMIGRANTS

1

In 1841, one in thirty-seven of the inhabitants of Mayo in Ireland came to England for summer work. They had to walk 120 miles to the east coast, then make a fourteen-hour crossing, and tramp to one of the southern or eastern counties of England. The crossing took from ten to thirty hours; they were densely packed on the open deck among cattle. It was impossible to reach water closets or drinking water. Filth and urine from the animals, human vomit and sea water combined to cake the travellers in a wretched paste. Commonly the harvesters arrived too weak to walk ashore, and had to be carried by the police. 'I undergo great hardships in going to England,' a Mayo labourer told a parliamentary commission. 'Nothing but the want of something to do drives me there. I would engage to work at home every working day in the year for £8, without food or support of any kind, and never think of going to England.'

The crossing varied in cost: some years it was two shillings and sixpence, other years it was a few pence. Nevertheless, a labourer needed at least £1 in his pocket to pay his way until he found work in England. The average wage in Ireland was tenpence a day. In the corn-growing counties of England, where the village communities had been destroyed by enclosure, temporary workers would be welcome at harvest time. They travelled and worked in gangs, hoping to make £5 or so in the season. Not all of them succeeded, and in the autumn they poured into London hoping for a free passage home under the Poor Law. Cobbett saw them: 'Hundreds of squalid creatures tramping into London . . . without shoes, stockings or shirts, with nothing on the head worthy of the name of hat, and with rags hardly sufficient to hide the nakedness of their bodies.' When they got home, they were confronted by their creditors, 'maybe half a dozen . . . each expecting to get part of what is due to him; one for con-acre, another for house-rent, and another for provisions on credit, and so on.'

There had once been a flourishing linen industry in northern Ireland, but after the Act of Union in 1800 it was exposed to the blast of competition from the English mills, and the weavers gradually lost their work. During the Napoleonic wars, Irish corn fed England, but once the wars ended ever more land was turned to pasture. The peasants, deprived of work, depended on the potato harvest of their rented scraps of land, and on the income from summer work.

It is not surprising, then, that many Irish families looked for permanent work in England. Ready to work for the lowest of wages, the men were taken on as heavy labourers in London and the industrial areas, while women and children worked as hawkers and pedlars, or in the mills, where the English were reluctant to work. By the 1830s the textile industry – the factory world – was heavily dependent on Irish immigrants. The flax mills of Leeds were kept going by them, and the Manchester cotton mills might have been uneconomic without a pool of desperate Irish workers, to keep wage rates down. They were used to break strikes: James Taylor, the owner of Newton Heath silk mills, told a parliamentary commission 'The moment I have a turn-out and am fast for hands, I send for ten, fifteen or twenty families as the case may be, the whole family comes, father, mother and children. I provide them with money.'

In this period, when machinery had taken over spinning but not weaving, the Irish also came in large numbers as handloom weavers. They were urgently needed, and manufacturers sent

72 'Owd Eccles' – Ephraim Eccles – was the last handloom weaver working in Darwen, Lancashire, when he was photographed in 1909.

agents into Ireland to ship families over for the work. Local relief committees in Ireland sometimes offered to pay one penny a mile, and the ferry passage, to families willing to travel to Manchester. Once in the factory towns, the Irish lived in the worst slums.

> They congregate together, and form in the town a number of distinct communities, each of which is a nucleus for the generation and diffusion of human miasma . . . their diet is of the lowest description and consists of potatoes, oatmeal, buttermilk and sometimes bacon . . . their great numbers have produced a competition with the English labourer, which has taught him how to live upon a lower scale of diet, and of household comfort, than he was wont to do.[1]

The potato crop in Ireland failed in 1822, and the hardship that followed pushed up the rate of immigration. There was plenty of work in England for those who would accept low wages: hodmen and scaffolding workers were needed as towns began to grow: construction workers were needed on the docks and canals. Eight new docks were built in Liverpool between 1815 and 1835, as Lancashire's exports boomed; they were built by Irishmen and worked by Irishmen. In many towns almost every bricklayer's labourer was Irish in 1835, and in Manchester Irishmen ran three-quarters of the market stalls.

Newcomers to English parishes were not entitled to poor relief: when trade slumped they were supposed to be sent back. But it was

73 Cellar dwellings, overcrowded and insanitary, were highly unpleasant.

cheaper, and more practical, for authorities to wink at the law. In 1834 one-fifth of the inmates of Manchester workhouse were Irish. with no strict right to be there.

Coming from illiterate peasant communities, used to generations of great hardship, these immigrants were not generally ambitious. Having achieved a basic standard of living they invested any surplus income in drink. The 'Little Ireland' in every large town became notorious. Friedrich Engels wrote that

> The worst quarters of all the large towns are inhabited by Irishmen. . . . He builds a pig-sty against the house wall as he did at home, and if he is prevented from doing this, he lets the pig sleep in the room with him . . . a heap of straw, a few rags, utterly beyond use as clothing, suffice for his nightly couch. . . . When he is in want of fuel, everything combustible within his reach, chairs, door-posts, mouldings, floorings, finds its way up the chimney.[2]

Many of the Irish lived in cellars originally intended as handloom workshops:

> Liverpool contains a multitude of inhabited cellars, close and damp, with no drain or any convenience, and these pest houses are constantly filled with fever. Some time ago I visited a poor woman in distress, the wife of a labouring man, she had been confined only a few days, and herself and infant were lying on straw in a vault, through the outer cellar, with a clay floor impervious to water. There was no light or ventilation in it, and the air was dreadful. I

74 But popular imagination, feeding on lurid sanitary reports, made them even more horrific than they were. Note, incidentally, the stub noses and simian upper lips in this crude sketch from *Punch*. These were meant to indicate that the figures were Irish.

had to walk on bricks across the floor to reach her bedside, as the floor itself was flooded with stagnant water. This is by no means an extraordinary case.[3]

It was reckoned that 39,000 people lived in the cellars of Liverpool, and 18,000 in the cellars of Manchester. Not that Manchester's 'Little Ireland' was much better if you lived above ground, according to Engels:

> Masses of refuse, offal and sickening filth lie among standing pools in all directions; the atmosphere is poisoned by the effluvia from these, and laden and darkened by the smoke of a dozen tall factory chimneys. A horde of ragged women and children swarm about here, as filthy as the swine that thrive upon the garbage heaps and in the puddles. . . . The race that lives in these ruinous cottages, behind broken windows, mended with oilskin, sprung doors, and rotten door-posts, or in dark, wet cellars, in measureless filth and stench, in this atmosphere penned in as if with a purpose, this race must really have reached the lowest stage of humanity.

In that he was wrong. They had escaped from something worse, and Ireland had still not plumbed the depths.

In 1845 the Irish potato crop failed. In 1846 it failed again. In 1840 Carlyle had said, 'The time has come when the Irish population must be improved a little, or exterminated.' Without potatoes, the time for improvement was gone.

> There is a horrible silence; grass grows before the doors; we fear to look into any door, though they are all open or off the hinges, for we fear to see yellow chapless skeletons grinning there. We walk amidst the houses of the dead, and there is not one where we dare to enter. We stop before the threshold of our host of two years ago, put our

75 The *Illustrated London News* gave graphic drawings of the effects of the famine: this is a funeral.

> head, with eyes shut, inside the door jamb and say with shaking voice 'God save all here'. No answer. Ghastly silence and a mouldy stench as from the mouth of burial vaults.

Thus John Mitchel described his visit to a village in the west of Ireland. In a country of just over eight million, perhaps a million perished.

> Cowering wretches almost naked in the savage weather, prowling in turnip fields and endeavouring to grub up roots that had been left . . . little children leaning against a fence – for they could not stand – their limbs fleshless, their bodies half naked, their faces bloated yet wrinkled and of a pale greenish hue – children who could never, oh it was too plain, grow up to be men and women.[4]

In 1846, 280,000 Irish arrived in Liverpool. The following year the figure was 300,000. The hope of most was to escape to America, and over the years perhaps a million succeeded. Official policy in England was to encourage them, for England did not relish a flood of starving immigrants. But many who came did not re-embark for America. By 1851 there were 500,000 Irish-born in England and Wales. A third of them were in Lancashire. One in every ten Mancunians, and one in every six Liverpudlians, was an immigrant from John Bull's other island.

76 A village in Galway, 1850. Those who have not died have fled.

They naturally went to the areas already heavily settled by previous immigrants. Sixteen years earlier, a cotton manufacturer had told a Poor Law inquiry

> On account of the number of Irish in Manchester, they feel almost as if they were coming to an Irish town and although they have little to give they give what they have. They will take in a family of fresh immigrants, though they have only one room and lie on straw themselves.

The unrelenting flood of newcomers made it impossible for living conditions in the Irish communities to improve. With ever-growing competition for work, English workers could not expect sustained improvements in their own wages.

In 1847, a year when trade was depressed, the House of Lords established a select committee to study 'Colonisation from Ireland'. They were told by an Irish Presbyterian clergyman that

> If you bring people over who have been accustomed to work for 6*d.* a day, and place them in competition with those persons here who are obtaining 2*s.* 6*d.* or 3*s.* or 5*s.* a Day, the necessary Consequence will be that those Irish Labourers will consider themselves well paid with 1*s.* or 1*s.* 6*d.* a Day, and your Labourers must come down to that standard. Either you will raise the Irish to the Condition of the English, or you will pull the English down to the Condition of the Irish.

As Ebenezer Eliot, the Chartist poet, put it in his *Miseries of the Poor*

> But wages grew scarce, while bread grew dear
> And wages lessened too,
> For Irish hordes were bidders here
> Our half-paid work to do.

It was not surprising that there should be conflicts between Irish and English workers. These culminated in a major riot at Stockport in 1852. 'Stockport,' wrote Engels,

> lies in a narrow valley along the Mersey, so that the streets slope down a steep hill on one side and up an equally steep one on the other, while the railway from Manchester to Birmingham passes over a high viaduct above the city and the whole valley. Stockport is renowned . . . as one of the duskiest, smokiest holes, and looks, indeed, especially when viewed from the viaduct, excessively repellent. But far more repulsive are the cottages and cellar dwellings of the working-class, which stretch in long rows through all parts of the town from the valley bottom to the crest of the hill. I do not remember to have seen so many cellars used as dwellings in any other town of the district.

By 1852 Stockport had some 60,000 inhabitants. The Irish population had risen from 300 to 14,000 in fifty years. Many of them had worked at first as handloom weavers, glad to make seven shillings a week for a fourteen hour day. But mechanical weaving had reduced that trade to starvation even by Irish standards, and the women and older children had gone to work in the mills. In many mills most of the workers were Irish. The town itself was turbulent: the eleven-strong police force could do little to quell the Saturday-night brawls, and the main sign of civic authority was the workhouse, known locally as the Bastille.

Employment in the United Kingdom cotton industry

	Factory workers	*Handloom weavers*
1810	100,000	200,000 (there is power spinning, but the cotton produced is all woven by hand).
1830	185,000	240,000 (the power loom has appeared, but more people are still hoping to make a living weaving).
1850	331,000	43,000 (factory weaving has taken over).

The election campaign of June 1852 was fought in Stockport on religion. Disraeli, mocking party managers in his novel *Coningsby*, had Tadpole urge the repeal of the malt tax. Taper, shocked, had a better idea. 'I am all for a religious cry. It means nothing, and, if successful, does not interfere with business when we are in.' That was in 1844. In the next few years religion played a significant part in English politics. The Roman Catholic population had been greatly increased by the Irish immigration, and in 1850 the hierarchy of the Roman church, destroyed in the Reformation, had been re-created so that the church 'may again flourish in the Kingdom of England'. The government, alarmed, made it illegal for Roman Catholic insignia and banners to be carried in public.

On Sunday 27 June 1852, the Catholic schools of Stockport held their annual procession of scholars. They refrained from carrying their flag, and were protected by a body of new immigrants. The march passed off without incident, but feelings were running high. A placard was put up around the borough calling English voters to reject the Whig candidate because of his sympathy towards Catholics: 'Will you throw away all you agree in and give Anti-Christ power to settle your differences? Anti-Christ drunk with the blood of your fathers? . . . The King of Rome will become the Sovereign of Britain'. The *Stockport Advertiser*, the local paper, supported the Methodist Tory candidate, and described the placard as reasonable.

Two days after the procession, Stockport erupted. Houses occupied by the English in Irish streets were marked with chalk and undamaged, while the rest were invaded and wrecked. A mob 300 or 400 strong literally drove the Irish out of the town, to camp in the woods and fields, and gutted their property. Two Roman Catholic chapels were destroyed. The *Stockport Advertiser* explained that this was not an anti-Catholic riot:

> The attack on the Chapels, which seems, at first sight, to suggest the impression that religious animosity might have had a good deal to do with the matter, we think is easily explained by the circumstance, that when the passions of the English got fairly excited, and they found how little there was in the shape of furniture to be destroyed in the wretched Irish dwellings they sacked, they felt the vengeance taken so utterly inadequate as to the provocation and insults they had received that they very probably attacked and demolished the Chapels as the only property belonging to the Irish which was of any value, and the loss of which would be a serious detriment or annoyance to their adversaries.

The riot lasted three days. At the end of it, *The Times* wrote,

> Our readers must have observed that the man who was killed was an Irishman; the 50 wounded, many of them very seriously, were Irishmen; the 114 prisoners were all Irishmen; the chapels that were gutted were all of them Roman Catholic; the houses that were ransacked and half-destroyed were all those of Irishmen. . . . How shall we solve this enigma? Were the Irish gutting their own chapels, breaking one another's heads, and turning their own houses inside-out?

The Times's concern for the safety of the Irish was widely shared. When the Irish themselves succeeded in bringing English rioters to trial alongside their own accused, the assize judge was careful to make an example of them:

> For the sake of public justice it is necessary to treat matters of this kind with great severity. For many years in this country we have not had outrages like these immediately directed against that religious liberty which it is the pride of England to possess.

Bigotry was condemned, and the security of the Irish community in England was guaranteed. They remained separate from the English population, distinguished by religion and way of life, generally working in the most unskilled trades and at the heaviest labouring work. Meanwhile in Ireland the tragedy went on. The famine was followed by large-scale evictions, as landlords set about improving their estates, and families were driven to live in ditches, or in temporary shelters on the edges of bogland. Alone among the countries of Europe, Ireland's population fell, until by the end of the century it was little more than half the pre-famine population.

There has been much debate over whether the coming of industry and the factory system was a curse or a blessing for working

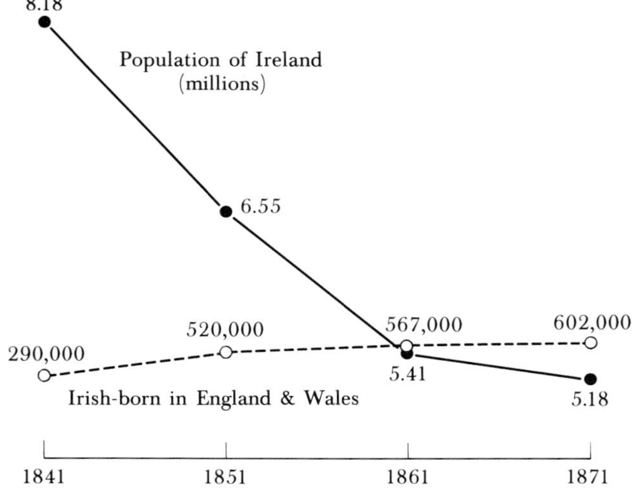

Figure 7 The population of Ireland, 1841–71.

people. The worst parts of the industrial towns were Irish ghettoes. It may well be that their existence held down the standard of living for English workers, but for the wretched inhabitants, anything was better than starvation at home.

Could England have become the first industrial nation without this pool of low-earning, hard-working toilers? And would they have been reduced to such a level, if commercial, industrial England had not wiped out the Irish economy?

Whatever was built in industrial England was built with Irish hands. Whatever was made of Ireland was made of English policy. The legacy of that rule still bleeds.

On 11 February 1886, *The Times* recorded

> Yesterday London from one end to the other experienced another sharp spasm of alarm with respect to rioters, and from the heart of the City to the far off suburbs preparations were made to meet hordes of ruffians on the march. That the lawless of the immense population of London should be awakened to their opportunities of plunder was to be expected after the experience of Monday, when the richest part of London was left entirely at their mercy. The tale of Monday's unchecked and uncontrolled march of plunder, and destruction, under the openly-preached doctrine of revolutionary social democracy, was carried into every slum of the metropolis, and every ruffian had taken to heart the doctrine . . . that the 'have nots' were many while the 'haves' were few, and that a show of revolution would cause property to change hands.

While the West End blazed with all the brilliance and wealth of England's commercial and imperial splendour, the East End was a seething mass of hopeless paupers, living in squalor, picking up casual work where and when they could find it, resorting, as everyone knew, to every kind of vice and crime for sensual gratification and the means to stay alive.

The riot of 1886 did not turn into the revolution feared by *The Times*, but the searchlight of the middle-class press was turned on the East End in an urgent search for causes and remedies. One writer in the *Pall Mall Gazette* identified what many began to think of as a significant factor in the equation of East End poverty:

> The foreign Jews of no nationality whatever are becoming a pest and a menace to the poor native-born East Ender . . . fifteen or twenty thousand Jewish refugees of the lowest type . . . have a greater responsibility for the distress which prevails than probably all other causes put together.

Jewish immigration into the East End had been going on for many years, but it began to rise dramatically after the accession of Czar Alexander III in 1881. For the great mass of the world's Jews were in his empire, and Alexander made it plain that they were not welcome there.

Russian Jews were obliged, unless they had special permission, to live in the Pale of Settlement. This stretched from the Baltic to the Black Sea, and included much of Poland and eastern Russia. There they lived in *shtetls*, small towns which were typically

> a jumble of wooden houses clustered higgledy-piggledy about a market place . . . as crowded as a slum . . . Hither come daily, except during the winter, the peasants and peasant women from many miles around, bringing their live-stock and vegetables, their fish and hides, their wagon-loads of grain, melons, parsley, radishes, and garlic. They buy, in exchange the city produce which the Jews import, dry goods, hats, shoes, boots, lamps, oil, spades, mattocks, and shirts. The tumult of the market-place is one of the wonders of the world.[5]

Within the closed world of the *shtetl* Jewish life flourished; Yiddish was the daily language, and Hebrew was reserved for prayer and the study of the Talmud. There the detailed commandments which governed pious Jewish life were widely observed and strictly maintained, from the pattern of daily prayer and the wearing of ritual garments to the eating of kosher food and the correct way of putting on shoes.

While many Jews were happy with this timeless world, others hoped to share in the enlightenment and prosperity which the nineteenth century offered. Jews began to form substantial communities in larger towns, such as Warsaw, Lodz and Vilna, and in the relatively liberal regime of Nicholas II many moved out of the Pale into Moscow and St Petersburg.

Alexander III put an end to that. Pogroms were encouraged – attacks by gangs of ruffians on the Jewish quarters of towns. In 1882 500,000 Jews living in rural areas of the Pale were forced to move into *shtetls*. Those Jews who had hoped to make a better life in Russia began to think in terms of flight – if possible to America. One emigrant who left in 1882 wrote in his diary

> Am I not despised? Am I not urged to leave? Do I not hear the word 'Yid' constantly? Can I even think that someone considers me a human being capable of thinking and feeling like others? Do I not rise daily with fear lest the hungry mob attack me? . . . It is impossible . . . that a Jew should regret leaving Russia.[6]

As the scale of oppression increased, so did the rate of emigration. There were some five million Jews in the Pale in 1897: between 1881 and 1914 more than two million emigrated. Most went to America, a land which seemed, from the accounts which circulated in Russia, to offer limitless opportunities. London was a stopping point on the journey, and about 120,000 made England their final destination. Most of the Jews who came to England passed through the East End of London.

My own grandparents went from Russia to the East End in this period, and their stories illustrate some of the elements that made up this migration. My grandmother, Leah Sandman, came in the hope of making a better life for herself. The eleventh of twelve children, she grew up in Lodz, near Warsaw, in a family of traders and artisans. All the children were expected to learn a trade; the most successful of her brothers ran a herring import business.

When it became clear that there was a very difficult future for Jews in Russia, one of Leah's brothers emigrated to Hull. He was a master baker, and his letters home showed that he was getting on well in England. Leah's mother was fearful at the growing scale of the pogroms, and so, when Leah, aged 15, and her sister Rachel, aged 17, begged to join their brother in Hull, the family agreed. They left in 1905.

Ever since the large-scale migration had begun, the English Jewish establishment had published warnings that Jews should stay away if possible.

> In order to avoid trouble in the coming days we beseech every right-thinking person among our brethren in Germany, Russia and Austria to place a barrier to the flow of foreigners to persuade these voyagers not to venture to come to a land they do not know. It is better that they live a life of sorrows in their native place than bear

> the shame of famine and the disgrace of missionaries and perish of destitution in a strange land.[7]

The warnings were ignored. It was relatively simple, with only a little money, to cross from Poland to Hamburg and take a ship to London or, in Leah's case, Hull.

Leah was a trained wig-maker, Rachel a needlewoman. They arrived in Hull illiterate, speaking only Yiddish, and with no idea of how they would manage. The journey had been their first experience of life outside a Jewish milieu. The ship itself was stinking and overcrowded, and the girls had been unable to eat the salt herrings provided as nourishment on the three-day journey: they were continually sick. Once in Hull, they looked to their brother for help. This did not work out, and once they had recovered their strength and confidence they went to the East End, where they found work and lodging.

The East End was, by then, alive with a flourishing immigrant community. The 35,000 East End Jews of 1881 had grown to over 150,000, working mainly in tailoring, boot and shoe making and cabinet making. They lived in densely overcrowded houses which had once been intended for middle-class families: attempts at slum

77 'Jewish immigrants just landed', from G. R. Simms, *Living in London*, 1902.

clearance had simply compressed ever more people into ever fewer dwellings, so that between 1871 and 1901 the average number of people in each dwelling had risen from nine to nearly fourteen. Rooms let for five shillings a week were sub-divided into cells rack-rented at a shilling a time.

Most of the jobs available were in tiny workshops. Over 70 per cent of the East End workshops employed less than ten workers, and conditions in these 'sweating dens' had been a subject for concern ever since the *Lancet* investigated them in 1884:

> In Hanbury Street we found eighteen workers crowded in a small room measuring eight yards by four and a half, and not quite eight feet high. The first two floors of this house were let out to lodgers who were also Jews. Their rooms were clean but damp as water was coming through the rotting wall. . . . The top room . . . had at times to hold eighteen persons, working in the heat of the gas and the stove, warming the pressing irons, surrounded by mounds of dust and chips from the cut cloth, breathing an atmosphere full of woollen particles containing more or less injurious dyes; it is not surprising that so large a proportion of working tailors break down from diseases of the respiratory organs.

Rachel, the needlewoman, would have looked for work in such a

78 Providence Place, Whitechapel, in 1905.

shop. Newcomers, or 'greeners', were expected to work for next to nothing until they had learned something of the trade; on average, they might find two days work a week. Rachel met and married Maurice Seifert, another migrant, who had become a presser. As a skilled man he could expect to make between six and nine shillings a day for an average of four days a week, in a city where the poverty line was reckoned at thirty shillings a week. They lived on herrings and potatoes.

These workshops were the backbone of a whole new industry, the ready-made clothing business. The *Pall Mall Gazette* (and others) had suggested that Jews were driving the East Enders out of their traditional occupations but, as Charles Booth explained in his *Life and Labour of the London Poor*, 'the ready-made clothing trade is not an invasion of the employment of the English tailor but an industrial discovery'. It was a discovery which went together with the ready-made shoe trade and the ready-made furniture trade, as the fruits of industrial wealth began to appear in the homes of everyday English families.

Multiple shops and chain-stores began to open in the towns and cities of England from the 1880s. The sewing machine had been invented in 1846; mass sewing and cutting became possible, and unskilled immigrants could rapidly learn to carry out a single operation at speed. After 1857 sewing machines were available for shoe sewing. Wholesalers on the borders of the East End were able to find sub-contractors prepared to work for very low rates, and for the first time new ready-made clothing and footwear became available at reasonable prices for ordinary families.

In the first half of the nineteenth century, clothing was a family's heaviest expense, after food; by the end of the century the average family could clothe themselves for less than they were spending on alcohol and tobacco. The 300 chain shoe-shops of 1875 had grown to 2,600 by 1900, and menswear shops spread nearly as fast.

The invention of the band-saw in 1858 heralded a similarly dramatic change in domestic furniture. Cabinet-making firms in the East End collected immigrants straight off the boats and put them to work on cheap furniture for the stores. This was a time when millions of families began to aspire to wardrobes and dining room tables. Solomon Nathan was one of the 'greeners' who found their way into cabinet making. He arrived at Tilbury under the impression he was in New York, and was found by one of the touts employed by a mass-production furniture shop. He was put to work at a bench for twelve hours a day, with a jug of water, a loaf of bread and a knife on a chain. A few years later, having changed his name to Nathan Solomon to sound more English, he was the owner of his own factory in Leeds, making walnut bedroom suites.

Some immigrants managed to establish themselves with remarkable speed. Leah Sandman was a trained wig-maker, a highly skilled task involving the insertion of each individual hair by hand. She found a ready-made market for her work; not only did every fashionable (or would-be fashionable) lady require a chignon but orthodox Jewish married women are required to wear a wig to conceal the beauty of their tresses. Four years after arriving in England she was able to open her own shop. Three years after that, when she was about to marry, she entered her future husband's shop and spilt fifty gold sovereigns onto the counter as her dowry.

Harry Drose, the man she was to marry, had fled to England as a refugee. He grew up with his mother in Kishenev, the capital of Bessarabia. In the later years of the nineteenth century the pogroms changed from beatings to massacres, and the pogrom of Kishenev in 1903 shocked the world. One survivor recalled, in a BBC radio programme, how

> I was chasing with the hooligans and see atrocities after atrocities, how they sling people down from the third floor. But one thing is in my memory for life, they got hold of a lady between 25 or 26, with a young child, they cut her breasts off and they took the child by the little legs and smashed it, you know to a brick wall, and killed it.

Harry was 16. His mother succeeded in smuggling him away, and they escaped to London. The boy was apprenticed to an East End jeweller, where he trained as a watchmaker, sleeping under the counter as apprentices did. By the time he met Leah he had taken the bold step of opening his own little shop outside the East End, in the City of London.

For Harry's mother, the world outside the East End was a hostile foreign land. While Harry was keen to get on, and make his way in the world, his mother refused to learn English or step outside the pseudo-*shtetl* which flourished in the streets of Whitechapel. There, where Yiddish newspapers were published and Yiddish theatre was performed, where the tiny synagogues of eastern Europe were reproduced and the pious life of Russian Jewry continued as before, she felt safe in a dangerous world.

Harry and Leah demonstrated their prosperity by taking a three-room flat all to themselves, with the expensive novelty of electric lighting, and hired a maid as a symbol of their intention to become middle class. A few years later they moved out, as many of the more ambitious immigrants were doing, and bought a house in the north London suburb of Clapton.

The process of assimilation was under way. It was an awkward progress. They moved into an area which was being colonised by

East End Jews, where they were among people whose food they could eat, and where they could buy kosher meat; but they also wanted to be accepted by the English community. Their children were not sent to a Jewish school but to an ordinary English school, where they began to feel that there was something degrading about coming from a family of foreign immigrants, even though many of the other children in the school came from the same background. Half-ashamed among the English of their Yiddish background, they were half-ashamed among the East End Jews of having moved out of the orbit of strict orthodoxy: Harry's mother would never come to see them. The tensions continued to grow as the family moved further out into the new Jewish suburbs which developed as the Underground pushed north, to Willesden and Golders Green. I grew up without ever knowing that my grandparents were illiterate Yiddish-speaking immigrants. It was not something to be proud of.

The pressures of assimilation were also being felt in the East End, where the demands of business were undermining religious orthodoxy. The Sabbath was the day of rest, when workshops closed: it was also the day of the *huzzar mart*, the pig market, when Whitechapel was buzzing with small masters desperately trying to hire workmen for their new batch of orders, and workmen desperate to be hired. Orthodoxy was also threatened by the desire of many Jews to make themselves less conspicuous. Hostility to the immigrants was being voiced more loudly, and in a symposium written in 1892 to support an aliens bill, a clergyman had spelt it out: 'Their alien looks, habits and language combined with their remarkable fecundity, tenacity and money-making gifts, make them a ceaseless weight upon the poor amongst whom they live.' Safety seemed to lie in avoiding such alien looks, habits and language.

The belief that Jewish immigrants had produced the squalor and distress of the East End was to some extent dispelled by the Aliens Commission report of 1903, which concluded that

> The development of the three main industries – tailoring, cabinet making and shoemaking – in which the aliens engage has undoubtedly been beneficial in various ways; it has increased the demand for, and the manufacture of, not only goods made in this country (which were formerly imported from abroad) but of the materials used in them, this indirectly giving employment to native workers.

But as industrial prosperity declined in the Edwardian years, with falling incomes and growing unemployment, the pressure to restrict immigration became irresistible. In 1905 the aliens bill

79 The poverty of the East End is captured in this photograph taken around Spitalfields in 1912 by Horace Warner. The lad is wearing the broad-brimmed hat of Polish orthodoxy, but if there is a Jewish 'money-making gift' it has not done much for him.

became law, and the Jews of the Pale stopped coming to England in significant numbers. Britain's proud boast, voiced by Palmerston, that 'Any foreigner, whatever his nation, whatever his political creed . . . may find in these realms a safe and secure asylum' was no longer true.

The Jews of the Pale continued to suffer under the Czars, the White Russians, the Bolsheviks, and finally the Nazis. By 1945 the five million who had lived there were reduced to perhaps 100,000. Of the rest, those who had not escaped (mainly to America) had perished, in pogroms and concentration camps.

While in England, the Jews had moved out of the East End, to make way for a new kind of immigrant.

3

Jatinder is a citizen of the world, and of nowhere. His family home is in a Punjabi village called Rampur. It is close to the small town of Nurmahal, the Palace of Light, built as a resting place for travellers by a Moghul emperor. His family were craftsmen, belonging to the Ramgarhia caste of carpenters and blacksmiths.

In the 1930s, Jatinder's great-grandfather went to Mombasa, in Kenya. Indian traders had operated in East Africa for hundreds of years; the connection was greatly strengthened by the British empire. Between 1896 and 1901, over 32,000 Indian labourers were brought to build a railway from Mombasa to Lake Victoria. More than 2,000 died of malaria, dysentery, scurvy and in other unpleasant ways – including twenty-eight who were eaten by lions. Many thousands more were invalided home, or accepted free passages back to India at the end of their contract. But 6,000 stayed on, and became the nucleus of a thriving business community. By 1939 there were some 50,000 Indians in Kenya, and restrictions on the right to own land had concentrated them in the towns.

Jatinder's grandmother stayed in Rampur with her son and daughters. In 1947, when India was divided into two states, Rampur was in the centre of a countryside in turmoil. Hindus and Moslems were at each other's throats – over a million died in ten days – and her 19-year-old son organised a terrorist band that went out killing Moslems. The next year he took his wife, newborn baby, sisters and mother to make a new start in Kenya.

Jatinder was born in 1956 in Nairobi, where the family was established running a large radio and record shop. Nine years later, when Kenya become independent, they had the choice of retaining their British citizenship, or choosing Indian or Kenyan passports. They elected to remain British. Since Swahili was being introduced as the language of instruction in Kenyan schools, Jatinder was sent to stay with relatives in India. He went to Chandigarh, the new city designed by Le Corbusier as the capital of the Punjab. There he went to school, and university.

The situation in Kenya became increasingly difficult for Asians. In the first two months of 1968 more than 12,000 were forced to leave, and claimed right of entry to Britain on the basis of their citizenship. In February an Immigration Act was rushed through the British parliament to take away that right.

Citizens of Commonwealth countries lost any right to come unless they were wives, children or parents of people already in Britain. Even holders of United Kingdom passports would only be allowed in if they could prove that they, their father or grandfather had been born in the UK. British citizens who lacked that 'close connection' would have to queue for one of a limited number of vouchers. In place of a right, they could ask for a privilege.

On 20 April 1968, Enoch Powell MP made the best-known political speech in England since the Second World War:

> Those whom the Gods wish to destroy, they first make mad. We must be mad, literally mad, as a nation to be permitting the annual inflow of some 50,000 dependants who are for the most part the material of the future growth of the immigrant-descended population. It is like watching a nation busily engaged in heaping up its own funeral pyre. . . . As I look ahead I am filled with foreboding. Like the Roman, I seem to see 'the River Tiber foaming with much blood'.

Between 1950 and 1968 the 'coloured' population of Britain had risen from about 100,000 to something over a million. A survey published in 1968 showed that 72 per cent of immigrants believed that there was discrimination against them when they tried to find jobs, and 69 per cent believed that there was discrimination against them when they tried to find somewhere to live. It also

Immigration to the United Kingdom 1948–76

	from West Indies	India	Pakistan	East Africa
1948	600			
1950	700	not available		
1952	2,200	not available		
1954	9,200			
1956	29,800	5,600	2,100	
1958	15,000	6,200	4,700	
1960	49,700	5,900	2,500	
1962	35,000	21,100	24,900	
1964	14,900	15,500	11,000	
1966	9,600	18,400	8,000	6,800
1968	4,800	28,300	14,900	18,843
1970	1,700	8,400	9,900	6,839
1972		10,000		34,825
1974		7,400		13,891
1976		5,700		24,000

showed that they were right. Powell's speech was a flamboyant attack on a race relations bill that would outlaw discrimination. The bill became law despite him.

Jatinder's father was able to retain control of his business in Kenya, but his wife and children were prudently installed in Chandigarh. On a visit to Nairobi, Jatinder applied for a voucher to enter Britain. When his application was accepted, he did not hesitate. He dropped his university course and went.

He already had relatives in Birmingham, Leeds and Bradford, an aunt in Leyton and a cousin in Southall. He arrived in 1976, and moved in with his cousin.

Almost half of the population of Southall in 1976 were of 'Afro-Asian origin'. One ward, Northcot, had twice as many 'blacks' as 'whites'. The majority were Punjabi Sikhs, 'Jat-Sikhs', from peasant families. They formed a self-contained community, running ethnic food shops, travel agencies, supermarkets, banks and every kind of trade.

The waves of emigrants from East Africa – a steady flow from Kenya, and a more sudden exodus from Uganda in 1972 – led to a dramatic increase in Asian businesses. The migrants from India, Pakistan (and the newly-independent Bangladesh) were generally peasant farmers, but the families coming from East Africa were used to a commercial life.

Britain had, in the mid-1970s, the fastest-shrinking small business sector of any advanced industrial country; small shops were closing down at an extraordinary rate. But the sub-post offices and corner grocers, the fish-and-chip shops and newsagents that were failing in the weak grasp of elderly English couples, were given new leases in the hands of young immigrant families prepared to work all hours and employ all the relatives God sends: 'How come every other corner shop in London is now run by an Indian family? Has there been an organised invasion, some conspiracy to oust every white face from local newsagents and replace them with brown ones?'

The *Evening Standard* article of December 1977, in which those words appeared, was based on an interview with Lakhsman Gadhvi, who had come from Kenya in 1973, settled in Enfield and eventually acquired a tobacconist's shop and the grocer's next door to it in Elm Terrace, Hampstead. Educated, speaking good English, with money in the bank and a determination to do well, he was alert to the possibilities of small shopkeeping: 'We work hard and make money. We are not beholden to anybody.'

As Asian faces became more common in the run-down corner shops, newspapers gave more prominence to stories of racial hosti-

80 Mr Gadhvi.

lity. The National Front began to announce overtly anti-black policies, and put up candidates on a 'send-them-back' platform.

In the summer of 1978, Brick Lane in London's East End was visited by a gang of 150–200 white youths who rampaged through it wearing Nazi insignia, throwing rocks and screaming abuse at the Bengali families who lived there. There followed militant declarations of self-defence by the Bangladeshi Youth Association: 'If they come again . . . if the police don't do anything to stop these thugs from coming down here in huge mobs, there will be a riot and there will be casualties. We will not take it lying down.' Gulam Mustapha, the secretary of the Brick Lane Mosque, was reported to be despondent: 'To defend yourself against hooligans is itself a crime so you've got no chance. There is no chance to survive.'

In different areas of England Asian communities have different characters. Sikhs, Hindus, Moslems have their own rich cultures and strong traditions; on top of that, the pattern of life in the terraces of Midlands factory towns is inevitably very different from that in suburban Ealing or the council flats of Bethnal Green. But however varied the traditions and aspirations of these communities, they share a common anxiety about their security. That anxiety, sharply reinforced by the National Front, dates from Enoch Powell's speech in April 1968, and the Immigration Act which had been passed two months before.

The Race Relations Act may have tried to outlaw racialism within the country, but the Immigration Act institutionalised racialism at its frontiers. The immigration laws cut deeply into the communities already in the country, partly because they affect the freedom of family connection, partly because of the constant reinforcement of the idea that non-whites are not welcome.

Jatinder had come to England partly as a youthful adventure, but partly also as part of his family's complicated strategy for survival, which entailed hedging bets in as many directions as possible. He remains in close contact with his father, who has held his place in Nairobi by becoming a publisher of Swahili and Congolese records. He is in close contact with his mother and sister, in India. Every year in the festival of Rakhi, he receives coloured threads from his sisters, to tie around his wrist as a symbol of their duty to him, and of his obligation to protect them. His brother came to join him in England, and found a job as a quality control supervisor at Hoover: 'He doesn't wear a turban any more. He doesn't believe in anything except money.'

81 Bengalis-in the East End took over the sweatshop industries that had been operated by Jewish immigrants.

In 1975 Gulam Mustapha was one of the organisers who arranged the purchase of the red-brick Mosque from the Jewish community. In those days it was a synagogue, although it had started life as a house of worship for an even older wave of migrants: it was built as a church by the Huguenots in 1743. Now it has a congregation of 14,000 Moslems. And while they are proud of the contribution they make to Britain, they are also conscious that they are a community apart.

Mr Gadhvi, in his Hampstead shop, keeps a weather-eye open for the day when he may have to take his money and go: 'our people are constantly reminding themselves: "Never forget the lessons of Africa".' Jatinder, who, when I met him, was working for Ealing Community Relations Commission, would half like to be his father's agent in England, half like to go back to Kenya, feels at home nowhere. Mr Mustapha is campaigning for Bengali to be taught in the schools of Bethnal Green, as an alternative to French and German. 'A person has to know his own language and his own religion. Otherwise he is a Mr Nobody.' He endorses the will of his children to become a permanent part of the British scene, but as one arm of their traditional family in Bangladesh.

A melting-pot it isn't.

Chapter 7
SHOPKEEPERS

1

Francis Place was a shopkeeper. When Napoleon was preparing to invade England, Place had a draper's shop at Charing Cross. He had also been the chairman of the general committee of the London Corresponding Society, which was outlawed in 1799 as treasonable and seditious. In 1807 Place became the leader of a group of shopkeepers and artisans who wrested political control of Westminster from the official Whig–Tory alliance. He stage-managed a campaign which brought about the repeal of the combination laws, and he was the man who wrote the 'people's charter' for the Chartists.

In the 1820s and 1830s, Place wrote his autobiography. His aim was to show that the London of tradesmen and artisans had been transformed in his lifetime. In his youth, he said, these people were ignorant, immoral, gross, obscene, drunk, dirty and depraved: and they had changed. To prove his point he described the London of his boyhood in close detail.

His father, a pauper child, had been apprenticed to a baker by the parish of Bury St Edmunds. When Francis was born, Mr Place was an officer of the Marshalsea court. Marshalsea was a debtor's prison, but any debtor who was not actually penniless, and who was unlucky enough to have a writ taken out against him in the Marshalsea court, was likely to be locked up in the basement of a 'spunging house'. There he would be charged exorbitantly for food and anything else he needed. If he demanded to be transferred to the squalor of the prison itself, he would be charged again. Francis's first home was a spunging house. His father lived well, on bribes and extortion, until the law was partly reformed in 1779. The family then took over a public-house in the Strand.

Francis was sent to school, to be given a tradesman's education: reading, spelling, handwriting and the 'rule of three'. He also learned how to fight, play street games and swim in the Thames.

At home, his father was an inflexible tyrant, punishing small faults with his fists, a stick, or a rope's end:

> In his opinion coercion was the only way to eradicate faults, and by its terror to prevent their recurrence. These were common notions, and were carried into practice not only by the heads of families and the teachers of youth generally, but by the government itself and every man in authority under it.

Boys were dressed like little men, with skirts to their coats, waistcoats, sheepskin breeches and three-cornered hats. Among the examples of popular debauchery, he describes how boys were permitted to spend the twelfth day of Christmas nailing people's clothes to pastrycooks' shops. The shops set out special displays of twelfth cakes, and Place's gang would hover around a shop on the corner of the Strand:

> At this time shop fronts were very clumsy things, and had about them a great deal of woodwork. . . . Each boy had a hammer and a quantity of short clout nails . . . a tap fixed the nail and a blow drove it home. Scarcely anyone could stop to see what was in the shop without being nailed, the tails of mens' coats and the gowns and petticoats of women were generally so firmly nailed that to get loose without tearing their clothes was impossible and the quicker this was done the less was the damage. . . . It frequently happened that when a person was nailed that he or she turned round either to extricate himself or herself or to attack the boys and were instantly nailed on the other side also. The noisy mirth these pranks occasioned was not confined to the boys who did the mischief, but was partaken of by grown persons, who ought to have known better, not by any means the lowest of the people, but by those who were well dressed.

Better dressed did not mean better behaved. There was no rigid distinction between the lowest of the people and successful tradesmen; a lifetime's journey from one gutter to another could easily include a few lucky years.

In 1785, aged 13, Place was apprenticed on the spur of the moment to a leather-breeches maker called France. Mr France was worth a good deal of money. His second and third wives had brought him, respectively, 'between one and two thousand pounds' and 'some five hundred pounds'. But money alone did not make a family respectable:

> By his first wife he had two sons and three daughters. At the time I was sent to him, his eldest daughter was and had been for several years a common prostitute. His youngest daughter who was about seventeen years of age had genteel lodgings where she was visited by gentlemen, and the second daughter who was a fine handsome woman was kept by a captain of an East India ship, in whose absence she used to amuse herself as such women generally do. . . . His eldest son was a first rate genteel pick-pocket, working at his

> trade of Leather Breeches making as a blind. . . . His other son had been a thief, was obliged to abscond, and at length to avoid punishment enlisted into a West India Regiment and went abroad where he died.

Mr France's workshop was home for his family and apprentices who worked there with journeymen twelve or thirteen hours a day,

82 London society was mirrored in this crowd at a cockpit, drawn by Rowlandson in 1808; a rowdy and excitable mixture, looking for excitement. Those who had come in poor hoped to leave richer. Some who had come in rich would leave having lost a great deal.

six days a week, when there was work. The cotton revolution was having an effect on prices, and leather breeches were being replaced by velveteen and corduroy. Mr France and his apprentices were reduced to making 'Rag Fair Breeches' – 'seconds' for the cheap second-hand shops of the Rag Fair district of London.

Francis had about eight shillings a week to spend, from his master and his parents. He could afford to join the high-living apprentice society of Fleet Street, entertaining prostitutes at parties, attending disreputable 'cock-and-hen' clubs, and he joined a cutter club racing an eight-oared boat on the tideway:

> The Cockswain was some years afterwards transported for a robbery – and the strokesman was hanged for a murder he did not commit. An attempt was made to set up an *alibi*, but it was said it could not be proved where he was, he being at the time committing a burglary with some of his associates.

You seized pleasure when you got the chance, for the world was liable to collapse under you at any time. As cotton breeches got cheaper, Mr France was obliged to 'shoot the moon' – dodge his creditors by clearing out in the night.

A short time after our removal my master surrendered himself in an action (*for debt*) and became a prisoner within the walls of the King's Bench. We had been for some time making breeches for workhouse

83 Fleet Market, built over the old Fleet ditch; a double row of stalls.

boys as journeywork for a contractor for which my master received only 8 pence a pair, even this sort of work was now at an end and my master and his family were reduced to the lowest state of poverty. He his wife and the two unfortunate children (*of his third marriage*) lingered on for another year when they all went into the workhouse where the old people shortly afterwards died. What became of the poor children I never heard.

Place's father, too, went to a debtor's prison when he lost the lease of his inn. He eventually moved from the Fleet prison to the Rules, an area around the prison where, for a fee, debtors were allowed to take lodgings. They were only allowed to leave the district on Sundays, when no one could be arrested for debt.

Place himself found what work he could as a journeyman, but as there was so little demand for leather breeches he learned to make them out of fabric. Combinations of workmen were illegal – it was the job of government, not the people, to determine the conditions

84 A tailor, from a book of trades of 1811.

of trade – but workers were allowed to join benefit societies. In the spring of 1793 the Breeches Makers Benefit Society revealed its secret function, and called a strike, in the hope of raising the rate of pay for what little work there was.

Place became one of the strike organisers. When the strike collapsed he was blacklisted. He was married and living in one room with his wife and child. They were starving, and the child died of smallpox. 'It is utterly impossible for anyone to tell how much we suffered during the six months which followed final conclusion of the strike.'

Combinations of workers were crushed: combinations of employers were allowed to flourish. Place had already seen the corruption which ran through petty officialdom, from his own father; his father, too, seemed to him a model of parliament's idea of authority – a great bully. Now corruption and tyranny touched him where it hurt: the employers combined to refuse him employment, and there was no one he could complain to or ask for help.

Eventually he was able to find work again; he also threw himself into the organisation of benefit societies among various groups of craftsmen. His landlord, a cabinet maker, was a member of the London Corresponding Society, which aimed at the reform of parliament. The only limitation on membership was a series of questions, the most important of which was: 'Are you thoroughly persuaded that the welfare of these kingdoms requires that every adult person, in possession of his reason, and not incapacitated by crimes, should have a vote for a Member of Parliament?'

In May 1794, when the society was two years old, Thomas Hardy, shoemaker, its secretary and founder, was charged with high treason:

> The violent proceedings of the government frightened away many of the members of the society and its number was very considerably diminished. Many persons, however, of whom I was one, considered it meritorious, and the performance of a duty to become members, now that it was threatened with violence, and its founder and secretary was persecuted.

Thus Place began his remarkable career as a political organiser on behalf of the radical shopkeepers and artisans of London. The government, terrified of the infection of French Jacobinism in its turbulent cities, acted to crush the society, but Place saw it as a force for stability:

> It induced men to read books, instead of wasting their time in public houses, it taught them to respect themselves, and to desire to educate their children. . . . They were compelled by . . . discussions to find reasons for their opinions and to tolerate others. It gave a new stimulus to an immense number of men who had been but in too many instances incapable of any but the grossest pursuits, and seeking nothing beyond mere sensual enjoyments.

The society was destroyed and outlawed before the end of the eighteenth century, but its impact had been widespread. It had alarmed the government enough to provide the excuse for a wave of oppressive laws, including the suspension of habeas corpus. It had so much popular support that there were reputed to be 300,000 people at its largest meeting, protesting at these laws and demanding universal suffrage. The register of one division of the society listed among its ninety-eight members nine watchmakers, eight weavers, eight tailors, six cabinet-makers, five shoemakers, four cordwainers, three carpenters, dyers and hairdressers, two merchants, ribbon-dressers, butchers, hosiers, carvers, bricklayers, frame-work cutters, breeches-makers, bedstead-makers

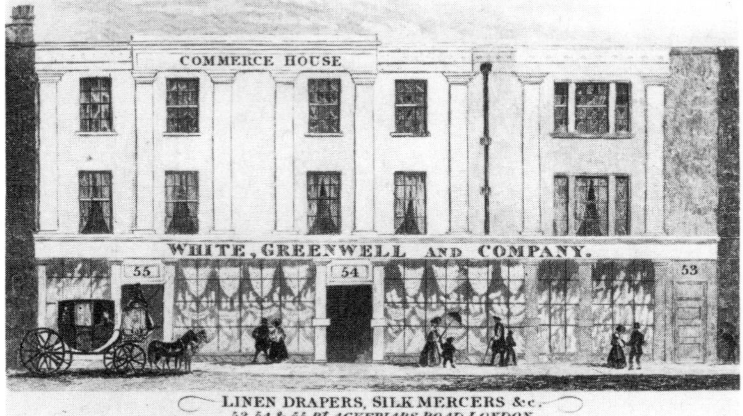

85 A draper's shop in Blackfriars Road, 1838.

and china burners, as well as a stationer, a hatter, a baker, an upholsterer, a locksmith, a wire-worker, a musician and a bookseller.

The original treason charge against Hardy collapsed, and long after the society ended, its principal members continued to celebrate the anniversary of his acquittal. Place did not normally go to these celebration dinners, but he attended in 1822. There he met two dozen old friends:

> Twenty at the least of them were Journeymen or shopmen at the time when they were delegates to the General Committee of the Society, they were all now in business flourishing men. . . . The society had been to a very considerable extent the means, and in some cases the whole means of inducing them to acquire knowledge the consequence of which was their bringing up a race of men and women as superior in all respects to what they would otherwise have been as can well be conceived. . . . I may I am sure safely affirm that the London Corresponding Society was a great moral cause of the improvement which has since taken place among the *People*.

The extent to which their businesses flourished could be seen on the streets. In place of the old shops, with ordinary house fronts, there were attractive shop fronts with gas-lit plate-glass windows. Place himself was proud of being in the forefront of the change. His own shop, opened in 1801, had the largest plate-glass windows in London 'if indeed they were not the first'.

Men who keep ledgers of profit and loss, and who have plate-glass windows to protect, are unlikely to be enthusiastic revolutionaries. When Place campaigned against the combination laws, he did so on the grounds that they encouraged dangerous underground associations. In a letter to Sir Francis Burdett, in 1825, he argued that:

86 A linen draper, from a book of trades of 1824.

> Men have been kept together for long periods only by the oppression of the laws; these being repealed, combinations will lose the matter which cements them into masses, and they will fall to pieces. All will be as orderly as even a Quaker could desire. He knows nothing of the working people who can suppose that, when left at liberty to act for themselves, without being driven into permanent associations by the oppression of the laws, they will continue to contribute money for distant and doubtful experiments, for uncertain and precarious benefits.

The virtues of a shopkeeper are not heroic. The new plate-glass shops needed hard work, creditworthiness, and a willingness to please the customer. Place made a fortune by knowing that 'the most profitable part for me to follow was dancing attendance on silly people . . . to have no opinion of my own, but to take a special care that my customers should be pleased with theirs.'

Place wrote about the licentious, half-criminal London of his boyhood with a mixture of relish and distaste. The rowdiness of that city was squalid and desperate, but his own radical vision had been created by it. It was a city which passed away in a single generation, as men like himself took their destinies into their own hands, and made themselves 'respectable'.

In revolutionary Paris, artisans and small traders were the driving force of the revolution, and set the style for a nation of 'citizens'. In radical London, the same kind of people learned the virtues of prosperity, and set the style for a nation of shopkeepers.

> Six or eight years ago, the epidemic began to display itself among the linen-drapers and haberdashers. The primary symptoms were an inordinate love of plate-glass, and a passion for gas-lights and gilding. The disease gradually progressed, and at last attained a fearful height. Quiet dusty old shops in different parts of town, were pulled down; spacious premises with stuccoed fronts and gold letters, were erected instead; floors were covered with Turkey carpets; roofs supported by massive pillars; doors knocked into windows, a dozen squares of glass into one; one shopman into a dozen. (Charles Dickens, *Sketches by Boz*, about 1835)

The linen-drapers rode to fortune on a flood of 'Manchester goods': sheetings and shirtings, webbings and velvets, the linens and drapes that were the glory of the industrial revolution, and that spread themselves over mattresses, tabletops, windows and torsos. With new kinds of goods to sell, the shopman had to become a salesman, dressing his window to excite the interest of passers-by, and 'pushing' lines to those who ventured in. The success of power spinning and power weaving demanded something approaching power selling. 'By increased skill the same amount of capital is made to do a greater quantity of work than before', explained the writer of a *Comparison between Large and Small Shops* in 1851. 'In fact the substitution of quick for slow sales is precisely like an improvement in machinery which cheapens the cost of production.' He went on to say that such shops created new demand, so that 'there have been improvements in the habits of the people, leading them to consume clothes and articles of ornament instead of ardent spirits'.

Since salesmanship was now the vital art, shops began to use their apprentices as counter-hands. When their indentures were complete, instead of becoming independent journeymen, they accepted posts as paid assistants and continued living-in at the shop. And with gas lighting, the counters they served at could be kept working until the last conceivable customer had gone to bed.

In 1825, when the Combination Acts were repealed, 20,000 shopmen of the linen-drapers, silkmakers, hosiers and lacemakers of London petitioned their employers for fixed hours, demanding that shops should close at 8 p.m. in the week, 10 p.m. on Saturdays, and an hour earlier in the winter. Almost sixty years later Thomas Sutherst wrote *Death and Disease Behind the Counter*, to show what happened to the counter-hand:

> He is forty years of age: he has had twenty-six years' experience of shop life. He is afraid he will not be able to stand it much longer. . . . Never worked less than 80 hours per week, but more frequently 90 hours per week . . . he feels at 40 that his health is broken. . . . He often pitied the young folks as he walked up and down and saw their pale, tired faces. . . . It is simply from bed to work and from work to bed the year round. No one dare complain for fear of dismissal without a character. . . . He noticed as a rule that young persons, male and female, are healthy and strong when they first come up from the country, but they invariably break down either before or at the end of their apprenticeship. He has known several instances where young men and women have been discharged for belonging to societies for enforcing their natural rights. . . . He should say that three-fourths of the assistants, male and female, are below the age of 21. As they get older they are sacrificed to make room for younger hands. Marriage under the present system of shop labour is discouraged.

This is from one of the dozens of case histories assembled by Sutherst to alarm a nation, not of shopkeepers, but of customers.

> We have only one assistant over fifty, and he is dying of consumption. . . . In the establishment at which I am now engaged, two have died from consumption during the last fifteen months, several have gone home ill. The majority spit phlegm.

Sutherst was president of the Shop Hours Labour League, started in 1881 to campaign for legislation to fix limits to shop hours. In one week of 1884 the League surveyed over 3,000 London shops, and found that about three-quarters of them were open after 9.30 in the evening. The League was trying to make a point, and it chose the districts it surveyed with care. The City and the West End were not touched; instead it examined Islington, Hackney, Hammersmith, Battersea, Stoke Newington, Poplar, Brompton, Lambeth, Bermondsey, Whitechapel, Borough High Street – all districts where new terraces of cheap red-brick housing had sprung up to house London's workers, who commuted to work on the early morning trains and trams. Wages were generally rising, and the fruits of mass-production and of empire were showing in lower food prices. A new world of working-class shopping had appeared. Lord Brabazon, an ardent campaigner for laws to restrict shop hours, insisted 'that none are more to blame than the working classes in this matter of the late shopping'.

But long hours of work were only part of the shop assistant's problems. Even in districts where shops closed at reasonable times, the living-in system meant that there was no escape from the regime of work.

87 P. C. Hoffman, in his shop assistant's uniform.

In 1894, P. C. Hoffman was engaged as an apprentice at a London emporium, the Holborn Silk Market. He was an orphan, brought up in the Warehousemen's, Clerks' and Drapers' School in Surrey. Although he had been educated to make a career in the wholesale or retail trade, and was well used to institutional life, living-in at Holborn came as a shock. He was shown his room, a small bedroom with a low ceiling, no curtains, a dirty window and a naked gas jet. There was no bed for him. He refused to share a bed, and so was put to sleep on the floor. At 11.15 came 'lights out', which was followed by a candle-light hunt for bugs and jesting sexual advances that quickly reduced him to tears.

Young Hoffman had entered an institutional world which was run like a workhouse, but which cultivated the appearance of servile gentility. Assistants were expected to wear frock coats and top hats; typical shop rules would include

> Young men must dress as respectably as when engaged – black coats and vests. Young men must not stand behind the counter (after closing excepted) or speak to customers with their coats off – fine 6*d*. Young ladies must wear black dresses made to clear the ground (showroom young ladies excepted), white linen collars and cuffs, and the hair arranged in a neat and becoming manner.

A shop's rulebook would commonly run to a hundred or more instructions, covering every aspect of life with military thoroughness. One list, quoted in a *Daily Chronicle* investigation in 1898, included:

1. The house door is closed at 11 p.m., Saturdays at 12 p.m. The gas will be turned out 15 minutes later. Anyone having a light after that time will be discharged.
2. Assistants sleeping out without permission will be cautioned twice and discharged at the third offence. . . .
6. Assistants are required to see that their looking glasses, drawers and wash-stands are in good condition when they first use them, as they will be held responsible for any damage afterwards. . . .
8. Bedrooms must be left tidy. No pictures, photos, etc. allowed to disfigure the walls. Anyone so doing will be charged with the repairs. . . .
23. No flowers to be put in wineglasses or bottles.

As Hoffman commented, the meanness of the 'no flowers' indicated the spirit of the system. His day began at 7.30 in the morning, when assistants had to put their trousers and jackets over their nightshirts and set the shop up for the day. Then they had to wash, dress, grab some bread and tea for breakfast and be in place for the shop to open by 8.30.

The whole day was spent under the eye of 'old Tommy', the silk buyer, who imposed fines for mistakes and who kept everyone in line with the colourful language of a sergeant-major. Dawdling over the twenty-minute lunch break, or ten-minute tea break, would call down Tommy's wrath – 'Damn your eyes, mister! Been on 'oliday, or did you 'ave a kipper for your tea, mister?'

Hoffman's wage was two shillings and sixpence a week, less twopence for boot cleaning ('they were never cleaned'), twopence for extra food (desperately needed), one and a halfpence library charge ('a few old books . . . Smiles' *Self-Help* and so on') and twopence as a compulsory donation to the Early Closing Association.

The Early Closing Association had begun life in 1842 as the Metropolitan Drapers' Association, an association of employers who wanted to reach agreement on limiting their hours. So long as some shops stayed open for late customers, all would, and more than half the shops in London stayed open until 10 p.m. even on Sundays – midnight on Saturdays. 'The results of this tyrranous sacrifice to the Moloch of business were mostly hideous and deadly', in the words of the association itself.

While the association had some success in the central area of London – Hoffman's establishment closed its doors at 7 p.m. – it made no headway at all where most customers were out at work all day. As shopping high streets developed all over the metropolis, and in every town, the pressure to stay open late grew even stronger. By the time the Shop Hours Labour League was founded, it was reckoned that, of the 100,000 shop assistants in London, 1,000 died of overwork each year, and another 3,000–4,000 were sent back to their homes in the country so ill that they had little chance of recovering. Sutherst's case studies stressed not only the 'death and disease' brought on by long hours of continuous standing in an atmosphere dank with the fumes of gas-lamps, but also the lack of time for education and improvement: 'no time for lectures whatever, we are worse than heathens', complained one assistant, 'we don't know anything of what is going on around us,' added another.

The moral, intellectual and physical decline of young assistants was seen as all the more significant in the later part of the century, when female shop assistants became more common. Lord Brabazon began campaigning for protective legislation because he shared a widespread belief that urban civilisation would, if uncontrolled, lead to a human calamity. The evidence was plain:

> Much of the social life and moral evil and degradation which pervades London is markedly due to the long hours of labour young men and ladies undergo in shops. Coming as they do from quiet, healthy country homes, and penned up in fetid atmospheres, they long for liberty, and very often grow weary of their bondage, and throw up in despair and disgust (especially the young ladies) their situations. Some of the greatest wrecks and waifs (male and female) in this great sink of London were once in shops.

He believed that 90 per cent of London's prostitutes had been shop assistants.

Moral protection was a two-edged sword, and shopkeepers defended the living-in system on the grounds that it guarded the moral welfare of young assistants – though there were stories that girls who asked for a rise were sometimes given a latch-key instead and were encouraged to supplement their income with a little night work. Hoffman joined the National Union of Shop Assistants, dedicated to overthrowing the system.

He worked in a number of London shops, including William Whiteley's store in Westbourne Grove, generally reckoned to have been the first department store in England. When he left, he had an interview with Whiteley, and told him that one of the objects of the Union was the abolition of living-in. 'Young man', came the stern reply, 'do you realise the grave moral responsibility that rests upon your shoulders in regard to that matter?' A few months later, Whiteley was shot dead by an illegitimate son he had fathered on one of his shop assistants.

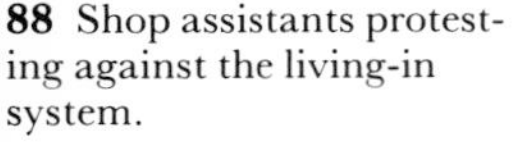
88 Shop assistants protesting against the living-in system.

None of the protective laws of the factory world applied to shops. Factory legislation existed to protect women and children; men were regarded as free agents, who had to bargain with their employers for the best terms they could get. The Truck Acts, which forbade the payment of wages in the form of food or lodging, did not apply to shop workers; they were not regarded as wage-earners. When the vote was extended to all men, in 1886, it did not include living-in shop assistants; they had no homes, and so could not register as voters. They were, said Hoffman, helots in their native land. The argument that men, as well as women and children, should be protected by the state was an attack on the Victorian idea that men should be free and untrammelled to make their own way in the world. It was an attack which was, eventually, to lead to the Welfare State. By a nice irony, even the slogan of that state's care – 'from the cradle to the grave' – came from behind the counter: it had originally been Whiteley's boast of the service offered by his store.

For shop assistants themselves, there was no possibility of 'Self-Help'. Hoffman became an energetic officer of the National Union of Shop Assistants, but it was a union which never developed any real strength. Its members would not fight for a living wage, because

> they would like others to think they were better off than they really were. At least they were rather ashamed of what they were being paid, for, after all, they had their pride. If the wage was light and the work was heavy, the frock-coat at least was highly esteemed and satisfyingly genteel. Proper deference was always paid to silk-faced respectability. Money was not everything.

89 Lipton's teas, 'Direct from the Tea Garden to the Tea Pot', were part of a revolution in shopkeeping. Lipton's stores were outlets for a world-wide trading company, and they were lock-up shops. No one lived on the premises. It was a change in the economics of shopkeeping, rather than union pressure, which destroyed the living-in system.

They tried to wage war on long hours and the living-in system, but in the end these were changed by economic pressures and the restrictions of the First World War, rather than by the shop assistants. Above all, they found it impossible to 'vote with their feet', by taking other work – not only because such work was hard to find, but because 'they had their pride'. Young drapers, it was true, might run away to join the Army – the 17th Hussars was known behind the counter as The Drapers – but once they had settled into the world of frock-coats and clean hands it was hard for them to consider the possibility of manual labour.

When the *Daily Chronicle* ran its exposure of shop life, it attracted many letters from assistants adding details of their own experience. In the stilted commercial prose they had been taught, young men wrote as though they were helplessly trapped in the institutions where they worked:

> I am compelled to live in the house upon nominal rations, insufficient to meet bodily requirements, having to expend part of my small salary to meet same. I am at present working fourteen hours per day, sixteen hours Saturday, till 5 p.m. on Thursday, for the exorbitant sum of ten shillings per week, board wage. I find it of no avail to complain, as I am told the usual remedy, viz, to leave. Out of my salary I am expected to keep up a gentlemanly appearance, to be honest, and to prepare for my dismissal when I become aged. Is there no remedy? Can any of your kind readers inform me how to free myself from bondage?

There were escapes, but they involved giving up the symbols of respectability, wearing rough clothes, getting dirty. Trained above all to sell, they were selling not only goods, the necessities of life, but also aspirations, images of the domestic stations along the road to gentility, a road paved with soft furnishings and snobbery, lined with 'the tea drunk by those who know' and 'the trouser press no gentleman should be without'. Living on commission, conscious that if they failed to sell to three customers a day they were out on their ears, they were their own best customers, totally committed to the idea that mankind is judged by appearances. As the *Daily Chronicle* described them, they were 'A forgotten and negligible class, living a hard and dreary and unhealthy life, a sacrifice to their own notions of self-respect and the throng of thoughtless purchasers to whom they are often less than nothing.'

3

When Mr T. left school in Salford, in 1936, he knew what work he wanted. He believed he had the makings of a commercial artist, and he wanted to paint posters for the cinema. He had spent hours in the new luxury Carlton in Cross Lane, where a sixpenny seat gave a continuous programme of Hollywood stars, newsreels of plutocrats at play, and the rich sound of Reginald Liversidge at the organ. He wanted to be associated with the world represented by the Carlton Cinema.

But Salford was not a gateway to that world. The slum streets around the cinema were full of men who should have been at work. Salford is the link between Manchester's cotton mills and the ship canal. In 1925 Britain exported £200 million worth of cotton goods. In 1935, it exported only £60 million worth. In human terms, that was represented in Salford by pinched families trying to live on a meagre dole. The means test inspector went from house to house, ordering families to sell anything of value before granting relief, and deducting a notional 'rent' from the payment if any grandparents lived with a family. Many families were broken up by this device.

The only jobs open were in a grocer's shop, or a pawnbroker's. Hoping that writing out pawn tickets would somehow lead on to signwriting, he took the pawnbroker's job, at ten shillings a week.

The broker's shop was an important part of domestic economy: families were often dependent on pawning the Sunday-best clothes on Monday morning, and hurriedly redeeming them on Friday or Saturday afternoon. That only applied, of course, to families who still had work. The very poor got no credit. Even if a woman brought a new suit in to pawn she might be turned away, if it had the wrong sort of label. Many cheap tailoring shops accepted trading cheques instead of cash, and the new suit might well be, as yet, unpaid for. Trading-cheque customers paid back a shilling every Friday night to the tally-man, commonly repaying twenty-one shillings for a cheque whose face value was £1. It seemed a cheap enough form of credit, unless you knew that the shopkeeper would only be able to redeem the cheque for sixteen shillings. Paying a guinea for sixteen shillings' worth of goods was one way of staying poor.

Since there was really no prospect of becoming a signwriter, Mr T. began to worry about his future. The pawnbroker would only pay a grown man thirty shillings which was less than a typical family man would expect on the dole. Fortunately, he was able to move to Burton's, the tailor, where his wages went up from ten to fifteen shillings, and he knew that as an adult salesman he would be able to make at least £3 a week.

Burton's was geared to providing respectable suits for respectable men – since they only accepted cash, a suit with a Burton's label was acceptable at any pawnbroker. Salford did not have many of these aristocrats of labour, and the Salford store was one of the least successful in the chain.

The shop's oak-panelled walls, oak-block floors and dignified glass-fronted cases were the same in hundreds of Burton's stores throughout the land. The factory-made suits were given their shape by canvas linings and pressing machines, not by the cut and stitching as in hand tailoring, but they looked smart, if a little wooden. The atmosphere in the shop was severely formal; even the juniors were called 'Mister', and the order of seniority was never forgotten for a moment. It determined who a member of staff could talk to, for everyone, including the manager, was a salesman, and the staff approached their customers in order of seniority. A salesman gave him helpful advice as they cycled home together, calling each other 'Mr P.' and 'Mr T.'

Mr T. was the last in the line to serve, and it was a long time before he had much chance to sell anything. From nine in the morning till eight at night (with a half-day on Wednesdays), while those above him attended to the customers, he was cleaning the cabinet fronts and waxing the floors. His spare time was spent reading company textbooks, with titles like 'Scientific Selling'. On Saturdays the shop stayed open until nine, but Mr T. then had to wait until the orders were ready for dispatch, and take them to the railway station so that they would be at the cutting room by Monday morning.

The illusion of traditional tailoring was preserved, with two or three weeks between taking a customer's measurements and giving him his suit – but if a customer was in a hurry, he could usually have it in forty-eight hours. Since most family men only bought a suit when they had to go to a funeral, this was important.

Younger men needed suits for more cheerful occasions. Before the First World War, a new suit was strictly 'Sunday-best', needed for church or chapel, but now it was more likely to be needed for Saturday night at the dance hall. Radios and gramophones had transformed popular music from street ballads and music-hall recitations, into big-band swing and crooned ditties. A smart suit was essential to cut any kind of a dash under the glittering ball of mirrors that hung from the dance-hall ceiling.

Divisions between rich and poor were deep, but divisions between one part of the country and another were beginning to

90 The multiple tailor's style in 1936.

diminish. Multiple stores of identical design sold identical goods from one end of the country to the other. From Newcastle to Brighton, the Saturday-night dancers wore the same tight-fitting jackets and baggy trousers on the male side of the floor, and the same styles of dress and hair on the female side. The aspirins from Boots, the supper out of tins from Liptons, the breakfast cornflakes from Home and Colonial, the shoes from Dolcis were the same wherever you went. Nearly 40,000 multiple shop branches covered the land. Radio and cinema provided the whole nation with the same dreams and idols, with the same jokes and news.

The coming of war reduced the variety of life still further. Rationing of food, and then gradually of clothing, footwear and other necessities, meant that in theory at least everyone was equal. Shopkeepers had to collect the ration coupons from their customers, and to withhold goods to which the customer was not entitled, no matter how much money was offered.

'Fair shares for all' was not the original purpose of rationing. When the Treasury first drew up its contingency plans for war, in 1929, it saw rationing as part of a programme to prevent inflation; fairness was rather a second thought. But in the event, a sense of social justice came to dominate the system. Rationing was not very successful in holding down prices; the price of clothes leapt up by 9 per cent in the nine months after they were put on the ration, in May 1941. But the scheme meant that no one could buy more than a bare minimum, unless there were good social reasons why they should be allowed to. The original clothing ration was fixed at a level that roughly corresponded to the amount that poorer people normally bought anyway.

To hold prices down, the government introduced a scheme in 1942 which encouraged manufacturers to produce particular garments from particular cloths at fixed prices. These garments were marked with a 'Utility' label, and they offered quite good quality at low prices. No one was obliged to buy Utility clothes, but their appeal was obvious, and they eventually accounted for 80 per cent of all clothes purchased.

An army of civil servants was set up to police the regulations. There were fiddles – some shop managers managed to operate a black market in coupons, and in the first year of clothes rationing 800,000 books of coupons were 'lost' and replaced. But the law was harsh: there cannot have been a single large multiple retailer that did not find some of its managers carted off to jail.

Mr T. spent the war in the Navy; when he came back to Burton's in 1946 the severest austerity regulations were being relaxed, but rationing was still in force. The Labour Party was elected in 1945 on a programme that would carry wartime planning into the peace: 'the establishment of a Socialist Commonwealth of Great Britain – free, democratic, efficient, progressive, public-spirited, its material resources organised in the service of the British people'. The only way of organising resources in the service of the British people was to retain complete control over buying and selling. In fact, the severest days of rationing were in 1947–8, when even bread was rationed, and the food ration was well below the wartime level.

The old maxim that 'the customer is always right' now made no sense. The customer was not free to make choices: the shop, following government controls, was forbidden to offer turn-ups on trousers or extra pockets, and the range of designs was severely limited. The customer was at the mercy of the shop, and might well have to wait nine months for his suit, and then find it was in a different material from that he had ordered. If he turned it down, he had to start all over again.

Not even the shopkeeper could evade the rules. In 1946 Mr T. got married. He had been obliged to spend his clothing coupons on his working uniform, black jacket, black vest, striped trousers. He did not feel he could get married in that – nor in his demob suit, the civilian uniform handed him when he came out of the Navy the previous year. His elegant appearance on the day suggested that he had found a way of evading the controls, but in fact he was wearing trousers borrowed from the shop manager's personal wardrobe, and his smart double cuffs were strips of starched linen from a shop-window dummy. If he had straightened his fingers, the cuffs would have dropped off.

'From each according to his ability – to each according to his need'. It was officially a slogan that belonged in the Soviet Union, but in fact it applied more in Britain than in Russia. The customers who could buy most in Mr T.'s shop were merchant seamen, who arrived in Salford with special allowances of clothing coupons because of their work.

Rationing had given Britain's poor a better diet and, through Utility schemes, better clothes and furniture, but now people lost patience. The black market flourished: 'spivs' offered their customers choices that shops were obliged to deny them.

Mr T. found that the suits his shop were offering had little appeal. Cast in the traditional mould – close-fitting, square-shouldered with waistcoats – they were the uniform of an old-fashioned respectability. Given the choice, people wanted something more relaxed, that would symbolise the future rather than the past. Americans, as everyone knew, had everything that Britain lacked – they had money, petrol, nylons, washing machines, refrigerators. Many young men wanted to escape from their demob suits into American-style loose-fitting drape jackets, with wide shoulders and no waistcoats. It was a democratic style. There was always a significant difference between the Savile Row suit and a working man's suit in the 1930s, but the loose drape jacket could be produced as successfully by a multiple tailor as by a master craftsman, if it was correctly cut.

Burton's, not knowing how to cut the new styles, began to slide towards bankruptcy. They tried to get it right, but their drape

91 The drape.

jackets tended to hang crookedly. In 1953 they were obliged to merge with Jackson's, a much smaller multiple which possessed the expertise to make the new style of suit, and dress the new style of man.

When Mr T. had first joined the firm, it catered to customers who knew their social place, and who chose their clothes accordingly. The suit was the badge that proclaimed 'this is a respectable working man'. In the 1920s and 1930s professional men and businessmen began wearing suits, but it was originally a costume for

92 The suit was a symbol of a working man in Edwardian England: here the agreement between the Labour and Liberal parties in 1910, when they decided not to stand against each other for election, is expressed entirely through their costumes.

the working man – Labour Party man, rather than a Liberal or a Tory.

By the 1950s, the dignified long coat, contrasting trousers and high hat of the middle-class gentleman had become a museum piece. Everyone wore suits. In this sartorial democracy, customers no longer knew their place. The only people seen on the streets in full-skirted jackets with silk facings were 'teddy boys'.

In 1959, when the Labour Party had lost three general elections in a row, *Socialist Commentary* commissioned a survey of political attitudes. The surveyor divided his respondents into 'middle class,' and 'skilled working class', and 'labouring working class', according to their jobs. But the classification made little sense to the people that he interviewed. About 40 per cent of the people he called working class described themselves as middle class. That, he concluded, was why the Labour Party had lost the election:

> The image of the Labour Party, held by both its supporters and its non-supporters, is one which is increasingly obsolete in terms of contemporary Britain. Both groups see Labour as identified with the working class – especially the poor and the labouring working class, and at the same time, many workers, irrespective of their politics, no longer regard themselves as working class.

The change was mirrored in a changing style of dress. Before the war, the cut of a man's suit was one indication of which street he lived in and how he earned his living – you could even guess how his home was furnished. But now the messages of dress were not so clear, for there was no clear story to tell, especially in the more affluent areas of the south and the Midlands. By 1959 four homes in five had television, and hire-purchase was widely available for such luxuries as carpets and three-piece suites.

The change that took place among customers was mirrored by changes in the hierarchy of the shop itself. No longer does a junior

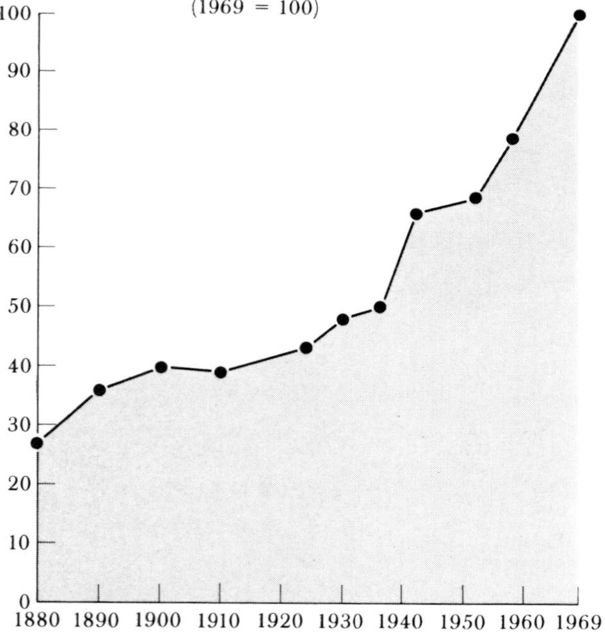

Figure 8 Real value of average weekly wages 1880–1969.

speak only to a salesman, and feel that it is a remarkable event to be addressed by the manager. Once the manager was the top salesman, expressing by his every move the perfect blend of deference and superiority which made his customers see him as the judge of their station – a feeling enhanced by the dignity of the shop. Now he is an instrument in a marketing strategy, and in the shop Mr T. manages, customers help themselves from open stands.

More than any other country in the world, Britain lives by large-scale retailing. The changing role of the shop manager, from

93 In 1977, Burton's dismissed 1,500 employees. (Reproduced by kind permission of the *Guardian*.)

apparent master of his establishment to a unit in the company selling plan, is part of a fundamental change in English life.

The growth of multiple shop branches, 1880–1976

1880	*1900*	*1920*	*1930*	*1950*	*1966*	*1976*
1,564	11,645	24,713	35,894	44,800	73,155	169,000

Between 1966 and 1976 the total number of shops in Great Britain fell from about 500,000 to about 400,000.

Respectability, responsibility, thrift and independence – all the virtues once associated with a Burton's suit – are musty qualities. In 1973, ten million suits were sold. In 1978 that figure fell to six million. And in 1978, twenty million pairs of jeans were sold. About half of Burton's 600 shops were closed in the 1970s. In those that remain, there is a new model of shop worker. Responsibility has become accountability: Mr T. is expected to provide his head office with daily breakdowns of sales and cash-flow. Respectability has become 'success': the kind of company car and the size of commission are the measures of people, rather than their accents or the way they dress. Thrift has been ousted by the pressure to buy, and Burton's now give credit to anyone who can produce a cheque card. As for independence: well, that was always a dubious virtue. In 1937 the National Union of Shop Assistants held a conference of Burton's branch managers, to try to win a fixed minimum rate for them. In the words of P. C. Hoffman

> The excuse put forward against agreeing to rates was that the managers as executive officers were members of the firm. But they could not engage or dismiss staff, they dressed their windows by pattern from Leeds, they could not buy cloth or clothes, though they must sell them and order them according to a system, they were liable to be shifted at any time from this place to that, their incoming and outgoing were regulated by an elaborate code, and inspectors and chief inspectors visited them and kept watch and ward over them to see all was going to plan.

Mr T. did not join the Union, either as an assistant or a manager. However slight his independence may have been, he felt that it was for a man to make his own way in the world, and strike his own bargains.

It was an attitude which, from Hoffman's point of view, extended the tradition of shop workers making sacrifices to their own notions of self respect. It was an attitude which kept Mr T. out of the Union. Until 1978: in that year, he did join the Union. For in that year, Burton's became a closed shop.

Chapter 8

MINERS

1

The Lambton family has farmed in Durham since the twelfth century. Six hundred years ago, according to legend, John de Lambton used to spend Sunday irreligiously fishing in the River Wear. One Sunday he caught an 'unseemly or disgusting' worm. He threw the horrid object down a well and told a friend that he thought he had caught the Devil. He became a reformed character, and went on a Crusade for seven years.

Deep under the land the worm flourished and grew, until it emerged as a terrible monster. John returned to find that the great worm was living in the Wear. It wrapped itself around a hill, or round a rock in the river, and had to be fed daily with the milk of nine cows, 'in default of which it devoured man and beast'.

John set himself to destroy the worm, but when he cut it with his sword, the parts rejoined and become more terrible. A witch gave him the secret that enabled him to succeed. He had a suit of armour studded with razor blades, and went to the rock where the worm came daily. Now, as it wrapped itself around the deadly armour, it was sliced into tiny pieces which fell into the current and were washed away.

The price of the witch's advice was the Lambton curse: no head of the house would die in his bed for nine generations.

In the centuries that followed, the Lambtons prospered as country gentlemen should. They became knights of the shire, representing Durham in parliament for generation after generation. When, in Elizabeth's reign, England began to run short of wood for burning, the Lambtons mined the rich vein of coal under their lands. Before the Civil War, Sir William Lambton shipped 30,000 tons a year down the Wear to Sunderland, 'the best coles in the country', it was said. But Sir William did not die in his bed.

Popular belief has it that the curse ended with General John Lambton, who took to his deathbed in 1794, armed to the teeth in case someone tried to budge him. General John was the first of the modern Lambtons. His deathbed was not in Lambton Hall; he had taken up residence in Harraton Hall, his mother's home, on the opposite bank of the river. The family was making a new start.

Two years before he died, a new Lambton pit was opened. The industrial revolution was creating a hunger for coal. There had been a limit on the depth of old pits, because underground water flooded them; but with new steam pumps it was possible to drive to deeper seams.

A new pit required new colliers and a new village to house them. Colliery villages were remote, isolated communities, regarded by the world outside as savage encampments. The new villages were inhabited by migrants; the agricultural parts of Durham generally had a shrinking population, but from 1730 to 1801 the population of the county rose from 97,000 to 160,000, as people came to the pits. Pitmen's children, according to a report in 1800, were put

Annual budget of a Durham miner, earning £32 a year, early 1790s

	shillings	
Rent	30	
Fuel	32	
Boots and clothes	100	
Barley	150	
Wheat and rye	50	
Oatmeal	104	
Meat	50	
Butter	50	
Milk	30	
Tea and sugar	40	
Candles, soap etc	30	
Potatoes	28	
(*total*)	694	(£34.14*s*.)

down the mine when they were 7 or 8 years old, and sometimes as young as 6. They grew up vicious, slovenly, extravagant and intemperate, 'almost from infancy habituated to frequent intoxication'.

Oh, the collier lad is a canny lad,
An' he's aalwes of good cheor,
Ah' he knaws how to wark, an' he knaas how to shork
An' he knaas how to sup good beor.

There was no shortage of beer money. Pitmen in Northumberland and Durham were hired by the year, and signed a bond which laid down the minute conditions of their work and pay. The contract was sealed with binding-money; this was originally a shilling, but competition for men was so fierce as new pits were opened that in 1800 a pitman could expect ten or twelve guineas, and four years later some coal-owners were offering binding-money of twenty guineas as well as gallons of beer. In the early years of the nineteenth century, pitmen's fortnightly pay rose by 30 or 40 per cent.

When George Parkinson wrote his *True Stories of Durham Pit Life*, he began with the cocky assurance of a pitman, schooled in the hard world underground: 'I may without presumption or needless apology present myself as the son of a Durham miner, born in 1828 in the colliery village of New Lambton, where my Father was also born in 1804.'

New Lambton was typical of the colliery villages of the great northern coalfield. One long row of low-roofed brick cottages formed the street, with a few shorter rows nearby. The street faced a meadow with a stream and an old mill, and the countryside around was wooded. A few minutes walk away was the beautiful and newly created Lambton Park. Optimistic that the mines would make their fortune, the family had pulled down old Lambton Hall in 1797, and set about turning Harraton Hall into Lambton Castle, a medieval fantasy. The pitmen, of course, had no place there.

> The only place for social gatherings or recreation was a public-house, formed by uniting two cottages, with a fenced cock-pit and a quoit ground at the front, and a quiet place for pitch-and-toss just round the corner, providing opportunities for votaries of those sports, which, with the tap-room as their centre, were often accompanied by drunken brawls and fightings with all the demoralising influences arising therefrom.

The tavern at the end of the row was a standard feature of colliery villages; it was also the 'tommy shop'. Pitmen were paid in tickets that had to be spent there. The tommy shop, normally run by a relative of the viewer (or agent) who ran the colliery, was notorious for overcharging and giving short weight, and colliers were usually heavily in debt to it.

Most of a pitman's life was spent underground. In 1800 the working day for small boys started at 2 a.m., when the caller-out came round. They were down the pit by three o'clock and did not return until after eight at night. They spent the time minding a door. As pits went deeper, and underground workings became more extensive, it was important to control the ventilating currents of air. 'Trapper' boys had to open the door when waggons of coal were coming, and shut it again quickly afterwards.

The waggons were drawn by horses, driven by lads aged about 11. Waggon drivers sat on narrow seats, and were likely to be injured by falling, or by being crushed against depressions in the roof. Spending such long hours in the timeless dark of the pit, boys reckoned the passing of their lives by counting their injuries: 'I never learned to read till last laming but one'.

At about 14, a boy would become a putter, manhandling the 'corves' or coal-baskets to and from the waggon train. At 21 he could expect to become 'a man for hisself', a hewer, picking away at the coal face, bent into an awkward space that would give him a

94 'Corves', baskets of coal, being lifted on and off waggons underground; from Hair's *Coal Mines*, 1844.

distinctive stance, like a question mark. The hewer was the man for whom the pit was sunk. It was his work that provided the basis of Britain's industrial revolution. But the work itself was unchanging from generation to generation. A hewer's day was shorter than a child's, but that was because he was working hard.

On Sundays the pitmen enjoyed the light of day. Then they put aside their working clothes of flannel for plush or velveteen breeches tied with ribbons, and posy jackets, heavily embroidered waistcoats. They arranged their hair in ringlets, and wore ribboned hats, with flowers in season. This was their dress for gaudy days, the pitmen's holidays, such as the day when the first cuckoo was heard.

Gaudy days were not mentioned in the pitmen's bond. There

was much that was taken for granted between pitmen and coal-owners, such as the right of the old and the invalid to occupy their cottages and enjoy the charity of their ex-employer. Established mining families considered it a sign of respectability to bind themselves year after year to the same pit, and the bond was a formal recognition of their station in society. They expected the coal-owners to respect their privacy and their privileges.

A new pit, with new pitmen, had no such sense of tradition. As increasing numbers of newcomers entered the bond, a new spirit of combination appeared underground. Combinations were made illegal in 1799, but in the unseen dark, from small beginnings, a union grew. Men were 'brothered'; 'the members of the Union bound themselves by a most solemn oath to obey the orders of the brotherhood under the penalty of being stabbed through the heart or of having their bowels ripped up'.

In 1810 the coal-owners decided to draw up a new bond that expired in April, instead of October. Demand was low in the spring, and they could afford to negotiate more carefully then. The new pits were producing coal faster than the market could bear, and coal-owners were feeling pinched. The master of Lambton was an 18-year-old lieutenant in the 10th Dragoons; his widowed mother had spent a fortune on building the castle, and was in debt. The Lambton pits were particularly unprofitable, because all the profits from the easily-won upper seam of coal had been squandered and now they were bearing the full cost of developing deeper seams in tough market conditions. A commercial report on the pits in 1810 spelt it out: 'as was then too generally the case in the Coal Trade, they had preferred present profit, to the future welfare of the concerns'. The pitmen signed the new bonds, and then realised their mistake. The union emerged, and for the first time revealed its strength. Throughout the whole of the northern coal-field, the pitmen downed their tools, and stayed home.

Breaking the bond was illegal, and the jails filled to overflowing. The Bishop of Durham's stables became an emergency prison for hundreds of men. Surprised by the unexpected power of this underground brotherhood, the coal-owners were forced to negotiate. The binding date stayed in April, but the bond itself was revised, and binding-money was fixed at five guineas. The bond was no longer a fixed statement of the age-old relationship between pitmen and coal-owners. It had become a negotiable contract of employment. A new age was beginning:

> When the spirit of mercantile speculation was once turned to the collieries . . . when competition on the market and the consequent diminution of profit, induced the owners to aim at making better

> terms with their men . . . the latter sought to strengthen themselves with the dangerous bond of combination. From that time a series of conflicts . . . ensued.[1]

Another sign of the new age was the growing scale of death underground. The occasional death of an individual pitman was so commonplace that, traditionally, no inquests were held or records kept, but the new deep pits were liable to devastating explosions that brought catastrophe to whole communities. Two explosions at Felling pit in 1812 killed 115 men and boys. Two years later the coal-owners brought Sir Humphrey Davy to design a lantern that would not ignite gas, and Lambton himself descended his pit to watch it being tried out.

John Lambton, who came into his estate in 1813, became personally very popular with his pitmen. He was an energetic fighter for the reform of parliament, using his family seat in the Commons to demand the vote for every householder in the country. Pitmen, like other working men, felt that parliament should be their protector, and hoped that reform would make it more responsive.

In August, 1819, the whole country was shocked by the 'massacre of Peterloo'. A crowd of perhaps 60,000 had gathered in St Peter's Fields, Manchester, to listen to the radical orator Hunt, and the mounted Yeomanry had charged into them, killing eleven and injuring over 400. Lambton was as fierce as anyone in denouncing the magistrates of Manchester. The radicals of Newcastle called a protest meeting, and, to their amazement, the 'savage pitmen' came pouring in. In perfect order and sobriety they swelled the number to between fifty and one hundred thousand. Back in their villages, they set up radical classes, and it was said that the radical paper, the *Black Dwarf*, could be seen 'in the hat-crown of almost every pitman you meet'.

The pitmen were learning new ways of organising and expressing themselves, instead of appearing as the riotous drunken horde that everyone expected. One of the main reforming influences was Methodism, which was actively making converts in colliery villages where no parson ever came. The Methodist leaders were alarmed to hear that pitmen were learning their political skills at Methodist meetings. The radical classes and class leaders were imitations of Methodist organisation. Converted men were not only learning how to act in a sober and responsible way, but also how to address public meetings. The Methodist Committee of Privileges issued a circular, warning against

> Tumultuous assemblies . . . calculated, both from the infidel

> principles, the wild and delusive theories, and the violent and inflammatory declamations . . . to bring all government into contempt, and to introduce universal discontent, insubordination, and anarchy.

The following year, a form of Methodism appeared in Durham which ignored such warnings, and revelled in tumultuous assemblies; Primitive Methodism. It was rejected by orthodox followers of Wesley, because it held mass open-air revivalist meetings which seemed dangerous to public order. These meetings were very popular among the pitmen: dramatic stormings of the soul, often held at night:

> The meeting was held by lantern light, so that the intense conviction and passionate earnestness of the preachers was heightened in their effect by the weird and solemn scene, until, a torrent of expostulation, warning, entreaty and appeal poured forth like a tempest upon the spell-bound multitude, a wave of indescribable emotion swept over them, and cries for mercy were on every hand.

George Parkinson was born when the epidemic of conversion was at its height:

> At Shiney Row, a village about a quarter of a mile away, the methodist revival had 'broken out', and the news spread to all the villages around. . . . One man at Lambton determined to see for himself what the strange news meant . . . on the Sunday morning, therefore, he walked to Shiney Row, and on entering the village met two men. To his great surprise, no dogs accompanied them; they were dressed in their better suits, and altogether had the appearance of men bent on important matters. 'W'y, whatton sort o' day had ye yisterda', lads?' he called out to the men . . . 'The Methodies hes getten in amang huz, and som o' huz hez getten in amang the Methodies. The bowling match didn't come off yesterday, because baith Harry and Tom was convarted last Sunda'. There hen't been a fight all the weekend.'

At one end of New Lambton Street stood the public house, 'with all the demoralising influences arising therefrom'. At the other end was erected the counter to those influences. Jacob Speed's cottage had its roof raised, and a projecting porch added, to turn it into a chapel. For the coal-owners welcomed the pitmens' conversions. The colliery viewer, Tom Smith, had the sense to recognize that the converted men were punctually at the pit on Monday morning, instead of lounging at the public house.

Conversion was spoken of as a new birth, out of which came a new man. A typical Primitive Methodist obituary reads:

> Born of parents in humble life, who wickedly abandoned their son to ignorance and crime . . . he became a new man in Jesus Christ. Old things passed away, and all things became new. The lion became as

a lamb, and the rude, untutored and rebellious spirit as that of a little child, for he was anxious to learn and ready to do the will of his heavenly father.

George Parkinson was brought up in this faith, in a community divided between those who went to the pub, and the new chapel folk, who were firmly putting aside the old ways. In place of the posy jacket, Sunday-wear became a black suit; in place of the cheerful, rowdy songs of the past, children were taught hymns encouraging an inner discipline like Isaac Watt's hymn of the sun:

When from the chambers of the east
His morning race begins,
He never tires, nor stops to rest,
But round the world he spins.
So, like the sun, would I fulfill,
The duties of this day,
Begin my work betimes, and still
March on my heavenly way.

George's parents were Methodist converts, and he was brought up to regard the chapel as the centre of domestic life. Since education was important to Methodists, he did not go down the pit until he was 9, and then by his own choice. He was eager to escape from school work, and be initiated into what seemed to him 'the mysteries and manly phraseology of a pit-boy's life'.

His first day remained vivid in his memory. His father went down with him, lowered in a basket of bricks, and he was seized with sudden fear as they dropped into the clanging darkness. 'Dinnet be flaid, hinney,' said his father, 'aw hev hald o' thee.' His grandfather was waiting at the bottom to lift him out. Giving him his candle stuck in a lump of clay, the old man said, 'Keep thi heart up, hinney: thoo'l mak' a good pitmen yet'.

George was to work as a trapper. After a few hundred yards they came to the door he was to mind. His father hewed a cubbyhole for the boy to shelter in, and left him in the dark, 'In a few hours I was quite at home in my work, and proud of doing it without a mistake.'

After an eight-hour stint at the face, George's father returned, coal-black. But George himself still had four hours more to work: 'My father stayed with me as long as he could, and as he rose to go home I saw the tears in his eyes and heard him, when a few yards away, say to himself, "Aw wish ye'd byeth been lasses".'

When George was born, the working day for a trapper was seventeen or eighteen hours, but it had been cut to twelve in 1831. Primitive Methodism had strengthened the spirit of combination among the men, and when the Combination Acts were repealed in

1825, Primitive Methodist hewers organised a legal union. In 1831 they called a strike, aiming to abolish the tommy shops and cut the working day for children, and to fight against the fall in pay which was being enforced as competition sharpened.

The men in the Lambton pits agreed to join the strike, but Lambton's agent, Henry Morton, set about cutting them out of the union. He agreed to the union demands, on condition that the men did not strike. They accepted the bond. The union leaders wanted peaceful discipline, but there were pitmen in the union who preferred the ways of the old brotherhood. Threatening letters appeared at Lambton:

> 3 April 1831
> John Radison you give these lines to the workmen or else you will suffer by the by. We suppose you are bound against your grements. You think you have done right but . . . if you don't come among the men the forst generall meeting you and your brother will ly in one Churchyeard and that will be such a church as a number of men like you has not lane in this long time.

When it was plain that the men were in danger, Lambton (now Lord Durham) arranged for a troop of Dragoons to be stationed nearby, to protect them.

The strike was successful, and other coal-owners were forced to accept the terms that Lambton had allowed from the start. The following year, the coal-owners refused to bind union members. Lord Durham did not insist that his own pitmen should be non-union men, but Lambton pitmen were no longer very welcome in the union. Durham's popularity remained high among them; he was the man who wrote the reform bill, and when he returned to the castle after the bill was passed, the pitmen took his horses out of their shafts, and hauled his carriage themselves.

The union tried to fight victimisation of its members by calling a second strike. At a great open-air meeting on Bolden Fell, their leader, Tommy Hepburn, spelt out what must be done.

> Let them, he said, make a few sacrifices, and twelve months would teach them a great deal. Things would come round in such a way that there would be no need of more miners than were ever employed in England before . . . it had been said that they ought to get knowledge and he would teach them how to do that. Let libraries be established among the collieries. . . . In conclusion, he urged them to part quietly, and let the world see their determination and good order.

The coal-owners followed the example set by Lord Durham the previous year. Refusing to deal with the union, they dealt with the strikers in their individual collieries. They offered terms, and if they were rejected, evicted the strikers and their families, and brought in blackleg labour from Ireland, Wales and the lead mines. The colliery villages were taken over by special constables and policemen imported from London, to enforce the evictions and protect the men at work.

Observers were astonished at the quality of the pitmen's furniture when they were evicted – almost every house had a four-poster bed, an eight-day clock and mahogany chests. There was little public sympathy for the strikers.

The Lambton method worked. By slicing the worm into many parts it was destroyed; by dealing with the strikers in their individual collieries, the union was broken.

But the spirit of combination survived. The breaking of the union left a bitter enmity between pitmen and coal-owners in many collieries. The influx of workers from other districts meant that there were too many pitmen looking for work – there were more men working underground in Durham than labouring in the fields on the surface. When the market for coal began to slump again, in the early 1840s, coal-owners looked at the fine print of the bond to find ways of saving money at the pitmen's expense.

The bond laid down the weight of coal in a tub; if the hewer produced short weight, he got nothing for his work. It was impossible for a hewer to know if the colliery scales were correct, or if coal was spilt. The bond laid down that if there was too much stone in a tub, the hewer got nothing; but working by the dim light of a Davy lamp it was hard to tell black brass from coal. If a hewer broke the coal into smaller pieces to check for stones, he was fined.

Once more the worm turned. The men began to re-combine, this time in a great national union, the Miners' Association of Great Britain and Ireland. This union was more powerful, and

95 The heading on the *Miners' Association Journal*.

better organised, than anything that had gone before, and it hired a solicitor to fight the bond in the courts. The coal-owners responded, in 1844, by refusing to continue the system of annual bonds. In its place, they offered a monthly contract under which men could be sacked at a month's notice and forced to leave their homes.

The union drew up a bond of its own, which would have guaranteed a minimum wage and allowed pitmen to continue renting their cottages after they stopped working, but the coal-owners were not speaking to the union. The pitmen all refused to sign the monthly contract.

From 5 April 1844, every pit in Northumberland and Durham stood idle. At their public meetings, the men declared, 'We are determined to be free . . . are we any longer to bear the yoke of bondage and toil in the bowels of the earth, as we have done?'

'He that oppresseth the poor, reproacheth his maker.' The leaders were once more the Primitive Methodists. The call was for order, sobriety, and God's justice for pitmen.

> Thou heard the Israelites of old,
> And led them to a blessed fold,
> Deliver us from slavery
> And set the sons of Britain free.

This time, Lambton pitmen stuck by their union. The first Lord Durham, 'radical Jack', had died in 1840, but his policy of ignoring the union and trying to split the men lived on. When the owners began to repeat the tactics of 1832, turning the pitmen out of their cottages, Lambton miners too were put into the lanes and fields. This time, though, it was not only the pitmen who were evicted. The coal-owners rejected all the antiquated feudal sentiment that lay behind the bond, and adopted a hard commercial view. The old, the injured, pregnant women were all hauled out (sometimes with real brutality), as the men of every village held fast to the union. They were left to manage as they could. The workhouses were closed against them. Lord Londonderry, the most powerful coal-owner of all, forbade the tradesmen in 'his' town of Seaham to give credit to strikers or their families.

There were individual outbreaks of temper by the pitmen, but they retained an astonishing discipline. 'Once more we appeal to you', the union wrote to the coal-owners, 'can we obtain an interview? Tell us how, and by what means.' There was no response. The great worm of combination would be cut up by inches, in a thousand different places.

The gentility of the reformed pitmen was no match for these

96 'Pitmen encamped', after being evicted in 1844; from the *Illustrated London News*.

tactics. On 13 August the union held a 'musical melange' in Newcastle to raise money for families starving after four months with no pay. Mr Sessford was at the pianoforte, there were performances by the Shincliffe Instrumental Band and the Bell Family Quadrille, and Mr Joseph Fawcett recited 'The Miner's Doom' in his pit clothes.

That night, at midnight, a special train arrived at New Lambton. Three hundred Welsh miners, women and children were taken off and hurried secretly into the pitmen's empty cottages.

The next day, the starving pitmen of New Lambton were begging for their jobs back. The strike collapsed in panic. Many who saw their jobs had been given to blacklegs rushed across the Tyne to become blacklegs themselves. The union fell apart, and was washed away.

> Was there ever so slaving and slashing a trade,
> Such a trade as this terrible hewing?
> I wish I'd been born to the plough or the spade,
> To building, or baking or brewing!

The bond was gone. Pitmen could not rely on traditional agreements for their protection: but neither could they rely on their own strength. They would have to find other ways.

From the children evicted in 1844 came a generation of leaders who aimed at putting the miner's case through the press and parliament. They were the new men created by Methodism, sober and responsible, claiming their place in the new civilisation of Victorian Britain.

In 1851 Britain celebrated that new civilisation in the Great Exhibition, whose object was, according to the *Edinburgh Review*, 'to seize the living scroll of human progress, inscribed with every successive conquest of man's intellect'. George Parkinson, who had never been more than twelve miles from his native village, could not resist its pull.

He explored the exhibition and the other sights of London. The day before his return, he fell into conversation with a well-dressed gentleman. Hearing that he came from Durham, the gentleman recited what he knew of the pitmen: their great appetites, their drinking and gambling, 'a strange class of people – rough, uncultivated, with a good deal of the savage about them'. After Parkinson had discussed the various things he had seen in the British Museum and other places, his companion asked what business he was in. '"Oh sir," I said, looking steadily at him, "It is my lot to be one of those rough, uncultivated, savage miners of which you spoke as the most brutal of Her Majesty's subjects."'

The old pitmen had vanished. Only their work remained.

Monday, 25 March 1913 was Fred Thompson's first day down New Lambton pit. He was just 14. His father was a hewer; so was his grandfather, killed by a fall of stone in 1909. Fred's two elder brothers were hewers, and one day he and his younger brother would be hewers too.

On Sunday night, when he came home from the pub, Fred's father had chalked the time of his shift on the door. At 4.30 in the morning the caller came down the row, knocking up the men for the day shift. Later in the week, some of the men would be too exhausted to answer, and would 'sleep the caller', but if men failed to turn out on a Monday it was because they had drunk too much on Sunday night. Sunday was, after all, the only day off, and the Primitive Methodists had not converted the whole village. The Thompson family was Church of England. They were conventionally religious – they all went to church on Sunday morning, and Fred was expected to spend all afternoon in bible class – but they were certainly not teetotal.

At five o'clock, the boy went out with his father to join the stream of men heading for the pit. He went through the darkness into the cage, with his father and his father's 'marrer' (mate), and plunged into the warmer world below, whitewashed and lit by naked bulbs. He proudly carried the symbols of his new status, an oil lamp, a 'bait box' containing bread and jam, and his bottle of cold tea.

Once down, he had to walk over a mile along the 'main road', trudging through water between six inches and a foot in depth, and trying to spot the places where the roof had become depressed through the pressure of thousands of tons of rock. Concentrating on walking safely along the invisible floor, which had buckled in places, he caught his unprotected head two cracks on the roof.

His first job was to separate the empty coal tubs from the endless rope that drew them along the main road, and yoke them to the ponies that hauled them to the coal face where the hewers worked.

At four in the afternoon, having worked for ten hours, he started on the long trudge back to the cage. By the time he emerged, the sun was low in the sky, and he walked back home through the gloom. There, the oil lamp was lit and supper was waiting. Meat was a luxury but the family ate well with leek or onion puddings and plenty of home-made bread. His father had got home first and already eaten. Fred sat down in his dirt, as he had seen his father do all his life, and when he had eaten he stripped off his pit clothes and got into the tub in front of the fire. His father never washed his back; there was a belief among hewers that washing weakened the spine. Fred had earned two shillings.

In 1916, Fred volunteered for military service. He was a hewer by then, working an eight-hour day at the coal face. As part of Britain's industrial backbone, he was exempt from conscription, and he was under no illusions about the war. His brother had been on the Somme, and had written home, 'stop where you are Fred – they kill them out here'. But the pit itself was no joy ride. Pony drivers were killed by being crushed against the roof, hewers were in danger from falls of stone. And hewing was pure muscle work. There was certainly skill required to work the seam in the right way, but hewers still had to grip their picks so hard that their hands swelled up with bruises, and they had to urinate on them to relieve the pain and carry on working. A hewer's position in the mine was decided by lottery, and if he was lucky he would draw an easy section – but if he was unlucky the coal would be hard, and his pay would be low.

Fred decided that he would take his chances with the Army. In any case, he did not want anyone to think that he was shirking his duty. But he would not be an infantry man. On the basis of his acquaintance with pit ponies, he was accepted as a trooper.

97 A pony driver, about 1920.

Many miners went into the Army, despite the importance of coal to the war effort. In the first year of war, the number of miners fell by a fifth. This was partly due to the patriotic enthusiasm of some colliery companies; Mr Killingback, a Nottinghamshire miner, remembers his father saying that their local colliery manager 'were a man for getting them into the army'. He had set up a cannon on a dais which he declared had been captured from the Turks in Gallipoli. The local kids who dared to climb under it discovered that it was inscribed 'Made in Birmingham'.

Mr Killingback was born in 1915, and grew up in the tense and difficult atmosphere that followed the 'war to end wars'. His father worked on the pit top at Shirland Colliery, and the family lived in a colliery row about a quarter of a mile from the pit. There were two identical rows of about two hundred cottages, each with two bedrooms and a garret. There were eleven children in the family when he was born, with four more to come. They slept five to a bed, crossways.

The village lived in the shadow of its master, J. T. Todd, the

98 Hewing at a low face, 1905.

managing director of the Blackwood Colliery Company. He lived near the village, 'with a quarter mile drive up to his big house. The iron fist. Everybody was scared more or less.' J. T. Todd had a hand in everything. His favourite sport was rugby union so he imported Welsh miners to form a team. 'That caused a lot of fighting.' There was a miners' welfare club; J. T. Todd more or less ran it. The steward was one of his hirelings.

The main events in a child's life in Blackwood were the Sunday-school treat, when the scholars were given tea and taken to a field for games; and Blackwood Wakes, on the nearest Sunday to the 19th of June, when a fair was held and every family tried to lay in a barrel of beer. There was also the annual sermon at the Wesleyan Sunday-school, when every boy appeared in his new suit for the year. Social life revolved around the chapel and, for the men, the club.

The traditional division between chapel and pub became much less important in the years after the First World War, as the Working Mens' Club and Institute Union began to make an impression on mining communities. The union had been started in

1862, by the Reverend Henry Solly, as an attempt to civilise the workers by providing a social life which would draw men away from the pubs and offer them the humanising influences of comfort, a good environment, contact with a better class of people, and the opportunity to engage in educational activities. The union remained largely London-based until it began to shed this patronising approach and concentrated on encouraging clubs run by the members themselves, with the emphasis on comfort, conversation and a quiet drink. The First World War, which stimulated a genuine comradeship in the trenches, produced a generation of clubbable men, and by 1922 there were over 1,150,000 members of affiliated clubs, including about 100,000 members of the newly-formed British Legion Clubs. 'It is but in recent years that working men's clubs have become any considerable part in the social life of the wage-earner', wrote the union's general secretary in 1922.

99 Members of the Working Men's Club and Institute Union on a conducted tour of the National Gallery.

> The Clubs and their members are no worse than their fellows, but a little bit better. It is the aim of the Union to speed this bettering, to see each Club-House high above and a constant example to the daily habitation of the workman. It is its aim to see the members in demeanour, in bearing, in tolerance and true courtesy, gentlemen who will leaven democracy with a new spirit, who will make manliness no enemy of courtesy, discipline no enemy to freedom, strength and depth of view no enemy of tolerance or free debate . . . it is not always an easy task . . . . 'Do you want to make the place a Chapel?' said a Durham miner to his President who had rebuked him for violence of language. 'No!' was the reply; '*just a club!*'

The Blackwood Club did not turn its members into gentle and peace loving men: Pitched battles with a neighbouring village were ended, not by moral reform, but by slum clearance. But it did shift the emphasis of trade unionism organisation away from the chapel, by providing an alternative meeting place that did not have the heavy drinking and rowdy traditions of the pub.

Everyone in the Killingback family had to work if they could: Mr Killingback's mother not only fed a large family and did all the washing for her family of miners, but used to go out wallpapering and take in sewing.

Mr Killingback's own first job was helping the butcher, after school and during the holidays. Most of the village food came from the co-op at the end of the row, but meat was freshly slaughtered by the butcher:

> I helped him to kill. Beast, pigs and sheep. I regretted it since I grew up. I didn't know it was cruel at the time. With beasts, they put a rope around the face and dragged them struggling to the slaughter house. They tied the rope to a ring in the floor. Then they used to poleaxe them, then shove a yard-long pole through the head. I got 1*s*. 2*d*. I gave my mother 1*s*. – I regretted that.

There was never enough money in the house. A brief post-war boom in demand for coal had been followed by a growing depression. The Versailles Treaty, which set out to 'make the Germans pay' for the war, obliged them to produce coal under conditions of near slavery, and cheap coal was also pouring across the Atlantic from America. A long lockout in 1921 ended with a fall in wages, so that at the end of that year miners' real wages were over 30 per cent lower than in 1914. It was rare for a miner to work a full week. Every Friday night the Killingback home was the scene of a blazing row that was rooted in the tension of poverty.

There was a brief improvement in miners' wages in 1923, when the French took over the Ruhr, and there was a collapse of German coal production, but by 1925 bad times were back. The coal owners demanded, as they always did in bad times, longer hours and lower wages. The miners appealed to the Trades Union Congress for support, and the government averted an immediate crisis by providing a temporary subsidy for the industry. But when the subsidy ran out, nothing had changed. On 1 May 1926 the miners were locked out. The TUC demanded that the government should help them, and when negotiations with the government broke down the TUC called a general strike. The strike was a nine days wonder. The TUC leaders were alarmed by the forces they had unleashed, and called the whole thing off on 12 May. But the miners fought on.

At Blackwood, the peace was kept by two policemen billeted at the butcher's house. They broke up the knots of men who congregated in the rows, or at colliery gates. Month after month the men marched begging from town to town, cadging money for soup kitchens. At school, boots were occasionally available. Since there were never enough to go round, they were put in a heap and the children were told to scramble for them.

At New Lambton, where Fred Thompson was a hewer once more, some of the men tried to form a 'non-political union' to get back to work. They began blacklegging. The pressures on family men were almost unbearable. Jack Davidson, who wrote a *History of the Northumberland Miners*, included his own childhood memory of the strike:

> Together with my friend Andrew Hall, also aged four years, we left the soup kitchen still feeling hungry, so we explored my mother's pantry. Save for some bread and an opened tin of condensed milk on the top shelf, it was bare. As we were both small we struggled and dragged what seemed then an exceedingly heavy chair into the pantry. With his assistance I reached the tin of condensed milk and though we only intended to take one or two spoonfuls, before we realised it we had consumed the lot. When we realised our 'crime' we ran out of the house leaving behind all the evidence of our raid in the pantry. Later that evening when I admitted my act to my mother and father instead of being chastised I was amazed to see my mother crying and my father with tears in his eyes; the only time I ever saw my father in tears.

The miners held out to November. Then they accepted the coal-owners terms: longer hours, and a cut in pay. Mr Killingback worked his first shift in 1929. He received just ninepence more than Fred Thompson had done in 1913. There was a constant bitter tension between the men and the management. A shift normally ended with the men bringing the full tubs of coal back to the pithead; the first job of the new shift was to ride them, empty, to the coal face. But if a shift was ending early, the men were never told. The manager waited until the tubs were emptied and back at the face before shouting 'Loose-all' and turning the men out. They had worked a little more than they were paid for, and had a long walk back.

When the under-manager at Blackwood retired, he carried on living in the village, but no one would talk to him. He spent the rest of his life in miserable isolation.

The miner's life began to change in the 1930s, when pit-head baths and coal-cutting machines began to appear in significant numbers. When a man could change out of his working clothes at the pit-head, and come home clean and bathed, his house was transformed. Pit-head baths came in very gradually, and even when they were available not all men could afford to use them, for there was often a charge. But where they were used, they enabled mining families to live the kind of ordinary domestic life that other workers had taken for granted for generations.

The other great change, the introduction of coal-cutting machines, came even more erratically. There were machine cutters in use before the start of the century, and when Fred Thompson started work in 1913, 8 per cent of the country's coal was mechanically cut. But it took ten years for that percentage to double, and another eight years for it to double again.

The machines did not make mining any safer: Fred Thompson

100 Before the coming of pit-head baths, miners washed at home. Where there were many boys in one house on different shifts, the pitman's wife would be preparing food and hot water all day and all night, cat-napping in her chair. There were women who only got to bed once a week, on Sunday afternoon.

101 (*left*) With clothes full of coal-dust to be beaten and washed, the home was an extension of the mine.

102 (*right*) A pit-head baths canteen in the 1930s. There were few places like this before the 1950s, where a miner could leave his pit clothes, shower, dress in clean clothes and have a pint of milk to clear the dust from his throat before going home.

was lamed operating one, and there were hideous accidents in which men were literally chopped to pieces. Miners were frightened, too, by the noise of the machine for it cut them off from the subtle pattern of creaks and groans that would tell them if the props were under too much pressure and likely to collapse, or a seam was about to slip. Suddenly the finely-tuned senses which kept them alive were blanketed. But the machines did mean that mining was no longer tied to the strength of a hewer's back. Between 1927 and 1938 the proportion of machine-cut coal rose from less than 25 to 60 per cent of all coal produced. In pits where mechanical cutting was introduced productivity doubled. Since pay was traditionally linked to the amount of coal cut, this was very welcome. Miners' wages had fallen more than any other group of workers in the late 1920s. By 1938, on average, they had nearly caught up with the rest.

But there was no great demand for the coal produced: in 1939, total production was still lower than in 1927. The improvement in efficiency meant fewer miners, not more coal. A quarter of the men who had jobs in the mines in 1927 had lost them by 1938. 'They always had a surplus of men at the colliery', said Mr Killingback. 'They wanted that surplus to keep things running smoothly.' If you were lucky enough to be working, you did not make trouble.

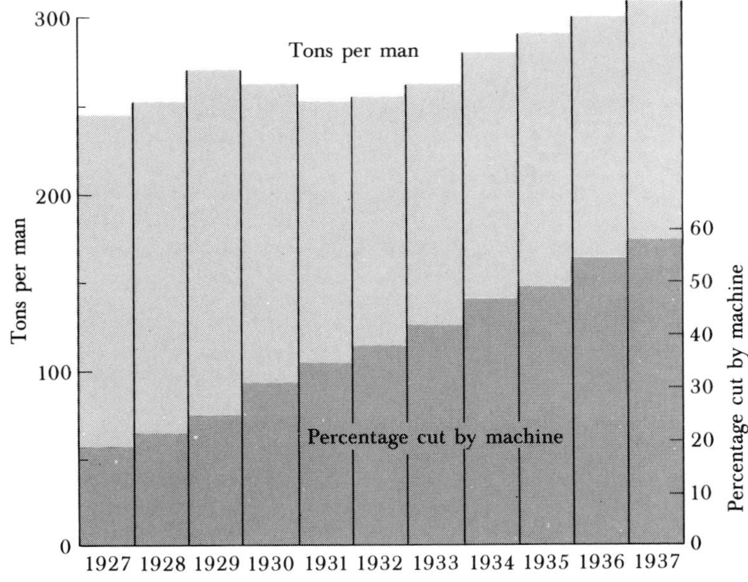

Figure 9 Productivity and the introduction of machine cutting.

The union at Blackwood's met in the miner's welfare, under the eye of J. T. Todd or his steward. For men like Mr Killingback, the union was less significant for its role in the running of the mine, than in the possibility it offered of an education and a career. There was, after all, no other way out of the mine, except on a stretcher:

> You're in a situation and you couldn't get out of it. Politics come to me in 1936, when I was 21. I remember reading G. D. H. Cole's *Short History of the British Working Class.* I loved talking politics – Communistic, not pit – and I really tried to get on in the union. I went to weekend schools, two-week schools, selection schools for day release, but I never made it. I really tried, but I never made it.

In 1938 he married: like most miners, he married a miner's daughter. He was offered a loan of £1,000 to buy a house, but seeing no possibility of repaying the money, he turned it down. He felt trapped. There was no accommodation available in the colliery houses, so he went to live with his brother in a neighbouring pit village. Blackwood's did offer him a house, but it was on a row right by the pit, squalid and ancient, covered in thick yellow smoke from the coke ovens. Eventually he found a small old cottage which he was allowed to take for five shillings and sixpence a week.

In 1939 came war and work; the country needed all the coal it could get, and suddenly there were too few miners instead of too many. Every male national service conscript whose number ended in nine was sent to work down a mine. This was still not enough, and so men whose number ended in zero were also drafted. These 'Bevin boys' were sent into isolated, closed communities, which still retained their nineteenth-century character in many ways. Geoffrey Keen was a factory worker from Ealing, and at 19 he was drafted into Kibblesworth Colliery, about five miles from New Lambton:

> In the village there were four centres of social life: the Plough Inn, the Colliery Welfare and the two Methodist Chapels facing each other across the main road. One could not help thinking about the hymn 'We are not divided, all one body we'. If by chance the two chapels turned out on Sunday at the same time the two congregations would walk as far as possible on the opposite sides of the road until they couldn't avoid crossing. There was considerable rivalry between the two chapels to win the allegiance of the new lads. I joined the choir at the Primitive Methodist Chapel where the spirit was absolutely amazing. The last bus left Newcastle at 9.00 p.m. and therefore people relied upon amusements within the village. There was a youth club at the Chapel but every door was open in the village (certainly every door belonging to a member of the primitive Chapel) and we could wander in and out. We had some great evenings of music and singing.

The government took control of the mines, as it had done in the previous war, but this time there was no going back to the system of private management. Nationalisation had been a goal of the union since the First World War, and the Labour government elected in 1945 was committed to it. 1 January 1947 was 'Vesting Day', when the coal industry, amid much official jubilation, was made the property of the National Coal Board.

Among ordinary miners, the change was not seen with total enthusiasm. The management did not change at many pits: the old staff remained in charge. A vast army of office workers were required to deal with the administration of the industry, and there were plenty of miners who felt resentful at their existence.

But the attitude of management changed on many issues. When Mr Killingback was down the mine before nationalisation, they struck a fault. The seam had slipped fourteen feet, and the mine had to be extended down to the new level. Everyone was sent home for three weeks – without pay. If that happened after nationalisation, everyone was paid. 'J. T. Todd would have turned in his grave.' There were paid holidays, and there was a new emphasis on safety, with steel supports and protective helmets. But the basic structure of a man's working life was unchanged: after earning good money on the coal face, he could expect old age, injury or coal dust to force him up to a low-paid surface job for his later years. And the pressure for efficiency meant that still fewer men were needed.

Fred Thompson's pit at New Lambton was closed, in the interests of efficiency, in 1963. New Lambton village was rebuilt with comfortable modern bungalows, but the pitmen were made redundant or, if they were young enough, moved to other collieries: Fred Thompson ended his working life as a 'lollipop man'.

Blackwood's too, is shut. Between 1965 and 1971, 229 British pits were closed down. Increasing use was made of automated machinery in the pits that stayed open. Mr Killingback's last job in the pit was as a technician, doing face repairs on hydraulic chocks – in his opinion the best job he ever had. It was utterly different from the hard slog of hewing – Fred Thompson says he wouldn't know pit work now.

The surviving mining communities are quieter, more domesticated places than they were when Mr Thompson and Mr Killingback started work. In their eyes, at least, the traditional pursuits still survived among the pitmen. 'They sup more now – can afford to', according to Mr Thompson. 'When you'd got a tanner and put it on horses it went down – now you put a pound on and it goes down just the same', says Mr Killingback.

But domestication has brought an end to other aspects of community life. When I went to New Lambton the Primitive Methodist Chapel was deserted and up for sale. The annual sermon at the Wesleyan Sunday-school in Blackwood is no longer a major social event. The tradition of earnest respectability has passed away.

Malcolm Bullough's Aunt Emily worked down the pit. Malcolm Bullough puts girders up at Ellington Colliery in Northumberland. He spoke with force, his eyes behind heavy glasses glaring, and wildly bristling eyebrows.

When I protested that women did not work in pits, I was firmly corrected. 'Them days they did. Those days they did. I'm goin' back a long time, ye knaa'. He was going back 140 years.

His grandfather came from Lancashire, with all his brothers, to work in the Northumberland coalfield. Aunt Emily was married to one of the brothers, Harry. She must have been born in the 1830s, and been older than Harry, for he lived long enough to tell his small great-nephew about her. 'She actually worked down a pit, me Auntie Emily'. There were indeed young girls working as trappers in the Lancashire mines until 1842.

In 1979, as I sat talking to three Ellington men in a comfortable living-room on a modern estate, the ghost of Aunt Emily was summoned to give evidence of the way miners have been made to suffer. Other ghosts, too. 'Oh, the old mine-owners treated us terrible. There was one man . . .' and I was given his name, his address, and the whole story of how he had walked five miles from a teetotal pit to get a drink, and had been seen staggering by the mine-owner's wife as she passed him on the road. When he got home he found his furniture dumped out in the street. He had been sacked and evicted. Every detail was given except the date. The only clue was that she passed him in a horse-drawn carriage.

The subject was the 1972 strike, the first national miner's strike since 1926. It was a strike that forged new instruments of union power: mass picketing, where over a thousand men at a time manned the picket line to physically block premises and confront the police with a show of force; flying pickets, sent out like commandos to stop the movement of coal wherever it occurred; 'secondary' picketing of premises owned by users of the coal, such as power stations. It was also a strike that demonstrated a solidarity between unions that had been missing in 1926: this time, the unions that were called on for help stayed on strike until the miners were satisfied.

We talked about the frustrations that had built up by 1972: about the power-loading agreement of 1966, which gave every miner a fixed daily wage, so that his income no longer depended on his skill and his luck in drawing a good coal face in the cavil, the lottery:

> As soon as ye got a good cavil, ye went to the store and ye got a suit and shorts and different things, ye knaa, and all the bairns got shoes. Now the next quarter ye got a bad cavil: that was when the bill came in, and ye had a job to pay that bill at times.

Under the power-loading agreement, a miner's income became a nationally negotiated weekly wage; it no longer depended on the luck of the draw. But from being a pieceworker, 'a man for hisself', he became a wage-earner, dependent on the strength of the union.

We talked about the effect of the agreement on the sense of community: how miners who had handed their skills and understanding on from one generation to another felt devalued by a weekly wage – a 'datal wage', they called it, a wage for office workers and men on light surface jobs. Neither skill nor effort was rewarded: 'It made a lot of lazy men'.

> In the piecework days a man had a good pride in his work. In my day, when I learned, there was na such thing as a training unit, ye learned the hard way. But if ye were interested in the job, ye took notice of what the older men told you. When ye went at the face they

used to give ye the information what they had learned. And that was the mining community passing information down, all the time. I can remember when I first started at the pit, one day, I was emptying me bottle of water out. And this old gentleman, he come up and he tapped us on the shoulder, he says, 'Son, never do that.' I says, 'What do ye mean?' He says, 'Emptying your water out.' I says, 'What for?' He says, 'You should never do that till ye get to bank [out of the pit]. You're all reet here, but ye never knaa what happens from here to getting in the shaft. Ye could be barred in, roof cave in, anything. You might be glad of that water.' You used to learn a lot off old pitmen – an old pitman, ye knaa, he used to tak a pride in his work. And that was the community of the olden days. PLA (the power-loading agreement) changed it. With the datal wage they're not learning. You used to cut the corners, ye knaa, ye would learn, off of old men, showing ye a trick. Since the PLA's come in, that atmosphere, some men, it's died.

There were other effects too, which the miners had not understood when they voted for the extra money the agreement represented: the closure of many small pits, destroying those communities, and the transfer of the men into larger pits, where they come for each shift in fleets of buses, so that even the pits that are open have their closeness broken. At the giant pit in South Shields, which runs five miles out under the North Sea, they call the men bussed in from Durham villages 'hillbillies', over-dramatising the

Figure 10 Pit closures in the north-east, 1957–78.

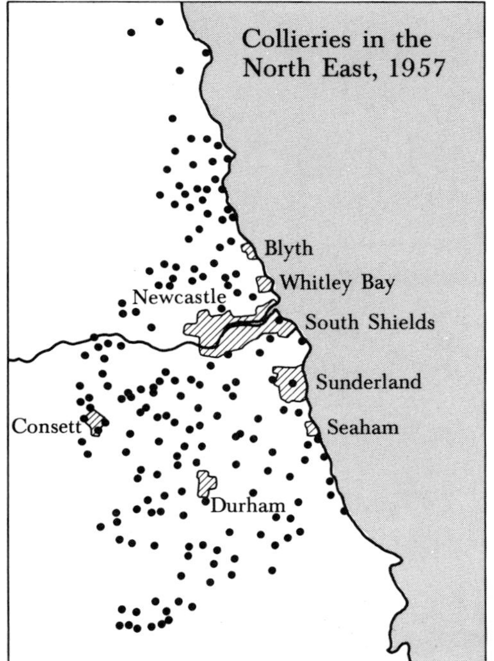

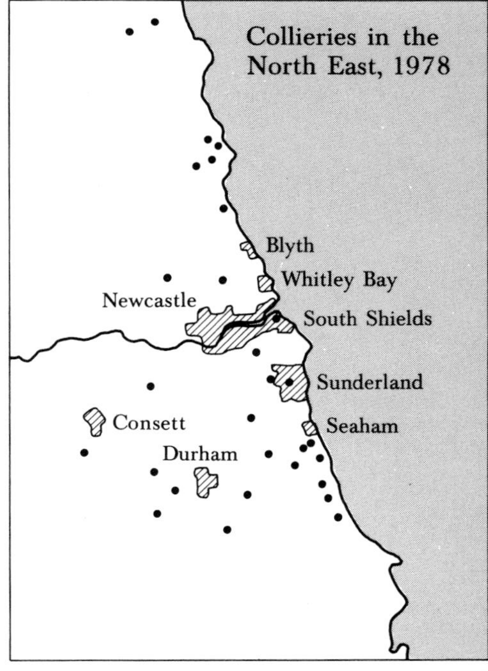

103 The need for water. In 1880 there was an explosion at Seaham. This empty water bottle was found with one of the pitmen who died entombed. The message, scratched on the tin with a nail, reads: 'Dear Margaret, There was 40 of us altogether at 7 a.m. Some was singing hymns, but my thoughts was on my little Michael that him and I would meet in heaven at the same time. Oh Dear Wife, God save you and the children, and pray for me. . . . Dear wife Farewell. My last thoughts are about you and the children. Be sure and learn the children to pray for me. Oh what an awful position we are in. Michael Smith, 54 Henry Street.' From *Explosions in Coal Mines*, W. N. and J. B. Atkinson, 1886.

104 A modern coal-face: a radio controlled shearer, with automatic hydraulic props above and a conveyor belt below.

isolation and simplicity of the communities from which they are brought. The Durham men respond by referring to the men from South Shields as 'sand-dancers', sharp sophisticates, with their highly mechanised pit, big-town entertainments and their shiftless habit of spending part of their working lives at sea.

In place of the spirit of community came the spirit of solidarity. The miners had been turned into industrial workers, and when their relative position in the pay-league fell they showed industrial workers what conflict could be. For with them on the picket lines stood the ghosts from their villages. When Malcolm Bullough stood howling at the mine deputies who tried to break through the picket lines to go to work in the pit, he was howling for Aunt Emily and the uncles and brother who died coughing their lungs out, at the mercy of the mine-owners. When Tommy Chester helped to organise picket shifts, he was doing it for 'hisself' and his 'marrers', and also for all the dead men who had been obliged to watch their children going hungry through the strike of 1926, for nothing at all. 'It'll nivver be forgotten. It'll always pass on. Nivver be forgotten. I've got a feeling in me mind, ye knaa, history will repeat itself. Hardship's got to come.'

The miners are living through the early history of industrialisation in our own generation. Their work has only just been fully mechanised – some pits still use picks and ponies. Their village communities are only now being broken up, and the 'olden days' are within the memory of men still at work. In their own lifetimes, they are being transformed from individual workers in a communal task, into wage-earners tied together by the solidarity of national mass unionism.

I have not met a single miner in the northern coalfield who would cheerfully send his son down the pit:

> I wouldn't want my son to suffer what I've had to suffer. Ye knaa what I mean. In wour pit we're lucky, just now we're on high seams. But I remember seams two feet high, and working lying in four inches of water, and things like that.

But the same man who said that, had a moment earlier been worrying about the decline of the industry:

> It doesn't matter if it's a Tory or Labour government, if they don't watch what they're doing we're going to hev no miners left. For the simple reason they're taking no influx of young lads; 'cause it's a job ye've got to train from being a young lad.

The miners' protests are compounded of many grievances: they are leaving one world and entering another, and it is a painful process. As Britain stumbles into the age of the micro-chip, the miners are seeing their communities overthrown by the industrial revolution.

References

Chapter 1 LABOURERS

1 *The Annual Register*, 1 March 1767.
2 D. Davies, *The Case of the Labourers in Husbandry* (Bath, 1795), p. 57.
3 W. H. Hudson, *A Shepherd's Life* (London, 1910), p. 133.
4 Wiltshire Record Office, WRO 413/23.
5 P. Lecount, *History of the Railway Connecting London and Birmingham* (London, 1839), p. 27.
6 H. Williams, *History of Watford, and Trade Directory* (London, 1884), p. 112.
7 W. Thorne, *My Life's Battles* (London, 1925), p. 28.
8 T. C. Thomas, *The War Diary of the 58th Labour Company* (Birmingham, no date), chapter 2.
9 F. P. Crozier, *A Brass Hat in No-Man's-Land* (London, 1930), pp. 108, 110.
10 Thomas, *War Diary*, chapter 5.

Chapter 2 SERVANTS

1 J. Macdonald, *Travels*, ed. J. Beresford (London, 1927), p. 12.
2 J. Hanaway, *Eight Letters to His Grace the Duke of* —— (1760).
3 J. O'Keefe, *Recollections* (London, 1826), vol. 1, p. 161.
4 *The Scots Magazine*, January 1760.
5 *London Chronicle*, 1761.
6 *Annual Register*, 11 May 1764.
7 Mrs John Sandford, *Female Improvement* (London, 1836), p. 141.
8 Leigh Hunt, 'The Maid Servant', in *Essays* (London, 1891), p. 60.
9 *Finchley Manual of Industry No. III, Household Work*, Finchley National and Industrial Schools (Middlesex, 1849), p. 23.
10 V. M. Firth, *The Psychology of the Servant Problem* (London, 1925), p. 29.
11 'Fine Ladies and Good Housewives', in *Once a Week*, 56, 1869.

Chapter 4 FACTORY HANDS

1 James Kay, *Moral and Physical Conditions of the Operatives Employed in the Cotton Manufacture in England* (Manchester, 1832), p. 24.
2 A. Ure, *The Cotton Manufactures of Great Britain* (1836), vol. 1, pp. 191, 193.
3 R. Mather, *Impartial Representation of the Case of the Poor Cotton Spinners in Lancs.* (London, 1780), p. 5.
4 *Leeds Mercury*, 15 January 1803.
5 Letter in *The Examiner*, 26 February 1832.

Chapter 5 SEAMEN

1 S. Leech, *Thirty Years from Home* (Boston, Mass., 1843), p. 40.
2 W. Richardson, *A Mariner of England 1780–1819*, ed. Spencer Childers (1908), p. 138.

3 *Five Naval Journals*, ed. H. G. Thursfield, Naval Record Society, vol. 91 (London, 1952), p. 159.

4 W. S. Lindsay, *History of Merchant Shipping* (London, 1874), vol. II, p. 538.

Chapter 6 IMMIGRANTS

1 L. Faucher, *Manchester in 1844*, trans. J. P. Culverwell (London and Manchester, 1844), p. 28 n.

2 F. Engels, *The Condition of the Working Class in England*, trans. and ed. W. O. Henderson and F. Chaloner (Oxford, 1958), p. 92.

3 *Second Report on the State of Large Towns* (1845), Appendix, Part II, p. 134.

4 J. Mitchel, *The Last Conquest of Ireland (Perhaps)* (New York, 1873), p. 247.

5 Maurice Samuel, *The World of Sholem Aleichem* (New York, 1943), pp. 26–7.

6 Dr George M. Price, 'Memoir', American Jewish Historical Association, December 1950, p. 101.

7 Ha Melez, XXII, 155, 1856, quoted in Lloyd P. Gartner, *The Jewish Immigrant* (London, 1960).

Chapter 8 MINERS

1 J. Holland, *Fossil Fuel*, 2nd edn (London, 1841), p. 298.

A Note on Sources

(Place of publication is London except where otherwise stated.)

Chapter 1 LABOURERS

1

I chose Stanwell because J. L. and B. Hammond used it as an example in their celebrated – and now largely 'discredited' – work, *The Village Labourer* (1911):

> The cottagers [they wrote] had to fence their allotments or forfeit them. Anybody who glances at an award will understand what this meant. It is easy, for example, to imagine what happened under this provision to the following cottagers at Stanwell . . . J. and F. Ride . . . Ann Higgs . . . R. Ride . . . Thomas King.

The sources to show what happened are now in the Greater London Record Office (Middlesex Records): a terrier of 1748, the parish registers and court books, the poor rate assessments, a number of deeds relating to Gibbons's and Hill's purchases and details of Gibbons's debts, the enclosure award in 1789 and a terrier of 1796. Voting details for 1768 are in the Middlesex Poll Book, and details of the Gibbons family are from historical notes, also in the Middlesex Records.

For a short, sharp statement of the contrary view to that taken here, that is, arguing that small farmers were not much affected by the enclosure movement and that the 'agricultural revolution' is something of a myth, see G. E. Mingay, *Enclosure and the Small Farmer in the Age of the Industrial Revolution* (1968). Mingay defines a 'small farmer' as one with between twenty and one hundred acres. Two-thirds of Stanwell's farmers held less than twenty acres in 1748 (i.e., of twenty-nine people holding over two acres, seventeen had less than twenty acres, and fourteen had less than ten acres). It was these very small arable occupiers whose fortunes were dramatically changed during the rest of the century.

For enclosures generally, I relied on W. E. Tate, *The English Village Community and the Enclosure Movement* (1967), and for the Wilkes election, on G. Rudé, *Wilkes and Liberty* (1962).

2

The story of the Tisbury riot is taken from *The Times* (3 November 1830–8 January 1831), Home Office papers (HO 40/27 and 52/11) and 'Machine-breaking riots at Pyt House Farm' in the *Wiltshire Archaeological Society Magazine* (XLVII, December 1936). I am particularly grateful to R. H. Jackson for his guidance on additional sources, including H. Graham's *Annals of the Yeomanry Cavalry of Wiltshire* (1886) and his own pamphlet for the Tisbury Local History Society, *Some Glimpses of The West Tisbury Story* (1975).

I gathered information on threshing machines from F. Atkinson, 'The horse as a source of rotary power', *Transactions Newcomen Society* (XXXIII, 1960–61); E. J. T. Collins 'Diffusion of the threshing machine in Britain 1790–1880', in *Tools and Tillage* (2, i, 1972); Stuart Macdonald, 'The progress of the early threshing machine', *Agricultural History Review* (23, 1975), and from a rather talmudic argument between Fox and Macdonald in *Agricultural History Review* (26, 1978), where they argue over just how many is many (Fox, 'The spread of the threshing machine in central Southern England'; Macdonald, 'Further progress with the early threshing machine: a rejoinder').

The central work on the Swing riots is *Captain Swing*, by E. J. Hobsbawm and G. Rudé (1969).

3

I am grateful to C. W. Clark, of Winchmore School, for guiding me to the sources for the Russell Wood disaster: *The Times* (12 November 1835) and the *County Press* (25 July, and 29 August 1835, 23 July 1836). 'Dandy Dick's' story was published as '*Navvies as they used to be*', in *Household Words* (21 June 1856).

Peter Lecount's account of building the railway was published in 1839, as the *History of the Railway Connecting London and Birmingham*. The best general account of navvies is *The Railway Navvies* by T. Coleman (1965).

There is interesting material on the composition of a later workforce in J. A. Patmore, 'A navvy gang of 1851', *Journal of Transport History* (vol. 5, no. 3, May 1962). H. Williams's recollections were published in his *History of Watford* (1884).

4

Will Thorne's autobiography, *My Life's Battles*, was published in 1925. Thorne became general secretary of the TUC, and then its chairman, as well as becoming a Labour MP in 1906. There is a valuable account of tramping labourers in 'Comers and goers', an essay by Raphael Samuel in H. J. Dyos and H. Woolf (eds), *The Victorian City: Images and Realities* (vol. 1, 1973). The structure of the Victorian building industry is discussed in P. W. Kingsford, *Builders and Building Workers* (1973) and J. Summerson, *The London Building World of the 1860s* (1973). The rebuilding of Birmingham is described in A. Briggs, *History of Birmingham* (vol. 2, 1952), and in J. L. Macmorran, *Municipal Public Works and Planning in Birmingham 1852–1972* (1973). There is an account of the Gasworkers' and General Labourers' Union in H. Pelling, *A History of British Trade Unionism* (1963).

5

There has been no study, so far as I know, of labour companies and battalions in the First World War.

Mrs Garnett's conversation with the navvy is mentioned in Coleman, *The Railway Navvies*. The lecture on 'The origin of labour in the Great War' was by Brevet-Colonel E. Gibb, and was published in the R.A.S.C. *Quarterly*, in July 1923. The simulation of trench warfare, described by Bruce Bairnsfather, is quoted in Charles Messenger, *Trench Fighting 1914–18* (1972). Details of the work of a forward battalion are vividly illustrated in J. L. Jack, *General Jack's Diary 1914–18* (1964). The story of the Manchester clay kickers is in A. Barrie, *War Underground* (1961) and in W. Grant Grieve and B. Newman, *Tunnellers* (1936). The war diary of the 58th Labour Company was published as *With a Labour Company in France* by T. C. Thomas. Brigadier Crozier is quoted in T. Wintringham, *Mutiny* (1936), which also discusses the demonstrations of 1919. Labour battalion casualties are mentioned in *G.H.Q. (Montreuil)* by 'G.S.O.' (1920). The use of Chinese labour by the British Army is examined in an unpublished PhD dissertation by N. J. Griffin of the University of Oklahoma (1973). *The Men Who Tidy Up* was published in 1917.

Chapter 2 SERVANTS

1

The most important modern work on eighteenth-century servants is J. J. Hecht, *The Domestic Servant Class in Eighteenth-Century England* (1956). John Macdonald's *Travels* were edited by J. Beresford and published in 1927. Hanaway's campaigning pamphlets were *Eight Letters to His Grace the Duke of——, on the Custom of Vails-Giving in England* (1760), and (under the alias of T. Trueman), *The Sentiments and Advice of Thomas Trueman* (1760). J. Townley's *High Life Below Stairs* was published in 1768.

2

The most useful modern book is P. Horn, *The Rise and Fall of the Victorian Servant* (1975). There is also valuable material extracted in F. E. Huggett, *Life Below Stairs* (1977), and F. Dawes *Not in Front of the Servants* (1973). I have relied on Pamela Horn's book for the quotations from Hannah Culliwick's diaries, which are in the Munby Collection at Trinity College, Cambridge. Rose Allen's *Autobiography* was published in 1847; Helen Forrester's, under the title *Twopence to Cross the Mersey*, in 1974; I am grateful to Miss J. Griffiths, of the BBC, for drawing my attention to this work. *A Short Account of the Progress of the National and Industrial Schools* was published in 1852; the four textbooks written for the school, the *Finchley Manuals of Industry (Cooking, Gardening, Household Work* and *Plain Needlework)* were written between 1848 and 1852.

3

Statistics on the numerical decline of domestic servants are taken from M. Ebery and B. Preston, *Domestic Service in Late-Victorian and Edwardian England, 1872–1914* (1976), as is the quotation from 'Once a Week'. The bulk of the story is told in Horn, *The Rise and Fall of the Victorian Servant*. Winifred Foley's reminiscences were published in *Useful Toil*, ed. J. Burnett (1974): Celia Fremlin's anthropological explorations were published in 1940 as *The Seven Chars of Chelsea*. The owner of the domestic employment agency quoted is W. A. Johnson, *The Servant Problem* (1922).

Chapter 3 SOLDIERS

1

The most important sources are the autobiographies of the men concerned: *Memoirs of the Extraordinary Military Career of John Shipp, late a Lieutenant in His Majesty's 87th Regiment* (1829, republished in an abridged form as *Paths of Glory*, 1969); *Narrative of the Eventful Life of Thomas Jackson, late Sergeant of the Coldstream Guards* (Birmingham, 1847), and Thomas Morris's *Recollections of Military Service* (1845, reprinted, ed. Brigadier P. Young, 1967). The Birmingham riot is reported in *The Times* (31 October, 1 and 2 November 1816). A great variety of autobiographical extracts are reprinted in J. Palmer (ed.), *The Rambling Soldier* (1977). Useful secondary sources are: H. de Watteville, *The British Soldier* (1954); J. R. Western, *The English Militia in the Eighteenth Century* (1965); J. Haswell, *The British Army, a Concise History* (1975); J. Laffin, *Tommy Atkins, the Story of the English Soldier* (1966); C. Barnett, *Britain and Her Army 1509–1970* (1970); A. Brett-James, *The British Soldier in the Napoleonic Wars, 1793–1815* (1970); Sir J. Fortescue, *A History of the British Army* (13 vols, 1899–1930).

2

A. G. F. Griffith's *Fifty Years of Public Service* was published in 1904. Timothy Gowing told his story in *A Soldier's Experience, or a Voice From The Ranks* (1883). Other contemporary material I used on the war came from Francis J. Duberly's *Journal Kept During the Russian War* (1855), and H. Clifford's *Letters and Sketches from the Crimea* (1956). Sergeant J. MacMullen published his analysis of recruits in *Camp and Barack Room; or, the British Army as it is* (1846). Of the many books on the Crimea war, I found the following particularly helpful: Dennis Judd, *Someone Has Blundered* (1975); R. L. V. Ffrench-Blake, *The Crimean War* (1971); C. Woodham Smith, *The Reason Why* (1953); P. Gibbs, *Crimean Blunder* (1960); and C. Hibbert, *The Destruction of Lord Raglan* (1961) – this is a joy to read.

3

Quotations are from: William Robertson, *From Private to Field-Marshal* (1921); John Baynes, *Morale* (1967); George Coppard, *With a Machine Gun to Cambrai* (1969); A. E. Ashworth, 'The sociology of trench warfare 1914–18' in the *British Journal of Sociology* (December 1968). Other books referred to include: Victor B. Carter, *Soldier True* (1963); Alan Lloyd, *The War in the Trenches* (1976); Martin Middlebrook, *The First Day of the Somme* (1971) and A. R. Skelley, *The Victorian Army at Home* (1977).

4

I am grateful to the officers and members of the East Finchley Branch of the British Legion for their help with this section. Details of army life are from Ian Hay, *The King's Service* (1939), Correlli Barnett, *Britain and Her*

Army 1509–1970 (1970), John Laffin, *Tommy Atkins* (1966) and Jock Haswell, *The British Army* (1975). Wingate's war is described in D. Halley, *With Wingate in Burma* (1944), and in the official history, S. W. Kirby, *The War Against Japan* (vol. 3, 1961). Ian Hay's *Arms and the Men* (1950) also proved a useful source.

Chapter 4 FACTORY HANDS

1

Robert Blincoe's story was first published in 1828. The man who wrote it up, J. Brown, a journalist campaigning against white slavery, had committed suicide in 1825. Blincoe's *Memoir* was reprinted in 1977 by Caliban Books, Sussex. S. D. Chapman, in *Early Factory Masters* (1967), makes a long attack on Blincoe's account of Litton, claiming that it is melodramatic and unreliable. He also defends Needham:

> Cruel punishments to children were not unusual in the eighteenth century, and two of those described in such horrific detail in the *Memoir* were, in fact, advocated by progressive educationists – notably Lancaster – at the beginning of the last century. Lancaster worked out an elaborate code of rewards and punishments, among which was 'the Log' a piece of wood weighing 4–6 lb, which was fixed to the neck of the child guilty of his (or her) first talking offence. On the least motion one way or another the log operated as a dead weight on the neck. Needham clearly tried to copy this progressive idea of the age. More serious offences found their appropriate punishment in the Lancastrian code: handcuffs, the 'caravan', pillory and stocks, and 'the cage'. The latter was a sack or basket in which more serious offenders were suspended from the ceiling. Needham clearly borrowed this idea, too, though his children are alleged to have been suspended by their arms over the machines.

Chapman also maintains that Litton Mill was atypical, starved of cash and financially unsound. Evidence given to parliamentary committees in 1816 and 1832, however, shows that similar conditions existed in some other mills, and it is significant, when one talks of financial soundness, that Needham stayed in business at Litton Mill while Messrs Lamberts of Lowdham Mill, and 'philanthropic' owners such as Oldknow at Stockport, and Davidson and Hawksley at Arnold, did not.

The indenture of apprenticeship quoted is between William Selman, husbandman, his son Richard, and Thomas Stokes, broadweaver of Wiltshire, signed in 1705. It is taken from P. Laslett, *The World We Have Lost* (1971). Details of Cuckney Mill from Chapman. Other useful works are J. L. and Barbara Hammond, *The Town Labourer* (1917) and their *The Skilled Labourer* (1919); M. I. Thomis, *The Town Labourer and the Industrial Revolution* (1974); W. English, *The Textile Industry* (1969); G. Unwin, *Samuel Oldknow and the Arkwrights* (1968).

2

The principal sources are by Frank Peel: *The Rising of the Luddites* (2nd edn, 1888, reprinted 1968), and *Spen Valley Past and Present* (1893). A modern work is M. Thomis, *The Luddites: Machine-Breaking in Regency England* (Newton Abbot, 1975). There is also much useful material in the Hammonds' *The Skilled Labourer* (1919); E. J. Hobsbawm, *Labouring Men* (1964); W. B. Crump, *The Leeds Woollen Industry* (1931), and, of course, E. P. Thompson, *The Making of the English Working Class*, which includes a careful study of the Luddites. The evidence of the Luddites to the examining magistrate is in the Public Record Office under KB/8/91, and HO/42 contains correspondence to the Home Office about the attack on Cartwright's mill. The story of the attack is told in Charlotte Brontë's novel *Shirley*, with characters very directly based on real life.

3

Reach's account of Manchester was edited by C. Aspin and published in 1972 as *Manchester and the Textile District in 1849*. Conditions of women workers are described in I. Pinchbeck, *Women Workers and the Industrial Revolution* (1930), W. F. Neff, *Victorian Working Women* (1929), and M. Hewett, *Wives and Mothers in Victorian Industry* (1958). Frank Peel's reminiscences are from *The Risings of the Luddites*.

The Chartist leaders were tried (and acquitted) for their alleged 'plot', and Fergus O'Connor's account of the trial (1843), includes interesting material from a central figure, Richard Pilling, who was a handloom weaver for twenty years and a factory hand for ten.

The uprising is examined in G. Kitson Clark, 'Hunger and politics in 1842', *Journal of Modern History* (vol. 15, no. 4) and A. G. Rose, 'The Plug Plot riots of 1842 in Lancashire and Cheshire', *Transactions of the Lancashire and Cheshire Antiquaries Society* (vol. 68, 1957), as well as in Thompson, *The Making of the English Working Class*. Much first-hand description, with letters from factory hands, is in the Public Record Office in boxes HO/45/249 A, B and C.

4

My principal sources of detailed information on Sam Page and the gun trade were *The Workers' Union Record* (1913–16), which is, I believe, only available in Birmingham Public Library, and an article by John D. Goodman on the Birmingham gun trade in *The Resources, Products and Industrial History of Birmingham and the Midland Hardware District*, ed. Samuel Timmis (1866), which was reprinted in *Arms and Armour* (7, iv, 1971, p. 79). There is also illuminating detail in an article by J. A. Hammerton and E. C. Middleton, 'The toy shop of the world', in the *Temple Magazine* (1900), and in Lord Cottesloe, 'Notes on the history of the Royal Small Arms Factory, Enfield Lock', *Journal of the Society for Army Historical Research* (vol. XII, 1933). The details of later nineteenth-century housing in Birmingham are drawn from *The History of Working-Class Housing*, ed. S. D. Chapman (1971). More general material on Birmingham comes from Asa Briggs, *History of Birmingham*, vol. 2. The quotations from Will Thorne come from *My Life's Battles*. I have also leaned heavily on 'The Labour Aristocracy in Nineteenth-Century Britain' by E. J. Hobsbawm, in *Labouring Men*. Details of the contents of a working men's institutional library are given in S. Shipley, 'The library of the Alliance Cabinet Makers' Association', *History Workshop Journal* (vol. 1, 1976).

5

In addition to Mark Stokes himself, my main sources have been K. Richardson, *The British Motor Industry 1896–1939* (1977), R. Jackson, *The Nuffield Story* (1964), and P. S. Andrews and E. Brunner, *The Life of Lord Nuffield* (1955). I also made use of the British Association study, *Britain in Depression* (1935). The study of tedious work referred to is S. Wyatt and J. N. Langdon, *Fatigue and Boredom in Repetitive Work* (1938). The story of the Siddeley apprentice is taken from *The Evening and the Morning*, a company publication of 1956. Material on Earlsdon is from *Warwickshire and Worcestershire Life* (June 1978).

Chapter 5 SEAMEN

1

The general works on the Spithead and Nore mutinies are G. E. Manwairing and B. Dobrée, *The Floating Republic* (1935), and J. Dugan, *The Great Mutiny* (1966). S. Leech's *Thirty Years From Home, or A Voice From the Main Deck* was published in 1844. Details of life in the Navy, and losses in the war, are from M. Lewis, *A Social History of the Navy 1793–1815* (1960). Charles Pemberton's story, *Pel. Verjuice*, was published in 1929. The story of the press gangs was written by J. R. Hutchinson, *The Press Gang Afloat and Ashore* (1913), and the importance of the impress service on the Tyne is made clear in C. Lloyd, *The British Seaman 1200–1860* (1968). Details of the Tyne impress are in S. Jones, 'Community and organisation – early seamen's trade unionism on the north-east coast, 1768–1844', in *Maritime History* (April 1973). *The History of Merchant Shipping and Ancient Commerce* is by W. S. Lindsay (4 vols, 1874–6). The Tyne strike of 1792 is documented in *The Times*, and referred to in A. Aspinall, *The Early English Trade Unions*, (1949). The courts-martial of the mutineers are preserved in Admiralty papers 1/5125, 5486, 1022 and 1023.

2

The history of the period is covered in A. G. Course, *The Merchant Navy: A Social History* (1963); P. G. Parkhurst, *Ships of Peace* (1962); C. Lloyd, *The British Seaman* (1968), and P. Kemp, *The British Sailor* (1970).

N. McCord, 'The seamen's strike of 1815 in north-east England', in *Economic History Review* (21, April, 1968), stresses the essentially moderate attitudes of seamen and magistrates in the strike. Nevertheless, the shipowners were cynically determined to have their own way, and their essential success determined the miserable position of seaman in the following half-century. W. S. Lindsay gave his recollections in *The Log of My Leisure Hours* (1868); J. Havelock Wilson gave his in *My Stormy Voyage Through Life* (vol. 1, 1925). Thomas Moore's pamphlet *Our Maritime Laws Considered* was published in 1852; in the same year, Lindsay produced *Our Navigation and Mercantile Laws Considered*. A biography of Moore, consisting of reprints of material by John Shaw in the *Hampshire Telegraph*, was published as *A Seaman's Friend* in 1876. An account of Samuel Plimsoll is given by D. Masters in *The Plimsoll Mark* (1955).

3

Most of the material in this section is taken from L. Yexley, *The Inner Life of the Navy* (1908). S. Bonnett, *The Price of Admiralty: An Indictment of the Royal Navy* (1968) is just what it sets out to be, and has interesting accounts of the way the Navy turned to iron and steam, and of naval punishments. Other material came from J. Winton, *Hurrah For the Life of a Sailor* (1977), P. Padfield, *The Battleship Era* (1972), Kemp, *The British Sailor*, and M. Lewis, *The Navy in Transition 1814–1864* (1965).

4

Fred Copeman's *Reason in Revolt* was published in 1948. Another eyewitness to the mutiny, L. Wincott, wrote *Invergordon* in 1931 and *Invergordon Mutineer* in 1974. He embraced the discipline of the Communist Party wholeheartedly, and his 1931 pamphlet claimed that the Party led the mutiny; a claim dismissed by B. Duncan, *Invergordon '31* (1965), and D. Divine, *Mutiny at Invergordon* (1970). Wincott became a Soviet citizen, and took part in the defence of Leningrad in the Second World War. He also spent eight years in a Siberian prison camp, an experience which he did not mention in his autobiography of 1974. T. Wintringham's *Mutiny* (1936) puts the mutiny in the context of general naval morale and resistance to sailing against Russia after the First World War. K. Edwards's *Mutiny at Invergordon* (1937), stresses the insensitivity and uncertainty of the Admiralty and its susceptibility to public and political pressures. S. Roskill, *Naval Policy Between the Wars* (1976, pp. 89–133), examines the mutiny from the official papers.

5

This section draws heavily on M. Middlebrook's *Convoy* (1976); it is the source for much of the detail, including the seaman who put a fiver in his discharge book. There are many other works on the war at sea: those which I found useful were J. Costello and T. Hughes, *The Battle of the Atlantic* (1977), M. Brown, *We Sailed in Convoy* (1942), D. Macintyre, *The Battle of the Atlantic* (1961), and *British Coaster 1939–1945* (1947), T. Cameron, *Red Duster, White Ensign* (1959), J. Creswell, *Sea Warfare 1939–1945* (1967), and D. Howarth, *Sovereign of the Seas* (1974).

There is much less, of course, on the Merchant Navy before the war: one of the strengths of Middlebrook's book is that it reaches into that part of the background. One work I did find useful is R. H. Thornton's *British Shipping*, in its 1939 edition.

Chapter 6 IMMIGRANTS

1

The two books on Irish immigration to Britain are both called *The Irish in Britain*; one is by K. O'Connor (1974), and the other by J. A. Jackson (1964). Seasonal migration was studied by B. M. Kerr in 'Irish Seasonal Migration to Great Britain 1800–38', *Irish Historical Studies* (3, 1943), and 'Irish immigration into Great Britain' (BLitt thesis, University of Oxford).

The Stockport riot was studied in some detail by M. Brock, 'Irish immigrants in Manchester, 1830–54' (BA dissertation, 1972, University of Southampton). Some details of the crossing to England are taken from H. S. Irvine, 'Some aspects of passenger traffic between Britain and Ireland, 1820–50', in *Journal of Transport History* (November 1960). Quotations from Le Chevalier de la Tocaye and John Mitchel are taken from *Two Centuries of Irish History*, ed. James Hawthorne (1966), based on a BBC Radio series.

2

The conditions in the East End, and the fears of a revolutionary upsurge, are described in detail in G. Stedman Jones, *Outcast London* (1971). Conditions in the Pale of Settlement are described in L. Greenberg, *The Jews in Russia* (vol. 2, 1951); M. Gilbert, *The Jews of Russia* (1976); I. Howe, *The Immigrant Jews of New York* (1976) and W. J. Fishman, *East End Jewish Radicals 1875–1914* (1975). Howe and Fishman also describe emigration routes, and the latter has much material on the attitude of English Jewry to the new immigrants. J. A. Garrard, *The English and Immigration 1880–1910* (1971) traces the pasage of the Aliens Act. V. D. Lipman's *Social History of the Jews in England* (1954) includes material on wages and conditions in immigrant workshops.

3

I have been helped by many people in my research for this section, especially Mrs Beryl Dhanjal of Ealing CRC, Dr Gulrez Shaheen, and Dr Anwar of the Commission for Racial Equality. I also learned much from Dilip Hiro's *Black British, White British* (1973), and R. Desai, *Indian Immigrants in Britain* (1971). W. Daniel's *Racial Discrimination in England* (1968) was based on the 1968 survey into racial prejudice. G. Delft, *Asians in East Africa* (1963), is a useful brief sketch of settlement in that area.

Chapter 7 SHOPKEEPERS

1

Francis Place's *Autobiography* was edited by Mary Thale (1972). The text is largely based on this edition, and also on Dorothy Davis, *A History of Shopping* (1966).

2

The general account is based on Davis, op. cit. Sutherst's *Death and Disease Behind the Counter* was published in 1884, the year after a collection of Brabazon's essays, *Social Arrows*, were published. P. C. Hoffman's autobiography, *They Also Serve*, appeared in 1949. The *Daily Chronicle* articles, 'Life in the shop' appeared in March and April 1898.

3

Mr T., who wishes to remain anonymous, gave me a great deal of help in writing this section. Books I consulted – their respective relevance is probably obvious – were: Robert Roberts, *The Classic Slum* (1971); The British Association, *Britain in Depression* (1935); M. Sissóns and P. French (eds), *Age of Austerity 1945–1951* (1963); J. B. Jefferys, *Retail Trading in Britain 1850–1950* (1954); Greville Havenhand, *Nation of Shopkeepers* (1970); P. C. Hoffman, *They Also Serve* (1949); A. G. Weidenfeld (ed.), *Better Living* (1949); A. Calder, *The People's War* (1969); W. K. Hancock and M. M. Gowing, *The British War Economy* (1949); A. Marwick, *Britain in the Century of Total War* (1968); M. Abrams and R. Rose, *Must Labour Lose?* (1960); Central Office of Information, *Britain 1948* (1948).

Chapter 8 MINERS

1

The tradition of the 'Lambton curse' is told in Sir T. Eden, *Durham* (vol. 2, 1952). The basic history of the coalfield and the miners' struggles is in E. Welbourne, *The Miners' Unions of Northumberland and Durham* (1921), and R. Fynes, *The Miners of Northumberland and Durham* (1873). The social background, and the impact of Primitive Methodism, is explored in R. Colls, *The Colliers' Rant* (1977). G. Parkinson's *True Stories of Durham Pit Life* was published in 1912. The relation of Lord Durham to his pitmen is discussed in L. Cooper, *Radical Jack* (1959), though from a very pro-Durham standpoint. The study of the Lambton pits referred to (1810) is in the Buddle Papers (vol. 3, pp. 193–207) in the North of England Institute of Mining, Newcastle, to whom I am most grateful for the opportunity to explore their archives. The obituary quoted is from the *Primitive Methodist Magazine*, June 1844.

2

I am grateful to Mr Thompson and Mr Killingback for their help with this section; I am also much indebted to Professor N. McCord, who suggested the significance of the development of club life. The history of working men's clubs I have taken from R. Price, *An Imperial War and the British Working Class* (1972), B. T. Hall, *Our Sixty Years* (1922), and G. Tremlett, *The First Century* (1962). I also referred to *The Official History of the British Legion* by G. Wooton (1956).

For general background to the story, I referred to A. Burton, *The Miners* (1976), J. Davidson, *Northumberland Miners' History 1919–1939* (1973), (which includes his own childhood reminiscence of hunger in the general strike), and H. Townshend-Rose, *The British Coal Industry* (1951). Geoffrey Keen's reminiscences were published in *Changing Kibblesworth*, by R. Dixon, E. McMillan and L. Turnbull, a pamphlet produced by Gateshead Metropolitan Borough Council Department of Education.

For a detailed account of life in the Durham coalfield, see D. Douglas's 'The Durham pitman', in *Miners, Quarrymen and Saltworkers*, ed. R. Samuel (1977).

3

I am heavily indebted to Mr V. Jupp and Mr E. Wade, both of the Open

University, for the insights they gave me and the contacts they helped me make. The distinction between 'hillbillies' and 'sand-dancers' is made in Mr Jupp's unpublished study of the effects of relocation of miners. I am also, of course, indebted to Mr Mahone, and all the other miners who have so willingly tried to explain things to me.

Index

To help the reader follow general topics through the book, the following thematic entries have been included in the index: dress, education, entertainment, food and drink, hours of work, housing, religion, transport, wages.

The subjects of the main chapter headings have not been indexed, so there are no entries for 'labourers', 'servants', 'soldiers', etc.

Numbers in **bold** type refer to illustrations.

Botulinum Toxin in Facial Rejuvenation

For
Paul, Fleur and Timothy Moriarty

Commissioning Editor: *Paul Fam*
Project Development Manager: *Shuet-Kei Cheung*
Project Manager: *Alan Nicholson*
Illustration Manager: *Mick Ruddy*
Design Manager: *Jayne Jones*

Botulinum Toxin in Facial Rejuvenation

Kate Coleman Moriarty BSc PhD FRSC FRCOphth
Eye, Oculoplastic and Skin Laser Surgeon
Eye and Oculoplastic Institute
Blackrock Clinic
Blackrock, Co. Dublin
Ireland

Mosby
Edinburgh London New York Oxford Philadelphia St Louis Sydney Toronto 2004

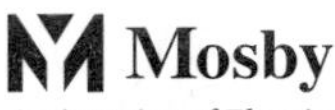

An imprint of Elsevier Limited

First published 2004

ISBN 0723433496

British Library Cataloguing in Publication Data
A catalogue record for this book is available from the British Library

Library of Congress Cataloging in Publication Data
A catalog record for this book is available from the Library of Congress

Note
Medical knowledge is constantly changing. Standard safety precautions must be followed, but as new research and clinical experience broaden our knowledge, changes in treatment and drug therapy may become necessary or appropriate. Readers are advised to check the most current product information provided by the manufacturer of each drug to be administered to verify the recommended dose, the method and duration of administration, and contraindications. It is the responsibility of the practitioner, relying on experience and knowledge of the patient, to determine dosages and the best treatment for each individual patient. Neither the Publisher nor the author assumes any liability for any injury and/or damage to persons or property arising from this publication.

Printed in Spain

The publisher's policy is to use **paper manufactured from sustainable forests**

Contents

Foreword

It is indeed a great pleasure for us to have the opportunity to write the foreword to this important handbook. Kate Coleman Moriarty has chronicled and catalogued her extensive observations following the treatment of her patients with botulinum toxin. These are displayed in an orderly fashion, allowing physicians to readily apply these pearls to the treatment of their patients.

We have used botulinum toxin injections to treat blepharospasm patients for more than 20 years. Now, just as botulinum toxin revolutionized the treatment of benign essential blepharospasm, it is launching non-invasive-techniques for facial rejuvenation into another era. Every physician and surgeon seriously pursuing rejuvenation of the facial structures must include chemodenervation as a cornerstone of their therapeutic menu. The effects of ablative and non-ablative laser therapies are enhanced with botulinum toxin Type A pretreatment. Combination therapy of botulinum toxin and filling agents yields prolonged effacement of glabellar furrows. The artful application of botulinum toxin not only reduces facial rhytidosis but repositions eyebrows, flattens pretarsal muscle folds and diminishes platysmal bands. Understanding the facial musculature allows the aesthetic physician to manipulate the balance of counteracting muscles and rejuvenate the face. This is the dawn of a new age of facial rejuvenation.

Stephen Bosniak, MD, FACS
New York, NY. USA

Marian Cantisano-Zilkha, MD
Rio de Janeiro. Brazil

Co-editors of *Operative techniques in ophthalmic plastic and orbital surgery*

Authors of *Cosmetic blepharoplasty and facial rejuvenation*

National Botox® Training Centers – New York, NY, USA and Great Neck, NY, USA

2003

Acknowledgements

Thank you to the kind patients who generously donated their photographs.

This book would not have been finished without the brilliance of John Savin, whose literary abilities are only matched by his golf prowess – thank you John for reading, editing, advising and transforming. Thank you to the staff of Elsevier for forbearance and guidance.

I would like to thank PAJ Moriarty for many things in my life, but of most relevance now is my gratitude for introducing me to botulinum toxin in the blepharospasm clinic of the Eye and Ear Hospital Dublin in 1988. A review of the patients in this clinic was the subject of my presentation to the Royal Academy of Ophthalmology in March 1988, the start of a deep curiosity in botulinum toxin. I would also like to thank the late Leo Koornneef and my friends JRO Collin, D MacNeill and Steve Bosniak for setting high standards, if only to aspire to their elevated heights of surgical and aesthetic perfection. Thank you Marian Cantisano-Zilkha for showing how the eye zone should be considered, surgery, make up, peels and all.

Thanks too to Chris Zachary and Roy Grekin for being so inspirational, the best teachers and simply the best at cosmetic dermatology. Thank you Rita Rakis for all the tricks!

A very special thanks is reserved for Maria Micheau. This book would not have been written without her inspiration, management, organization and motivation.

Thank you to the highly skilled Airmid McSeain and Andrea McAlister for being so much fun to work with and so supportive and dedicated.

Kate Coleman Moriarty

Introduction

Botulinum toxin has been used to minimize wrinkles since 1990. In some patients it smoothes frowns and lines miraculously, but in others the price of eliminating wrinkles is an exhausted haggard appearance – younger perhaps, but lifeless and dull. The art of good botulinum toxin (BTX) treatment lies in predicting in every individual the precise response to a precise injection. Patients have to be made aware of the expected outcome, and offered a choice of treatment combinations, or alternatives if these are necessary.

For success, the correct muscle fibers have to be injected with the correct dilution of botulinum toxin. However if all patients attending for frown management received the same set of injections at the same dose, only some 30% would be happy; 30% would be uneasy about the consequences of their treatment (uneven brow elevation, excessive brow arching, heavy lids); and 40% would look tired, heavy-lidded and puffy-eyed for 3 months.

The clinical guidelines offered here should ensure that practitioners become confident in the good cosmetic use of BTX, and that their carefully selected patients remain safe. Emphasis is placed on the customized choice of treatment and alternatives are suggested for those who are not treatable by BTX.

The ability to select the right treatment has to be learned, and then, with experience, becomes almost intuitive. It requires a close analysis of facial features and their relationship to each other. Good BTX treatment must always make the patient look better, though not necessarily younger: the aim of this book is to show how this can be achieved.

■ **The art of good botulinum treatment is always to make the patient look better, but not necessarily younger.**

1 Historical background

The *Clostridium* family of bacteria, common to most environments, produces spores that on germination release some of the deadliest toxins known to mankind. *Clostridium welchii* contaminates wounds and caused the infamous gas gangrene of World War 1: *Clostridium botulinum* produces botulinum toxin – a powerful neurotoxin.

Clostridium botulinum was first identified in 1897, in Belgium, by Professor Emile van Ermengem who was investigating fatal cases of food poisoning following the consumption of macerated ham. It was named after the disease it causes, botulism, a lethal form of food poisoning originally associated with sausage meat (botulus is Latin for sausage). In the same year, an antiserum for botulism was made.

There are seven known serotypes of botulinum toxin (A, B, C, D, E, F, and G). Serotypes A, B and E cause the classic food-borne disease with a flaccid paralysis of motor and autonomic nerves. Type B was first discovered in 1910, and the isolation of Type A began in the 1920s. During the Second World War research continued into this potent neurotoxin as a possible agent ('agent X') for biological warfare. Most of this work was carried out at the chemical warfare laboratories of Fort Detrick, Maryland, and Porton Down in the UK. Porton Chemicals was bought by Ipsen pharmaceuticals in 1989 and is the source of Dysport®, one of the commercially available forms of botulinum toxin.

Dr Alan Scott, an ophthalmologist from the Smith-Kettlewell Eye Research Foundation, became interested in substances that caused transient muscular paralysis. He acquired botulinum toxin Type A from Fort Detrick, and performed the first clinical tests on humans in 1978. His results in the treatment of strabismus (an abnormal contraction of the extra-ocular eye muscles) were published in 1980 and led to the extensive use of botulinum toxin Type A by ophthalmologists in the treatment of blepharospasm (an abnormal involuntary twitching and contraction of the facial muscles around the eye), hemifacial spasm and cervical dystonia (abnormal spasm of cervical musculature) (see Chapter 10).

The astute observation by Dr Jean Carruthers, an oculoplastic surgeon in Toronto, of the incidental rejuvenating effects of botulinum toxin on patients with facial dystonia, was shared with her husband, Dr Alastair Carruthers, a dermatologist. At the same time, similar observations were being published by Professor Nick Lowe and others.

Thereafter the story is well known. With good medical training and the correct selection of patients, botulinum toxin can be given easily, safely, and repeatedly.

2 Botulinum toxin: mode of action and serotypes

A working knowledge of the pharmacology of botulinum toxin is essential to understand the contraindications and complications of treatment with it. For an excellent analysis of its pharmacology, the reader is referred to Huang, Foster and Rogachefsky (2000, see Bibliography).

Botulinum neurotoxins are polypeptides. Botulinum toxin comprises a protein molecule (150kd) which can be cleaved into a heavy (H)(100kd) and a light (L)(50kd) chain (Fig. 2.1). These chains are normally held together by a disulphide bond, which is heat labile. Disruption of this bond inactivates the neurotoxin. This explains why botulinum toxin must be stored at the correct temperature and reconstituted carefully, preserving the integrity of the two-chained molecule (see below).

Botulinum toxin induces paralysis by blocking the release of acetylcholine at the skeletal neuromuscular junction, thereby inhibiting the transmission of nerve impulses across the synaptic junction to the motor end plate. There are seven serotypes of botulinum toxin, five of which are effective at the human neuromuscular junction (BTX A, B, E, F and G). The different serotypes act by cleaving different proteins at the presynaptic vesicle.

Three types of botulinum toxin are currently available commercially: Botox® and Dysport® (both botulinum toxin Type A); and NeuroBloc® (botulinum toxin Type B).

Allergan in Westport, Ireland produces Botox®. Dysport® is produced by Ipsen Pharmaceuticals, UK, and NeuroBloc® is produced by Elan, Ireland. Product specifications are given below. NeuroBloc® is licensed for use in cervical dystonia under the name of Myobloc® in USA.

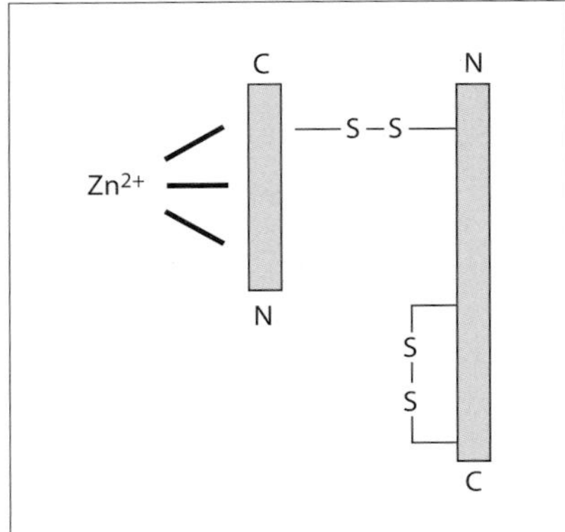

Fig 2.1 Diagram of botulinum toxin molecule showing heavy and light chains. After Aoki, R. The development of botox – its history and pharmacology. Pain Digest 1998; 8:337–341 by permission of Springer–Verlag.

MUSCULAR CONTRACTION: NORMAL CHOLINERGIC TRANSMISSION (SEE FIG. 2.2)

Voluntary muscle contraction is a response to stimulation by action potentials passing along a nerve to the muscle. Once these action potentials reach a synapse at the neuromuscular junction, they stimulate an influx of calcium into the cytoplasm of the nerve ending. This increase in calcium concentration allows acetylcholine to fuse with the membrane, using a protein complex, before crossing the synapse and fusing with nicotinic receptors on the muscle fiber. The protein complex consists of three types of protein: VAMP (synaptobrevin), SNAP-25 (synaptosomal associated protein), and syntaxin.

THE MODE OF ACTION OF BOTULINUM TOXIN (SEE FIG. 2.3)

Acetylcholine depends on a protein complex for its release from the nerve ending into the synapse. Botulinum toxin, using a specific enzyme in the light (L) chain, interacts with one component of the protein complex of the nerve terminal, thereby inhibiting the discharge of the acetylcholine. The protein attacked is specific to the different serotypes of botulinum toxin. BTX-A blocks SNAP-25, while BTX-B blocks VAMP. This explains why the development of antibodies to BTX-A (Botox® or Dysport®) does not preclude a good clinical result from BTX-B (NeuroBloc®).

Both the heavy (H) and light (L) chains of the botulinum toxin molecule are needed to block the release of acetylcholine. The H-chain attaches the botulinum toxin to the nerve membrane, allowing the L-chain to be transported to its site of action – the protein complex. The L-chain enzyme then cleaves the protein specific to the particular neurotoxin. Neuromuscular transmission ceases and the target muscle atrophies reversibly.

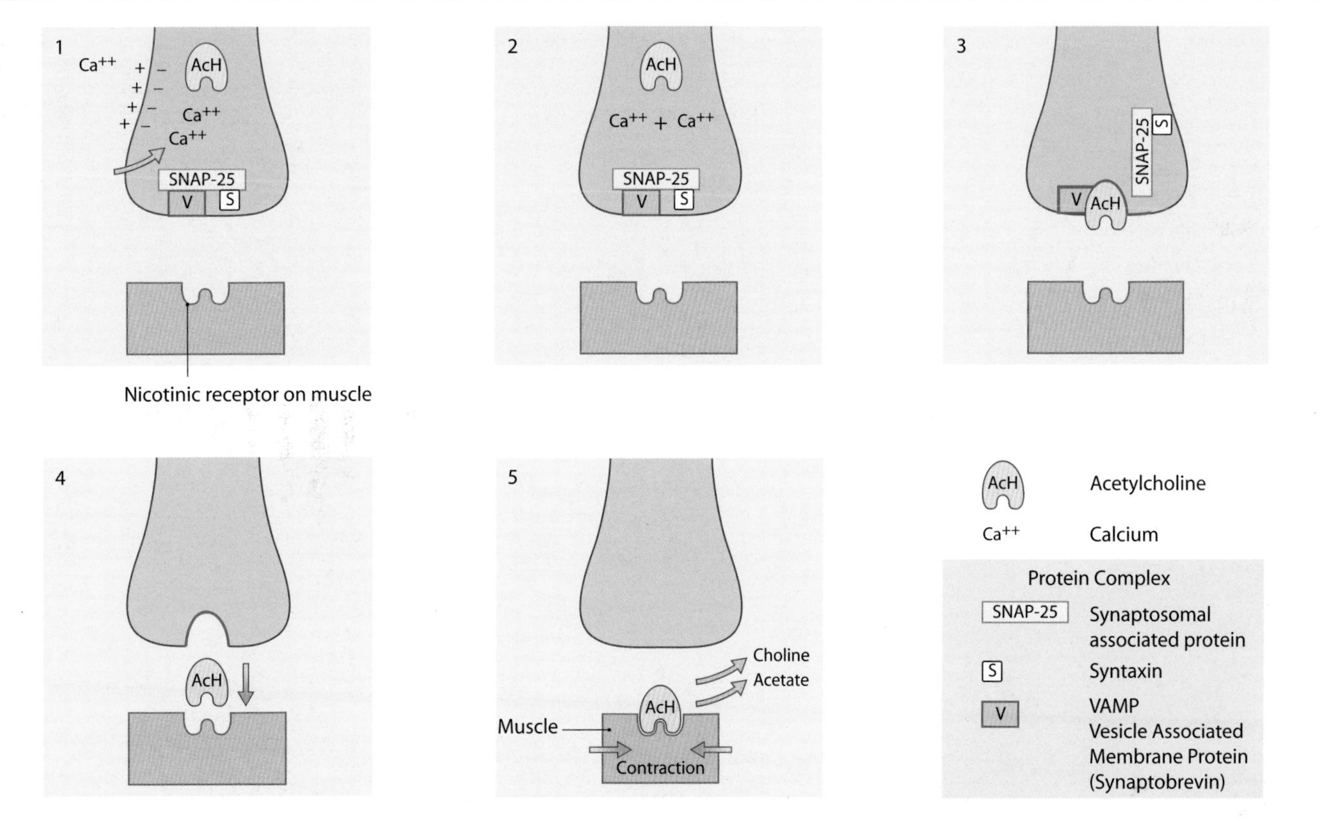

Fig 2.2 Normal cholinergic transmission. 1, A signal passes down the cholinergic nerve, causing calcium to pass through the depolarising presynaptic membrane; 2, The calcium then triggers the binding of the acetylcholine molecule to a protein membrane complex; 3, The protein membrane complex allows the acetylcholine to pass into the synaptic cleft; 4, The acetylcholine travels across the synapse to a nicotinic receptor on the muscle, where it stimulates contraction before disintegrating into acetate and choline.

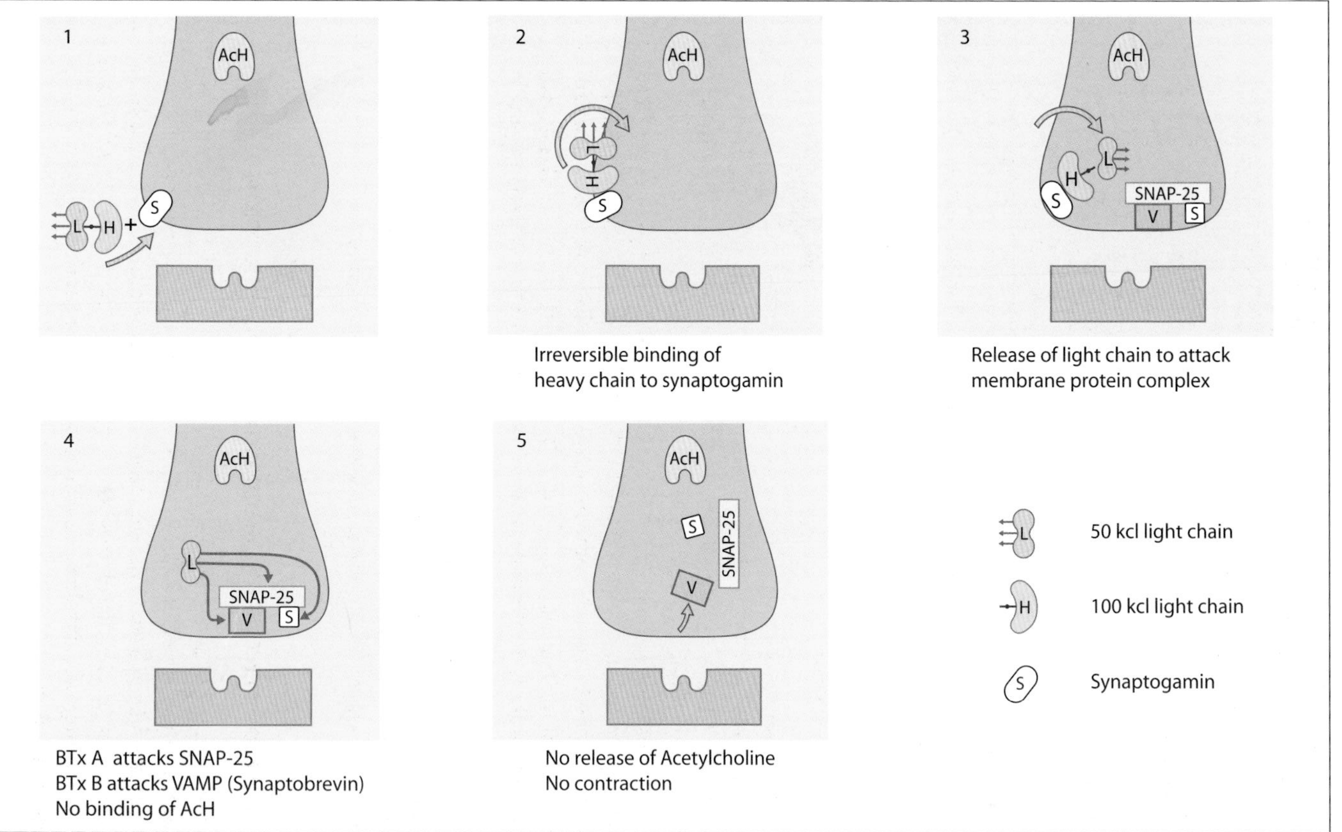

Fig 2.3 Action of botulinum toxin at the neuromuscular junction. 1, The heavy chain of the BTX binds to synaptogamin on the presynaptic membrane; 2, The heavy chain/synaptogamin complex enables the BTX light chain to enter the cell; 3, The light chain attacks the membrane complex and disables it so that *no acetylcholine binds*; 4, BTX-A attacks the snap-25 protein of the membrane protein complex while BTX-B attacks VAMP (synaptobrevin); 5, There is no release of acetylcholine.

If botulinum toxin is not handled correctly before injection, the fragile bond which holds the L and H chains together may split, preventing the H-chain from being able to guide the L-chain to the correct protein inside the terminal, and rendering the molecule ineffective.

USER TIP

Botulinum toxin acts only on the neuromuscular cholinergic receptors unless given in very high doses, when autonomic effects may be possible.

USER TIP

Botulinum toxin acts by blocking the release of acetylcholine from the pre-synaptic terminal of the neuromuscular junction.

MUSCLE RECOVERY

The precise way in which muscles recover after an injection of botulinum toxin is still unknown. Cleavage of the protein complex is irreversible, but the changes following botulinum toxin use include a proliferation of axonal nerve buds to the target muscle and the regeneration of muscle end plates.

Muscle function takes between 24 hours and five days to cease; in contrast, recovery takes from six weeks with NeuroBloc®, and an average of 14 weeks with Botox® and Dysport®. Some muscles, the frontalis in particular, remain paralyzed in some patients for as long as five months after only one treatment. Prolonged paralysis results in muscle atrophy which has been shown to last years in the forehead musculature.

The orbicularis oculi muscle requires three to six months to recover its function but, even then, the muscle returns to only 70-80% of its original bulk. This explains the fact that a single treatment can help the 'crow's feet' of patients who are reluctant to engage in a series of treatments.

THE DEVELOPMENT OF ANTIBODIES TO BOTULINUM TOXIN

The development of antibodies to one serotype does not preclude an effective response to another one. Research suggests that the development of these antibodies is related both to the frequency of administration of BTX and to its concentration. Ideally, therefore, good therapy should be spaced at a minimum of 12-week intervals, and should use the lowest concentration effective for that duration of action.

USER TIP

Avoid the development of antibodies by using the lowest dose recommended for the site, with a minimum treatment interval of 12 weeks.

BOTULINUM TOXIN SEROTYPES

Botulinum Toxin Type A (BTX-A) (Botox®, Dysport®)

BTX-A cleaves SNAP-25 at the neuromuscular junction, preventing the release of acetylcholine. It is the most widely available botulinum toxin and has been used by the author since 1988. All treatments in this book refer to BTX-A with the exception of a report below on BTX-B.

Two forms of BTX-A are currently available: Botox® is produced by Allergan Inc.; and Dysport® by Ipsen Pharmaceuticals. The author has used Dysport® since 1988 and Botox® since 1990. At the time of publication, Dysport® is widely used in Europe and South America, while Botox® is available in the USA as well as in Europe. Allergan was awarded FDA approval for the cosmetic treatment of glabellar lines in May 2002, and, as Botox® Cosmetic, BTX-A is sold in the USA for this purpose.

Botulinum Toxin Type B (BTX-B) (NeuroBloc®)

BTX-B acts on a different cytoplasmic protein complex. The secretion of acetylcholine is disrupted when the light chain of the BTX-B molecule cleaves a protein called synaptobrevin, also known as vesicle associated membrane protein (VAMP). Clinical trials have shown BTX-B to be effective for the treatment of patients with cervical dystonia, including those resistant to BTX-A. BTX-B is produced by Elan, Ireland, and is called NeuroBloc®.

In a recent trial of NeuroBloc® for rhytids, 30 patients were treated at a dose recommended by Elan as the equivalent of doses usually used for Dysport® and Botox® (to be discussed in detail in Chapters 4, 7, 8 and 9). It was found that, unlike BTX-A, muscle inaction begins within 24 hours – the average for BTX-A being three to five days. Diffusion of toxin from the injection site was similar to that of Dysport®. Patients noted that BTX-B stung more than BTX-A but were pleased by the speed of its effect and by the outcome.

The greatest difference in clinical effect was its duration of action. The effect of BTX-B, at doses expected to be similar, lasted for only 6 weeks (unpublished results, Author) and this is in keeping with other reports. Both toxin serotypes 'wear off' within a few days: i.e. once muscle function has started to return, it recovers completely over a short period. The second phase of the trial is now underway, examining the cosmetic effects of BTX-B at the concentrations used for cervical dystonia.

3 Clinical indications and usage

THE INDICATIONS FOR USING BOTULINUM TOXIN

The cosmetic indications for botulinum toxin are listed in Table 3.1. Non-cosmetic indications for botulinum toxin include the following: strabismus, hemifacial spasm and blepharospasm, spasmodic torticollis, focal dystonias such as writer's cramp, post facial nerve palsy synkinesis, migraine, hyperhidrosis, bruxism and esophageal achalasia. (For further discussion of non-cosmetic indications, see Chapter 10).

How to choose between Botox®, Dysport® and NeuroBloc® for rejuvenation

The choice between BTX-A (Botox® and Dysport®) and BTX-B (NeuroBloc®) will be based on the duration of action required, unless the patient already has antibodies to BTX-A.

Table 3.1. The cosmetic indications for botulinum toxin

Crows feet (periocular rhytids)	Pebbly chin
Vertical (glabellar) frown	Nasolabial folds
Horizontal (frontalis) frown	Jaw line (platysma
Wrinkles on nose	Venus rings (horizontal neck rhytids)
Upper lip rhytids	Turkey neck (vertical platysma bands)
Vermilion border	Décolleté
Angle of mouth	Scar management

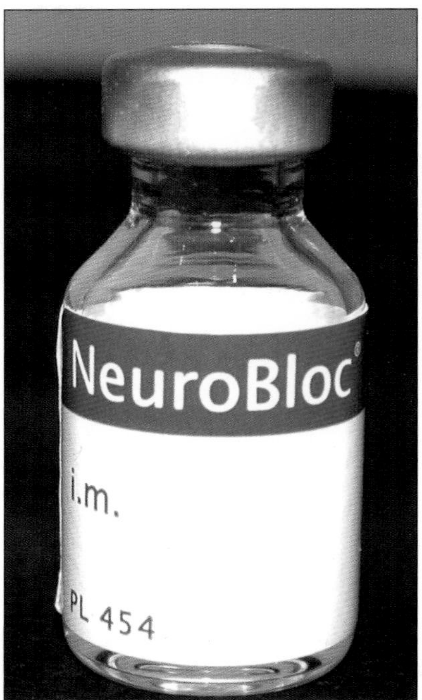

Fig 3.1 Bottle of NeuroBloc®

NeuroBloc® (at a concentration of 200 units per 0.1ml) is the toxin of choice for shorter periods of action (Fig. 3.1). Some patients (and practitioners) are nervous of the outcome of their first treatment and may be happy to have an effect lasting six rather than 12–14 weeks. Others need to use their facial muscles professionally and are happy to induce muscle atrophy for a limited period e.g. while 'resting' between film productions. This encourages their wrinkles to flatten, while retaining the ability to retrieve full facial expression when desired. It is also possible that even shorter actions will be available with further modifications of the dose. It is worth noting that inadequate storage of Botox® or Dysport® (e.g. at an incorrect temperature), or excessive dilution, also shortens the duration of their effect.

USER TIP

NeuroBloc®, at a concentration of 200 units per 0.1 ml, is the first choice for a duration of action of six weeks. Botox® and Dysport® both last for 12–14 weeks.

Botox® or Dysport®?

Botox® Cosmetic (Fig. 3.2) is the only botulinum toxin Type A currently licensed for cosmetic use in the USA for the treatment of the vertical glabellar

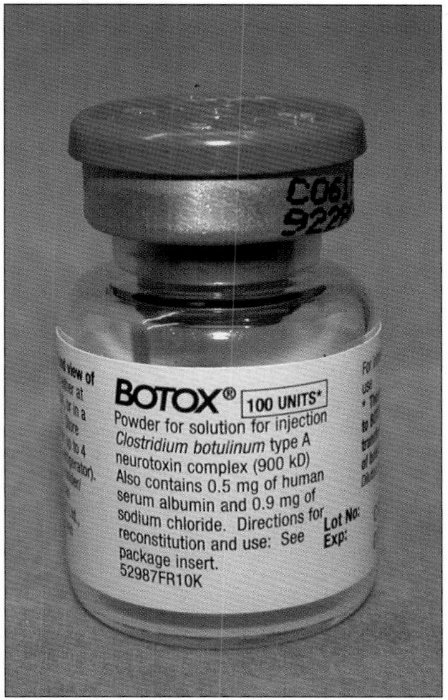

Fig 3.2 Botox® Cosmetic

frown. The rights to Dysport® in the USA have been acquired by INAMED Corporation (Zyplast, Zyderm) and licensing is expected in the near future. Both are widely used in Europe. Dysport® is licensed for cosmetic use in Brazil and Mexico.

In Europe, the choice lies between Botox® and Dysport®. Research shows both to be equally effective in comparable doses for cervical dystonia and facial rejuvenation. The author's experience with both types of BTX-A for rejuvenation and blepharospasm indicates that Dysport® (Fig. 3.3) may be more effective in patients with blepharospasm who have had an incomplete result with Botox®. Both Dysport® and Botox® have similar durations of action, their effects wearing off after 12 to 14 weeks. Dysport® tends to diffuse to more muscle fibers per site of injection than Botox®.

These qualities are useful for the beginner who may find it easier to start with Botox® around the eyes and Dysport® to the frontalis. An experienced practitioner with a busy BTX-A practice may choose between the two on economic grounds only – both are currently available at the same price in Ireland.

From a practical point of view, an inexperienced practitioner, with few patients and an irregular demand for BTX-A, may initially prefer the storage qualities of Dysport® (see Chapter 4) though the larger vial of Botox® makes preparation and dilution easier.

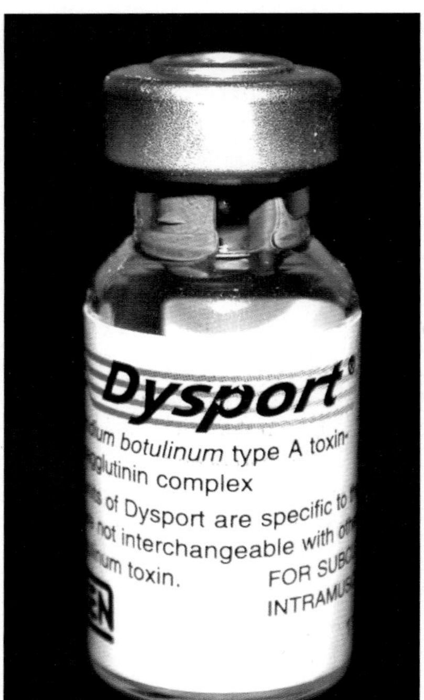

Fig 3.3 Bottle of Dysport®

CONCENTRATIONS

Botulinum toxin is the most potent toxin known to mankind. It functions at very low concentrations and so can be assessed accurately only in terms of lethal dose unit per Swiss-Webster mouse. One mouse unit (mu) is the median intraperitoneal dose required to kill 50% of a batch of 18 to 20g female Swiss–Webster mice (LD50) over three to four days.

The types of mice used by Allergan, Ipsen and Elan differ and so the units discussed are NOT interchangeable. One vial of Botox® contains 100 mu, while one vial of Dysport® contains 500 mu: one vial of NeuroBloc® contains 10,000 mu. This variability of assay, coupled with the absence of a definitive human assay, means that the doses used have to be based on clinical experience. Clinical efficacy is directly related to the degree of dilution of the toxin, the muscle targeted and the volume injected.

The potency of one vial of Botox® is not the same as that of one vial of Dysport®. Several studies suggest that 3–5 units of Dysport® equate with one unit of Botox®. NeuroBloc® is said to measure up against Botox® at the ratio of 1 unit of Botox® equaling 50 units of NeuroBloc®.

The concentration of Botox® has changed since it was introduced to Europe in 1989. The original batch of 150 g of pure crystallized toxin was prepared by Dr Schantz in 1979. Botox® is a vacuum-dried form of purified BTX-A, produced by cultures of the Hall strain of *Clostridium botulinus.* It is isolated as a crystalline protein complex from the culture solution by a series of acid preparations, and then redissolved in a solution containing saline and albumin. It is then filtered using a sterile technique before vacuum drying. This author's experience with Botox® from 1989 to 1997 was with the original Schantz preparation. In 1997, a new batch was prepared by Allergan with different labeling. This batch, in current use, contains 20% less protein than the original one and so is less likely to stimulate an albumin-related allergic response. However, the author noticed an immediate reduction in the duration of effect of the 'new' Botox® and concluded it to be weaker than the original batch. Several observant patients in the author's clinic, who had been treated every 14 weeks for two years, complained in the same month of a reduced effect though they were unaware of the change in batch. The author's practice changed, from using a regular dilution of the Botox® vial with 3.5 ml (as previously published) to a dilution with 2.5 ml, in order to reproduce the same results. Subsequent reports from the USA have suggested the new batch was associated with an increase in side effects (e.g. ptosis) and so was assumed to be stronger. These reports, in fact, support the belief that the new batch is more dilute, because it is well documented now that greater dilutions diffuse more widely and are more likely to produce side effects.

The author continues to dilute Botox® with 2–3 ml for routine rhytid management (depending on the site) and has detected no further changes in concentration.

- **Botox is produced by a precipitation technique and freeze-dried to a powder.**
- **Dysport is produced by column-based purification and freeze-dried to a powder.**
- **Neurobloc is a high molecular weight BTX-B that is not lyophilized but a buffered intact protein complex in liquid form, at a pH of 5.5.**

DOSAGES

Bolinum toxin Type A

This book gives doses in milliliters of reconstituted solution as opposed to 'units' of BTX-A. One ml syringes are recommended (Fig. 3.4, see also Chapter 4) allowing doses of 0.025 ml to be given safely. Always keep an eye on the hub of the syringe and the volume used while injecting. The doses

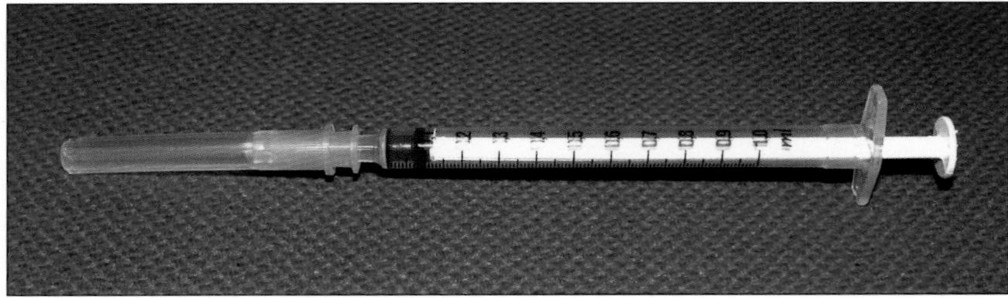

Fig 3.4 One-ml syringe

recommended relate to the experience of the author, with thousands of patients undergoing repeated cosmetic treatments over six years (and over 14 years for blepharospasm patients). The concentration used per injection site will be described in detail in Chapters 4, 7, 8 and 9.

Botox® and Dysport® are both reconstituted to give an equal effect per ml. In this book, 0.1 ml BTX-A refers both to Botox® (reconstituted with 2.5 ml) and Dysport® (reconstituted with 3 ml). The difference in concentration is because a vial of Dysport® is stronger than a vial of Botox® (although the price per vial is equal), and so requires greater dilution for effect. Allergan (Botox®) and Ipsen (Dysport®) have developed different individual 'mouse units' of concentration. These are not interchangeable and refer to different quantities.

A vial of Botox® contains 100 (Allergan) units, whereas a vial of Dysport® contains 500 (Ipsen) units. Measurement of dose per site in units could therefore be hazardous in countries where both products are available. Measurement in volume allows the practitioner to get a 'feeling' for the different doses per site. The practitioner can observe a treatment in volume as opposed to having to convert volume to units during treatment e.g. 0.1 ml to a site can be observed, rather than thinking 'this is 4 units Botox®' or '16.6 units Dysport®'. With practice, the concentration can be adjusted to modify the effect of treatment further.

USER TIP

Think in vol/ml solution and not units/BTX-A when injecting a patient. This allows good control and safety as one eye should always watch the volume gauge.

USER TIP

2.5 ml to Botox® correlates with 3 ml to Dysport®, giving equal doses per 0.1 ml injected.

0.1 ml Botox® (4 Botox® units) = 0.1 ml Dysport® (16.6 Dysport® units)

Botulinum toxin Type B (NeuroBloc®)

NeuroBloc® was launched in Europe in March 2001 for the treatment of cervical dystonia. It is presented in a ready-to-use solution and can be stored for 2 years if refrigerated. It is available in three vial volumes (containing 2,500, 5,000 and 10,000 units) and each vial contains a slight overfill. Although it is effective for 12–16 weeks in the treatment of cervical dystonia, at concentrations equal to that of Botox® (i.e. one unit Botox® = 50 units NeuroBloc®), its duration of action for cosmetic use in the author's clinic was six weeks. Current trials with this new product are examining the effect of increasing concentration on duration of action.

- **Botox® units are not equivalent to Dysport® units: Allergan (Botox®) and Ipsen (Dysport®) have developed different individual 'mouse units' of concentration which are not interchangeable.**
- **Botox® and Dysport® vials contain different quantities in units and are the same price per vial.One Botox® unit is 3-5 times stronger than one Dysport® unit. One Botox® vial has 100 units but one Dyport vial has 500 units.**
- **Low concentrations diffuse further than high concentrations.**
- **High concentrations last 12 weeks, low concentrations often wear off sooner.**
- **In this handbook, Botox® and Dysport® are both reconstituted to give an equal effect per ml.**
- **Dose should be measured in volume, rather than units, in order to avoid confusion. This also allows an eye to be kept on the syringe gauge while injecting a precise volume.**

The preparation of the toxin and of the patient are discussed in Chapter 4.

4 Preparation, storage and injection technique

USER TIP

NEVER handle botulinum toxin without surgical gloves.

PRESENTATION

Botox®

Botox® is delivered in an insulated container. It is presented as 100 units of freeze dried powder in a glass vial. The vials frequently look empty to the inexperienced eye, as the powder tends to rest in their bottom angle (Fig. 4.1).

There are strict guidelines for storage of botulinum toxin in order to prevent denaturation and maintain maximum efficacy. Botox® should be stored, before reconstitution, either frozen at minus five degrees (-5°) centigrade or in a refrigerator at 2–8° centigrade until reconstituted. Once reconstituted, Botox® must be stored at 2–8° centigrade (refrigeration temperature). Inexperienced practitioners can use a thermos flask or a vaccination transporter (Fig. 4.2) to maintain the solution at 2–8° if a refrigerator is not available in the clinic. This is effective but the temperature may vary and, if ice is used, may even be too cold. There is minimal evidence that freezing reconstituted Botox® solution preserves its efficacy and Allergan do not recommend this. Freezing may in fact accelerate denaturation of the product, greatly reducing its duration of efficacy after injection. In the author's experience, Botox® that has been partially denatured by being stored at the wrong temperature (e.g. leaving the bottle

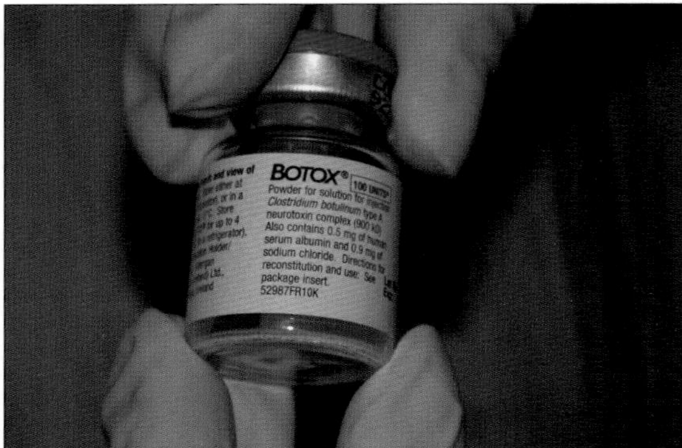

Fig 4.1 Powder at the bottom of a Botox® vial.

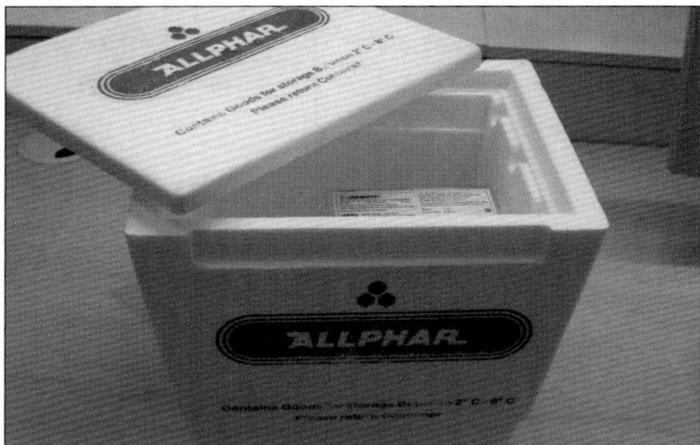

Fig 4.2 Insulated container.

on a table instead of in the refrigerator) will still achieve some effect but of a reduced duration.

Dysport®

Dysport® comes in a plastic hinged box containing two glass vials (Fig. 4.3). Like Botox®, it is a freeze-dried powder that clumps at the bottom of the vial. Dysport® does not have to be stored in a deep freeze but, once reconstituted, it must be kept at 2–8° centigrade. Ipsen recommend using it within eight hours of reconstitution. Reconstituted Dysport® should not be frozen.

NeuroBloc® (Myobloc in the USA)

NeuroBloc® is a liquid and comes in vials of three different sizes: 2,500 units (0.5 ml), 5,000 units (1.0 ml) and 10,000 units (2.0 ml) (see Fig. 3.1). It can be

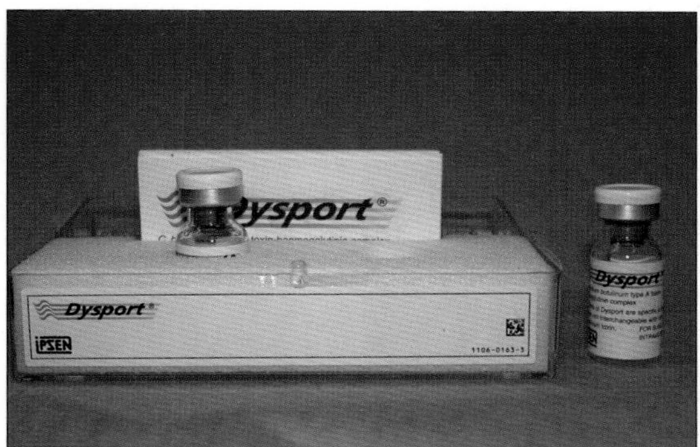

Fig 4.3 Plastic box of Dysport® with 2 vials.

stored in unopened vials, in a refrigerator at 2–8°, for up to 18 months, and at room temperature for 8 hours. If diluted with saline, it should not be stored for longer than 8 hours. NeuroBloc® should not be frozen.

RECONSTITUTION

The rubber seal on the vial should be wiped with an alcohol swab before using a 5 ml syringe to inject the desired volume of normal preservative-free saline. A green 25-gauge needle is inserted carefully through the center of the bung. Especial care must be taken with Botox® bungs which freeze solid as the needle can easily enter at an angle, releasing pieces of rubber into the solution.

USER TIP

Never agitate botulinum toxin solution when reconstituting it.

The product is vacuum-sealed. Air can be injected into the vial to avoid too rapid a reconstitution, and a thumb can be placed under the plunger of the syringe to control the rate of release of saline onto the powder (Fig. 4.4). The saline must not gush in and agitate the solution mechanically. Rotating the vial during injection also assists a gentle reconstitution.

TRANSPORT

Both Dysport® and Botox® can be transported after reconstitution if the solution is not agitated. The author used to work in an outlying clinic and used a cold packed vaccine insulation box for transport. Ideally Dysport® and Botox® should be reconstituted after the journey. Agitation denatures the toxin and greatly reduces its duration of action

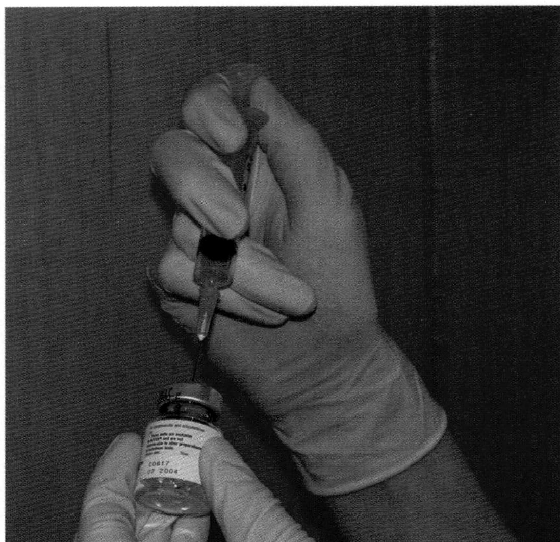

Fig 4.4 Controlled reconstitution.

INJECTION TECHNIQUE

Almost all of the injections mentioned in this book, unless specifically stated otherwise, are intramuscular and not subcutaneous.

The author's experience is based on the initial management of patients with facial dystonia. Such patients suffer from involuntary and irregular contraction of one or several groups of facial muscles, often involving the orbicularis oculi and orbicularis oris. The impulse, once sparked, is thought to travel from muscle fiber to muscle fiber by the sequential depolarization of adjacent fibers (ephaptic transmission). BTX-A injections are placed in such a way that they achieve the maximum blockage of impulse transmission with the minimum of side effects, by giving BTX-A to muscles along the line of transmission.

The placement of BTX-A around dangerous areas, such as the corner of the mouth where inadvertent diffusion to the levators of the labii superioris will cause drooling, requires careful analysis of the degree of diffusion of the injection by dose and by depth of injection. Intramuscular placement is essential for maximum effect and control, but subcutaneous treatment can be used gently in these areas.

USER TIP

All injections of BTX-A referred to here are intramuscular unless otherwise stated.

INJECTION

We recommend using one ml tuberculin or insulin syringes. These are essential for the dose to be gauged accurately during injection. The doses recommended in this book are given in units of volume. The finest mark on a one ml syringe is 0.01: we often recommend using 0.025 ml (more later).

USER TIP

Always watch the gauge of the syringe while injecting.

DOSAGE

The vial can be diluted with preservative-free normal saline to achieve the desired concentration. The doses recommended for cosmetic use have been established independently by several workers over the last six years and, while now based on experience, were initially derived from the doses used for blepharospasm (Chapter 10).

Jean and Alastair Carruthers made their original observations about the ability of Botox® to smooth rhytids while treating a patient with blepharospasm induced by facial palsy. Blepharospasm due to orbicularis oculi spasm is treated with injections into the muscle above and below the eye. The information leaflet provided with each vial of Botox® or Dysport® gives the optimal dose recommended to relax each part of the orbicularis muscle. For blepharospasm, Allergan recommend a dilution of 2.5 ml to give 4 units per 0.1 ml. Dysport® recommend a dilution of 2.5 ml to give 20 units per 0.1 ml.

USER TIP

Botox® Cosmetic has been licensed for the management of the glabellar frown (see Chapter 8). Specific directions for dosage are provided.

A review of the literature provides information on the dosage preferences of a variety of practitioners. The author has validated the doses suggested in this book over the course of more than 10,000 treatments given since the cosmetic use of Botox® was suggested in the early nineties. With experience, the reader should get a feeling for the required dose in each patient – as part of the 'art of botulinum' – and may well modify these doses accordingly. The following guidelines based on the author's experience may be useful:

- **Aim to use the smallest volume of the lowest concentration necessary to provide paralysis of the target muscle for at least 12 weeks.**

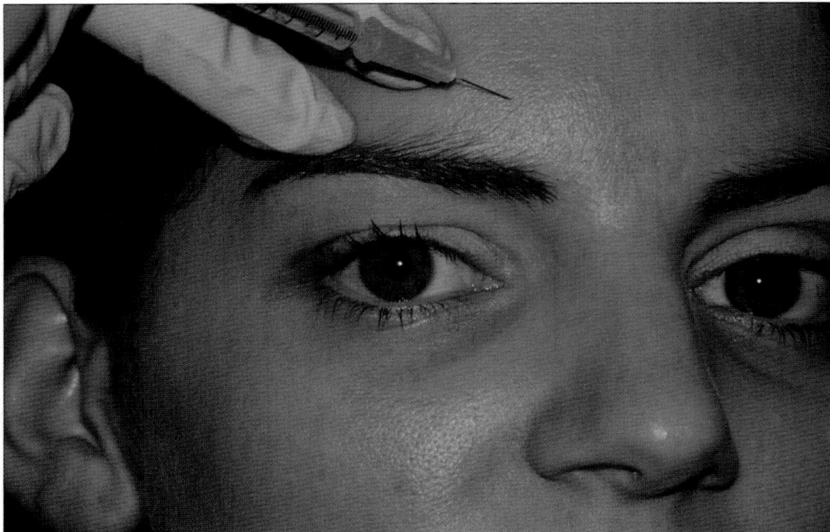

Fig 4.5 Injecting at 1cm over superior orbital rim.

- **Decide in advance how far you want the injection to diffuse.**
- **Remember that, on average, 4 units in 0.1 ml of Botox® will diffuse 1 cm; 20 units of Dysport® in 0.1 ml will diffuse 1.5 cm; 20 units of Dysport® in 0.05 ml will diffuse less far; as will 2 units of Botox® in 0.05 ml.**
- **Select the injection site so that treatment will not extend beyond the desired diffusion zone e.g. 0.1ml Botox® injected one centimeter above the superior orbital rim (not brow) to treat the glabellar muscle. This avoids diffusion towards the levator muscle (Fig. 4.5). Likewise, inject Dysport® 0.05 ml one centimeter from the lateral canthus (outer corner of the eyelid) to avoid diffusion medially. This is dealt with in detail in later chapters.**
- **Base your choice of dosage on the recommendations given in Chapters 7, 8 and 9. Most receive the same dose for the same rhytids; but one aim of this book is to teach how to treat the unpredictable minority too.**

USER TIP

Concentration of botulinum toxin:
Too weak = short duration of action
Too strong = risk of increased side effects

Increased Diffusion

GOOD FOR:

- **Treatment of frontalis**
- **Extended treatment of crow's feet (inferolaterally over zygomatic arch)**

Reduced Diffusion

GOOD FOR:

- **Lateral canthus**
- **Pre tarsal orbicularis**
- **Close to superior orbital rim**

USER TIP

Increased volume dilution per unit botulinum toxin means increased diffusion.

ASPIRATION

Always use gloves for self protection. The solution should be aspirated freshly for each patient, although some doctors recommend pre-aspiration of botulinum in several one ml syringes, and then storing them in the refrigerator. Manufacturers recommend a single vial per patient which must be used within four hours of reconstitution.

Botulinum toxin is potent and very expensive, so each drop must be used to its maximum effect. Even 0.0125ml is effective in certain sites.

Take care to remove the 25-gauge needle from the bottle after aspiration, particularly with Dysport® where the combination of a small vial and a viscous solution encourage seepages from the needle.

Once aspiration is complete, attach a 30-gauge needle to the hub of the syringe. Take care that the batches of needles and syringes fit well together, and beware attachments so loose that the toxin dribbles from the hub during injection. This is wasteful, and may be hazardous if the leaked fluid contacts the patient's face (ingestion of botulinum toxin droplets have been suspected of causing mild gastroenteritis). Clear the air bubble from the syringe using minimal agitation. This requires more care with Dysport® because of its greater viscosity.

USER TIP

Wipe away any spilled botulinum toxin with a hypochlorite solution

INJECTION TECHNIQUE

First, study the face and the muscles of the area to be injected (see Chapters 7 and 8). An inexperienced worker should mark the injection sites with a washable skin marker, having first wiped the sites with an alcohol swab. It is important to sterilize the skin at the injection site, as many patients wear a make-up foundation. Local granulomas or erythematous nodules can develop at injection sites (Fig. 4.6), but the author has never seen areas of infection or cellulitis related to an injection. Some practitioners suggest that alcohol denatures the toxin. If this were so, then every injection site swabbed with alcohol during a treatment session should have a similar effect on the toxin at the time of injection. The author, however, has seen no difference in the effect of BTX when given simultaneously to sites which have been swabbed (forehead) and have not (eye zone in patients who find the alcohol too irritating and are simply swabbed with saline).

Botulinum toxin can be injected intramuscularly or subcutaneously. Most doses in this book, however, are based on intramuscular injections, and have been derived from experience with blepharospasm. Subcutaneous injections are also effective but need more injection sites to allow for maximum absorption. Pre-tarsal orbicularis injections are usually given intramuscularly

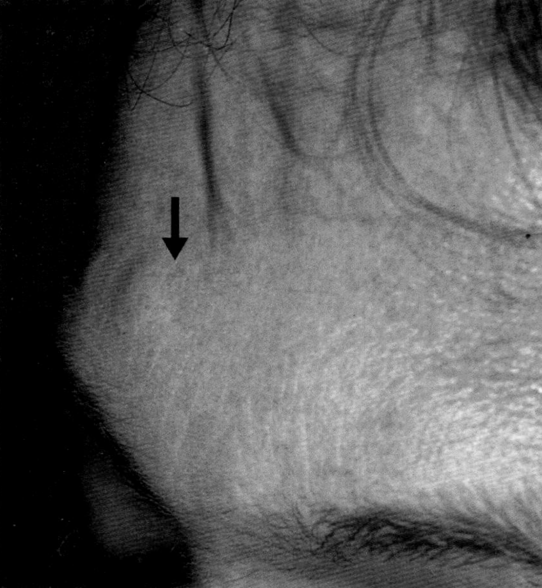

Fig 4.6 Granuloma on forehead at site of Botox® injection (arrow).

as the skin here is only 0.5 mm thick. Intramuscular placement stings less, and produces less local erythema. However it carries a slight risk of causing intramuscular bruising.

USER TIP

Avoid the supraorbital nerve, vein and artery complex when injecting the glabellar area. Study the anatomy and, if in doubt, feel for the supraorbital notch (not always present) under the medial aspect of the brow.

Start with the frontalis zone. Ask the patients to frown while assessing the bulk of muscle contraction, then relax the patient and inject at the point noted. Gently tip the periosteum with the needle, withdraw slightly, and inject while watching the syringe gradations. With experience, one soon becomes familiar with the muscle bulk, and the periosteum is rarely touched. Take care to point the needle away from danger and in particular avoid pointing it towards the orbital septum when injecting the lateral canthus.

It is sometimes useful to hold the muscle site between two fingers, especially in the glabellar area (Fig. 4.7).

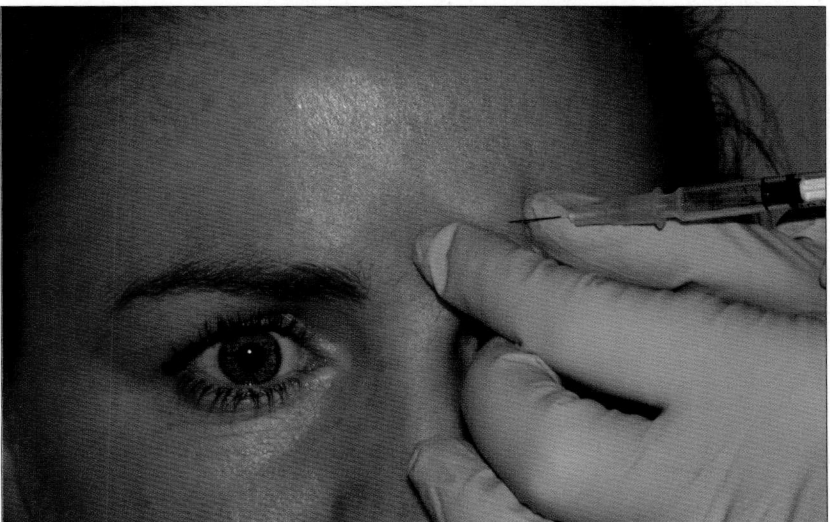

Fig 4.7 Holding the muscle between two fingers when injecting the glabella.

USER TIP

Spread the lateral orbital skin between two fingers to observe the orbital veins clearly and take care to inject around these.

USER TIP

Steady the injecting hand by resting the little finger on the face while spreading the skin with the other hand. Resting the little finger of the injecting hand against the face, or the other hand on the face, also helps to avoid sudden movement by the patient towards the needle (Fig. 4.8). Look carefully for and avoid superficial veins.

PAIN

Botox® stings more than Dysport®, and NeuroBloc® more than Botox®. Topical anesthesia makes no difference to the pain of intramuscular injections, although it should be used for other injections – see Chapter 11. Slow insertion of the needle can greatly reduce the perception of pain, possibly by minimizing the mechanical stimulation of cutaneous pain receptors.

In the author's clinic experimental reconstitution using saline preserved with 0.9% benzyl alcohol (Wigmore pharmacy) has been found to stop the stinging. There have also been reports of reconstitution with lidocaine (lignocaine) to minimize pain but the efficacy of this has not been tested by the author.

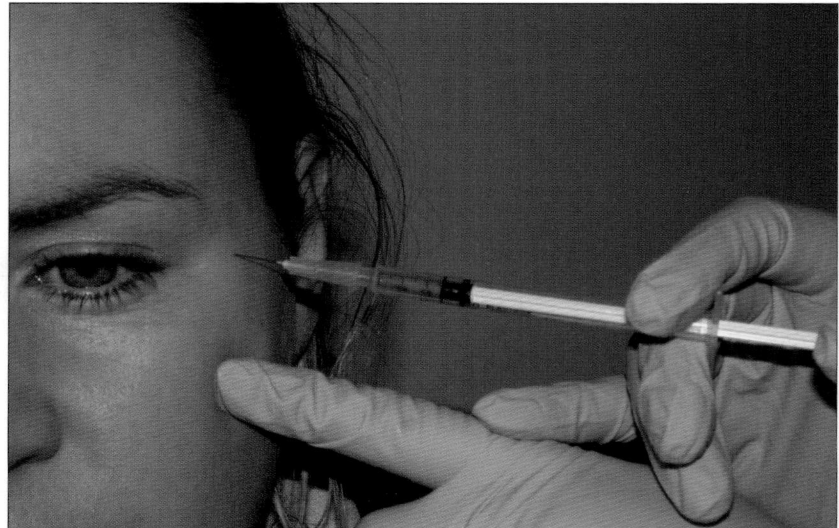

Fig 4.8 Steady the injecting hand, and avoid sudden movement by the patient towards the needle.

POST-INJECTION

The patient should be asked to press on the site with a tissue immediately after the injection – even while other sites are being treated. This minimizes bruising. Any bruising that occurs should be treated immediately with an ice pack from the freezer. Camouflage cream or make-up is then applied before the patient goes home.

Some experts believe that flying or lying down after treatment causes untoward diffusion and hence side effects such as ptosis. However, the author has had no cases of ptosis in over 10,000 treatments, and has seen no evidence to confirm this theory.

DURATION OF APPOINTMENT

An average botulinum appointment lasts a maximum of 10 minutes. This excludes the first counseling visit (often 90 minutes) but includes reading and signing the consent form, the injections and settling the account. A nurse practitioner may prepare the patient, thus reducing the time spent with the practitioner.

Table 4.1. A comparison of the different commercially available botulinum toxins

	Botox®	Dysport®	NeuroBloc®
Presentation	Single 100 unit vial (frozen)	Two 500 unit vials (refrigerated)	0.5 ml, 1.0 ml or 2.0 ml vials (refrigerated)
Form	Freeze dried powder	Freeze dried powder	Liquid protein complex
Reconstitution	0.9% preservative free saline	0.9% preservative-free saline	May be further diluted with 0.9% preservative-free saline
Recommended storage before reconstitution	One year frozen at = ≤5° or one year refrigerated at 2–8°	One year refrigerated at 2–8°	18 months under refrigeration at 2–8° or 8 hours at room temperature If diluted, no more than 8 hours at either room temperature or under refrigeration
Recommended storage after reconstitution	Four hours at 2–8° Should not be frozen	Eight hours at 2–8° Should not be frozen	

5 Patient selection

Some patients have a clear idea of their requirements and a good aesthetic sense. Others trust their doctors to advise them on 'what looks good'. They may come for treatment only because they were told to do so by their friends or their parents. If so they may resent a treatment to which they are not fully committed.

The golden rule here is that if patients are not going to derive any *perceivable* pleasure from botulinum toxin, then their expenditure will not be properly rewarded. Their trust in their physician will be reduced, almost as if they had been 'sold' a dress in a shop that they did not really want – such shops are rarely revisited. It is important not to be influenced by such patients' demands. If a decision is made by the physician to refuse treatment, then at least no harm is done. The botulinum treatment cannot be 'undone' one week later if the patient is unhappy with the outcome (even though the physician had already described the implications of treatment clearly). Above all, remember that no one *needs* botulinum toxin.

HOW TO IDENTIFY SUITABLE PATIENTS

- **Listen to their presenting complaint and then, while still looking at the patient, decide quickly whether it can be treated with botulinum toxin or not.**
- **Continue the consultation while carefully assessing the patient's psychological suitability (more below).**

- **If, on first impression, the patient seems suitable, spend time providing verbal and written information about the treatment (this can be done by a trained nurse).**
- **Always examine patients closely – as described in the following chapters – and discuss the likely outcome of botulinum toxin injections with them.**
- **Be sure that your patients understand what has been said fully before they sign the consent form.**

Physical assessment is an art, which becomes intuitive with experience. A variety of different complaints are dealt with in detail in this book with all their caveats. Time must be taken over the initial examination and in order to be certain that the patient will be happy after treatment.

SELECTION PROCESS

All new patients must be assessed physically and mentally. Written information about botulinum toxin should be provided at the time of consultation and patients should have time to digest this before an opportunity is provided to ask the physician any relevant questions. Practice nurses (Chapter 12) should be able to identify most patients suitable for botulinum toxin, and so do not have to spend time counseling those the practitioner is likely to decide not to treat. The alternative is to assess patients first and then send those selected for treatment to the aesthetic nurse for photography and counseling. When the patients return to the practitioner, it will be possible to double-check that the risks and likely outcomes are fully understood before the consent form is signed.

THE INITIAL PHYSICAL ASSESSMENT

With experience, it is possible to decide at a glance whether or not botulinum toxin will help a patient. A 29-year-old non-smoker, for example, with crow's feet that only wrinkle when she is smiling, will do very well. Botulinum toxin will rid her of wrinkles completely. On the other hand, her twin, who smokes and uses a sun bed for a permanent tan, may have wrinkles at rest with an early reduction in lower lid skin tone. Time must be spent explaining to her that she may possibly be disappointed with botulinum toxin – the injections might help to stop the clock and avoid new rhytids, but without alternative treatments (including sun protection, laser resurfacing, stopping smoking) she will continue to have her wrinkles.

The decision must be made, prior to treatment, as to whether botulinum toxin can eliminate rhytids, reduce them and prevent further rhytids, or whether another type of treatment is necessary. Consider whether patients are likely to look unusual after treatment e.g. with peaked brows or tired appearance with heavy brows. Would they be better to avoid treatment altogether, to have gradual treatment over a few weeks, or to have a different treatment?

The initial assessment must be followed by a physical examination but obvious contraindications should be detectable at this stage. Some signs immediately indicate or contraindicate treatment; for example, it is best to decline treatment where a patient has no specific complaints but decides that 'the doctor knows best', and presents for botulinum toxin with the vague aim of 'looking better'.

The patient should have given an accurate age and history of smoking (though some do not!) and a full medical history should reveal no obvious contraindications such as myasthenia gravis, pregnancy etc. (see Chapter 6).

At this stage, the physician should:

- **Observe the face, neck and hands of the patient while the patient is animated (talking).**
- **Look for the signs summarized in Table 5.1**
- **How old does the patient look? Is this older or younger than expected?**
- **Is the skin on the face sun-damaged?**
- **Consider the patient's profession. Many actors will not benefit from paucity of facial expression.**
- **How does the skin behave with facial expressions?**
- **In particular, observe static wrinkles around the eyes and on the forehead, whether these change with the facial expression and, importantly, whether**

Table 5.1. Signs to be observed quickly before a full consultation takes place

Consider the following:	Look for:
General skin condition	Sun damaged, pigment spots, poor tone.
Age	Cardiovascular status, skin perfusion, overall tone and skeletal structure.
Brow position	Examine lash/brow distance. How does it change with expression? Are the forehead wrinkles the result of 'holding' brows?
Crow's feet	At rest or in motion? Do they extend down towards the perioral lines when smiling?
Hooding	Is there a fold of skin at the corner of the eye that disappears when the patient lifts the brow?

patients tend to hold their brows in continuous suspension by wrinkling their forehead, thereby hiding any underlying dermatochalasis (excess skin folds on upper eyelids).

- **Are crow's feet present only when the patient smiles?**
- **Are wrinkles present at rest?**
- **Do the wrinkles continue over the zygomatic arches?**
- **Is there 'hooding' of the skin above the corners of the brows?**

INDICATIONS FOR TREATMENT

Wrinkles on the face

It is good if the wrinkles are dynamic i.e. only appear with frowning and smiling. Treat these.

If the patient has wrinkles at rest and is sun damaged or simply elderly, care must be taken to emphasize that botulinum toxin will reduce lines around the eyes and forehead but will not eliminate them.

Glabellar rhytid (vertical frown)

Consider the following points:

- **If the frown is dynamic i.e. visible only in motion, the result of treatment may well be a good one.**
- **If the furrow is present at rest: warn the patient that it may not be completely eliminated.**
- **If the patient has heavy brows (seen especially in men), treatment of the frown may increase the sagging medially.**
- **Examine the brow–lash distance? (Fig. 5.1). If low, regardless of age and skin tone, treatment may cause descension of the medial brow over the orbital rim, causing an unusual 'tired' appearance.**
- **Are the patient's brows asymmetrical in motion? If so, the results of treatment will be asymmetrical too unless this is taken into account.**
- **Does the patient have an active frontalis? If so, treatment of the vertical furrow alone may cause the lateral brow to elevate, creating an unattractive peaking of the brows. Such patients should have a different treatment or their full forehead zone treated.**

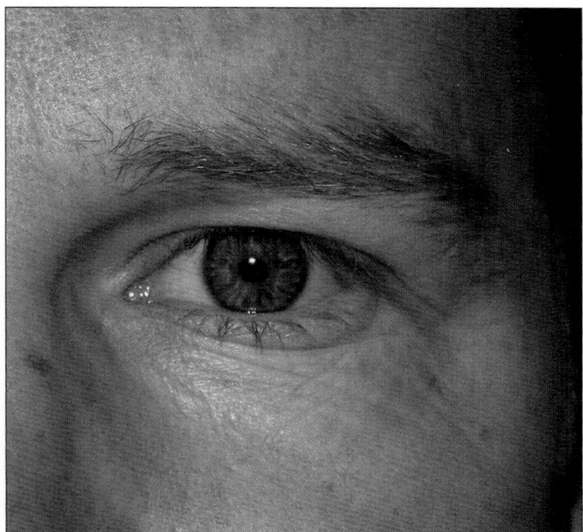

Fig 5.1 Patient with low lash–brow distance.

Horizontal rhytids (frontalis)

Consider the following points:

- **Eyebrow position: Patients with a good lash/brow distance at rest, will do well with treatment.**
- **High eyebrows: relaxing the horizontal rhytids will prevent the high resting tone of the brows, particularly in patients over 50 or those with sun damaged skin.**
- **Active brows with changes in facial expression: if such motility is culturally influenced, as, for example, in France, the patients may be unhappy with the loss of facial expression.**

Crow's feet

- **Wrinkles in motion only – such rhytids are ideal for treatment.**
- **Wrinkles at rest – aim to discuss modification and prevention in detail with the patient.**
- **Wrinkles extending over zygomatic arch, increasing with smiling, and usually seen in older patients: extra care must be taken. Botulinum toxin treatment alone can create an incongruous appearance: no crow's feet when smiling, but wrinkles extending from the cheekbone to the perioral smile lines. This can even**

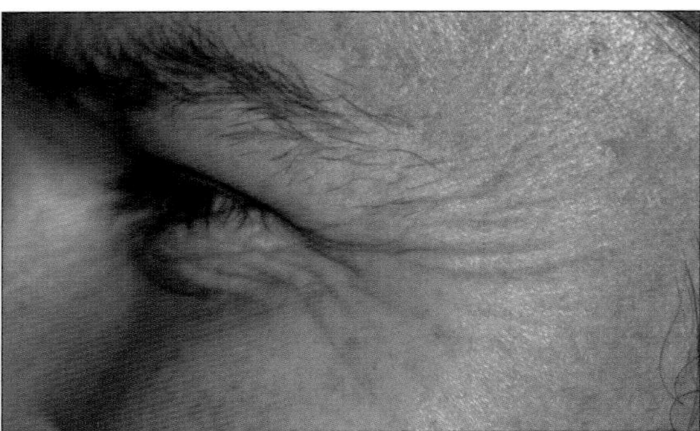

Fig 5.2 Patient with hooding of lateral brows.

create a 'Mickey Mouse' appearance – a flat area around the eyes surrounded by extended perioral smile lines.

- **Hooding of lateral brows (Fig. 5.2): this is usually due to loss of tone and descension of the lateral brow and temporal forehead. The 'wrinkle' under the hood will remain after treatment. It is important to explain to the patient that other treatment (e.g. endoscopic brow lift, carbon dioxide laser resurfacing) is indicated and that botulinum toxin will not remove the particular rhytid.**

Psychological assessment

The physician must develop a keen instinct when assessing patients for cosmetic botulinum toxin, in particular, the patient's psychological suitability and comprehension.

Aesthetic treatments, unlike medical ones, are not essential and can be refused at any stage. The initial consultation should identify patients who are poorly equipped psychologically to deal with changes in their appearance.

Every patient is entitled to follow up consultations once they have received a treatment, regardless of the medical necessity of the visit. If a patient becomes distressed by the new shape of their eyebrows, it is important to be available to counsel and reassure them until the effect of the botulinum toxin has worn off. This may even entail daily appointments for the first week, followed by weekly appointments for reassurance until the toxin has worn off.

Guidelines applicable to all cosmetic medical and surgical treatments

An astute, experienced, telephonist will screen out many unsuitable patients. The next point of contact in a cosmetic practice may be the practice manager, who books appointments and deals with patients' accounts. They too are trained to detect patients who may have unrealistic expectations, or show poor comprehension. Patients frequently see an aesthetic nurse before their medical consultation. An experienced practice nurse can cancel a treatment plan for an unsuitable patient. The patients who eventually see the physician are usually ideal for treatment, but some are still deemed unsuitable at the time of consultation because of unachievable expectations or more frequently, lack of psychological reserves to deal with a risk at that particular moment in time. Such patients may have their first treatment postponed and be given an appointment for review. A typical reason for postponement would be a recent bereavement.

There are obvious reasons for refusing certain patients even though they are physically suitable for botulinum toxin, but more subtle ones should also be considered.

The decision not to treat is always based on the possibility that the patient will not be happy with what the treatment will do – even if they think they will!

- **Ask yourself, before every new treatment, will this make this patient happy?**
- **If not, why not?**

Some reasons for poor patient satisfaction despite a good result

Low intelligence

Patients who cannot understand risks or side effects despite repeated explanations often reveal themselves only after the first treatment, by telephoning the next day to say that it 'hasn't worked', or 14 weeks later to complain that the 'wrinkles have returned' despite advice about the time of onset and duration.

Unreasonable expectations

Patients with unreasonable expectations often argue with the physician. For example, if shown how the brows might peak if their glabella alone is treated, they might disagree and continue to request the glabella treatment on its own. Do not treat these patients!

Some cosmetic surgery patients are highly manipulative. There may be a pattern of missing or changing appointments, insisting that they have canceled when they had not, and misquoting the secretary about the instructions given. Such patients are often extremely nice to the physician but create havoc with the nurse and manager. Once such a pattern of behavior has emerged it is wise to try to stop further treatments or fail to make appointments available.

Some manipulative patients like to 'test' their doctors. Patients who are deceitful about their medical history (e.g. concealing previous cosmetic surgery despite obvious scars) may conceal other facts. There are numerous anecdotes about patients attending hospital under a pseudonym for cosmetic procedures. In one case, the patient suffered a myocardial infarction at the time of the procedure, having denied a previous history of the heart disease in case the cosmetic surgery was refused, attending under a pseudonym.

Care must be taken to document in detail all consultations, with written information, photography and a good signed consent form. Certain patients may deny ever being given information and have been known to misrepresent medical advice, slandering the physician. Such patients typically slander other colleagues to the physician e.g. 'I went to Dr X but it didn't work'. Most colleagues are proficient, and it may be prudent to be alert to the motives of patients who complain about them. The easiest solution is NOT to treat difficult patients in the first place.

The close friends of patients or their siblings can also have unreasonable expectations. One sibling, with a family resemblance, may marvel at the other's result, and expect the same cosmetic result. It can be hard to point out that their sibling is a natural beauty with symmetrical features and good skin tone, whereas they, although rather alike, have lower heavier brows with asymmetrical frontalis action and sun damaged skin!

Some patients are referred by other patients, expecting the same result as their friend. Care must be taken to explain the expected differences in results, while never referring to their friend or acknowledging that their friend really is a patient.

Depression

Depression is greatly underdiagnosed. Both reactive and endogenous types are relative contraindications to treatment. A depressed patient may speak slowly, and seem 'flat' during the consultation. They may have suffered a recent bereavement, separation or divorce. Those who experience such life crises often review themselves. They notice their appearance, decide that they have 'let themselves go' and fix up a botulinum toxin appointment. Some become tearful during the consultation.

There are two good reasons for not treating depressed patients. The first is the risk associated with every procedure. An unusual complication could deepen their depression. The other is that many patients, even mildly depressed ones, have poor powers of concentration, so they find it hard to assimilate medical advice.

The subject of their depression may be gently broached. Cosmetic treatment options can be discussed but accompanied with a suggestion to postpone the treatment until they are better. Psychological and medical counseling may be recommended, perhaps with a referral to their G.P. for a psychiatric referral. Time is well spent discussing the way the body behaves with depression, and the forms of treatment available. These patients usually return when they are better and are often suitable then for cosmetic procedures.

It is true that some depressed patients do cheer up when botulinum toxin eliminates their frown, but care should be taken about the timing of such treatments.

Dysmorphophobia

This disorder is rare but seen at every cosmetic clinic. It has various degrees of severity and patients require a psychiatric referral – if they will agree to one. Avoid treating such patients without a report from their psychiatrist.

An example of a dysmorphophobic patient is one who came for the management of a 'wrinkle'. There simply was no wrinkle where they pointed. In another, the normal lower lid Morgagnian crease (between the pretarsal and tarsal orbicularis) was the offending wrinkle.

Such patients often refuse to look in the mirror during the consultation, and almost always become distressed if attempts are made to photograph them. It is useful to remember that even though the defect identified by the patient is not apparent to an objective viewer, the patient may continue to view it as a problem whether it is treated or not. Some patients will have received numerous cosmetic treatments elsewhere at enormous expense. The ethics of this are debatable.

USER TIP

Avoid joint consultations i.e. seeing two friends at the same time. Welcome a 'second ear' if necessary and let a friend sit in, but it is difficult to assess a patient's mental suitability for a procedure when speaking to two people at once.

6 Contraindications and complications

The selection of patients for treatment with botulinum toxin is described in detail in Chapter 5. Some well-established contraindications must always be kept in mind.

ABSOLUTE CONTRAINDICATIONS

Anything that interferes with the predicted response to botulinum toxin, which inhibits the release of acetylcholine at the neuromuscular synapse (Fig. 6.1).

Drugs and disorders which also reduce acetylcholine at the motor end plate, amplifying the action of BTX.

- **Eaton Lambert antibodies. Note a history of cancer, metastases and general lack of wellbeing which may suggest a diagnosis of Eaton Lambert syndrome (see Neuromuscular disorders).**
- **Aminoglycosides (gentamycin, streptomycin, kanamycin) act on the presynaptic neurone.**

Drugs and disorders which alter the response of the motor end plate, amplifying the action of BTX

- **Myasthenia gravis alters and reduces the acetylcholine receptors on the motor end-plate (see Neuromuscular disorders).**

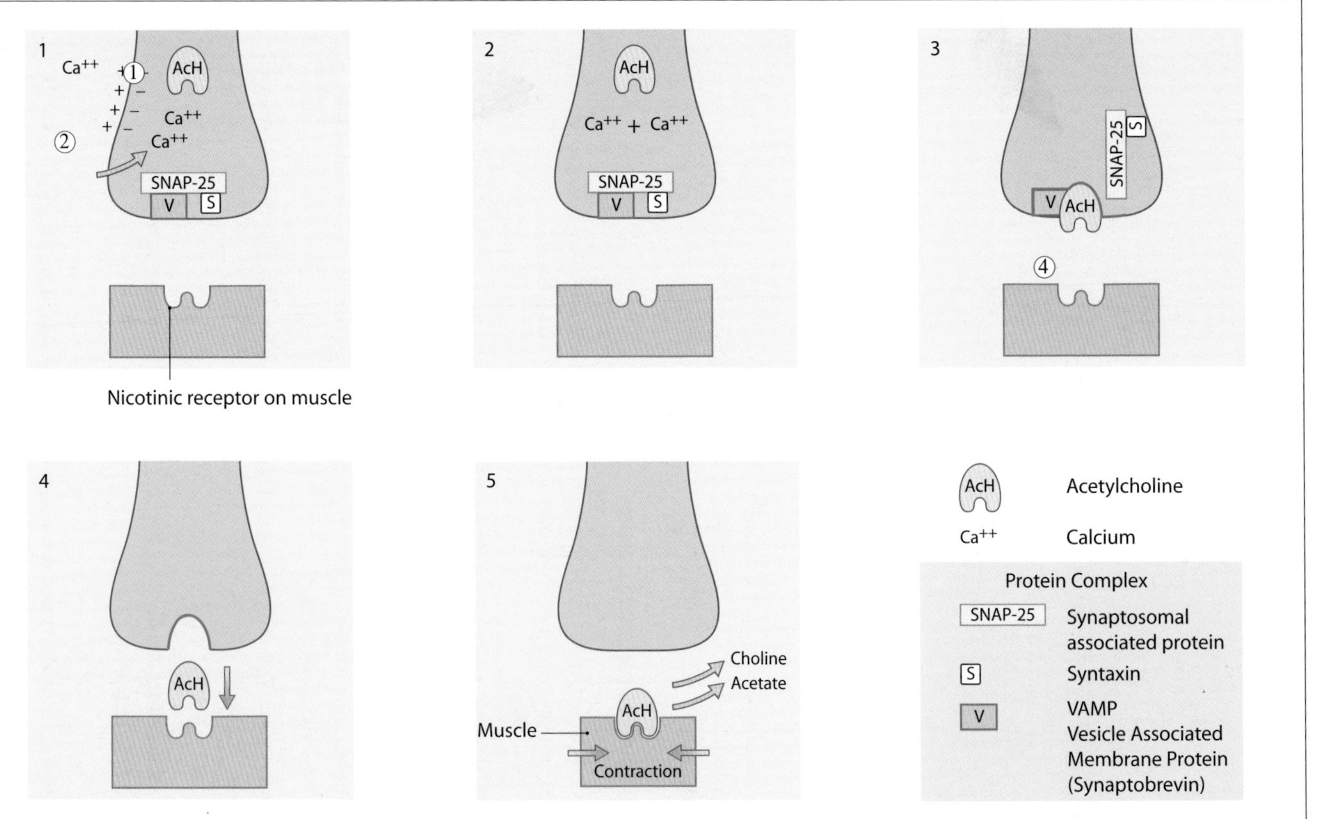

Fig 6.1 Normal cholinergic transmission and action of botulinum toxin at the neuromuscular junction: effects of drug and disease interactions (circled numbers). ① Calcium channel blockers: aminoglycosides, ciclosporin; ② Tumour antigen antibodies block calcium channels (Lambert Eaton syndrome); ③ Block binding of BTX heavy chain to synaptogamin: chloroquine and hydroxychloroquine; ④ Block nicotine receptors: antibodies, e.g. myasthenia gravis, D-penicillamine; 5, Post synaptic acetylcholine antagonist: tubocurarine, gallamine, pancuronium. Agonist blocker: succinylcholine.

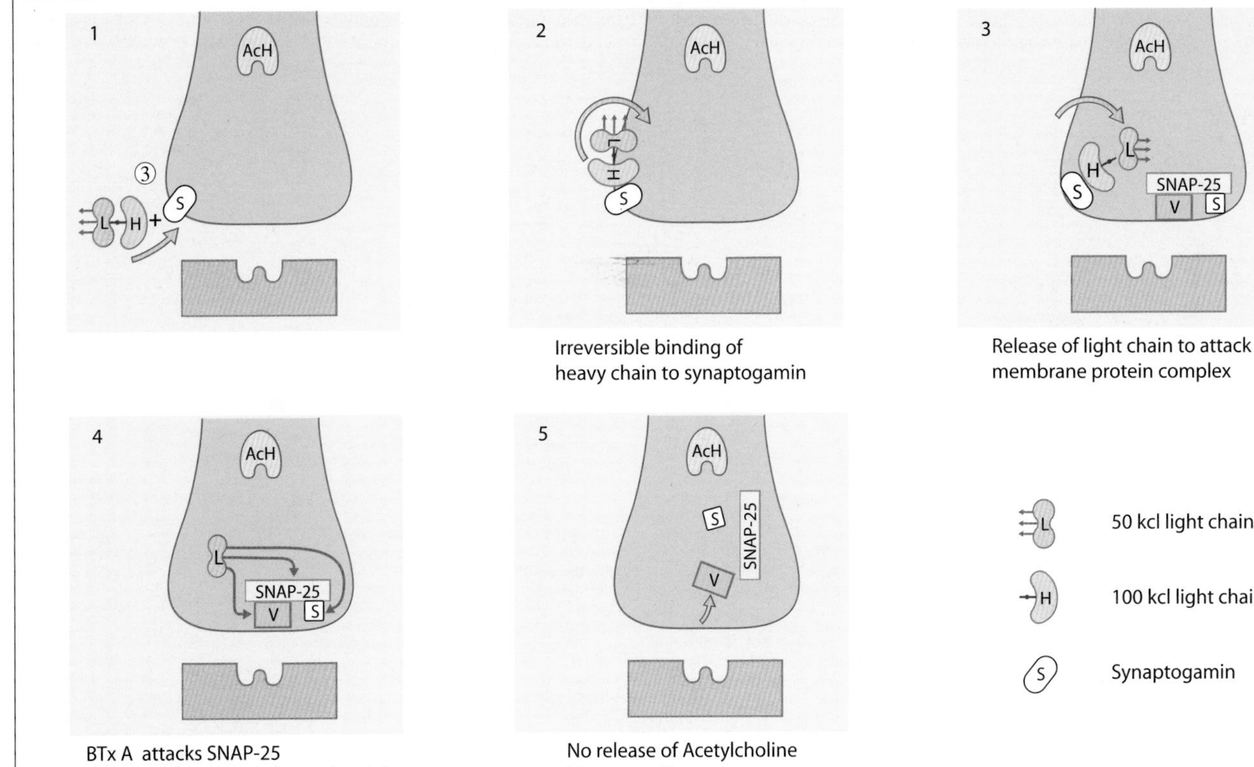
1
AcH
3
L
H
+
S
2
AcH
L
H
S
Irreversible binding of
heavy chain to synaptogamin
3
AcH
L
H
S
SNAP-25
V
S
Release of light chain to attack
membrane protein complex
4
AcH
L
SNAP-25
V
S
BTx A attacks SNAP-25
BTx B attacks VAMP (Synaptobrevin)
No binding of AcH
5
AcH
S
SNAP-25
V
No release of Acetylcholine
No contraction
L
50 kcl light chain
H
100 kcl light chain
S
Synaptogamin

Fig 6.1 *Cont'd.*

- **Medication with succinylcholine (an agonist blocker) produces a prolonged depolarization with reduced contraction.**
- **Tubocurarine, pancuronium and gallamine are antagonist blockers that compete with acetylcholine for end-plate receptor sites.**
- **D-penicillamine can produce myasthenia gravis-type antibodies.**

Drugs which reduce the action of botulinum toxin

The antimalarials chloroquine and hydroxychloroquine, and the immunosuppressant ciclosporin can reduce the action of botulinum toxin.

Neuromuscular disorders

It is of paramount importance to avoid botulinum toxin in patients with neuromuscular disorders. Many such disorders are inherited and so a thorough family history must be taken with this point in mind.

General and local anesthesia

Administering botulinum toxin at the time of general or local anesthesia gives less predictable results. Avoid injecting botulinum toxin to the eye zone in patients who have had local anesthesia for blepharoplasty.

Also avoid giving botulinum toxin in the post-operative phase where there is local oedema, in order to reduce the risk of distal diffusion and, for example, perioral palsy.

Pregnancy and breast feeding

The teratogenicity of botulinum toxin has not yet been established and so it is contraindicated in pregnancy and during breast-feeding.

Allergy

A history of allergy to any ingredient in the formulation, including albumin.

Infection at the proposed injection site

Contraindications:

- **Eaton Lambert syndrome**
- **Myasthenia gravis**
- **Neuromuscular disorders (check family history)**
- **Aminoglycosides, e.g. streptomycin, gentamycin, kanamycin**
- **Certain drugs used during anesthesia, e.g. succinylcholine, tubocurare**

Contraindications (*continued*):

- **D-Penicillamine – used in rheumatoid arthritis**
- **Chloroquine, hydroxychloroquine (antimalarials)**
- **Ciclosporin (immunosuppressant)**
- **Pregnancy**
- **Infection**

USER TIP

Search the patient's history for any hint of muscle or nerve weakness that they may not be aware of. Enquire about episodes of intermittent drooping of the eyelid.

USER TIP

Take care to document that the patient has denied any contraindications.

RELATIVE CONTRAINDICATIONS

Many patients who come for botulinum toxin treatment for rhytids are self-referred. Their motivation is based either on a drive for self-improvement or a desire to 'have what their friend has had', i.e. a wrinkle-free forehead. Reserve judgment on their suitability for treatment until a careful assessment has been carried out. This is dealt with in detail in Chapter 5, and most of the side effects discussed in the present chapter can be avoided by rigorous patient selection. In addition, patients must be provided with detailed written information about the poisonous nature of the botulinum toxin as well as about the other risks associated with treatment.

If fully informed, most patients have reasonable expectations. Once in possession of all the facts, they are in a position to decide what risks to take and when. They may be happy to risk walking down the aisle with a camouflaged bruise, or may prefer to postpone this risk until after their 'big day', and opt to keep their frown instead. If their treatment will be unpredictable (e.g. the treatment of a deep frown in a patient with moderate lash/brow distance and a moderate transient risk of immobile brows) then let them know about this. They can always change the date of their appointment to avoid it clashing with a big occasion.

USER TIP

Avoid treating patients who cannot fully understand the risks being discussed.

Table 6.1. Patients' complaints after injections of botulinum toxin (BTX) for their rhytids.

Complaint	Most likely cause
It didn't work!	BTX denatured.
It didn't last!	BTX too dilute or too old.
I'm still frowning!	Patients don't understand what you have told them about their low brows and the treatment of frown! (see Chapter 8)
Patient looks tired	BTX to forehead causes brow ptosis.
My eyes are swollen!	Due to protrusion of upper and lower lid orbital fat and skin from weight of flaccid brows and flaccid lower septum.
Peaked eyebrows	BTX over 75% of medial brow only.
Hollow socket	BTX to inferolateral canthus in certain patients.
Epiphora	BTX over lacrimal pump.
Severe bruising	BTX over branch of maxillary vein.
Unnaturally wide lateral palpebral aperture	BTX to pretarsal orbicularis muscle.

Table 6.1 lists the most frequent complaints encountered in the author's practice during more than 10,000 treatments with botulinum toxin for rhytids. During this time the incidence of complaints has dropped dramatically, probably as a result of more rigorous patient selection and counseling.

PATIENT COMPLAINTS

Complaint: 'It didn't work'

Dysport® and NeuroBloc® usually start to work within 24 hours, but it is advisable to warn patients that results are not immediate, and that they may notice nothing for up to five days.

It is possible to get a bad batch of toxin, albeit very rarely. Both Allergan and Dysport® will replace a faulty vial immediately, free of charge. Take care not to agitate the solution and to follow storage guidelines carefully (see Chapter 4). The most likely cause for a failure of the toxin to work is inappropriate handling of it.

See the patient as soon as possible. Confirm that treatment has not worked. It is wise to examine your files for other patients who received treatment from the same batch. Offer to re-treat at no extra cost and re-examine within two weeks. If there is still no effect, the patients may be resistant to the toxin and will have to pay for any further treatment using an alternative toxin.

USER TIP

Advise patients to re-attend with their complaint – but not earlier than one week, and not later than three weeks.

Complaint: 'It didn't last'

Examine the patient if possible, but this complaint is usually made at a follow-up visit. Check the batch used and the other patients treated with it. The patient is usually right. The most likely cause will be excessive dilution of the botulinum toxin or denaturation by agitation or the wrong room temperature.

Reassure the patient. Resist any temptation to re-inject within 12 weeks in order to avoid the risk of stimulating antibody formation (see below). Use a different strength, or more sites, next time.

Complaint: 'I'm still frowning'

Examine patients within three weeks but not before 10 days. This allows the toxin to take effect. Give more botulinum toxin if stray residual active fibers are genuinely visible. Spend more time on counseling if the result is what you have aimed for i.e. some residual brow movement and lift in a moderate- to low-browed patient.

Do not give more toxin to the lateral frontalis against your better judgment. A tired-looking patient will be far less happy than a partially frowning one.

Complaint: the patient looks tired

This is due to an unexpected lack of brow movement in a moderately low-browed person. It can also occur when botulinum toxin diffuses too far medially. The tonic orbicularis under the eyelid is loosened, allowing the infra-orbital fat pad to protrude.

Spend time reassuring patients that the maximum effect is transient, and that the extra muscles involved have received only the 'edge' of the treatment as the toxin diffused. This means that they will recover much sooner that the central muscles, and that a tired look rarely lasts for more than four weeks. Increase brow movement with scalp aponeurosis exercises.

Complaint: 'My eyes are swollen'

A sudden onset of swelling and puffiness around the eyes, if pathological, is almost always due to allergy (associated with itch, hayfever etc.) or infection (associated with erythema, pain, temperature). In the author's experience a local allergic reaction to botulinum toxin is uncommon although it can occur in those who react to albumin. Care must be taken with patients in the 60+ age group. Such patients have greatly reduced skin elasticity and tone. This results in sagging of the forehead skin (causing brows to drop) and sagging of the periocular skin (causing upper and lower lid bags). Many patients use their frontalis muscle to suspend the sagging brows and upper lids. They hold their forehead muscle in a permanent frown, causing high arching brows and nice deep upper lids. Treatment of such a frown with BTX will automatically relax the frontalis, throwing their brows down and their lid skin onto their lashes.

These patients may complain of droopy lids and 'swelling' over their eyes due to BTX, when in fact it is simply the skin sagging because the brow position has been lowered. Try to demonstrate this possibility to the patient by manually pressing their brows down. Avoid BTX unless blepharoplasty and/or brow lift has been performed.

Swollen eyes after Botox® mean that the natural orbital fat and skin folds have protruded. Demonstrate this to the patient by asking them to look in a mirror with their head tilted upwards, a position that allows the fat to sink back into the sockets. Also lift the brows up actively with your hands while they watch the effect in the mirror. Reassure as above.

Complaint: peaked eyebrows

This is dealt with in Chapter 8. Incomplete paralysis of the frontalis muscle is often chosen to achieve a natural effect. The aim is to retain some forehead movement while freezing the frown. The problem is that residual active frontalis fibers may sometimes, unpredictably, distort the shape of the brows. A symmetrical treatment may result in asymmetric brow peaking (Fig 6.2). Some patients have naturally asymmetrical eyebrows: others experience contra-lateral overaction of untreated frontalis fibers as the opposite side fails to respond to stimulation. This is common in squint patients whose eye muscles work as part of a yoke mechanism. Contraction of the medial rectus on one side is associated with contraction of the contra-lateral lateral rectus. Under-activity of one muscle e.g. the lateral rectus due to abducens palsy, will result in over-activity of the opposite medial rectus (Herring's law).

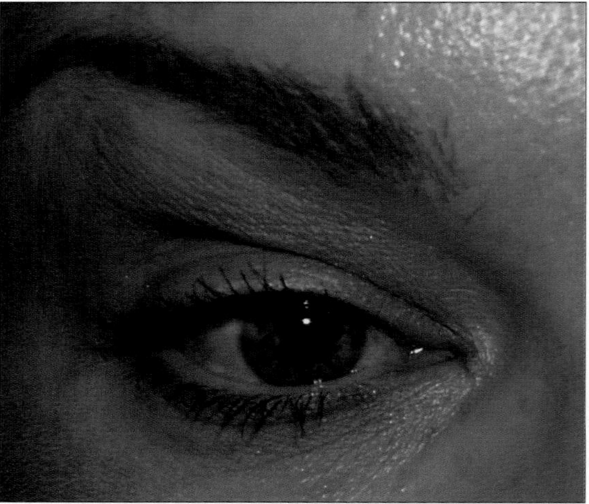

Fig 6.2 Unnatural brow peaking following botulinum toxin to glabella in a patient with overactive lateral frontalis fibers.

Examine your patients carefully before starting treatment. Try to predict asymmetry. It is best to give an initial symmetrical treatment with a view to 'balancing' the effect within two weeks of the first treatment. Very little botulinum toxin is needed to achieve the correct effect e.g. 0.025ml (see dose box) subcutaneously. Avoid using too much as this can cause brow ptosis.

Complaint: a droopy eyelid

Ptosis is the term used for a droopy eyelid. The distance from the lower lid margin to the upper lid margin (the palpebral aperture) varies. Some patients have visible sclera below and above their limbus (edge of the cornea). This may occur in myopic patients with naturally large eyes; in patients with thyroid eye disease; or in those with unusually shallow orbits.

The eyelid is elevated by the levator palpebrae superioris muscle (normal range is 17mm from looking down to looking up) and Müller's muscle – a supra-tarsal collection of involuntary smooth muscle fibers. The voluntary levator muscle elevates the lid, while Müller's muscle is responsible for fine tuning lid height and 'setting' it. Müller's muscle is only responsible for 2 mm of lid height and paralysis, e.g. in Horner's syndrome, therefore causes only 2 mm of ptosis.

The upper eyelid margin of most patients rests 2 mm below the limbus and is symmetrical. Unilateral ptosis will often result in a raised eyelid on the other side and, likewise, the illusion of ptosis can be created by unilateral lid retraction causing lowering of the opposite lid (Herring's law).

USER TIP

Always look for lid symmetry before giving botulinum toxin.

Congenital ptosis is relatively common, and age-related ptosis even more so. The latter is due to involutional weakening of the levator muscle attachments. It can be subtle at first i.e. less than 1 mm, and is usually associated with elevation of the lid crease as the skin-muscle attachment separates from the original crease. Ptosis is often worse in the evening and, in age-related ptosis, the eyelid will be lower than the normal lid on looking down. It is important to note that patients with levator aponeurosis disinsertion (age-related ptosis) usually raise their eyebrows to 'hold' the lid height. This can be a subtle change and failure to detect it prior to botulinum toxin treatment will result in the unmasking of a pre-existing ptosis.

There have been several reports of ptosis due to botulinum toxin, but some of these refer to brow ptosis, not to true ptosis. Brow ptosis will occur in any patient with an overactive frontalis muscle and involutional descent of the brows. It is not due to botulinum toxin to eyelid muscles although brow ptosis can lead to an eyelid being pressed to a lower height by the simple effect of the weight of the brow on it. This can be identified by replacing the brows manually and observing the return of normal lid height.

True ptosis following botulinum toxin is due to inadvertent treatment of the levator palpebrae superioris muscle. Reported incidents occur if toxin diffuses through the orbital septum and usually last less than two weeks. The incidence is low and the author has not seen a case in 14 years of experience with botulinum toxin, perhaps as a result of avoiding the levator muscle and never injecting medial to the lateral orbital rim. Unless experienced, practitioners should also avoid injecting the corrugator muscle from the inferior aspect of the brow, particularly in patients with a low lash/brow distance.

Treatment of botulinum-induced ptosis is reassurance, reminding the patient that it will recover as the BTX wears off. Recovery is reported to occur between 2 weeks and 3 months. Some recommend using apraclonidine 5% (Iopidine®) eye drops to stimulate Müller's muscle. This will result in a temporary elevation, but only of 2 mm. Apraclonidine is an alpha-adrenergic stimulator used to reduce intra-ocular pressure and has several ocular side effects: its use in the treatment of transient ptosis occuring as a result of cosmetic application of botulinum is therefore questionable. The risks posed to the eye by use of apraclonidine must be balanced against the fact that the ptosis will undoubtedly recover when the botulinum wears off.

Complaint: a watery eye

Epiphora means a 'watery eye'. It is an unusual complaint but can either be due to paralysis of the lachrymal pump or to paralysis of the lower lid orbicularis.

Paralysis of the medial pre-tarsal orbicularis prevents the suction of tears into the lacrimal sac that normally occurs with blinking. It is often seen with Bell's palsy. It can be avoided by not injecting botulinum toxin medial to the mid-pupil line.

Another cause of epiphora is excessive laxity of the inferior pre-tarsal orbicularis. The resting tone of the muscle is reduced and so the height of the lower lid drops. The increased palpebral aperture may undermine the normal tear film. The tear film break-up time may increase and the ocular area exposed to the atmosphere may be too great for the volume of tears produced. This results in inadequate lubrication of the eye (a dry eye) BUT manifests itself as epiphora. When the eye is dry, the blink reflex causes the lid to pass over a dry surface, creating 'microscratches' on the cornea. This stimulates trigeminal nerve fibers and results in tears, and a watery eye. Unfortunately this reflex flow of tears is often not enough to cure the

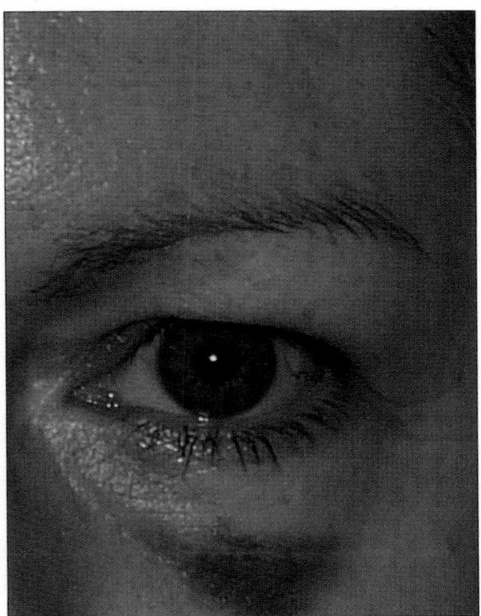

Fig 6.3 Bruising following botulinum toxin injection to lateral canthus for crow's feet.

dry eye and may be accompanied by a gritty sensation. Remember that a reduction in the tear film, and mildly dry eyes, are common in menopausal women.

The treatment of epiphora due to pump inaction is to wait until the botulinum toxin wears off. The treatment of a dry eye is lubrication. Recommend over-the-counter preparations such as Tears Naturale®, Artelac® or Liquefilm Tears®. More viscous agents, such as Vidisic® gel or gel tears, help if the patient is outdoors and at night. Lacri-Lube® (petrolatum eye ointment) may be recommended in severe cases for use at night. If these measures fail, consider referral to an ophthalmologist for other types of management such as temporary lachrymal plugs.

Other complaints in Table 6.1

These are dealt with in Chapters 7 and 8. Experience in the art of botulinum toxin usage will help to avoid them. However, bruising due to damage to intramuscular arterioles is completely unavoidable. Figure 6.3 shows a recent patient who had botulinum toxin prior to lower lid blepharoplasty. Recommend a suitable camouflage cream.

SIDE EFFECTS

The side effects of botulinum toxin are usually minimal: one of the deadliest poisons known to mankind is also one of the safest when used correctly.

Resistance

Most reported side effects follow the injection of toxin at high doses for the treatment of cervical dystonia and other large muscle disorders. Antibody production has not been reported in patients receiving less than 50 units Botox®. In one study, the production of immunoglobulin G autoantibodies occurred in 4.3% of patients receiving botulinum toxin for torticollis. Those who have developed antibodies to Type A should still respond to other serotypes. It is noteworthy that no resistance has been reported in patients receiving botulinum toxin for aesthetic reasons, but as patients receive higher doses to include neck rhytids, the risk of resistance must be kept in mind. Current advice is to avoid repeating injections within three months and to avoid booster injections.

USER TIP

Lessen the risk of developing resistance by avoiding booster injections and treatments less than three months apart. Use the smallest dose necessary.

General

Patients have complained of generalized side effects, such as an influenza-like illness and headache. Certain rare side effects, such as generalized muscular weakness, are believed to be due to the dissemination of botulinum toxin via the blood stream. Botulinum toxin does not cross the blood /brain barrier.

Dysphagia can occur after the injection of botulinum toxin for cervical dystonia, and is due to local diffusion from the injection site. The use of low volume doses at high concentrations will limit this. Dysphagia has been reported following cosmetic use in the neck: neck weakness has also been reported. These symptoms usually subside after two to three weeks.

Bruising is an inevitable side effect of any intramuscular injection. Cutaneous vessels can be seen and avoided, but patients must accept the risk of ecchymoses from hidden vessels. Bruising in the lower lid can track down to the neck. Compress the injection site immediately after treatment and apply ice. Avoid injecting patients taking aspirin, non-steroidal anti-inflammatory preparations or *Ginko biloba* – a homeopathic inhibitor of platelet function – in order to reduce the risk.

7 The management of crow's feet

'Crow's feet' are the wrinkles that form with age at the outer corners of the eyes. They are due to contraction of the orbicularis oculi muscles (Fig. 7.1). Their treatment with botulinum toxin is usually straightforward but certain aspects must be considered carefully first.

The functions of the orbicularis oculi muscle are to close the eye, to drain the tear film, and to create facial expressions. Contraction of this muscle can also drag on the lateral third of the eyebrow, contributing to drooping of the brow with age. In addition, the resting tension of the orbicularis oculi muscle can increase with age and character.

Many patients keep tension at the lateral canthal angle constant, and so have pleasant 'smiling eyes'. This tension can be important to the appearance of the patient: it results in rhytids, but also supports an ageing midface in some patients. It can also prevent the protrusion of age-related lower lid 'bags' (orbital fat) by supporting the orbital septum.

Injections of botulinum toxin will smooth out the rhytids and make the skin look younger, but patients may begin to look 'thin' around their eyes as they lose muscle bulk after repeated injections. They may also look 'drawn' or tired as their mid-face falls over the zygomatic arch. Such changes usually do not become apparent until several treatments have been undertaken. The loss of tension can reverse with time as the orbicularis muscle rarely atrophies permanently; this has been shown by the results of long-term botulinum toxin treatment of orbital blepharospasm.

This chapter covers the assessment and treatment of crow's feet. It is important, however, to re-examine patients before every treatment and to

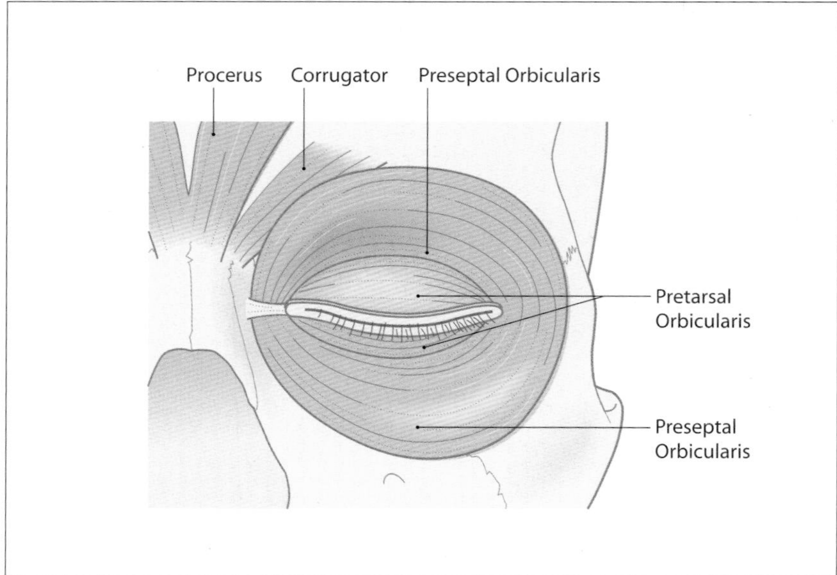

Fig 7.1 Anatomy of orbicularis oculi muscle. After Zide BM and Jelks GW (1985) Surgical Anatomy of the Orbit. Raven Press Books, Ltd. New York. With permission of Barry M Zide.

make sure that they will still look well because of it. Make certain that the botulinum toxin can do for the patient what the patient expects.

USER TIP

Botulinum toxin will paralyse the orbicularis muscle, making it flaccid and even atrophic. This will stop wrinkles, but the loss of muscle tone will not suit everyone.

PATIENT EXAMINATION

- **Examine patients both from the front and the side.**
- **Examine them at rest and when smiling.**
- **Try to imagine what relaxation of their orbicularis muscle will do to their appearance.**

WHAT TO LOOK FOR WHEN EXAMINING A PATIENT

- **Examine the tone of the orbicularis oculi muscle and the position of rhytids.** Are the wrinkles deep? Spread the skin gently between your fingers. Are they still very obvious? If they are, tell patients that they might not notice much effect from the treatment. Advise them about laser resurfacing and skin management (Chapter 11). If the wrinkles are mild, advise patients that they might get a permanent effect with time and good skin care. (Fig. 7.2ab)

- **Examine the facial skin and muscle tone** by asking patients to smile while pressing lightly on the zygomatic arch with two fingers. This stops the orbicularis muscle from contracting and so simulates the paralysis of botulinum toxin.
- **Patients with severe sun damage or poor skin tone** (often older patients) will observe that, on smiling, the cheek and orbicularis oculi muscles elevate the

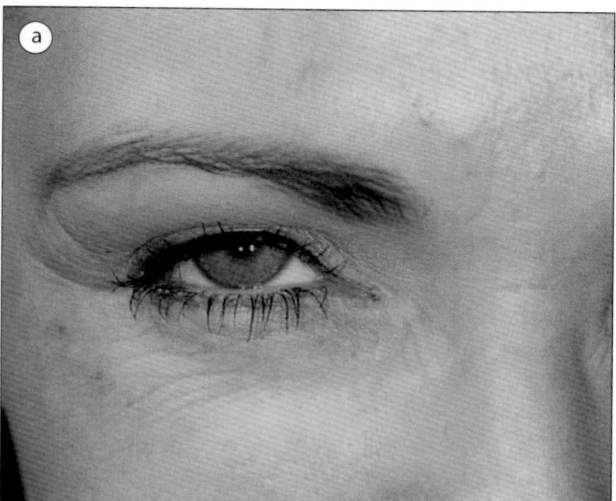

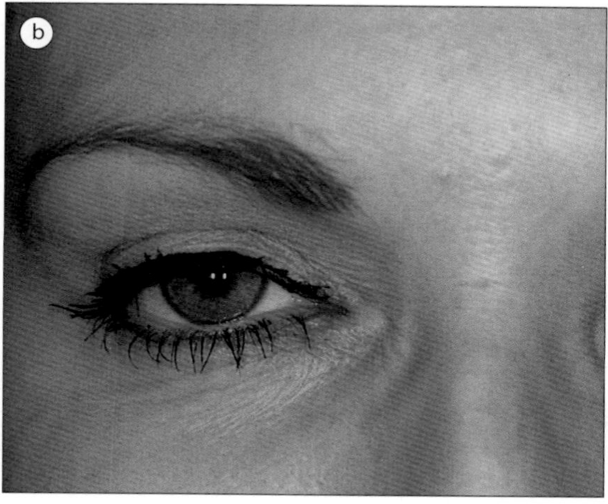

Fig 7.2 Before (a) and one year after (b) Botox® to crows feet and forehead.

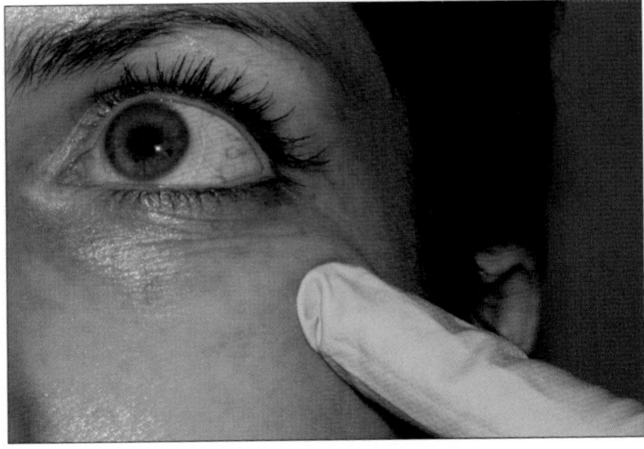

Fig 7.3 Patient with poor skin tone and wrinkles at rest. Ask patient not to smile. Push skin up over zygomatic arch. Demonstrate to patient the wrinkles that occur at the crow's feet due to deterioration of skin tone. These will also occur when the patient smiles and their smile 'pushes' the cheek up, even when BTX has paralysed the lateral orbicularis oculis.

facial skin and send it into folds around the lateral orbit. Show patients that this will also happen after botulinum toxin treatment to the crow's feet (Fig. 7.3), otherwise they will think that the injections have not worked. It is often wisest not to treat such patients unless they have had surgical or laser correction of skin tone (Chapter 11).

- **The Mickey Mouse sign:** occasionally patients (especially men over 50 with good skin tone) notice that smiling causes their wrinkles to 'bunch up' at the level of the zygoma after treatment of their crow's feet. This can create a curved wrinkle running from the lower orbital rim, out along the inferior border of the orbicularis oculi, over the zygomatic arch, to the top of the orbicularis oris (the Mickey Mouse smile). The periocular fibers have atrophied as planned, but the resting skin tone prevents elevation of the periocular skin and muscle on smiling. The excessive tone of the orbicularis oris, however, associated with thinning of lateral orbicularis oculi fibers, makes the smile appear much wider than the upper face. Take care with such patients.
- **Examine the contour of the socket.** Is it shallow, allowing anterior displacement of orbital fat and bags? Does the inferior orbital rim protrude? Is it recessed behind the level of the anterior surface of the cornea? This may also be assessed by the 'pencil test'. Ask the patient to hold a pencil vertically against the anterior cheekbone. If this passes in front of the cornea (Fig. 7.4a), then the patient has good lower lid skeletal support. If the pencil only reaches the lash margin (Fig. 7.4b), then the patient is at risk of developing sagging of the lower lid and widening of the palpebral aperture if botulinum toxin is injected for pretarsal orbicularis wrinkles.
- **Examine the distance between the lash margin and the lower orbital rim, which increases with age.** A short distance means that the patient may have botulinum

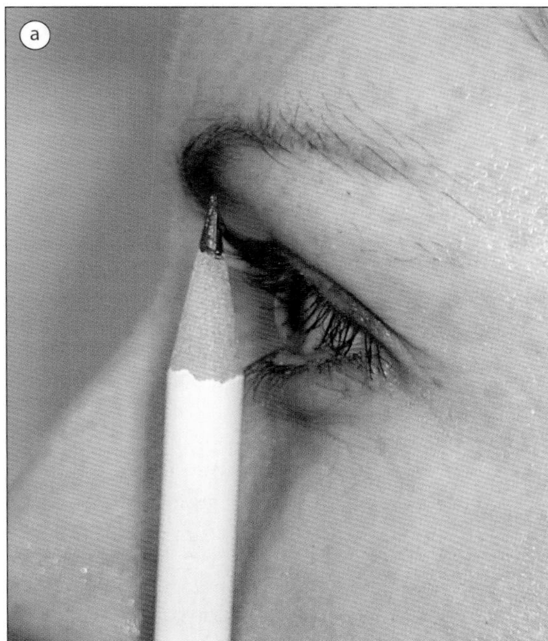

Fig 7.4a Example of bone structure where a pencil will pass from the maxilla in front of the cornea.

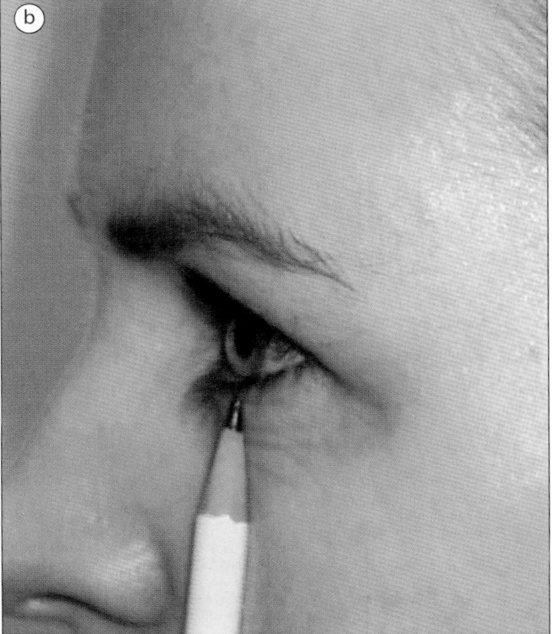

Fig 7.4b Some patients have a maxilla which recedes from the inferior orbital rim. A pencil will pass from the maxilla through the eye. This means that infero-orbital contents (muscle and fat) are prone to bulging in front of the orbital rim, creating 'bags'.

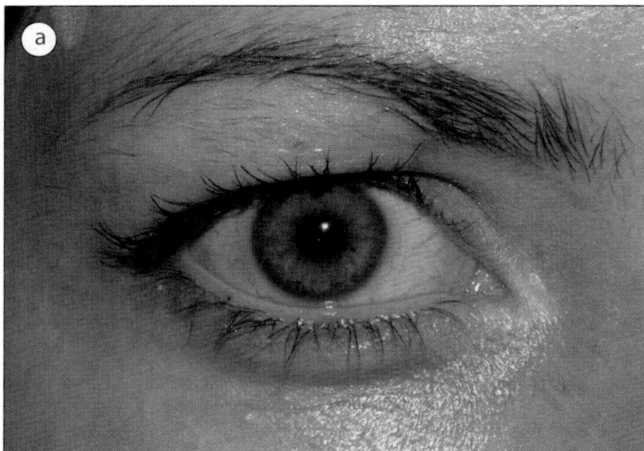

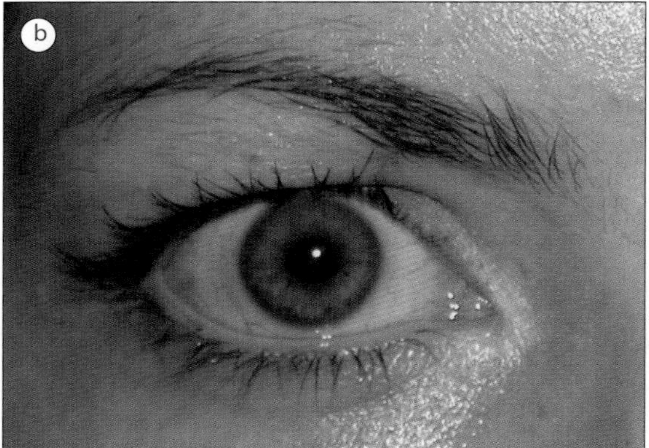

Fig 7.5 Short orbital rim–lash distance allows safe botulinum toxin to the preseptal orbicularis if hypertrophied. (a) is before Botox® and (b) is after Botox®.

toxin successfully to pretarsal wrinkles without protrusion of orbital fat or folds of skin (Fig. 7.5ab).

- **Examine the height and width of the zygomatic arch.** Does the orbicularis muscle sag between the cheekbone and the eye? Will this area develop a hollow appearance if the muscle becomes thinner? Such a hollowing can be unattractive if accentuated (Fig. 7.6). Discuss this and inject more laterally to avoid diffusion to the 'hollow'.
- **Take especial care over patients with large eyes and wide high cheekbones** (e.g. fashion models – Fig. 7.7). They are also, because of their large eyes, at high risk of sagging of the lower lid. The lower lid normally elevates with smiling as the palpebral aperture narrows and the orbicularis oculi contracts. Botulinum toxin will allow a more wide-eyed smile. This is often attractive, but never when

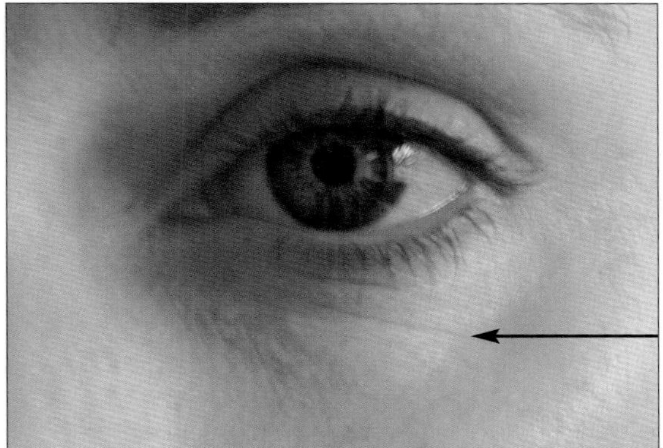

Fig 7.6 Hollowing after botulinum toxin (BTX) treatment. Avoid giving BTX on, or medial to, the infraorbital zygoma in a patient with high broad cheekbones. This would cause atrophy of overlying orbicularis and subsequent hollowing. Note hollowing (arrow).

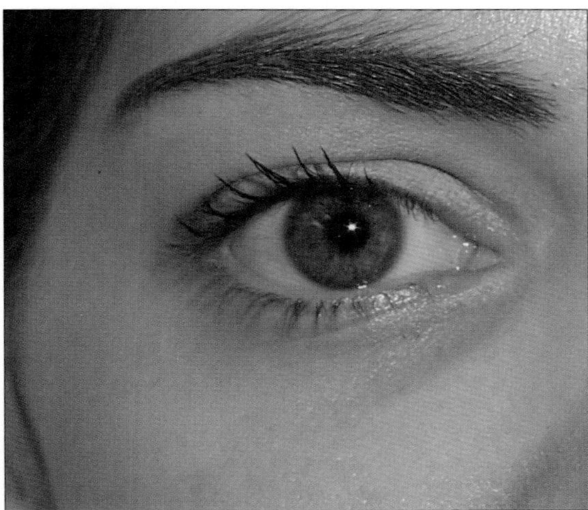

Fig 7.7 Large eyes, wide high cheekbone: botulinum toxin close to the lower lid will weaken elevation of the lower lid and may increase the lateral palpebral fissure, creating a flat lateral lid instead of being angled above the height of the medial canthus.

the lateral corner of the lid falls below the medial, creating a pseudo lateral canthus inversus.

- **Look for a weak orbital septum or protruding orbital fat pads.** Ask patients to put their chin *down* and then to look up into the mirror – this will accentuate lower orbital fat pads. If fat protrudes, *do not* treat the skin under the eyelid as the subsequent loss of tone will cause temporary deterioration of the bags. These patients should have lower lid blepharoplasty and understand that only the wrinkles at the sides of their eyes will benefit from botulinum toxin.

Table 7.2. Side effects of botulinum toxin injections into the orbicularis oculi for crow's feet

Problem	Cause	Management
Thinning of muscle over zygoma	Injection in a patient with high, broad cheek bones	Inject more inferolaterally, below the zygomatic arch
Failure of lower lid to ascend with smile	Diffusion of BTX to pre tarsal orbicularis	If looks well, repeat! If not, inject more laterally next time
Watery eye (epiphora)	Diffusion of BTX towards lacrimal pump preventing tear drainage	Avoid pre-tarsal orbicularis medial to mid-pupillary line
Hooding	Wrinkle due to sagging skin and not orbicularis contraction	Counsel patient carefully. Recommend brow lift surgery or cheat with hyaluronic acid
Large fold of wrinkles below zygoma (Mickey Mouse sign)	Patient has good result but poor skin tone, causing wrinkling of lower face only with smile	Discuss carefully. Patient may benefit from full face resurfacing or face-lift. BTX may be contraindicated otherwise.

Side effects of botulinum toxin treatment for crow's feet

These may occur if the injections are placed in the wrong part of the muscle, given at the wrong dose, or given with unrealistic expectations. They are listed in Table 7.2.

Tear film

Botulinum toxin to the eye zone can affect the tear film in two ways: the need for tear film may increase, and the drainage of tears may be reduced.

Increased need for tear film

Weakening of the pretarsal orbicularis widens the palpebral aperture (as discussed above). This may aggravate an already compromised tear film by increasing the area requiring lubrication and by reducing the rate of reflex blinking. Such patients may complain of a dry gritty feeling or, more likely, of watery eyes. This is because drying of the eye causes the eyelid to scrape over the cornea and sclera, creating micro-epithelial defects and a sensation of grittiness. The resulting corneal stimulation provokes involuntary epiphora and a watery eye.

These patients should increase their artificial lubricants or lubricate occasionally with a gel substitute until the botulinum toxin wears off. Many lubricants are available without prescription and the trick is to use them frequently initially, then to wean them off according to symptoms.

Reduction of drainage of tears

Botulinum toxin can be injected into the pretarsal orbicularis to reduce a hypertrophic orbicularis muscle and early 'bagging' (Fig. 7.8). However it should never be injected close enough to diffuse towards the lower lid punctum. This would paralyze the lacrimal pump, causing a watery eye – unless, luckily, the patient was already suffering from a dry eye.

The lacrimal pump (Fig. 7.9) comprises fibers from the orbicularis that insert onto the vertical portion of the canaliculus and the lacrimal sac. Blinking contracts these fibers and dilates the canaliculus and sac. This creates a negative pressure drawing the tears along the lower lid margin into the lacrimal sac. Paralysis of the lacrimal pump occurs naturally in patients with facial nerve palsy. Treatment, if indicated, is by means of a glass tube (Lester Jones tube) inserted from the medial canthus to the nasal cavity.

Temporary paralysis of the lacrimal pump by botulinum toxin can be avoided by staying lateral to the mid-pupillary line, and by using low doses of high concentrations. This treatment is not recommended for the novice practitioner.

Lower lid bags (dermatochalasis and/or orbital fat)

Avoid injecting botulinum toxin medial to the outer orbital rim in patients with excessive lower lid skin and fat (Fig. 7.10) as this will cause sagging of the orbicularis muscle with protrusion of the inferior orbital fat. Remember, too, that botulinum toxin will diffuse to different degrees in different patients.

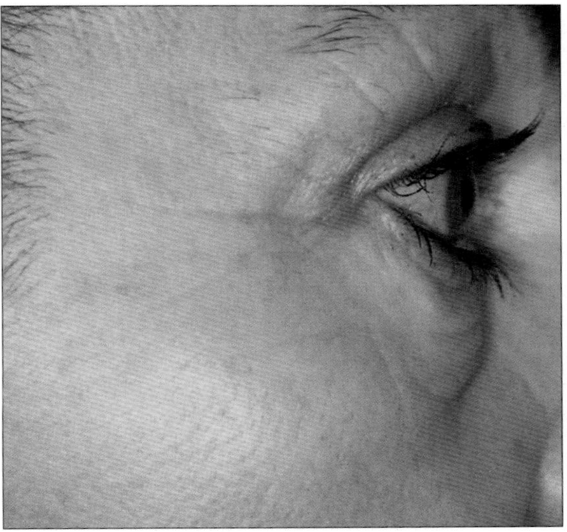

Fig 7.8 Hypertrophic orbicularis muscle.

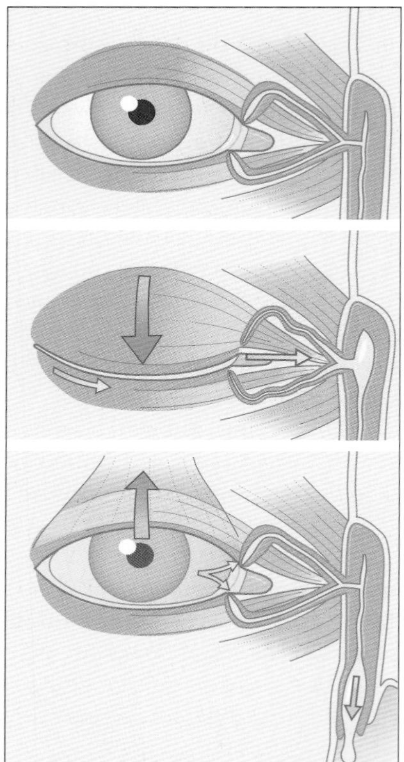

Fig 7.9 The lacrimal pump. Contraction of orbicularis fibers with blinking dilates the vertical portion of the canaliculus, creating a negative pressure which 'sucks' the tears into the lacrimal sac. After Zide BM and Jelks GW (1985) Surgical Anatomy of the Orbit. Raven Press Books, Ltd. New York. With permission of Barry Zide.

I have injected thousands of patients but was recently surprised to discover this side effect in a female smoker in her mid-forties with marked solar elastosis. I injected botulinum toxin as usual, including one centimeter inferolateral to her orbital rim. She developed temporary heavy bags under both eyes as the toxin diffused towards the pretarsal orbicularis bilaterally. Fortunately, she only received the 'tail end' of the diffused toxin here and the effect wore off after a few weeks, long before the rhytids returned. It is very unusual for that level of diffusion to occur and her poor skin quality was a contributory factor, but be warned! The same patient unfortunately refused to allow publication of her photographs.

Discuss blepharoplasty with such patients and demonstrate what they can expect from botulinum toxin alone.

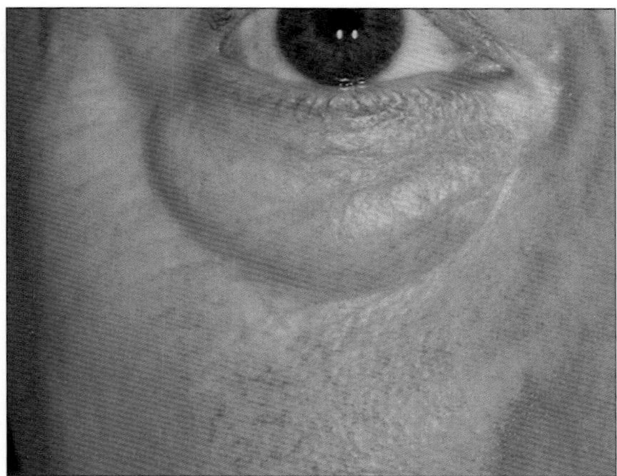

Fig 7.10 Lower lid 'bags'.

Hooding

Some crow's feet will persist despite botulinum toxin. These include the skin folds at the outer corners of the lids due either to brow ptosis or to sagging of the temporal frontalis muscle or both (Fig. 7.11). Discuss this with the patient and suggest correct treatment of these wrinkles. Mention that 'cheating' with hyaluronic acid will also be effective (Chapter 11).

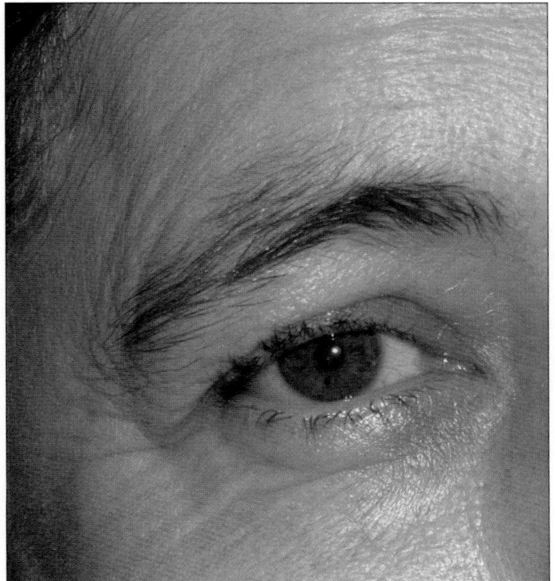

Fig 7.11 Eyebrow ptosis.

Table 7.1. Categories of crow's feet and their treatment

Type of crow's feet	Management
Wrinkles in motion	Botulinum toxin
Fine lines at rest	Botulinum toxin, collagen stimulation
Deep wrinkles at rest	Botulinum toxin, laser resurfacing, coblation
Deep wrinkles at rest with hooding	Botulinum toxin, laser resurfacing, hyaluronic acid, brow repositioning.

Method of treatment

Crow's feet may be categorized and treated accordingly, as shown in Table 7.1.

DOSE BOX

Botox®: 2.5 ml dil to 100 units vial = 4 units in 0.1 ml
Dysport®: 3 ml dil to 500 units vial = 16.6 units in 0.1 ml

Once the patient has been prepared, informed, examined, photographed and has consented, the recommended doses are as follows (drawn on photographs):

- **wrinkles in motion (Fig. 7.12): 0.05 ml x 2 each side.**
- **wrinkles in motion with lateral depression of brow (Fig. 7.13): as above with 0.025 ml lateral to point of contraction.**

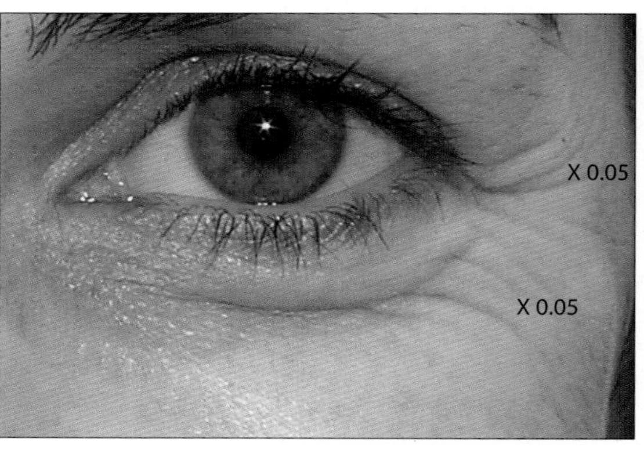

Fig 7.12 Injection sites and dose for a young patient with wrinkles in motion.

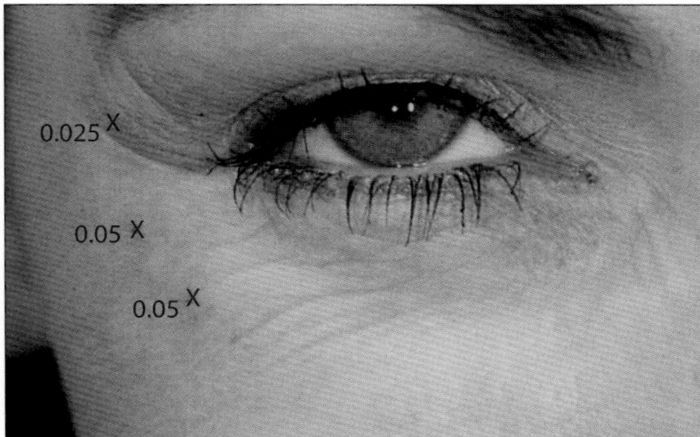

Fig 7.13 Injection sites for wrinkles in motion and at rest with wrinkles below lateral brow.

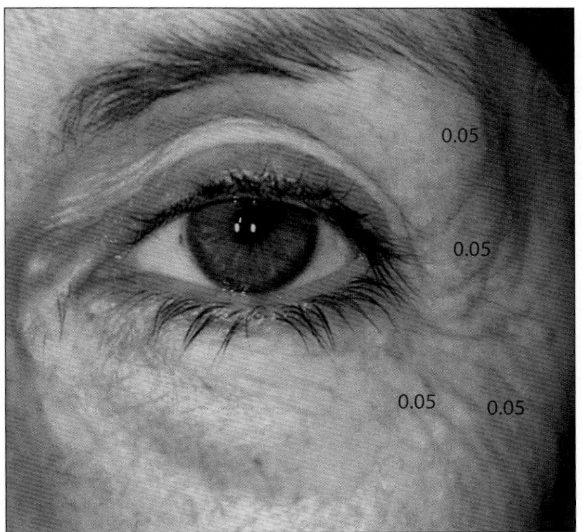

Fig 7.14 Deep wrinkles at rest extending over zygomatic arch. X, 0.05 ml.

- **wrinkles at rest extending over the zygomatic arch (Fig. 7.14): as above with 0.05 ml one cm inferolateral to lateral canthus.**
- **wrinkles at rest with orbicularis hypertrophy and no contraindication (see above) (Fig. 7.15): 0.0125 ml above and below pretarsal crease, lateral to the mid papillary line.**
- **high wide cheekbone (Fig. 7.16): 0.05 ml at outer canthus and 0.05 ml 0.5 cm below zygomatic arch.**

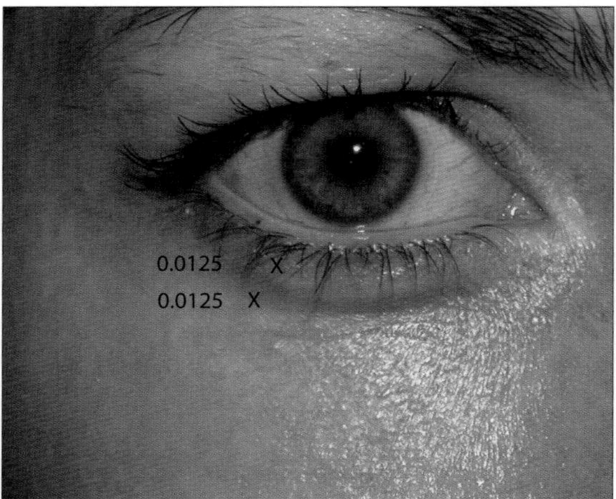

Fig 7.15 Treatment of crows feet with orbicularis hypertrophy.

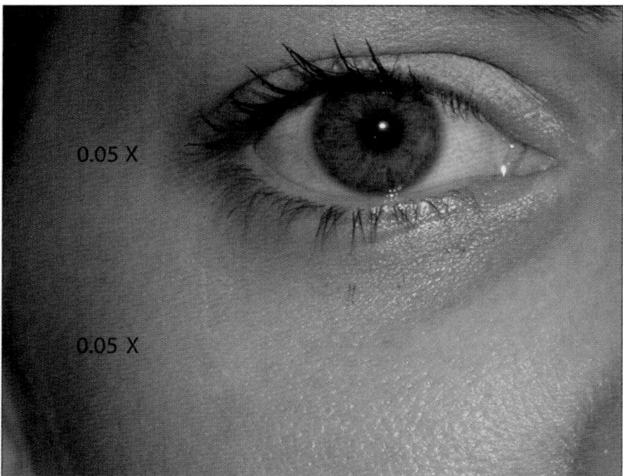

Fig 7.16 Treatment of high wide cheekbones.

8 Management of forehead wrinkles

Botulinum toxin is widely known to be an excellent treatment for smoothing out both vertical and horizontal forehead lines. Patients often ask for it to be used to treat their vertical (glabellar) frown, their horizontal lines, or put in a general request for improvement. It is important to find out at an early stage whether they are looking for total immobility of the forehead (this is often not possible – as explained below) or simply for a natural-looking effect with some residual forehead expression and greatly reduced wrinkles.

Forehead wrinkles are due to a combination of genetic and environmental factors, especially damage from light ultraviolet light. The contributions of both must be analyzed when patients attend for treatment. Make sure too that they do not expect the ablation of furrows as this requires CO_2 laser resurfacing for maximum effect.

Botulinum toxin to the mid-forehead can lead to permanent atrophy of the muscle fibers, with an excellent long-lasting result. This usually occurs after five or six treatments at 14-week intervals. The glabellar muscles always seem to recover after treatment but can, with time, diminish in size and function. Most patients continue to return for glabellar and crow's feet treatment, with an annual 'top up' to the mid-frontalis.

Treatment of the frontalis will inevitably affect the shape of the brow. This must be assessed carefully and discussed with the patient. The treatment of horizontal lines alone may avoid changes to the brow, but once the glabella has been treated, the frontalis must be balanced with the treatment.

Remember that the shape of the brow is subject to fashion. The author prefers the current trend for a female brow to have a slight arch at the junction of the medial two thirds to the lateral third. More modern trends include a horizontal brow that elevates laterally. It is essential to avoid a 'Dr Spock' effect with a peak to the brow, usually achieved by the unopposed action of the frontalis on the mid-brow, and most likely to occur when the glabellar muscles are treated independently (see fig 6.2).

Tell your patients what to expect from botulinum toxin at this stage, and discuss how their foreheads might alter with age. Let them know that, although an injection might provide a nice temporary brow lift, in the long run this might have to be maintained by surgery.

Select patients as described in Chapter 5, and take great care to avoid treating the forehead of a patient with the rare neuromuscular disorder known as chronic progressive external ophthalmoplegia (CPEO). Remember that such patients may not yet have been diagnosed. Examine the eyes and eyelids of every new patient for signs of abnormal muscle function. If in doubt, refer to an ophthalmologist for examination before any treatment is attempted.

- **Chronic Progressive External Ophthalmoplegia (CPEO) is a rare neuromuscular disorder that causes progressive immobility of all the external ocular muscles and of the levator muscles of the eyelids. Patients eventually need an operation to attach their frontalis muscles to their eyelids (by a subcutaneous sling) so that they can open their eyes and see. The initial presentation is often a symmetrical ptosis with brow elevation.**

ANATOMY OF FROWN MUSCLES

An intimate knowledge of the anatomy of the forehead is essential for successful treatment. There will always be a few patients with variations on the normal anatomy, but the typical muscle attachments are shown in Figure 8.1. In particular note the following:

- **The frontalis muscle originates from the galea aponeurosis (near the hair line) and stretches to an insertion into the skin and the orbicularis oculi at the level of the eyebrows.**
- **The frontalis does not cross the midline and is separated by a central muscle-free zone at the base of the nose (Fig. 8.2). Movements of the galea aponeurosis unaccompanied by movement of the frontalis will cause wrinkling of the forehead skin, especially in patients who can voluntarily 'wiggle their ears' or 'move their scalp'.**
- **The bone at the base of the nose is covered by the procerus muscle (skin attachments only), blending into the corrugator muscle at the level of the**

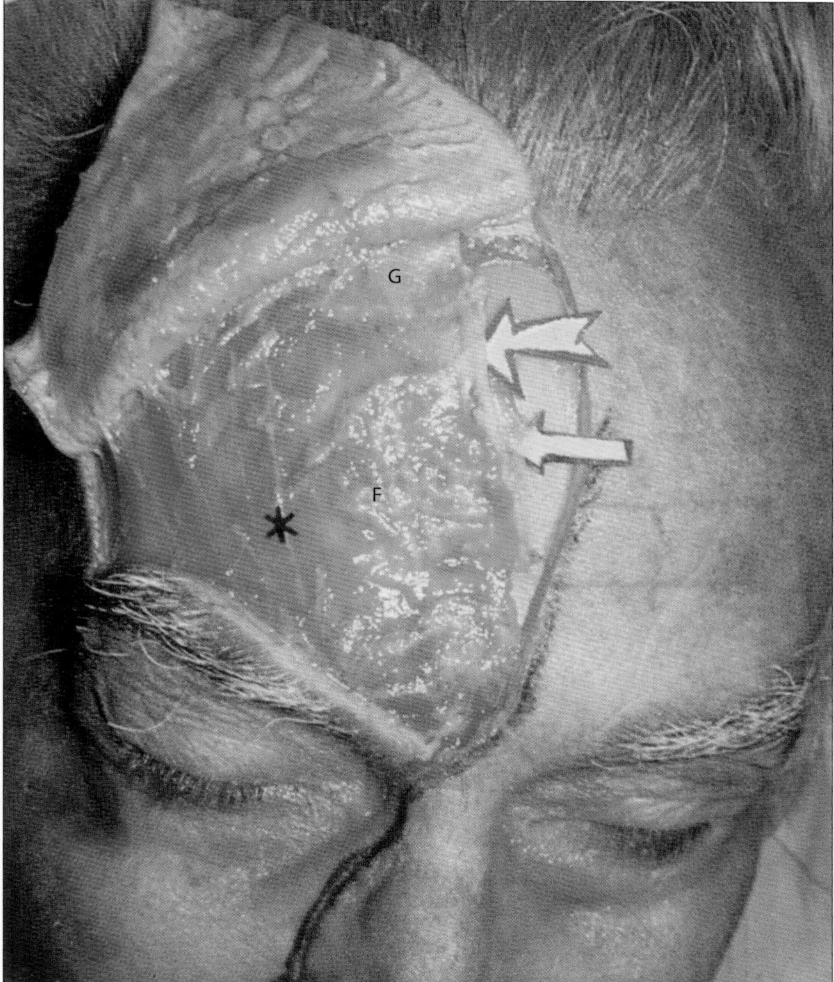

Fig 8.1 Anatomy of the forehead. The vertical fibers of the frontalis muscle (F) insert into the skin and orbicularis oculi at the level of the eyebrow. The frontalis muscle, innervated by a branch of the seventh cranial nerve, originates from the galeal aponeurosis (G). The red arrow tip is inserted below the galea. The black arrow tip lies beneath the periosteum of the frontal bone. Note the sensory nerve (*), a branch of the supraorbital nerve coursing over the muscle. The frontalis muscle usually does not cross the midline. From Zide BM and Jelks GW (1985) Surgical Anatomy of the Orbit. Raven Press Books, Ltd. New York. With permission of Barry Zide.

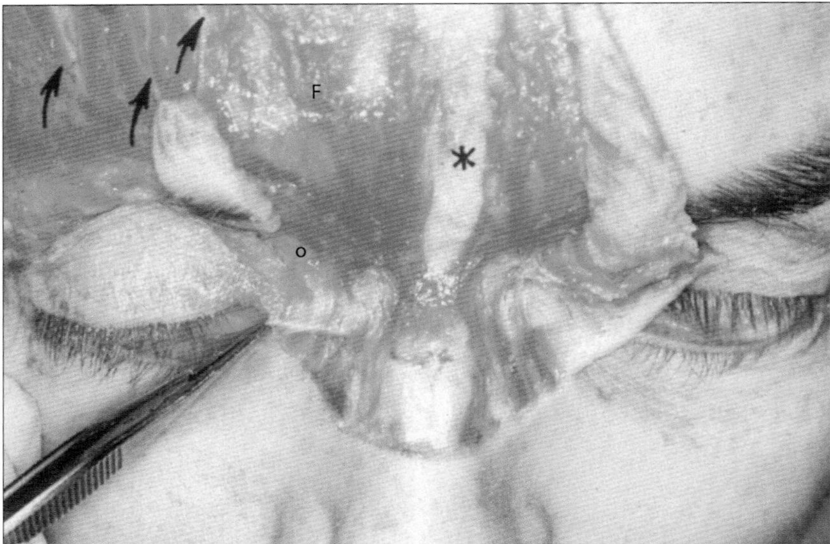

Fig 8.2 Note that the frontalis fibers do not cross the midline. Note the paired frontalis muscles (F) with their central muscle-free zone (*). The supraorbital nerves are noted coursing upward (small arrows). The forceps grasp the anterior portion of the medial canthal tendon. Note the orbicularis oculi fibers (o), some of which originate from this tendon. From Zide BM and Jelks BW (1985) Surgical Anatomy of the Orbit. Raven Press Books, Ltd. With permission of Barry Zide.

eyebrows, and the medial fibers of the orbicularis oculi below the medial part of the brow (Fig. 8.3).

- **The corrugator muscle arises from the nasal process of the frontal bone. It is responsible for drawing the eyebrows together, creating the vertical glabellar rhytid. The corrugator lies deep to the frontalis, the procerus, and the supraorbital nerves and arteries. It attaches to the skin above the medial aspect of the eyebrow.**
- **The vertical fibers of the orbicularis oculi, which run superomedial to the medial canthal tendon, attach to the medial brow and are known as the depressor supercilii. The angular veins are embedded in this muscle.**

EXAMINATION OF BROW/FOREHEAD RHYTIDS

- **General appraisal**
- **Specific glabella (vertical frown) examination**
- **Specific forehead (horizontal frown) examination**

Fig 8.3 The glabella complex. After Zide BM and Jelks GW (1985) Surgical Anatomy of the Orbit. Raven Press Books, Ltd. New York. With permission of Barry M. Zide.

General appraisal

- **Eyebrows**
- **Hairstyle**
- **Ptosis**
- **Dermatochalasis**

First examine your patient carefully and decide what botulinum toxin can do for his or her particular type of lines. Decide at this stage whether or not botulinum toxin treatment will eliminate the wrinkles. Will laser resurfacing be needed? Will the vertical lines also require a filler? (Chapter 11)

Eyebrows

Examine the eyebrows. Are they heavy or groomed? Some brows look as if they have descended because of their excessive growth of hair. Simple contouring of the brow with tweezers can give the illusion of a lift and instantly take years off the eyes (Fig. 8.4ab). A visit to a reputable beautician may be recommended in order to acquire a professional shape, which the patient can easily maintain thereafter.

Hairstyle

Discuss this with the patient. If a fringe (bangs) is being worn, will the effects of botulinum toxin be noticeable? Is the patient happy to have botulinum toxin to

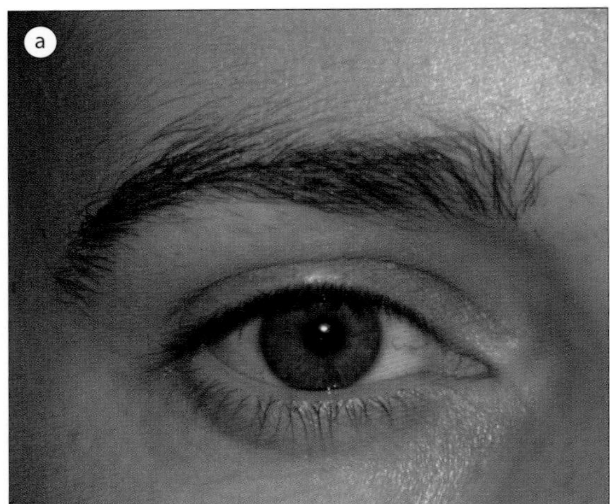

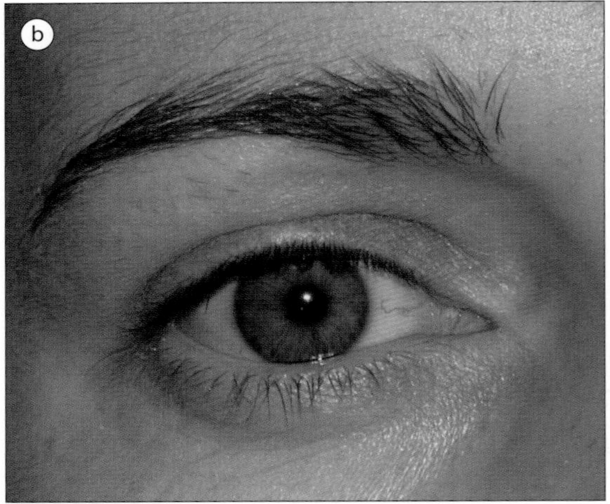

Fig 8.4 (a) before and (b) after eyebrow contouring.

prevent further ageing of the forehead, regardless of whether or not it can be seen?

Ptosis

Always examine the patient for signs of ptosis (a droopy eyelid). This is common in patients over 60 years old, and is usually unilateral or asymmetrical. The levator aponeurosis, which opens the eyelid, and which is also responsible for the 'lid crease' by its superficial insertion into the orbicularis muscle and skin, slips up under the orbital rim (and eyebrow) with age or trauma. This causes a slight drooping of the eyelid that worsens on

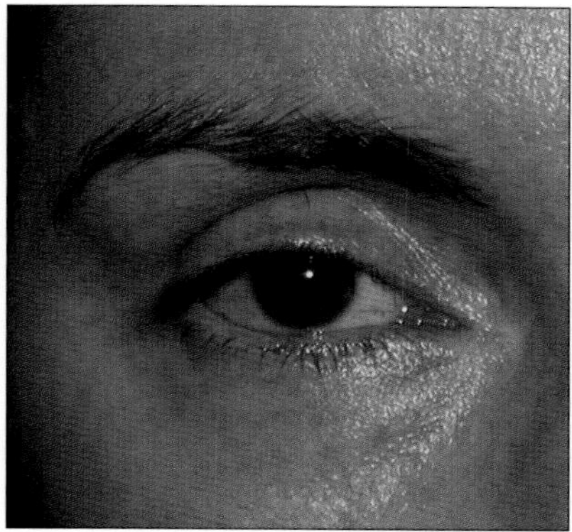

Fig 8.5 Levator aponeurosis disinsertion. Note high lid crease and ptosis.

looking down and when the patient is tired (Fig. 8.5). Patients then compensate by tensing the frontalis muscle, developing high arched eyebrows, deep frontalis furrows, and deep upper lids, which droop sleepily. The lid crease is often noticeably higher on the affected side (normal 7–10 mm, symmetrical).

In these patients, botulinum toxin to the frontalis muscle will remove the frown but also drop their eyebrow. This may result in an immediately obvious ptosis (even though it was already present). Patients will also complain of swollen upper lids as their brow descends. The ptosis is often asymmetrical, sometimes unilateral and sometimes occurs in young people following trauma. It will be hard to convince these patients that the botulinum toxin did not cause the initial ptosis. Examine carefully before treating!

BASIC PTOSIS EXAMINATION

- **Observe the patient in the primary position (looking straight ahead).**
- **Measure the palpebral aperture – the distance from the lower lash margin to the upper lash margin at the midpoint of the pupil.**
- **Place a finger over the patient's brow to stop it from moving.**
- **Ask the patient to look down. Place the zero point on a fine ruler over the upper lid lashes before immediately asking the patient to look up. Now measure the point on the ruler where the lash margin is.**
- **The result is the levator muscle function (normal is 15–18 mm).**

Dermatochalasis (eyelid bags)

The term dermatochalasis refers to age-related wrinkling and sagging of the skin over the eyelids. Examine carefully for brow elevation with overaction of

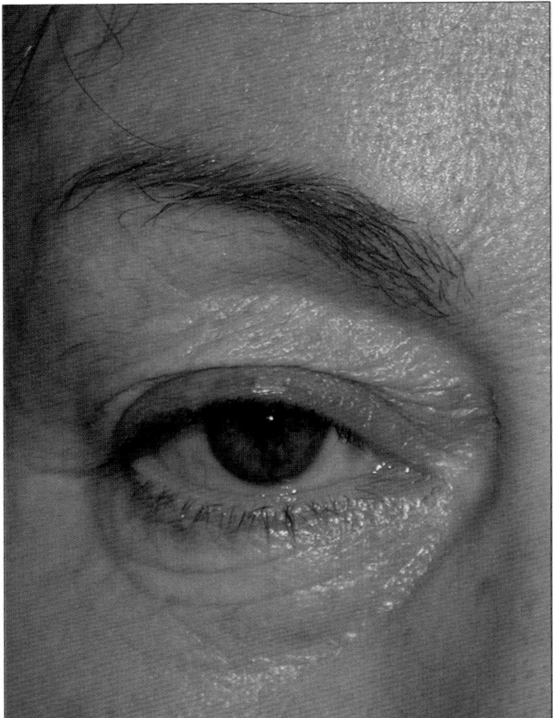

Fig 8.6 High raised eyebrows with forehead wrinkles and upper eyelid bags, and weight-induced ptosis.

the frontalis compensating for the 'heavy skin' and subconsciously lifting it off the lids (Fig. 8.6). Botulinum treatment to the frontalis may unmask the dermatochalasis and give the illusion of 'swelling' of the upper lid skin.

Examination of the glabellar frown

The glabella is the area between the eyebrows. A deep rhytid, the glabellar crease, may occur in isolation (Fig. 8.7); with a parallel but usually shorter rhytid (Fig. 8.8); or with curved rhytids under the medial brows (Fig. 8.9). A vertical glabellar crease is usually associated with hypertrophy of the medial corrugator fibers.

Horizontal glabellar rhytids ('Bunny lines') are due both to dynamic and static factors. The dynamic cause is contraction of the procerus muscle (there is no frontalis here). The static cause is sagging of the forehead skin and muscle with age, overhanging the base of the nose (Fig. 8.10).

The medial fibers of the frontalis elevate the brow but overlie the brow depressor and the corrugator. Treatment of the corrugator should avoid the brow elevator fibers.

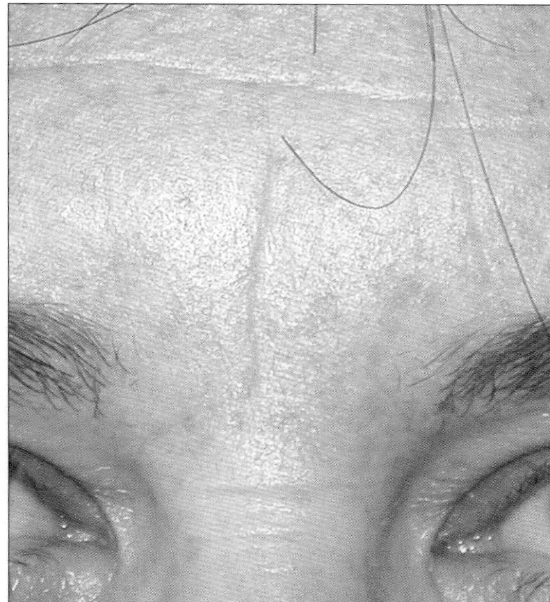

Fig 8.7 Single vertical frown line in a 40-year-old woman.

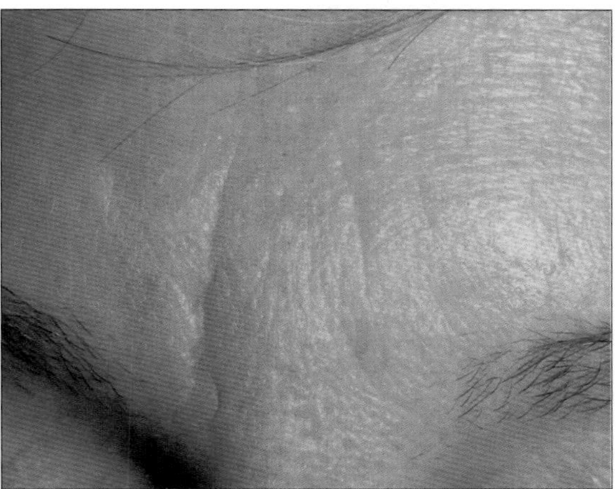

Fig 8.8 Parallel vertical frown lines.

Examination of the horizontal frown

Examine the brows carefully. First, demonstrate the effect that botulinum toxin to the forehead would have if brow tone were to be weakened. To do this, ask the patient to close both eyes and then to open them very slowly while looking in the mirror. This may require repeated attempts, but show the result to the patient in the mirror (Fig. 8.11)

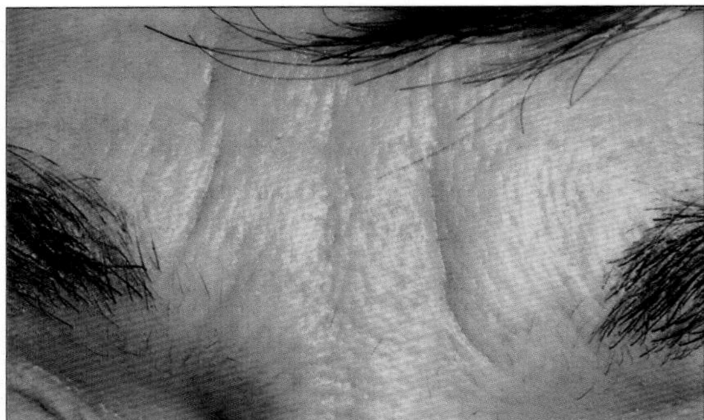

Fig 8.9 Curved vertical frown lines

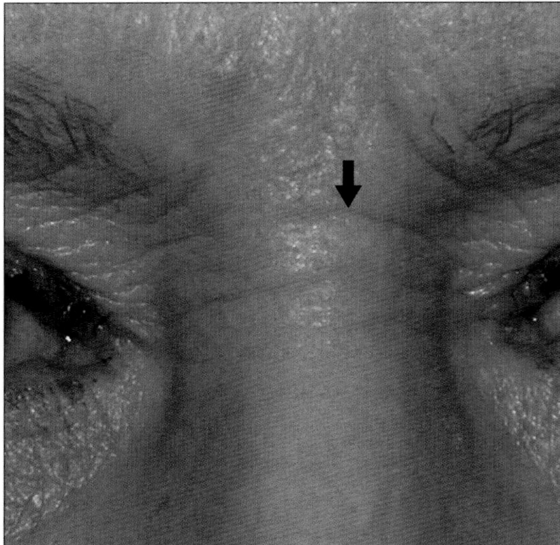

Fig 8.10 Bunny line.

Examine the upper lid crease once this has been achieved. If the lid crease is unaltered by their resting brow, then the patient is suitable for full botulinum toxin treatment. If the lid crease has become full due to dermatochalasis or mild brow ptosis, recommend a limited botulinum toxin treatment to the upper forehead and advise the patient that some movement of the forehead will remain.

BROW EXAMINATION

- **Observe where the horizontal and vertical forehead rhytids lie. Are they due to excessive brow elevation? Is the patient holding an excess of upper lid skin off**

Fig 8.11 Ask patient to close both eyes (allowing eyebrows to drop) then to open eyes slowly while looking in a mirror. This demonstrates the probable resting position of the brows after botulinum toxin A to the frontalis muscle.

their lids? Explain to the patient that botulinum toxin may make them look too 'tired' or 'heavy lidded'. They will be open to a partial effect or surgical alternatives.

- **Tug on the skin below the brow to check for laxity. Does the brow droop at the sides? Tell patients that they might get a temporary elevation of the lateral brows after treatment (Fig. 8.12) but that this is not always repeatable as some frontalis fibers eventually atrophy.**
- **Ask patients to elevate their brows. Are they symmetrical? (Most are not). Point out any asymmetry.**
- **When the brows are elevated, do they 'peak' at any point? Some patients have naturally pointed brows which, if unmasked with botulinum toxin, look unattractive (Fig. 8.13ab). The currently fashionable arch lies at the junction of the medial two thirds and the outer third of the eyebrow – but fashions change.**
- **Ask the patient to frown (Fig. 8.14ab). Which fibers contract? Some patients actually elevate their medial brow by contracting the corrugator, raising the brow superomedially. Others tend to drag the brow down.**
- **Decide whether or not the patient would benefit from an endoscopic brow lift or blepharoplasties (Fig. 8.15ab). Discuss this with them and refer if necessary. Explain the improvements possible from botulinum toxin without surgery (use your hands to stabilize the medial brow, for example, while the patient raises the brow).**

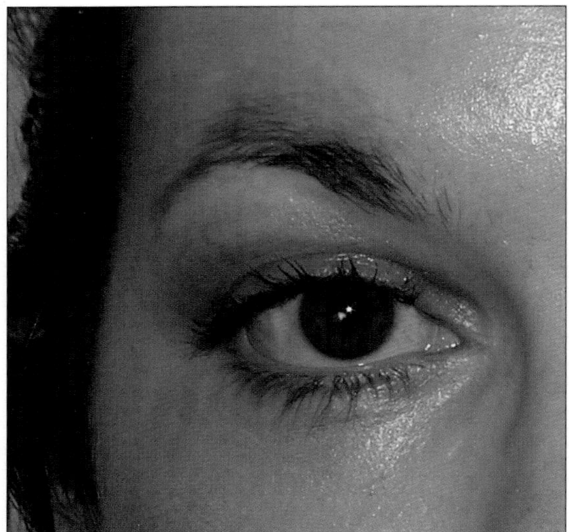

Fig 8.12 Temporary elevation of lateral brow, creating a pleasing arch after Botox® to the glabella. Note post–laser resurfacing erythema (10 days post–laser).

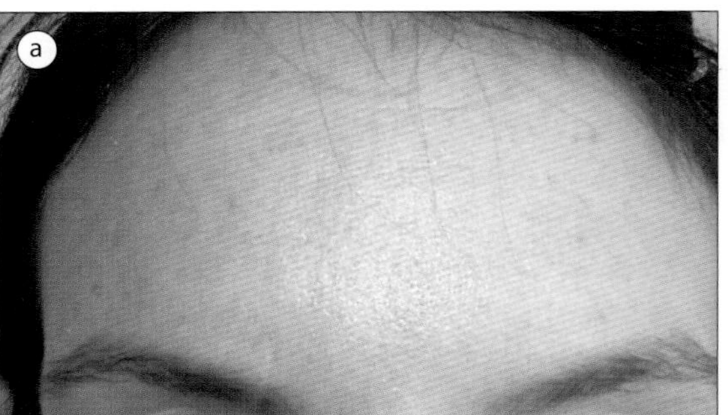

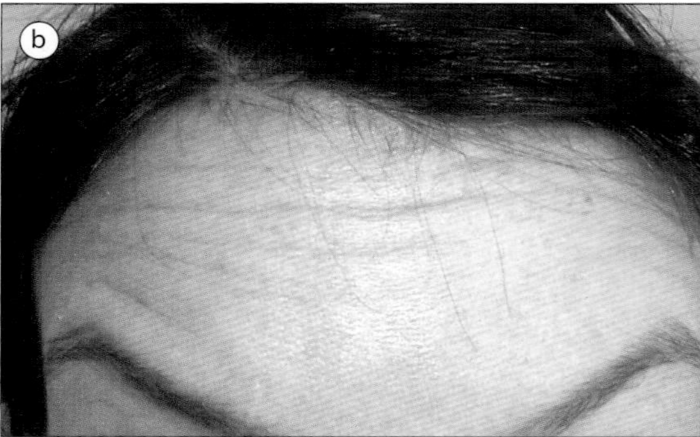

Fig 8.13 A patient with natural peaking of her eyebrows (a) at rest and (b) when asked to elevate brow during pre-treatment consultation.

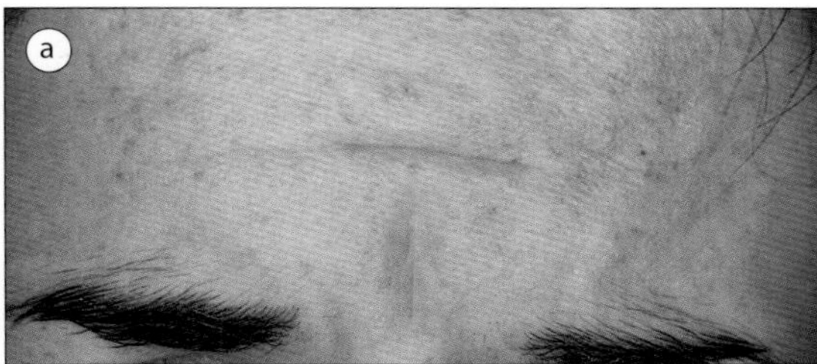

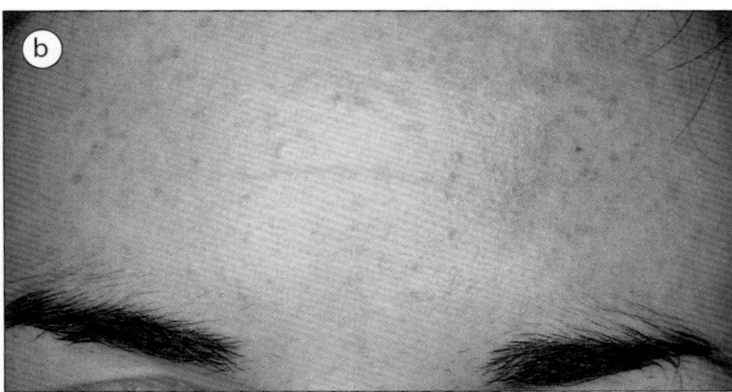

Fig 8.14 (a) before and (b) after Botox® for frowning. Patient is trying to frown in photo 8.14b.

- **On the follow-up visit, before the next treatment, ask patients to place their fingers over their brow muscles and feel the contraction as they frown. They will often notice that the lateral fibers of the frontalis have strengthened, squeezing the corrugator toward the glabellar area. Some patients may tolerate botulinum**

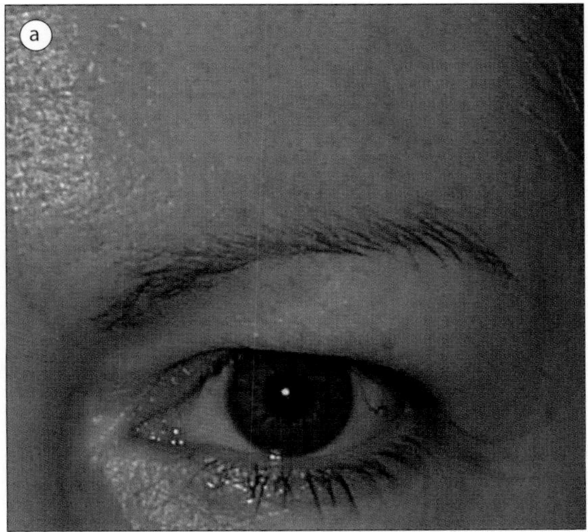

Fig 8.15 (a) before and (b) after upper blepharoplasty and internal brow fixation.

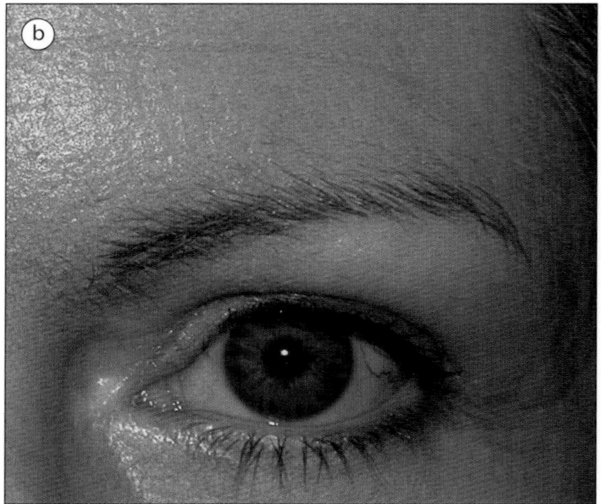

Fig 8.15 *cont'd.*

toxin to this lateral area, but most will look tired, with total inaction of their frontalis if treated.

PRINCIPLES OF FOREHEAD RHYTID TREATMENT

- The mid-frontalis may eventually atrophy, requiring less treatment.
- The glabellar complex rarely atrophies.
- Treatment changes with time as the muscle response alters.
- Untreated muscle can hypertrophy with time e.g. the lateral frontalis.
- Treatment depends on brow position and the presence or absence of blepharochalasis.
- Avoid ptosis by not injecting beneath the superior orbital rim.
- Allow for one centimeter of diffusion of toxin when injecting (more with Dysport®).
- Avoid peaked brows by treating the frontalis two centimeters above the possible peak.
- Avoid intramuscular injections close to or in the brow.
- Discuss brow movement at length with the patient.

RECOMMENDED TREATMENT OF FOREHEAD WRINKLES

DOSE BOX

Botox®: 2.5 ml dil to 100 units vial = 4 units in 0.1 ml
Dysport®: 3 ml dil to 500 units vial = 16.6 units in 0.1 ml

Treat the forehead as a single zone to achieve a balanced effect. Consider the optimal glabellar treatment and then treat the frontalis accordingly.

BASIC GLABELLAR TREATMENT (FIG. 8.16)

- **Treatment of a glabellar rhytid:**
- **The essence of treatment is to paralyze the contraction of the corrugator muscle while allowing acceptable brow movement WITHOUT descent of the medial brow or ascent of the lateral brow!**

Inject 0.1 ml botulinum toxin one centimeter above medial brow (line of medial canthus). ALWAYS aspirate first to avoid the supraorbital complex. Inject 0.05 ml at base of nose below brow level (to diffuse to procerus and brow depressors). Inject 0.05 ml one centimeter above base of corrugator muscle (ask patient to frown and palpate each time before injection).

ADVANCED GLABELLAR TREATMENT

With experience it is possible to increase the concentration of the botulinum toxin while reducing the volume. Injections can then be placed below the brow, up towards the corrugator muscle and above the trochlear tendon towards the medial brow depressor fibers. Great caution must be taken not to enter a blood vessel in the very vascular area of the superomedial orbit. Inaccurate dosage

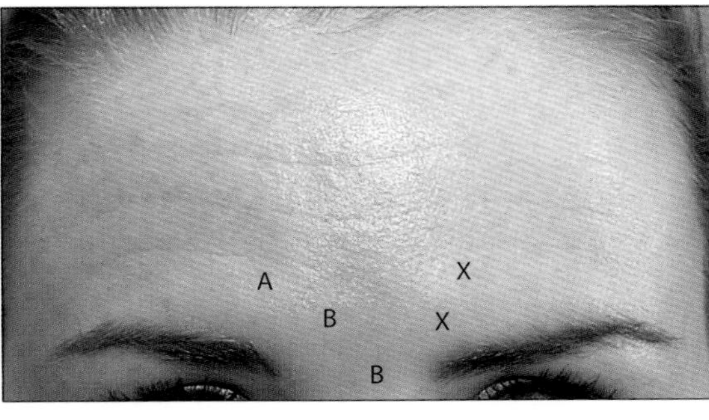

Fig 8.16 Suggestion for glabellar treatment in inexperienced hands. A, 0.1 ml; B, 0.05 ml.

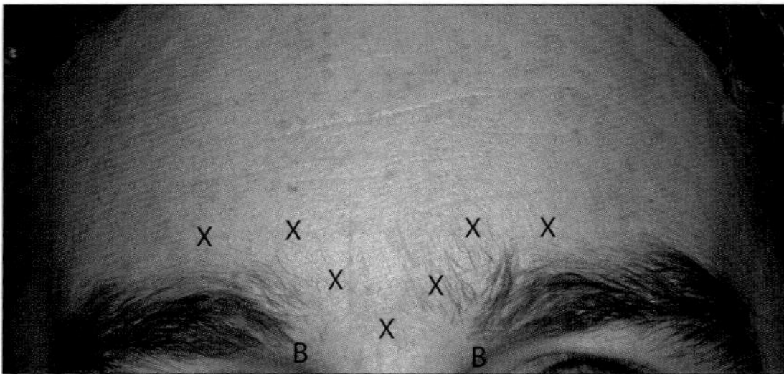

Fig 8.17 Suggested injection sites for optimal glabellar treatment in experienced hands. Site B is at high concentration and low volume. Do not try unless comfortable with diffusion distance as ptosis will be likely.

may cause toxin to diffuse towards the levator muscle, causing ptosis, and toward the superior oblique muscle, causing diplopia. Outstanding results may be achieved in this fashion, with subtle elevation of the brows and smoothing of all furrows. However this technique should be undertaken only by those completely familiar with anatomical variations in this area who are experienced enough to assess the degree of diffusion of the different concentrations accurately. (Fig. 8.17)

IMPORTANT CONSIDERATIONS FOR GLABELLAR TREATMENT

- **Injecting botulinum toxin below the orbital rim greatly increases the risks of true ptosis (a droopy eyelid) due to diffusion of toxin towards the levator muscle of the lid.**
- **The corrugator may be approached from below the medial brow by an expert, thereby avoiding the elevating frontalis fibers. Lower doses at higher concentrations are recommended – but only in experienced hands. (Fig. 8.18)**
- **The supraorbital artery, vein and nerve lie on the corrugator muscle and must be avoided. Palpate the supraorbital notch (not always present), in the bone at the medial brow. This is the line of the supraorbital complex (2.7 cm from midline).**
- **The angular vein traverses the area below the medial brow, the site of the depressor supercilii.**

BASIC FRONTALIS TREATMENT

I examine the frontalis region by asking the patient to frown repeatedly, allowing me to identify the strong points of the frontalis. I inject the bulk of the muscle adjacent to the rhytid. I inject 0.01ml intramuscularly in the central zone as shown (Fig. 8.19) and then inject 0.05ml to the other areas to give

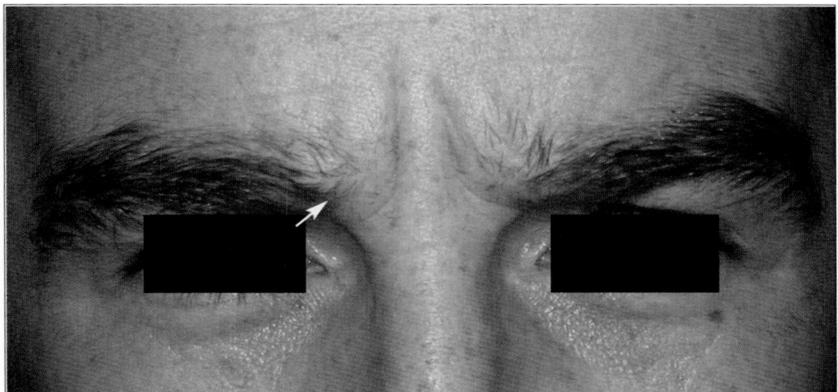

Fig 8.18 Extra treatment to corrugator – only for experienced practitioners. Deep approach to currugator muscle.

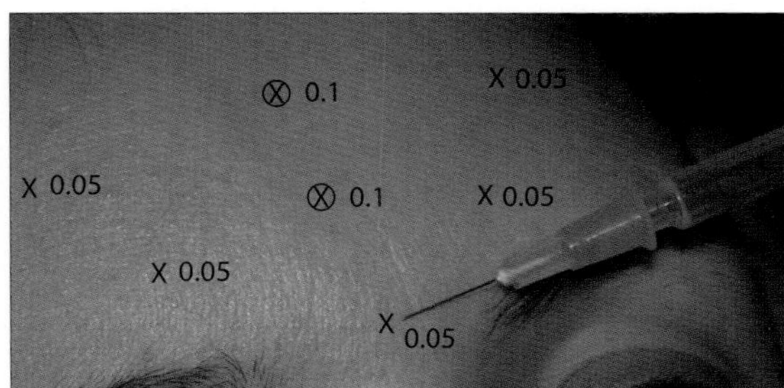

Fig 8.19 Basic frontalis treatment. (X), 0.1 ml, X, 0.05 ml.

symmetry. I sometimes give 0.025ml subcutaneously above the lateral brow to soften rhytids whilst retaining frontalis action. On follow up visits, I frequently inject 0.1ml into the scalp aponeurosis to discourage hypertrophy and an overaction of aponeurotic fibers which would result in excessive scalp movement relative to the atrophic frontalis muscle (Fig. 8.20).

USER TIP

Tell the patient that the treatment sites will be different each time because the muscles will recover differently.

TREATMENT OF RHYTIDS

Different types of rhytids may be treated as follows:

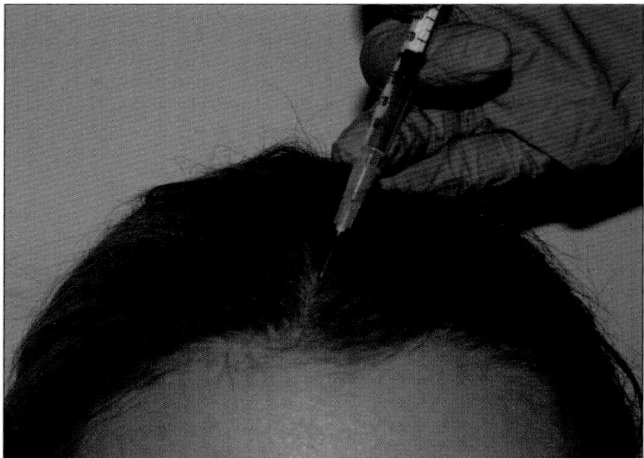

Fig 8.20 Injection of scalp aponeurosis.

Simple forehead lines in motion, none at rest (20 – 30 years) (Fig. 8.21)

If the brows are firm, then treat the complete frontalis. Expect a semi-permanent effect within 2 years as the frontalis muscle atrophies.

Young patients with firm brow attachments are easy. Inject the glabellar area as shown in Figure 8.16, along the line of the corrugator. Treat the frontalis as shown to prevent peaking of the brows. Injection sites are chosen to allow for diffusion of the toxin within one centimeter of the site. This allows treatment of the procerus medially, sometimes incorporating some overlying frontalis fibers

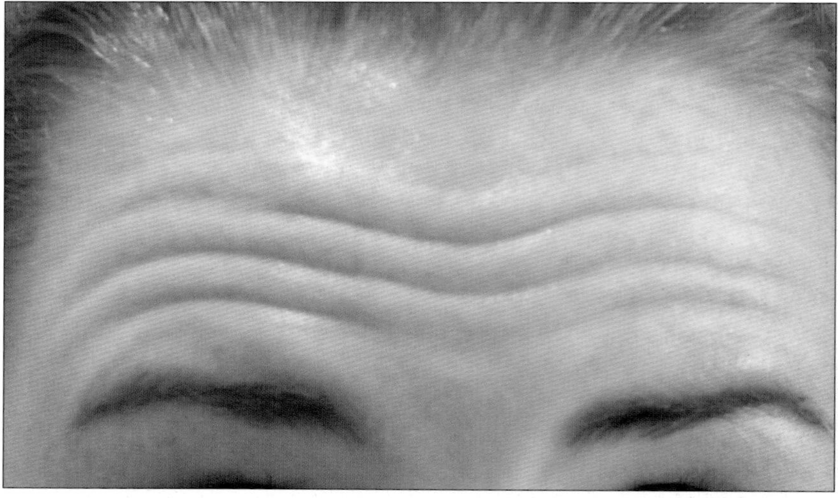

Fig 8.21 Simple forehead lines in motion, none at rest (20–30 years).

with diffusion towards the brow depressor, counteracting brow depression medially at the most nasal aspect of the brow.

Simple forehead lines in motion, none at rest (20-30 years) (Fig. 8.22)
Short brow lash distance with slightly mobile brows. Avoid lateral frontalis and treat superolateral frontalis instead. Treat medial brow depressors.

Forehead lines at rest and in motion (Fig. 8.23)
Treat as above but classify rhytids. If severe, advise about CO_2 resurfacing.

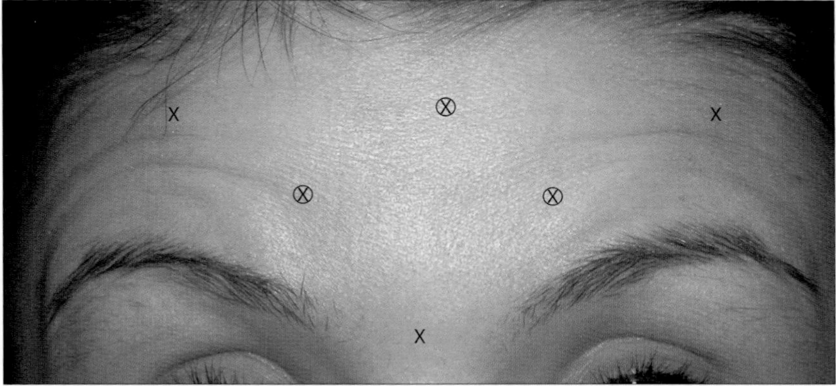

Fig 8.22 Wrinkles in motion in a 20 year old woman with short lash–brow distance and mobile brows.

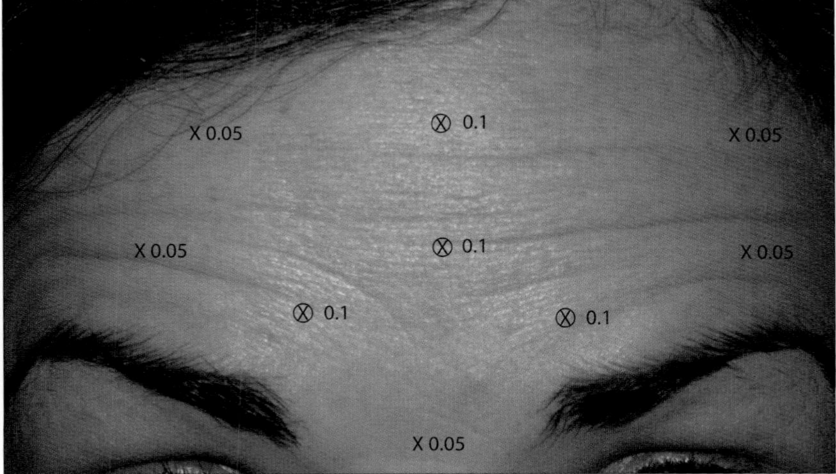

Fig 8.23 Patient over 40 with high arched brows and wrinkled forehead. X, 0.05 ml, (x), 0.1 ml.

High arched brows with furrowed horizontal lines in patient over 35 (Fig. 8.24)

Take great care. This patient is typical of those who can become extremely distressed if they lose the deep appearance of their upper eyelids as the frontalis becomes paralysed with botulinum toxin. The heavy brow can sometimes weigh upon the upper lid simulating ptosis; but when the brow is gently lifted by the examiner's finger, the lid will return to its normal position.

Discuss surgical correction at length (Chapter 11). Consider botulinum toxin treatment to the upper rhytids, retaining the elevating action of the lower frontalis fibres. Offer filler to the glabellar crease and the fine lines over the lateral brow.

The male forehead (Fig. 8.25)

The male brow tends to be horizontal with a short lash brow distance. The muscles may be bulkier than those of the female forehead and sometimes need greater doses. Treatment of the glabellar area alone can lead to a feminising arch and must be avoided unless requested. The male forehead is also prone to a receding hairline. Such patients may require extensive volumes of botulinum toxin to treat the occipital portion of the frontalis, otherwise they will return with frontal furrows.

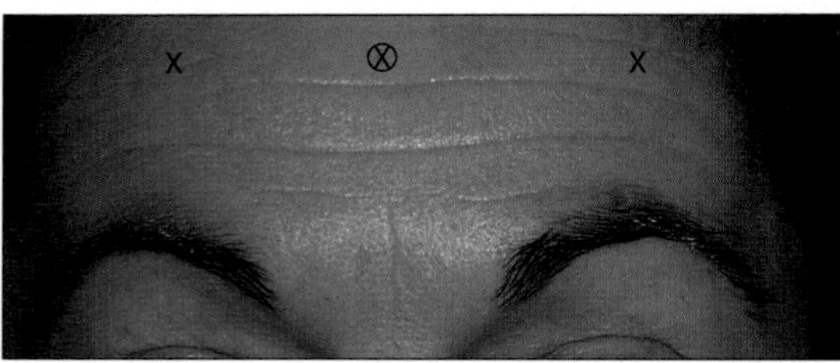

Fig 8.24 Patient over 35 with high arched brows and wrinkled forehead. Retain brow height by avoiding BTX to brow area (i.e. lower half of forehead).

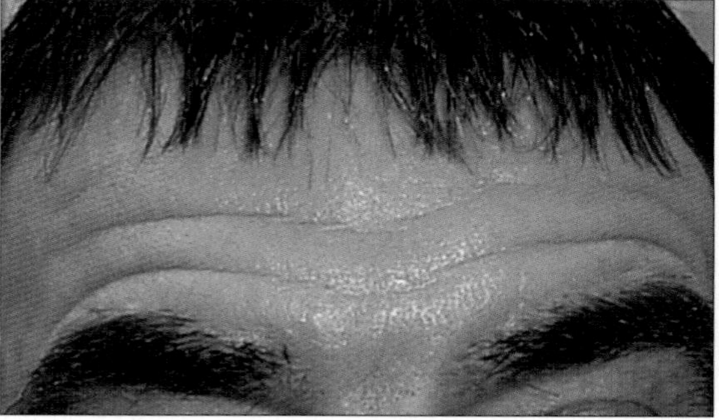

Fig 8.25 Typical heavy male forehead.

9 Treatment of the perioral region, the neck and scars

DOSE BOX

Botox®: 2.5 ml dil to 100 units vial = 4 units in 0.1 ml
Dysport®: 3 ml dil to 500 units vial = 16.6 units in 0.1 ml

A good knowledge of the anatomy of the perioral region is essential before undertaking botulinum toxin treatment. The orbicularis oris responds well to botulinum toxin but great care must be taken to limit diffusion into the surrounding muscles (Fig. 9.1). This can be achieved by using a higher concentration of the toxin, at a smaller dose. Treatment of the wrong muscle fibers can lead to dribbling, difficulty in drinking water, slurred speech and asymmetrical smiling.

Patients with facial hemispasm frequently require botulinum toxin to a focus of spasm over the elevator of the lip. This leads to a depression of the corner of the mouth and drooling of saliva (Fig. 9.2) but patients would usually rather have an embarrassing dribble than an uncomfortable spasm and twitching of the side of their face. However this complication MUST be avoided in a cosmetic practice.

AGEING OF THE PERIORAL REGION AND NECK

Ablating wrinkles does not always make a patient look younger. When considering rejuvenation of this area, examine the overall tone of the musculocutaneous complex. Also examine the skeletal support, the dentition and the shape of the nose.

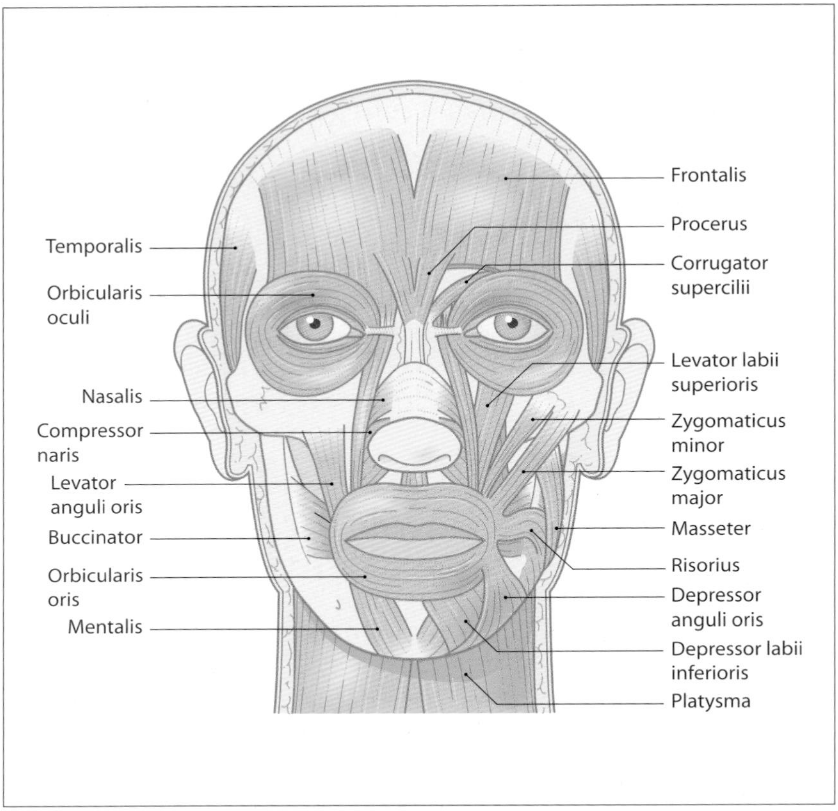

Temporalis
Orbicularis oculi
Nasalis
Compressor naris
Levator anguli oris
Buccinator
Orbicularis oris
Mentalis
Frontalis
Procerus
Corrugator supercilii
Levator labii superioris
Zygomaticus minor
Zygomaticus major
Masseter
Risorius
Depressor anguli oris
Depressor labii inferioris
Platysma

Fig 9.1 Anatomy of perioral area. After Zide BM and Jelks GW (1985) Surgical Anatomy of the Orbit. Raven Press Books, Ltd. New York. With permission of Barry M Zide.

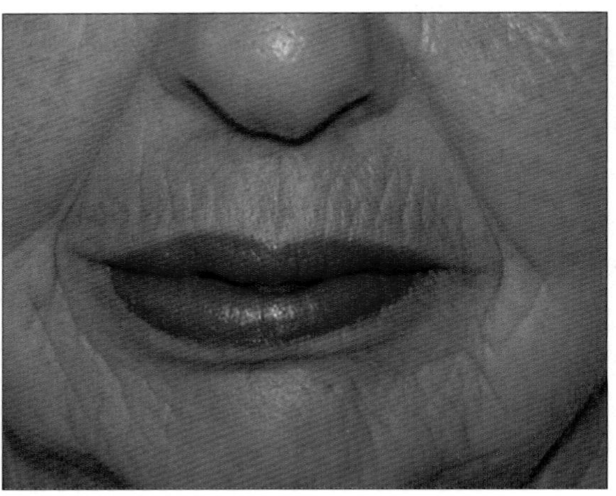

Fig 9.2 Mouth droop following botulinum toxin for severe blepharospasm.

Research has confirmed that ageing causes an antero-postero recession of the facial bones, which contributes to sagging. The distance from the nose to the vermilion border increases with time. The vermilion border itself shrinks, the lips lose volume, and tend to turn downwards instead of up and out.

The lip depressors and elevators induce wrinkles at the corners of the mouth and 'marionette lines'. The mentalis muscle encourages the tip of the chin to turn upwards, creating the mental fold and sometimes a 'pointed' chin. Recession of the jaw will accentuate the wrinkles, from the corner of the mouth to the chin.

The platysma muscle will eventually draw the sides of the mouth towards the jaw, and this, along with facial sagging, creates jowls. Increased resting tone of the platysma creates vertical bands (turkey neck) along the line of action, and 'venus rings' i.e. horizontal banding, perpendicular to the line of action.

The tip of the nose becomes pulled down with time (pointed nose) and the descent of the mid-face, coupled with recession of the facial bones, deepens the nasolabial folds.

TREATMENT

Botulinum toxin causes a flaccid paralysis of muscles that have been injected, and so induces a mild elongation as the muscle spindles stop contracting. This is particularly obvious in the vertical muscles of the face e.g. in the upper lip. Examine the patient carefully and consider the likely effect of elongating a perioral muscle before injecting it. If the patient already has a long nasal–vermilion distance, for example (Fig. 9.3), then treating upper lip wrinkles with further relaxation of the muscle will not produce a good

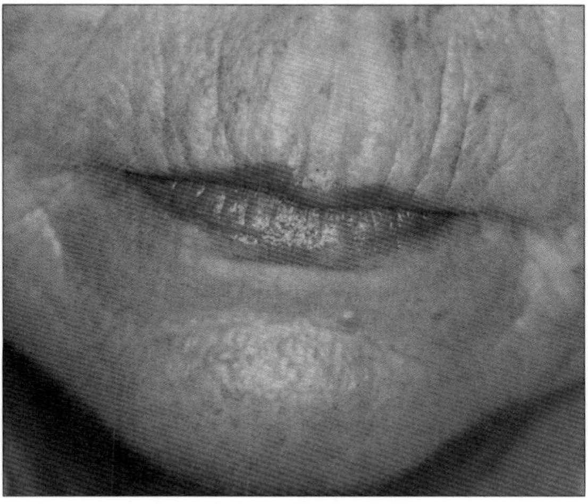

Fig 9.3 Long upper lip with wrinkles.

appearance. Treatment of the nasolabial fold will also lengthen the upper lip. These patients can be offered alternative treatments such as surgery, CO_2 resurfacing and fillers (Chapter 11).

PERIORAL INDICATIONS

- **Upper lip rhytids**
- **Lower lip rhytids**
- **Pebbly chin**
- **Elevation of lip corner**
- **Reduction of nasolabial folds**

Upper and lower lip rhytids

Moderate rhytids, particularly in non-smokers, can be discouraged with a small volume of botulinum toxin injected away from the vermilion border (Fig. 9.4). Limiting the contraction of the orbicularis oris will always curtail its true function as a sphincter around the mouth for articulation and eating. Patients often notice a weakening of their ability to 'pout' and, even though they seldom actually slur their speech, they sometimes experience the sensation of slurring.

More profound side effects occasionally occur and patients must be warned about these. Milder sensations of poor articulation often wear off over the first few weeks. It is often easiest to counteract the risks by using a milder phased treatment augmented with resurfacing or fillers.

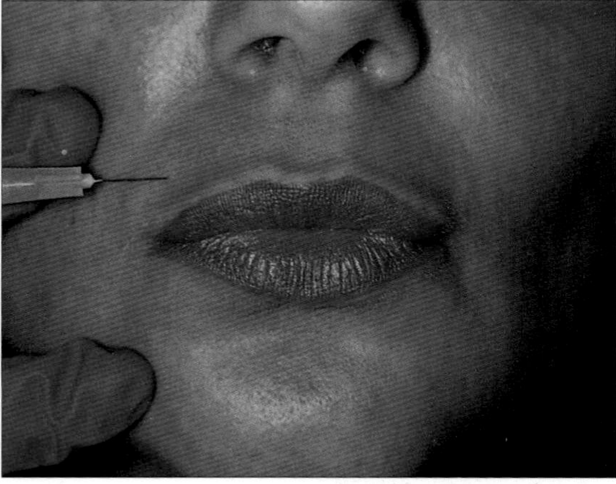

Fig 9.4 Botulinum toxin to the upper lip.

Whenever possible, encourage CO_2 resurfacing of the rhytids for at least a 50% long term improvement (Chapter 11), or, if an instant remedy is desired, inject hyaluronic acid into the valley of the rhytid. Some patients benefit from both; but never at the same time in the lip or nasolabial fold area.

If necessary, no more than 0.0125 ml of botulinum toxin per site (at the above dilutions) is recommended. Using a lower volume at a higher concentration is also valuable, but difficult to manipulate at first, and is perhaps best tried by an experienced operator.

USER TIP

Avoid injecting fillers and botulinum toxin into the perioral area at the same time. Botulinum toxin can elongate and flatten the lip, requiring a different level of filler. The filler may also appear as nodules if given to an area which subsequently flattens with botulinum toxin.

USER TIP

It is sometimes safer to treat deep upper lip rhytids with laser resurfacing and/or injections of hyaluronic acid than with botulinum toxin, because of the twin risks of weakening the lip sphincter and elongating the lip (Chapter 11).

Vermilion border

Fine 'bleeder' lines at the vermilion border can be injected with 0.0125 ml of botulinum toxin (Fig. 9.5). I avoid injecting rhytids farther away from the vermilion border at the same time. This minimizes the laxity of the lip and the risk of side effects. I tend to inject intramuscularly, although other experts have had excellent results with subcutaneous injections in the 'danger zones'.

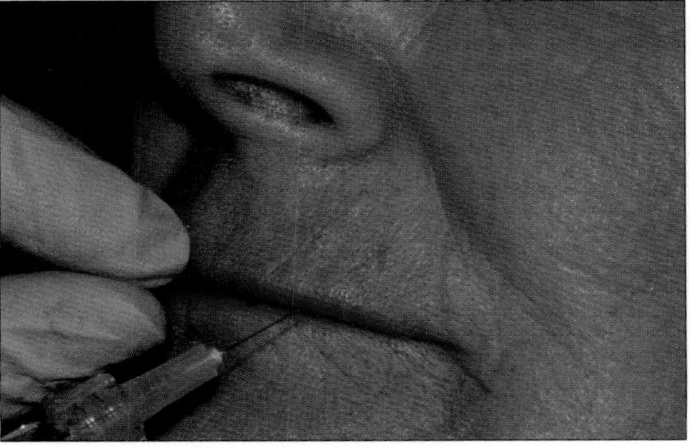

Fig 9.5 Treating 'bleeder lines'.

Corner of mouth (Fig 9.6)

Botulinum toxin to the depressor of the angle of the mouth can achieve a sought-after upturn of the outer corners, which can be nicely augmented with hyaluronic acid. I have achieved good results with 0.05 ml. The depressor anguli oris is intimately associated with the underlying platysma and the adjacent depressor labii inferioris. Unwanted diffusion to the depressor labii inferioris will result in an inability to purse the lower lip, asymmetry when smiling, and even dribbling when drinking. Some experts recommend avoiding these side effects by injecting subcutaneously and not within one centimeter of the angle.

USER TIP

For peri-oral treatment, if in doubt, start with a low dose and low dilution of botulinum toxin, given subcutaneously. Review the patient within 2 weeks and give more if necessary.

Nasolabial folds

Injections of botulinum toxin have been used to treat deep nasolabial folds and nostril flares. I tend to treat the folds with Perlane® (Chapter 11). I have seen photographs of the impressive results obtained by Dr Le Louarn of Paris, who recommends a low volume of highly concentrated Dysport® (personal communication). Ipsen Pharmaceuticals will publish these results shortly.

Pebbly chin and mental crease

Botulinum toxin is excellent for smoothing the mentalis muscle, the main muscle responsible for wrinkling of the chin (Fig. 9.7). It is important to warn patients that the result may be asymmetrical at first, as the toxin may diffuse

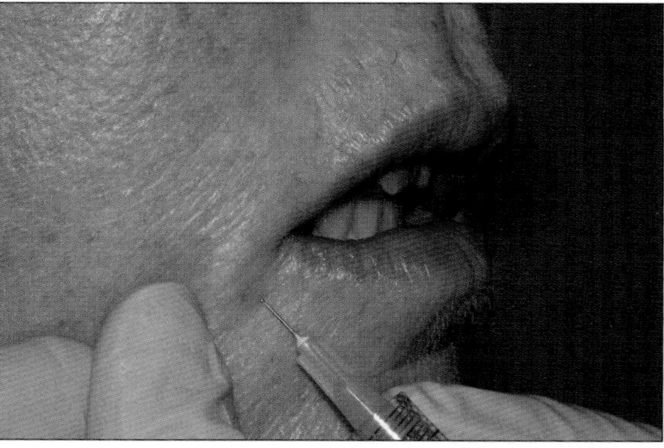

Fig 9.6 Treating the corners of the mouth.

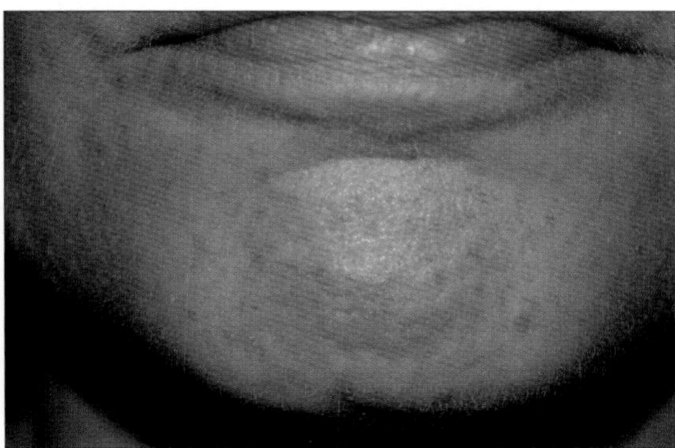

Fig 9.7 'Pebbly' chin.

irregularly towards one head of the muscle. I recommend starting with a low dose (0.025 ml) and increasing this until the desired effect is achieved. Insert the needle directly in the center of the tip of the chin, withdraw slightly having reached the periosteum, and inject 0.025 ml initially. Consider subsequent subcutaneous injections of 0.0125 ml to the overlying depressor anguli oris.

The mental crease deepens with age as the tip of the chin elevates (a 'Wicked Witch' chin). Subcutaneous injections of 0.0125 ml along the crease help to shorten it (Fig 9.8). Hyaluronic acid (especially Perlane) will fill it instantly.

BOTULINUM TOXIN TO THE NECK

Botulinum toxin is very effective at neutralizing the pull of the platysma muscle under the chin and so preventing horizontal banding lower down on the neck (Fig. 9.9). It is also effective in the treatment of 'turkey neck' – the vertical folds of platysma lying between the mandible and the clavicle.

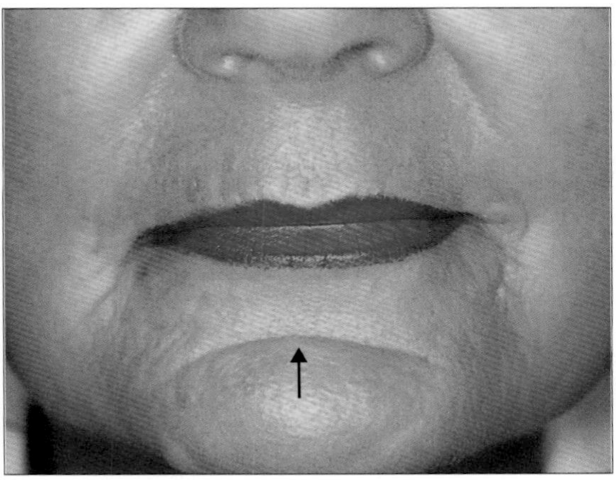

Fig 9.8 Horizontal crease in chin.

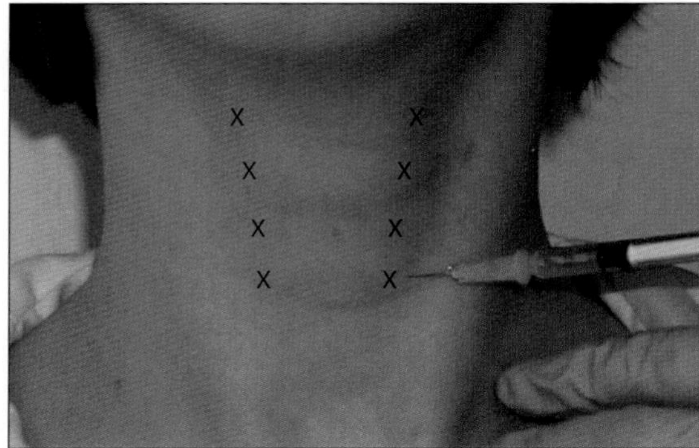

Fig 9.9 Horizontal neck wrinkles. X, 0.05 ml.

The platysma spreads out from its origin at the base of the mandible and parotid fascia, down the neck and along the pectoral fascia. A reduction in the pull of the platysma tends to give the illusion of elevating the lower facial muscles and, in some patients, even of a reduction in their marionette folds.

Care must be taken to prevent diffusion of the toxin towards the esophagus, which is extremely sensitive to it, as there have been several reports of unexpected dysphagia from earlier treatments, using doses similar to the frontalis ones. Care must also be taken to avoid the larynx as hoarseness has also been reported, along with difficulty in lifting the head.

The subcutaneous injection of 0.05 ml of botulinum toxin is recommended. Divide the prominent area visually into units, and aim to space the injections 1.5 cm apart. Treat only the 'band' that is obvious at rest sitting upright, and not the flat part of the platysma that protrudes on effort. Treatment of the band often suffices and reduces the volume of botulinum toxin required (Fig. 9.10).

Finally, remember that some patients with prominent neck banding and 'jowls' would benefit from a lower facelift. Always discuss this surgical option with them and then refer them to a plastic surgeon.

BOTULINUM TOXIN FOR SCARS

Patients who normally heal well in other parts of their face tend to heal badly if they have a linear scar perpendicular to the direction of pull of a facial muscle. Muscle pull stretches and thins scars, which often remain red. This is particularly true for the frontalis muscle. The muscle can also pucker and 'dip', particularly in the perioral region and when parallel to the muscle action e.g. after a midforehead brow lift.

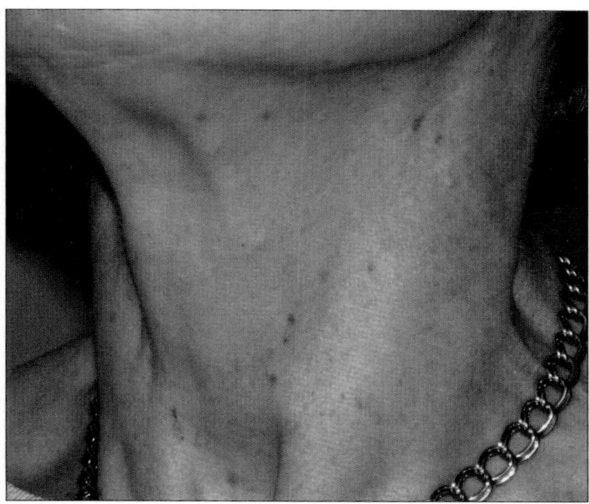

Fig 9.10 Platysma: vertical neck wrinkles. Note injection marks.

The traditional way of correcting unsightly forehead scars has been to re-excise them, taping the incision firmly with steristrips and then bandaging the forehead for up to six weeks in an effort to keep tension off the margins of the scar. Botulinum toxin will provide a tension free zone for up to 14 weeks (sometimes longer in the frontalis area). NeuroBloc® will create the same effect for 6 weeks.

Frontalis scars

Inject the frontalis muscle evenly across the whole forehead, as in the treatment of rhytids (Fig. 9.11). This keeps tension off the scar while preventing asymmetry of the forehead, which would occur with injections localized to the scar itself. Make sure that every centimeter along the scar receives botulinum toxin, giving it at 0.5 cm on either side of the scar. The dose per site used is 0.05 ml.

Peri-oral scars

Great care must be taken to avoid the toxin diffusing towards the lip elevators or sphincter muscles of the mouth. Begin with the lowest dose, and increase this until an effect is achieved. Review the patient after 10–14 days to decide on this. Figure 9.12ab shows a scar that followed a road traffic accident, in a patient who requested laser resurfacing. Examination showed that the scar was much more unsightly 'in motion', i.e. while the patient was talking, than 'at rest'. Botox® 0.0125 was therefore injected on either side of the scar, at sites one centimeter apart. The scar appeared to flatten over the next week and the

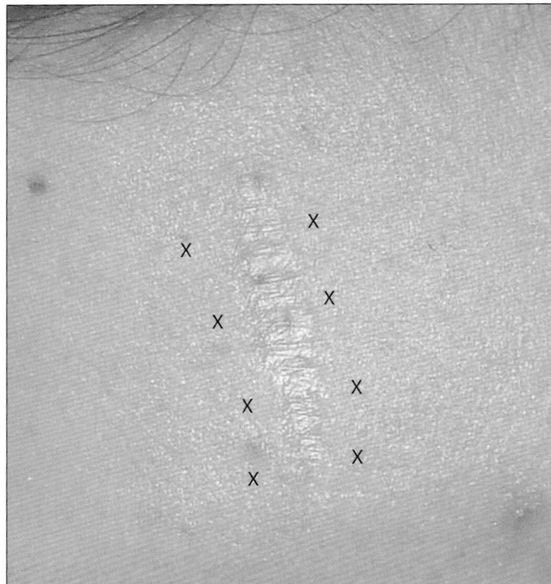

Fig 9.11 Typical forehead scar for excision and botulinum toxin treatment. X, 0.05 ml.

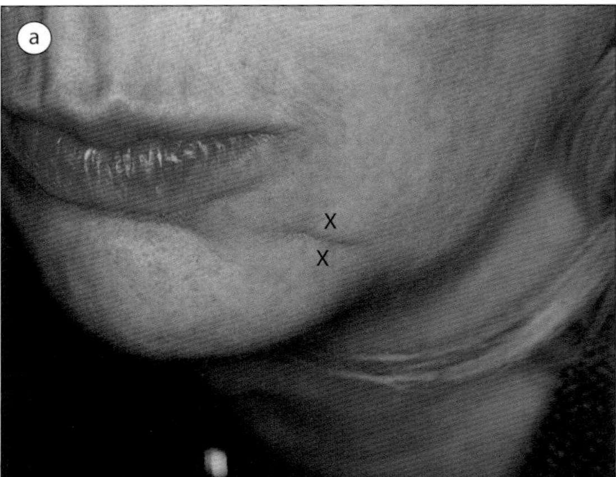

Fig 9.12 (a) before and (b) after botulinum toxin to scar on chin. X, 0.0125 ml.

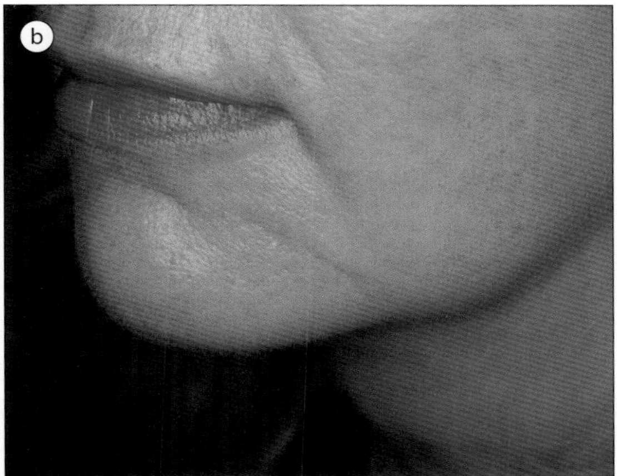

Fig 9.12 *cont'd.*

patient was extremely happy. Follow up treatment with the same dose, 14 weeks later, gave the patient the feeling of a 'drag' on that side of her mouth. This could not be detected on examination, but the botulinum treatment schedule was modified to annual sessions with occasional injections of hyaluronic acid if required (Chapter 11).

DÉCOLLETÉ

Excellent results from the botulinum treatment of décolleté wrinkles have been reported by Dr Petra Becker-Wegerich of Düsseldorf (personal communication). The author has not tried this but has seen impressive photographs of the results.

10 Other indications for botulinum toxin

An excellent summary of this subject can be found in the 'Handbook of Botulinum Toxin Treatment' by Peter Moore (see bibliography).

Botulinum toxin blocks the release of acetylcholine from cholinergic nerve terminals. This action at the neuromuscular junction weakens striated muscle, but it can also affect other cholinergic terminals such as those of the sympathetic and parasympathetic systems. This can lead to autonomic dysfunction – for example there have been reports of gall bladder dysfunction – and opens up possibilities for several uses in areas other than those listed below (Table 10.1).

Botulinum toxin was originally licensed for the treatment of strabismus after pioneering work by Dr. Alan Scott of the Smith Kettlewell Eye Research Foundation in San Francisco. Injecting the toxin into an overactive extraocular muscle causes it to relax. The first strabismus patient was injected in 1977 and, by 1982, Dr Scott had also treated patients for nystagmus, hemifacial spasm, lid retraction, torticollis and spasticity of the legs.

The initial license for botulinum toxin was for strabismus; and this was followed by licenses for dysthyroid ophthalmopathy, nystagmus and medical tarsorraphy. Since then botulinum toxin has been the treatment of choice for blepharospasm and hemifacial spasm. It is widely used for dystonias and new applications are constantly emerging. Recent work has focused on its non-muscular effects, such as those on the skin.

Table 10.1. Current uses for botulinum toxin.

System	Disorder
Gastrointestinal	Dysphagia
	Achalasia of the cardia
	Hypertrophic pyloricstenosis
	Hirschsprung's disease
	Anal fissure
	Hemorrhoids
	Proctalgia fugax
Ophthalmic	Blepharospasm
	Nystagmus
	Oscillopsia hyperlacrimation
	Medical tarsorraphy strabismus
Sweating	Hyperhidrosis
	Gustatory sweating
Abnormal movements	Palatal tremor
	Limb myoclonus
	Head and neck tremor
	Tics
Dystonias	Cervical dystonia
	Oromandibular dystonia (Meige's syndrome)
	Laryngeal dystonia
	Limb dystonia
	Hemifacial spasm
Palsies	Cerebral palsy
	Post Bell's palsy synkinesis
	Facial palsy (for symmetry)
Other	Myofascial pain
	Migraine
Cosmetic	See elsewhere in this book

STRABISMUS

In strabismus (a squint) there is an imbalance in the way the extraocular muscles contract. This can be congenital and appear in childhood, causing an eye to turn in (esotropia) or out (exotropia). Other causes include nerve palsy. Both eyes work together as a result of neural signals traveling simultaneously to the agonists of one eye (e.g. the medial rectus) and to the antagonists of the other (e.g. the lateral rectus). The intensity of the signal is balanced between opposing muscle groups (Herring's law). An excessive relaxation of one muscle (for example, from a right sixth nerve palsy) can lead to an excessive contraction of the opposite antagonist (in this example, the right medial rectus muscle), causing the eye to squint towards the nose.

The eyes must be straight for proper vision to develop, as the visual cortex of the brain requires a sharp image from each eye (until around 8 years of age) to mature properly. If an eye squints, then it will become amblyopic ('lazy') if not straightened in time, and never develop its full visual potential. This effect can be reduced by occluding the opposite eye, by using certain glasses or by surgery. In a developed eye, strabismus (e.g. from a sixth nerve palsy) leads to double vision as the image falls on different points in the two eyes.

The treatment of strabismus may be cosmetic, but initially is aimed at developing normal vision and preventing diplopia. Traditionally, a 'tight' contracting muscle was 'cut' surgically and repositioned. Alan Scott discovered that a 'tight' muscle could be relaxed temporarily by injecting botulinum toxin.

Such injections for strabismus are usually given under electromyographic control, with an electrode being inserted into the muscle, under topical anesthesia. Botulinum toxin is particularly useful for the treatment of paralytic nerve palsies. It is used to assess the degree of the palsy, by relaxing the opposite contracting muscle and reducing the work that the paralyzed muscle has to do.

The main benefit of botulinum toxin in strabismus stems from its use as an adjunct to conventional squint management, for example by predicting postoperative diplopia. Other types of restrictive squints benefit too, as do certain types of nystagmus.

IDIOPATHIC BLEPHAROSPASM AND HEMIFACIAL SPASM

Botulinum toxin is the treatment of choice for dystonic movement disorders. These are due to a functional defect in the interneural circuitry of the brain and spinal cord, sometimes related to problems with the basal ganglia.

Idiopathic blepharospasm may begin in childhood with twitching and excessive blinking. Usually however it presents in the fifth to seventh decade, and is more common in women than men.

Idiopathic hemifacial spasm may follow irritation of the facial nerve by a branch of the anterior or posterior inferior cerebellar arteries. Spasm occurs in the muscles supplied by the facial nerve. It is seen rarely with posterior fossa tumors but, in childhood, is always associated with intracranial pathology. The spasm may improve during moments of excitement, and during periods of concentration, for example on mental arithmetic or other activities. It can spread from one muscle group to a neighboring one, and may be provoked by irritation such as that associated with a dry eye.

Botulinum toxin can be injected into the orbicularis and other spastic muscles; but first the focal point of the spasm has to be established. The injections are placed so as to discourage transmission of the impulse between muscle groups, especially in facial hemispasm where contraction of the orbicularis oris can spread to the orbicularis oculi. The treatment schedule selected will depend on the degree of spasm. Most patients return within three months for repeat injections, the doses used being titrated against the side effects, such as ptosis.

SPASMODIC TORTICOLLIS AND OTHER DYSTONIAS

Spasmodic torticollis (cervical dystonia) is the most common type of dystonia. It usually presents in the early 40s and may be preceded by trauma. It can also be transmitted as an autosomal dominant trait, sometimes in association with bilateral tremor of the hands.

Tonic spasm of the neck muscles is associated with jerks or tremor. Seventy percent of patients suffer from pain, and there may be associated brachial symptoms (paraesthesiae or pain radiating to the arm and hand). Functional impairments include difficulty in looking at the road while driving and in placing food in the mouth during a jerk. Many patients are overwhelmingly embarrassed by their condition.

Some patients develop tricks to overcome the spasm, such as sucking a pen, but botulinum toxin injections have revolutionized management, replacing most surgical alternatives. Cases unresponsive to botulinum toxin may benefit from systemic medication with anticholinergics (e.g. trihexyphenidyl (benzhexol)), or benzodiazepines such as clonazepam, carbamazepine and baclofen.

HYPERHIDROSIS

The treatment of hyperhidrosis with botulinum toxin was first suggested in the early 1800s by a German physician, Justinus Kerner, who noted that his patients with botulism sweated less than usual.

Primary idiopathic hyperhidrosis is a common cause of excessive sweating of the palms, axillae, face (Frey's syndrome, gustatory sweating) and feet. It can be embarrassing and disabling enough to warrant medical management. Traditional treatments have included topical aluminium chloride salts, oral anticholinergic drugs and tap water iontophoresis. Surgical treatment is based on removing the nerve supply to the glands (endoscopic transthoracic sympathectomy) or a local excision of the axillary sweat glands. Surgery has only a 66% success rate because of post-operative compensatory hyperhidrosis. Its side effects include Horner's syndrome, gustatory sweating, neuralgia and pneumothorax.

Botulinum toxin inhibits the release of acetylcholine at the eccrine sweat glands and this has revolutionized the management of hyperhidrosis. The treatment is easy to master, particularly when guided by the Minor

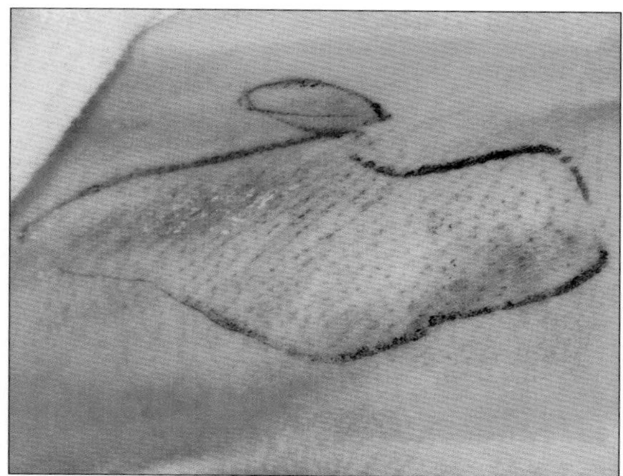

Fig 10.1 Starch iodine test to axilla for botulinum toxin treatment of hyperhidrosis.

starch-iodine test (Fig. 10.1), though with experience this is not necessary. The area to be treated is divided into a grid pattern along which the toxin is injected. The response is dose related: 50 units of Botox® or 50 units Dysport® injected subcutaneously across a grid in each axilla will usually stop sweating for 8 months.

Treatment of the palms has to be intradermal to avoid transient neuromuscular weakness, but this is painful and requires a nerve block. However, the results are even better than those for axillary hyperhidrosis, though it is recommended that the two hands are treated three weeks apart because of possible weakness.

11 Other solutions

- Hyaluronic acid
- Laser resurfacing
- Laser blepharoplasty
- Combination treatments
- Face-lift, brow lift
- Microdermabrasion
- Chemical peels
- Skin protection and rejuvenation products

INTRODUCTION

Botulinum toxin is good at preventing wrinkles in certain age groups. It is the ideal treatment for 'wrinkles in motion' and can even dissolve 'wrinkles at rest' in patients with good skin tone (see Fig. 7.2ab). However patients with poor skin tone, and deep crow's feet at rest will not get a good response from botulinum toxin alone (Fig. 11.1). Those with furrowed brows but a low lash–brow distance, poor tone of their forehead skin, and/or an excess of upper lid skin (dermatochalasis), will actually look worse if they lose further muscle tone after botulinum toxin. They need an alternative treatment.

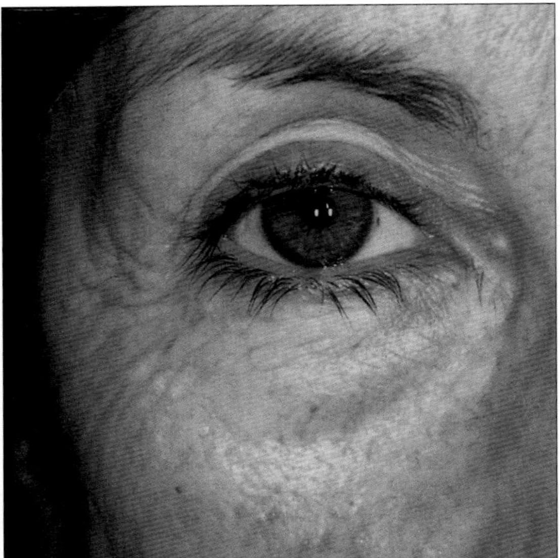

Fig 11.1 Deep crows feet at rest (static rhytids)

Ageing skin sags for several reasons. The skin loses collagen, becoming thinner and less transparent as the parallel collagen fibers become cross-linked and misaligned. This is greatly accelerated by smoking and exposure to ultraviolet A and B rays. The time at which ageing starts is genetically predetermined: if a mother doesn't have a wrinkle until the age of 55, then her daughter with the same genes and habits may not either. Clearly the extent to which the skin ages also depends upon environmental factors. If a mother has had an excessive exposure to the sun and smokes, she will probably become severely wrinkled within a short time when she begins to age at 55. On the other hand, if her daughter – with the same genes – avoids UV damage and smoking, she may well retain the tone in her skin for much longer.

It is sensible to educate all botulinum toxin patients on the subject of skin protection and recovery ('stopping the clock'). Aesthetic nurse practitioners may spend time assessing the patient's skin regime and, if necessary, Retin-A® can be prescribed.

Ageing of the face is also due to the recession of its skeletal support. The antero-posterior diameter of the skull lessens with time, and this encourages sagging in spite of an otherwise excellent skin tone. The diameter of the orbit increases from superomedially to inferolaterally, reducing support for the orbicularis oculi muscles and skin. Traditional cosmetic surgery replaces this lost support by excising skin and muscle (face lift, blepharoplasty). More recently, implants, such as malar and chin ones, have been used. Laser resurfacing can tighten and 'lift' sagging structures. Brow lifts are being replaced by brow repositioning (internal brow fixation or an endoscopic brow lift), while blepharoplasties often include lateral canthal tendon plication to tighten the sagging areas over an expanded orbital rim.

There is currently a movement towards the replacement of lost collagen and fat by fillers that replenish the tone of the skin and plump up lips, as well as supplementing lost skeletal support.

The ways in which patients should be selected for botulinum toxin are discussed in detail in Chapters 5,7,8 and 9. Some alternatives are discussed here.

HYALURONIC ACID AND OTHER FILLERS

USER TIP

Fillers are an essential part of a good cosmetic botulinum toxin practice.

'Fillers' are volume-replacing products that can be inserted or injected into the skin. The principle behind their use is that, with age and sun damage, the face loses volume and so the skin sags.

Fillers are an essential part of a botulinum practice. Like botulinum toxin, they are injectable and associated with almost no downtime. Unlike botulinum toxin, the most advanced fillers give an instant result. Within minutes a patient can leave the office looking up to ten years younger. This sort of result is often addictive and many of our patients routinely book in for a 'top up' of their filler at the same time as their follow-up botulinum appointment. Current legislation in Ireland prohibits the injection of botulinum toxin by a nurse practitioner, although this is allowed under medical supervision in other countries such as the UK. Nurse practitioners are, however, allowed to inject fillers and to inject submucosal anesthesia (but not nerve blocks).

Hyaluronic acid

Hyaluronic acid occurs naturally in the body and is the main component of the vitreous gel of the eye. It was originally derived from cockerel combs but is now produced synthetically. Since the 1980s it has been used extensively in cataract surgery to prevent the cornea collapsing and to protect the corneal endothelium during surgery. It is now available in different consistencies for intraocular injection. Restylane® was developed by an ophthalmologist in QMed for injection into the skin.

Hyaluronic acid is a pure substance and the incidence of allergic reactions to it is very low. Patch testing is not required.

Many other fillers are currently available on the market. Having started with collagen (Zyplast® and Zyderm®) and Softform® implants, the author now favors hyaluronic acid, which is not yet freely available in the USA. However similar results can be achieved with collagen, albeit for a shorter time and with increased side effects. Fat transplantation offers a permanent solution, but is a semi-surgical procedure requiring time off work, and often more than one treatment session.

Hyaluronic acid is available in several forms, including two ranges: Perlane®, Restylane® and Restylane fine line® by QMed (Fig. 11.2), and Hylaform Plus®, Hylaform® and Hylaform fine line®. Juvederm® appears to have a similar effect although its duration of action is less well established. Perlane®, Restylane®, and Restylane fine line® last for nine months. Their molecules are gradually absorbed and replaced by water, which maintains the volume enhancement until the molecular framework collapses (Fig. 11.3). Hylaform Plus®, Hylaform® and Hylaform fine line® last for only six months but have their own advantages.

The author's personal choice of product, based on experience, is currently as follows:

- **Perlane® appears to be the most viscous, most enduring and the best for deep rhytids.**

Fig 11.2 Photo of Restylane®, Perlane® and Restylane® fine line. Courtesy of Q-Med, AB, Uppsala, Sweden.

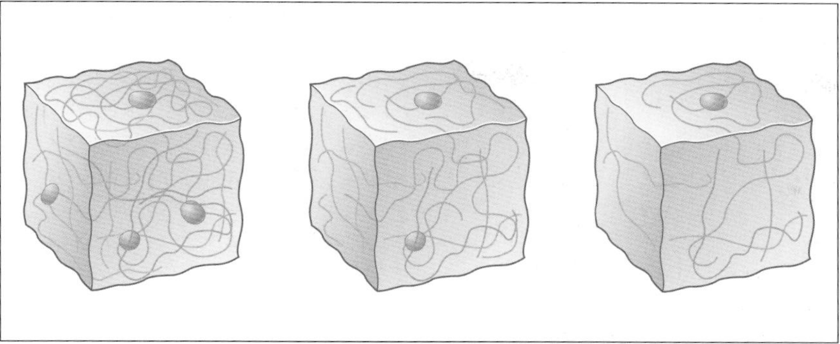

Fig 11.3 Structural framework of Restylane® and Perlane® molecules. Initial volume is maintained throughout the degradation phase.

- **Restylane® is of moderate viscosity, long lasting, good for deeper and superficial injections and the most versatile (deep, superficial and lips).**
- **Hylaform Plus® is less viscous than Perlane®, making it ideal for smooth insertion into lips.**
- **Hylaform fine line® and Restylane fine line® come with a 32-gauge needle and smoothly fill fine superficial rhytids, e.g. crow's feet.**

Indications

The choice of product depends on the area to be filled and on the volume required. Patients may also be restricted financially in their choice of treatment which can be adapted in order to give the best value for their money. For example, Perlane® may be best for deeper rhytids, but if a patient has both superficial and deep rhytids (e.g. a glabellar crease and nasolabial folds), and can only afford one syringe, 0.7ml of Restylane® may be used to treat both. Patients can be advised to plan for a full Perlane® syringe in the future, and they should be made aware that the deepest rhytids compress the gel most quickly, and require a top-up sooner. If there are no budgetary constraints, open as many syringes as are necessary to achieve the desired result (Fig. 11.4ab). Failure to do so always leads to a dissatisfied patient.

It is important to analyze the facial features and then tell patients exactly what volume is required for an optimal result, e.g. 2 x Perlane® 0.7 for deep nasolabial folds; 1x Hylaform Plus® 0.75ml for lips; 1x Hylaform fine line® for cheeks. They will then appreciate that suboptimal results will be achieved with less, and will not telephone the next day to say 'the lines are still there' if they buy only one syringe.

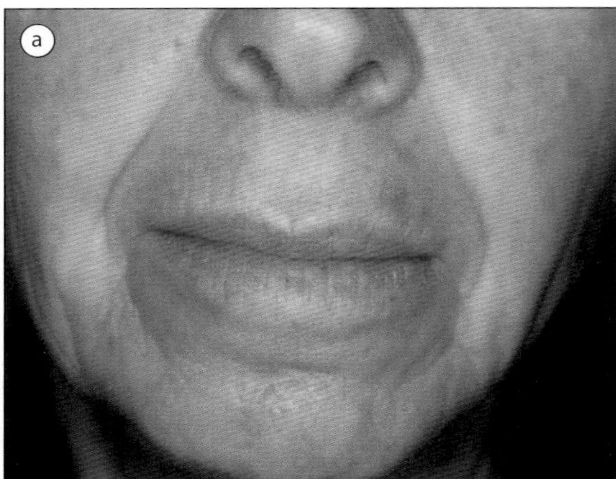

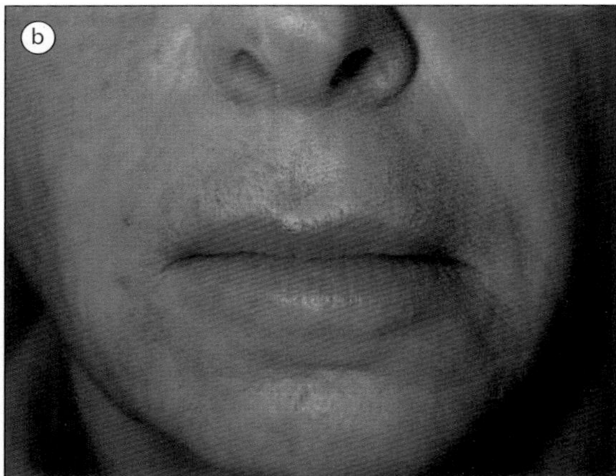

Fig 11.4 Before (a) and after (b) four syringes of 0.7 ml Restylane®.

Patient Preparation

Injections of hyaluronic acid are sore – the pain being a sensation of pressure rather than the 'sting' of botulinum toxin. Injections are usually superficial and so can be effectively anesthetized topically with Emla® or Amotop®. Deeper injections, for example to the lips, can be very painful. It is recommended that a local anesthetic is infiltrated submucosally first.

Patients should be warned that preparation takes at least 30 minutes. They should arrive early, in order that the nurse can apply Emla® and cover (with OpSite® or cling film) the area to be treated. They can then relax before treatment. For the lips, tetracaine gel is applied to the gums after these have been dried with a swab. A dental syringe with a short 30-gauge needle is used to infiltrate Citanest® (or lidocaine (lignocaine)) submucosally in the fornix. This works in 10 to 20 minutes. Sterex® antiseptic cream is applied after the treatment and patients are allowed to apply make-up.

Nasolabial folds

Some nasolabial folds, particularly those associated with a short upper lip, respond well to botulinum toxin treatment. Deeper folds, in older patients, are best treated with a face-lift, although it is not uncommon for a deepening of the nasal end of the fold to persist after an effective operation. Most patients presenting for botulinum toxin are not ready to consider major surgery at the time of their initial consultation, and are thrilled to have a short term 'cheat' with Perlane®.

Superficial filling can be very effective (Fig. 11.5ab) and achieved either with Perlane® or Restylane®. Deep filling may take more than one session (Fig. 11.6ab). We place Perlane® in the superficial dermis, deep to the epithelium. Deeper placement often fails to 'lift' the skin and may be 'lost' towards the sinuses. Warn patients that this layer will become slightly

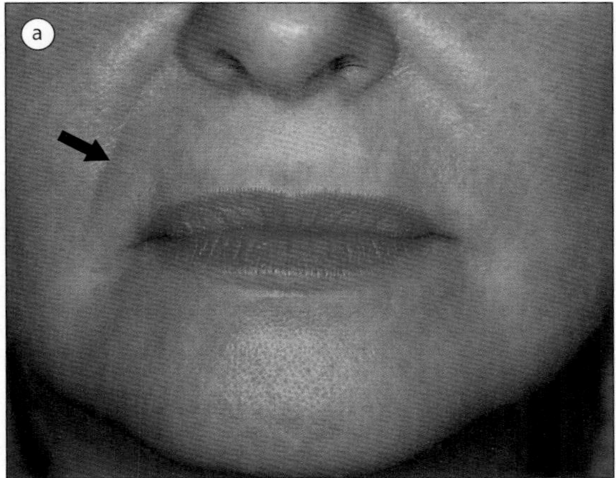

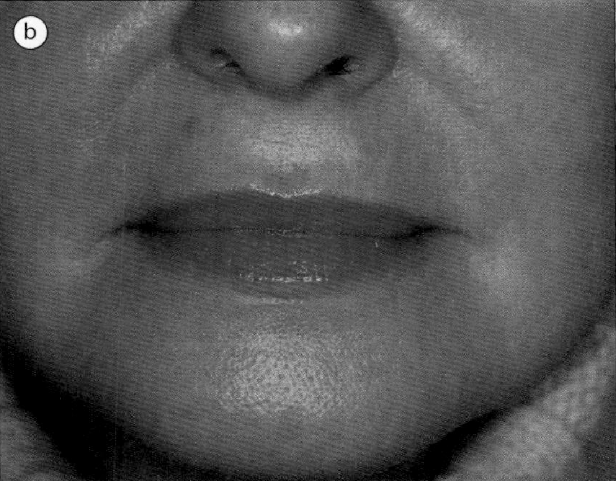

Fig 11.5 Before (a) and after (b) treatment of fine nasolabial line with 0.4 ml Restylane®.

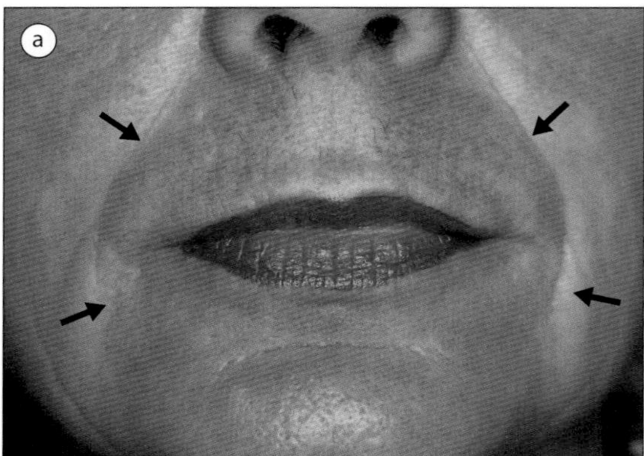

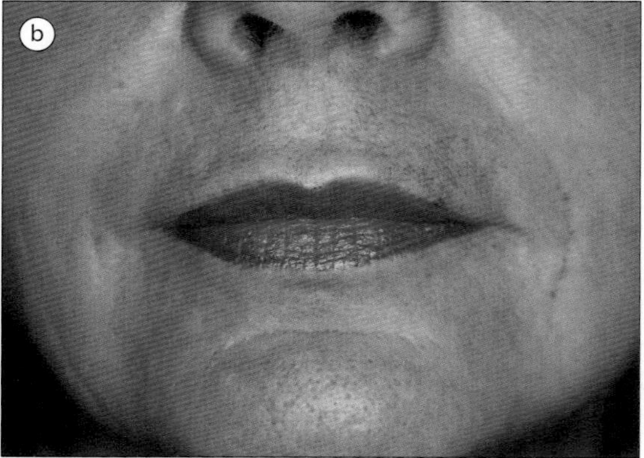

Fig 11.6 Before (a) and after (b) treatment of deep nasolabial folds with Perlane® 0.7 ml.

compressed by facial movements and recommend a top-up over the same layer after six weeks. This compensates for the compression of the initial layer and achieves a long-lasting effect.

Marionette lines

These can be improved greatly by lower face-lift surgery. Some patients tend to slide their lower jaw back, emphasizing the downturn of the corners of the mouth. Discuss the need for a dental opinion with such patients and refer them back to their own dentist if appropriate. The treatment of marionette lines with a filler is rewarding (Fig. 11.7ab). As with the resolution of a frown, the elimination of these descending lines can alter a patient's countenance and create the illusion of lifting the whole face. The author prefers Perlane® or Restylane® for this area.

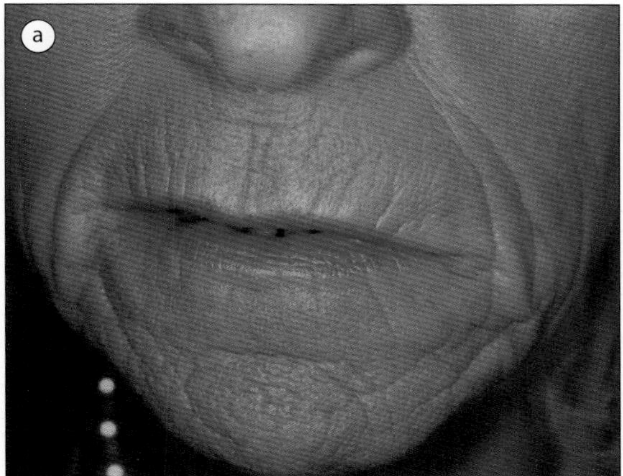

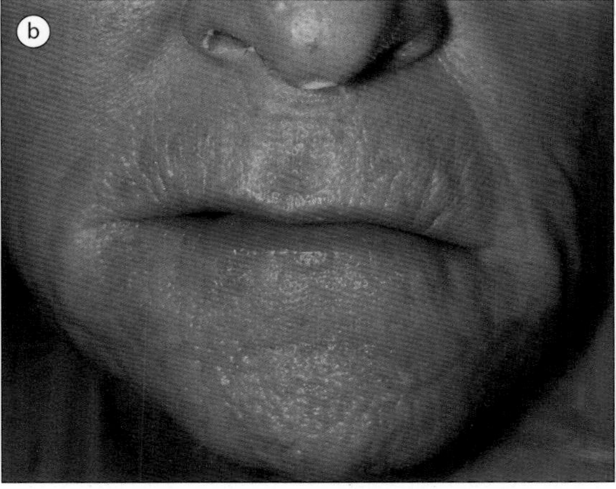

Fig 11.7 Before (a) and after (b) Restylane® to marionette and perioral lines.

USER TIP

Do not overfill an area of skin with hyaluronic acid as this can cause local necrosis and bruising. It is better to bring the patient back after six weeks for further treatment to the same area. This allows for some compression of the initial gel and achieves a greater 'lift'.

Glabellar crease

The treatment of a glabellar crease with botulinum toxin is discussed in detail in Chapter 8. Hyaluronic acid offers an instant 'fix' if a patient is waiting for procerus and corrugator muscle bulk to diminish. It is also ideal for those who are unsuited to full-blown botulinum treatment because of brow ptosis. The author favors Restylane® for this area but has often placed some 'left-over' Perlane® in the deeper dermis, or Hylaform fine line® more superficially. Fine rhytids respond very well to Restylane® or Hylaform®. Usually less than 0.2 ml of hyaluronic acid is needed to treat this area. A small syringe (e.g. 0.4 ml) can be opened and sometimes the remains can usefully be placed periorally or nasolabially.

The upper lip

Patients complain of upper lip rhytids (especially smokers), or of a thinning of the upper lip, or both. The nose-lip distance elongates with age and some plastic surgeons shorten this surgically with an elliptical excision of skin from under the nose. Most patients are unaware of this elongation.

Look carefully before the anesthetic is applied or injected. Ask the patient to pout and observe the gaps between the fibers of the orbicularis oris. Examine the distance from lip to nose. Look for rhytids at rest, and deeper rhytids in motion. Examine the symmetry of the lips and discuss this with the patient.

Care must be taken with 'wrinkles in motion only': inject Restylane® or Hylaform® into the gap that is seen with pouting (Fig. 11.8). Inject the superficial dermis and take care not to leave a bleb above the surface of the skin at rest. If a 'lump' forms, massage the area between two fingers and disperse the gel. Instruct the patient to do the same over the following few days.

'Wrinkles at rest' are best treated with a combination of laser resurfacing and Restylane®. Many patients will go ahead with fillers while waiting for the right time for resurfacing.

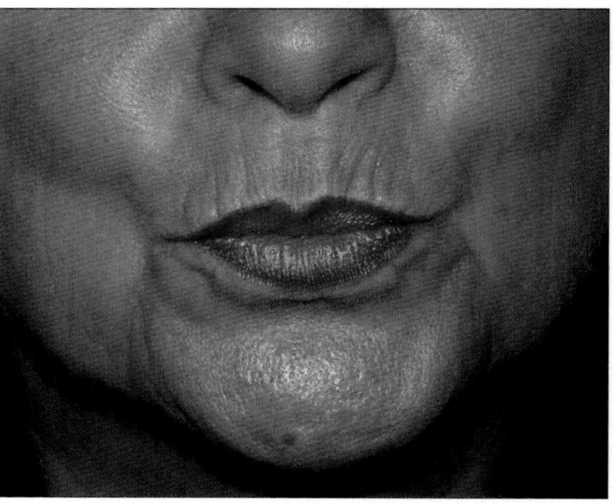

Fig 11.8 Wrinkled upper lip emphasized by pouting.

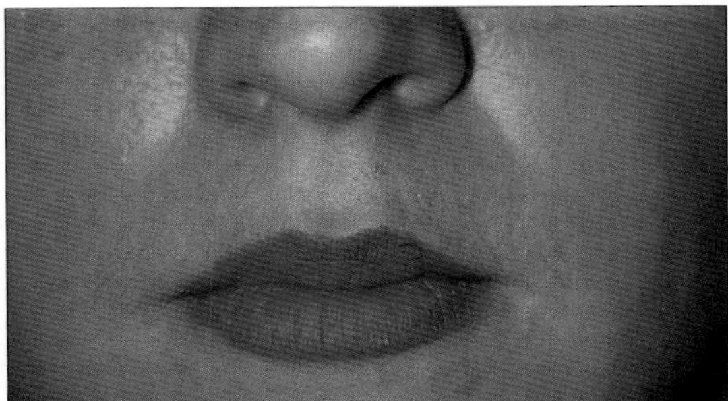

Fig 11.9 Cupid's bow/philtrum.

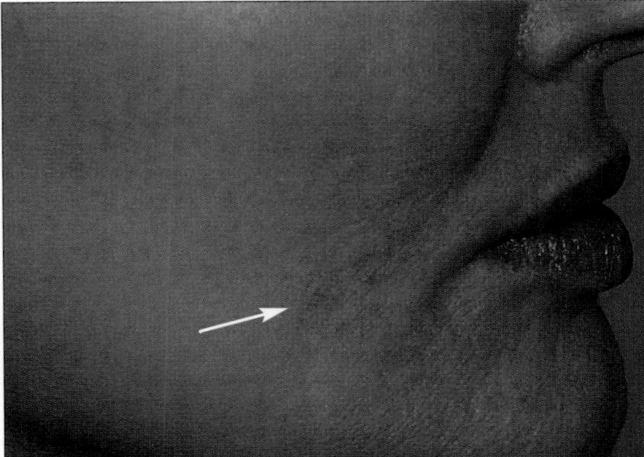

Fig 11.10 Fine line injections.

Increasing the convexity of the upper lip with injections between the orbicularis oris fibers shortens the lip nicely and improves its appearance. The philtrum can be reconstructed, again rejuvenating the lip instantly (Fig. 11.9), and a small amount may also be placed at the Cupid's bow.

Deep 'rhytids at rest' can be kept at bay with Hylaform fine line® injected very superficially into the epithelium (Fig. 11.10).

Lip enhancement depends largely on taste. The author prefers not to enhance an upper lip that will protrude noticeably above the lower one, even if the upper is much thinner. It is not always possible to guarantee vertical volume and, in particular, with certain types of dentition, the gel can expand the lip anteriorly. The vermilion border alone may be enhanced for a subtle improvement (Fig. 11.11ab). Restylane® is excellent for providing symmetry to lips. It is also useful for patients with cleft lip deformities and, when layered with Perlane®, a nice anterior displacement of the upper lip can be achieved.

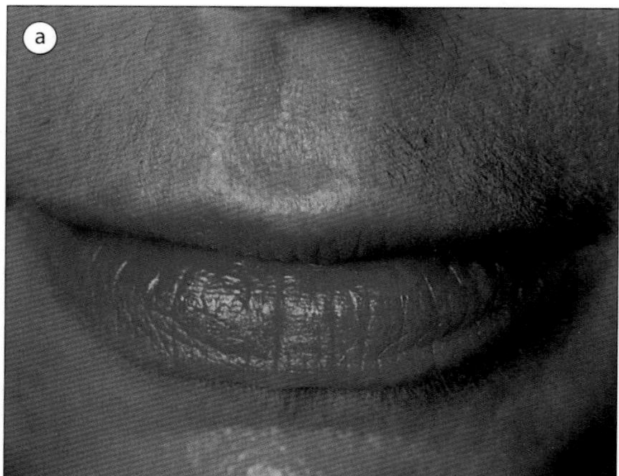

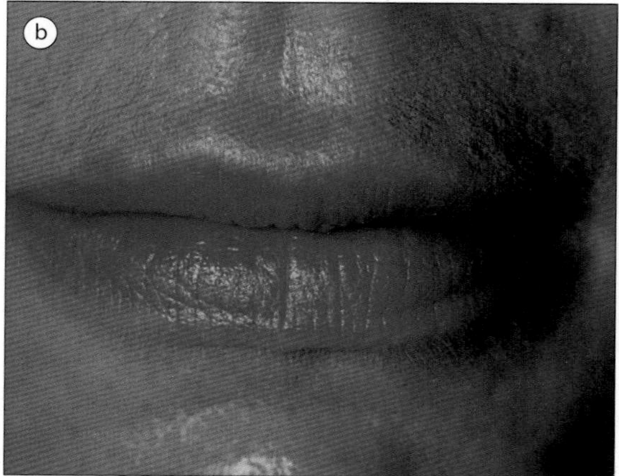

Fig 11.11 Before (a) and after (b) Restylane® to vermilion border, upper lip, prior to hair removal laser to upper lip.

Scars

Hyaluronic acid is useful for the volume expansion of scars (Fig. 11.12ab). Treatment with botulinum toxin is dealt with in Chapter 9.

Crow's feet

Botulinum toxin will erase some crow's feet and laser resurfacing will erase the rest. It is important, however, to identify 'hooding' before treatment. Patients with a fold of skin at the outer corner of their eyes will be disappointed with botulinum toxin if it is not demonstrated to them that their fold is due not to

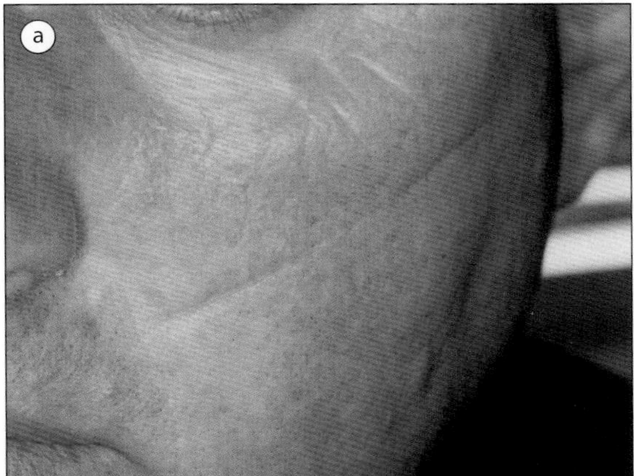

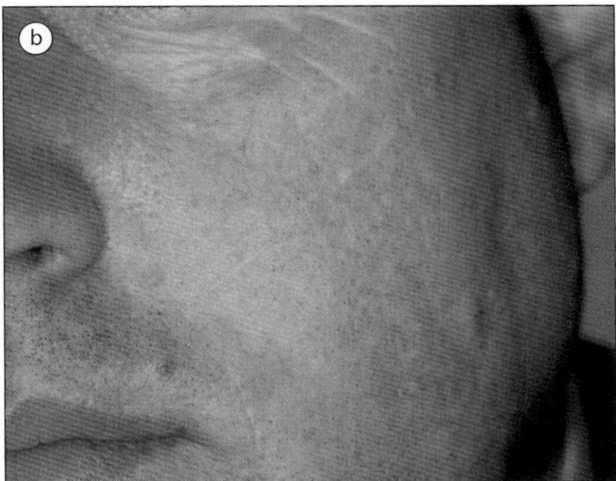

Fig 11.12 Before (a) and after (b) Perlane® to facial scar.

contraction of the orbicularis oculi, but to sagging of their lateral brows and temporal areas. In this case, the correct treatment is by an endoscopic brow lift. Temporary correction may be possible by upper blepharoplasty, with extension of the scar along the crease, or sometimes with internal brow fixation. (Fig. 11.13ab).

Patients with hooding can sometimes cheat with Hylaform® or Restylane fine line®. The 32-gauge needle is inserted just below the epithelium, and gel is injected along the rhytid. Another method is to place a series of gel micro-blebs. The result is an instant improvement although some patients experience temporary edema at the injection site. Fine line gel is also good for infraorbital rhytids, although laser resurfacing may be preferred rather than risk irregularities in the fine periocular skin.

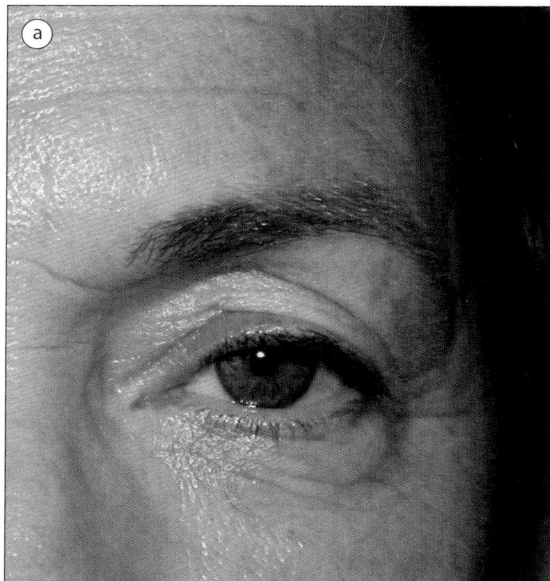

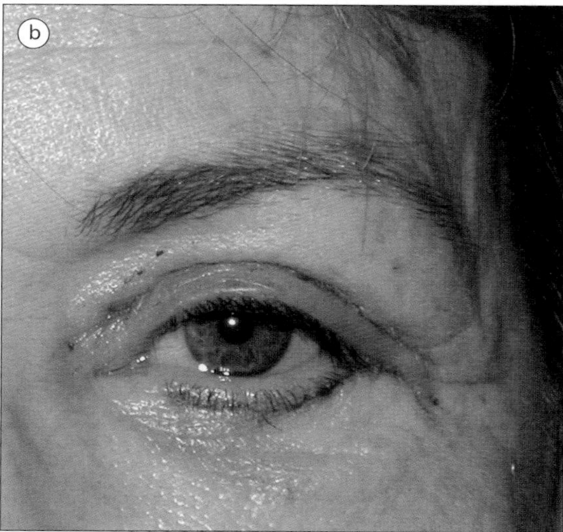

Fig 11.13 (a) Before internal brow fixations, upper blepharoplasty, lower transcutaneous blepharoplasty and lateral canthal tendon plication. (b) scar at 6 days post-op. Note extended scars to treat 'hood'.

The chin

The use of botulinum toxin is an effective way of reducing 'pebbly chin' (see Fig. 9.7). Perlane® or Restylane® may be recommended for irregularities in this area, particularly over dimples.

Cheeks

Botulinum toxin is not indicated for sagging cheeks: the treatment of choice is a face-lift. Laser resurfacing will also tighten the cheeks significantly but there is a growing movement towards volume enhancement with hyaluronic acid. Dr Rita Rakus, London (personal communication) recommends a grid pattern of enhancement across the full cheek. The author has had considerable success with Hylaform® and Restylane fine line® to the fine rhytids of the cheeks, particularly those lying lateral to the orbicularis oris (see Fig. 11.10).

USER TIP

Avoid placing hyaluronic acid in the epithelium of a nasolabial rhytid or the cheeks if the skin is fine and translucent (e.g. in a model). Translucent skin will show a grey/white mark of gel at the injection site.

LASER RESURFACING

Botulinum toxin is excellent for 'crow's feet in motion' and may diminish some 'rhytids at rest' with time. However the complete removal of crow's feet is best achieved with laser resurfacing or Coblation. Laser resurfacing is the treatment of choice for perioral rhytids, with or without fillers.

Three main types of lasers are used for resurfacing:

- **Carbon dioxide (e.g. Sharplan Feathertouch®, Coherent Ultrapulse®)**
- **Erbium**
- **Combined carbon dioxide and erbium.**

All of the results shown in this book were achieved with the Feathertouch laser.

Patient selection is discussed in detail in Chapter 5, but make sure that the patient is informed about static wrinkles and laser resurfacing before giving botulinum toxin. Failure to do so will lead to unrealistic expectations and disappointment.

USER TIP

Botulinum toxin is essential for the long-term results of the laser resurfacing of crow's feet. Counsel patients carefully about the natural return of rhytids after the laser resurfacing of crow's feet without paralysis of the orbicularis oculi (Fig. 11.14 abc). Suggest botulinum toxin injections are given a week before, and three months after treatment, as part of the resurfacing procedure.

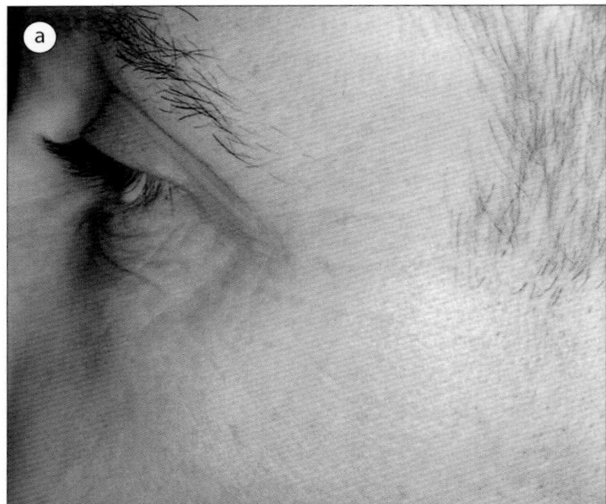

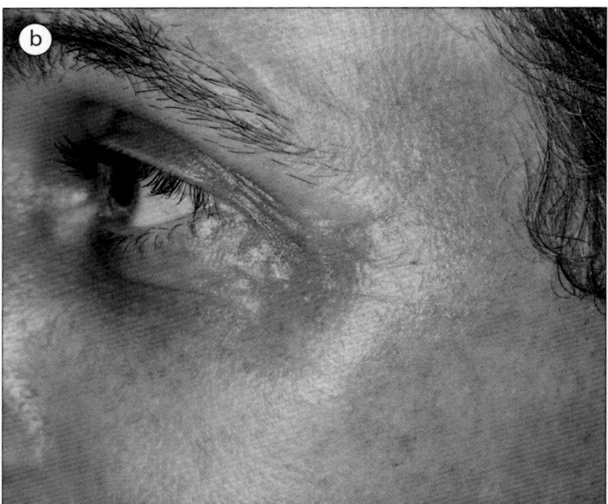

Fig 11.14 (a) before CO_2 skin resurfacing, (b) 6 weeks after CO_2 resurfacing: note return of crows feet, before Botox®, and (c) 6 weeks after Botox®, 12 weeks after CO_2 resurfacing; note wrinkles have disappeared.

Most patients who require botulinum toxin for crow's feet are happy to have the injections once they understand that their 'wrinkles at rest' may diminish and that the 'wrinkles in motion' will improve greatly. Most do not want the downtime of laser resurfacing. It is important at the initial consultation, however, to offer resurfacing as a long-term solution. If your practice is not involved in resurfacing, it is important to provide the following information – and a referral, if requested, to a laser practice.

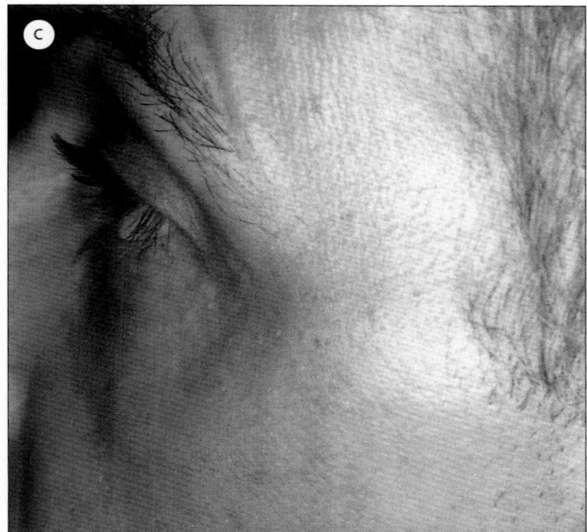

Fig 11.14 *Cont'd.*

Basic facts about laser resurfacing for wrinkles

- **A laser vaporizes the superficial layer of the skin, carrying the wrinkled layer with it.**
- **Treatment is under local anesthetic and takes 15 minutes for crow's feet.**
- **The skin will heal in six to ten days.**
- **The skin will have a dressing or ointment on it.**
- **Following treatment, the skin will be red, brown or even paler than before.**
- **Freckles will be obliterated, providing a contrast with freckled skin.**
- **Treatment itself is painless but simple analgesics may be needed over the first 24 hours.**
- **The patient must rest in an elevated position and apply cold packs for the first 24 hours.**
- **The patient must be available for post-treatment examinations by the practice nurse – daily if necessary – for six to ten days.**
- **Ideally the patient should take two weeks off work and socializing, although some can return to work with camouflage make-up after six days.**
- **The initial results will be greatly improved after three months when new collagen has been formed in the skin.**

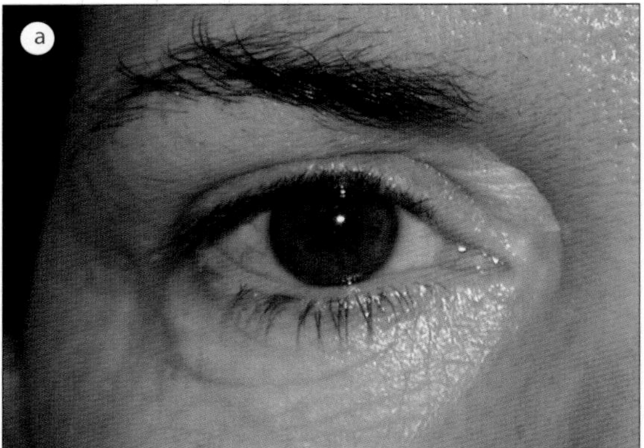

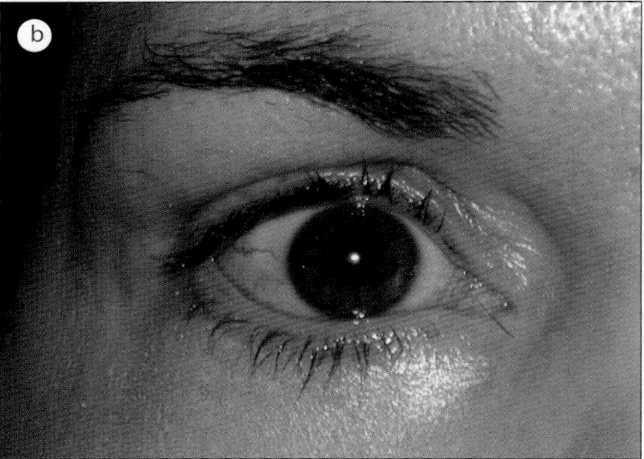

Fig 11.15 Before (a) and (b) 4 weeks after CO_2 resurfacing to eye zone, endoscopic brow lift and upper blepharoplasty.

- **Botulinum toxin is essential to keep the skin flat until this happens (Fig. 11.15ab).**
- **The patient must avoid sunburning the new skin while it is healing.**
- **The patient must appreciate that sun exposure at six weeks will darken the treated area. The use of a sun block is very important even though the pigmentation is reversible.**
- **Complete eradication of rhytids is not uncommon, but the patient should be warned to expect only a 50% improvement of the deeper ones.**
- **The patient will still benefit from hyaluronic acid injections for volume replacement to the lip as the 'new collagen' is never enough.**
- **Non-lasered skin can be blended with the treated area by using intense pulsed light (IPL), Retin-A®, AHAs, microdermabrasion, chemical peels and sun block.**

UPPER LID BLEPHAROPLASTY

Ageing patients who have an excess of skin over their upper lids (dermatochalasis) will often elevate their brows subconsciously using the frontalis muscle. This lifts the skin off their lids, restores the deep crease, and takes 'the weight off their lids'. This excessive brow elevation will cause deep horizontal frown lines to develop. Such patients often ask for these wrinkles to be removed with botulinum toxin (as discussed in detail in Chapter 8). However treatment of the frontalis with botulinum will drop their brows to their normal position and accentuate the dermatochalasis. It is important to explain to these patients that they will look tired and older if their frown is paralyzed. They must choose between frown lines and an upper blepharoplasty. Some patients may also need brow repositioning if their brows have sagged.

Some patients complain that using botulinum toxin for their forehead made their 'lids swell'. This is because a loss of brow elevation may also allow normal orbital fat to protrude. Figures 11.16ab and 11.17ab illustrate pre- and post-laser blepharoplasty patients. Making transcutaneous incisions and vaporizing excess fat using a CO_2 laser reduces hemorrhage, edema and recovery time.

If your practice does not perform oculoplastic surgery, then the following information may be given to patients, along with an appropriate referral.

Basic facts about upper lid blepharoplasty

- **Blepharoplasty means the excision of skin and/or fat from the eyelids.**
- **An incision will be made in the lid crease.**
- **The surgery takes place under local anesthesia and lasts for between 30 and 60 minutes.**
- **Stitches will be removed between 4 and 7 days after the operation.**
- **The scar will usually be hidden in the crease (Fig. 11.18).**
- **The patient must rest in an elevated position for the first 24 hours.**
- **Rest is important for the first 4 days to prevent late complications such as hemorrhage.**
- **One week off work usually suffices.**
- **The most common complication is bruising (reduced with laser incision).**
- **Rare complications include infection, prolonged swelling and hematoma formation.**
- **Results last until ageing causes further sagging of the skin i.e. forever in some patients and at least 10 years in most.**

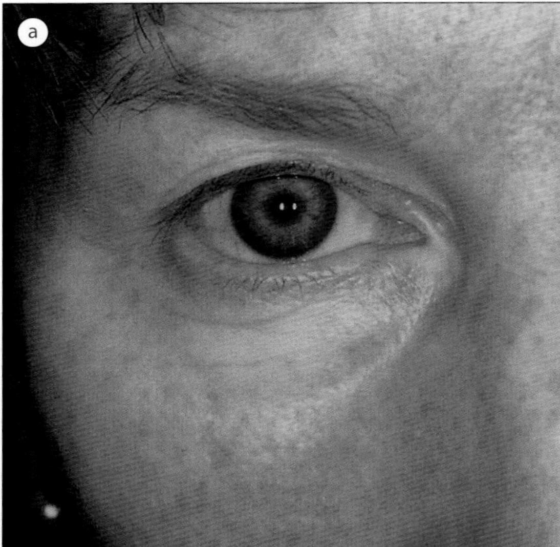

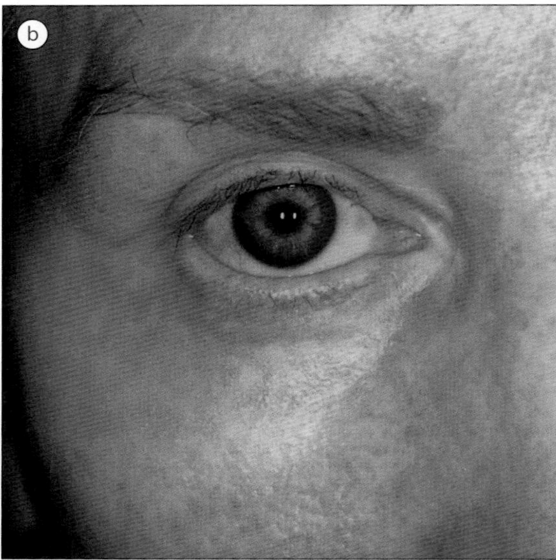

Fig 11.16 Before (a) and three weeks after (b) CO_2 laser blepharoplasty to upper lids with internal brow fixation, and lower lid transconjunctival blepharoplasty with CO_2 resurfacing. Note: erythema at 3 weeks in type 1 skin.

Lower lid blepharoplasty

Ageing causes the skin under the eyes to sag. Laxity of the orbital septum behind the skin and muscle also allows the lower orbital fat pads to protrude, emphasizing the 'bags', which are often held in the orbit by the tone of the

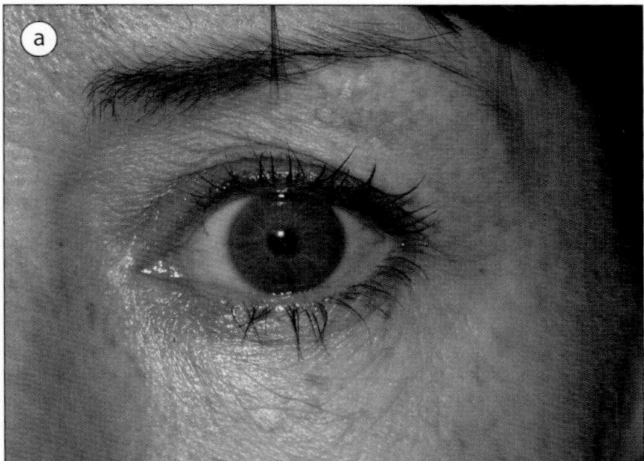

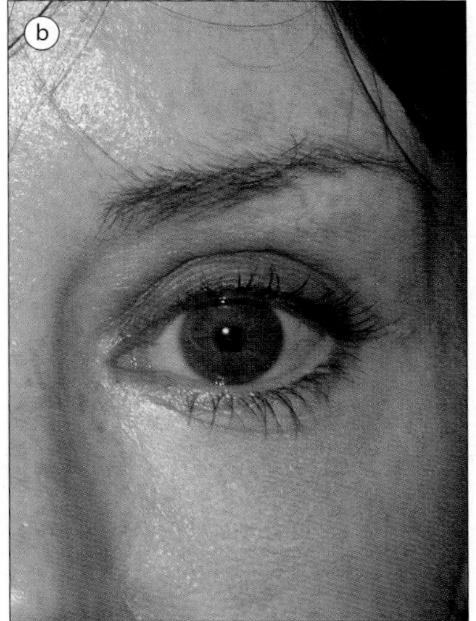

Fig 11.17 Before (a) and three weeks after (b) CO_2 laser blepharoplasty with lower lid transconjunctival blepharoplasty and eye zone CO_2 laser resurfacing. Note pink discolouration that usually fades over 6 weeks.

orbicularis oculi muscle. It is very important not to inject botulinum toxin into the lower lid orbicularis muscle if it seems to be restraining fat in this way. Such patients must be told that they can only have their lateral rhytids (crow's feet) treated if they have lower lid blepharoplasties.

Traditional lower lid blepharoplasty is transcutaneous, through an incision underneath the eyelashes (sub-ciliary) (Fig. 11.19). A skin/muscle flap is raised, the fat is excised, and the flap is trimmed and sutured. Limitations of this procedure are a visible scar, a tendency to pull the lateral eyelid vertically and so

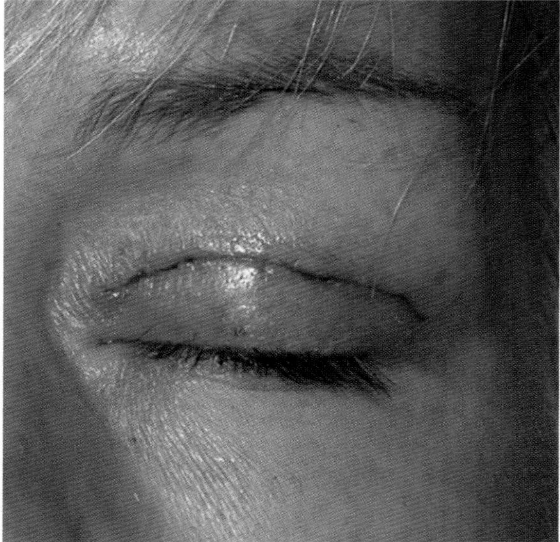

Fig 11.18 Typical lid crease scar day 6 post blepharoplasty.

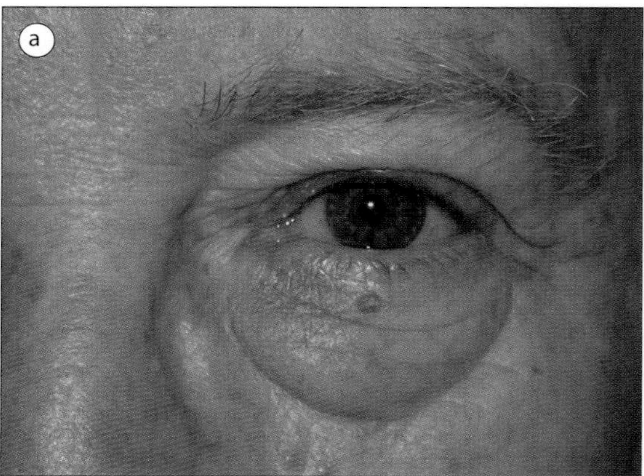

Fig 11.19 Before (a) and after (b) traditional transcutaneous blepharoplasty with subcilary incision.

'round' the lateral canthus, and increased problems with hemorrhage and bruising.

This procedure may be restricted to those who are not suitable for laser resurfacing e.g. sun bathers with sun damaged skin on their faces and no desire to blend old skin with new; patients with excessive orbicularis folds who require muscle shortening; and the many men who would find it embarrassing to wear make-up to hide the erythema that follows resurfacing.

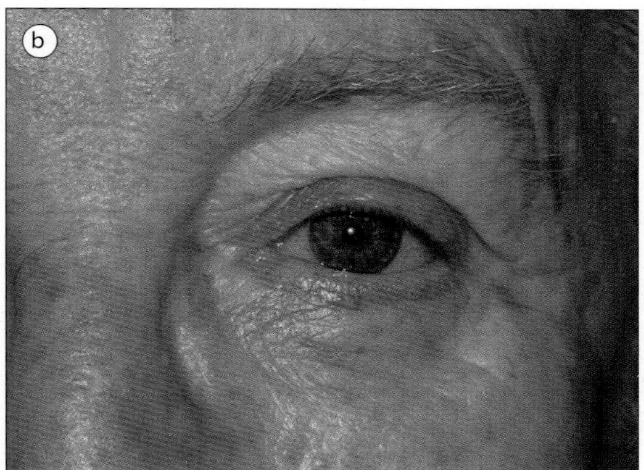

Fig 11.19 *Cont'd.*

USER TIP

Do not inject botulinum toxin into the lower eyelids if there is an excess lower lid skin and fat. This causes the prolapse of fat, with protrusion of 'bags', until the orbicularis muscle tone returns.

The author prefers to perform transconjunctival fat removal. An incision is made through the conjunctiva in the lower lid fornix. Fat is then vaporized. This may be done without skin resurfacing (Fig. 11.20ab – thyroid) but most patients want their skin tightened too, and two passes with the Feathertouch® CO_2 laser can achieve this (Fig. 11.21ab).

Basic facts about lower lid blepharoplasty

- **This is the removal of lower lid fat bags with tightening of the skin.**
- **Skin can be tightened by a cut under the eyelashes or with a laser.**
- **If the skin is cut, the sutures will be removed between 4 to 6 days. There will be a fine scar, which can easily be concealed with an eyeliner pencil. Most people should take one week off work**
- **If the skin is lasered, there will be no scar but the resurfaced skin will take six to ten days to heal. Post-operatively the resurfaced skin may be red, brown and then pale (as above). Make-up can be applied as camouflage as soon as the skin has healed. Most people should take two weeks off work.**
- **The eye may be bloodshot after the surgery – due to bruising.**

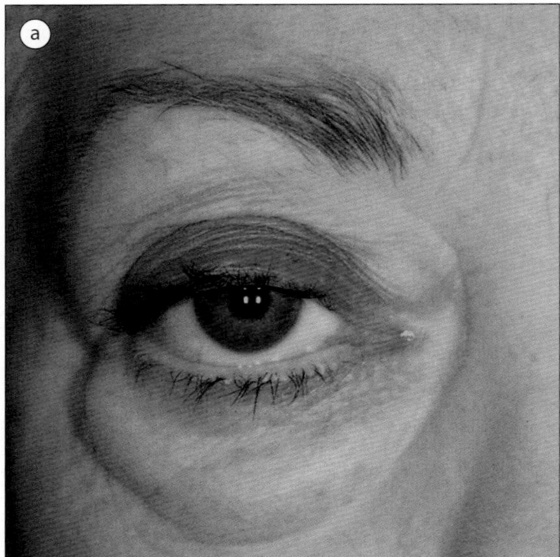

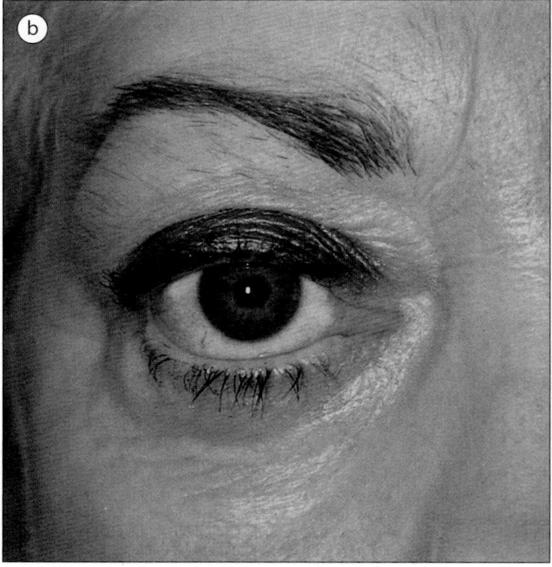

Fig 11.20 (b) transconjunctival fat removal without skin/muscle excision or CO_2 laser resurfacing in a patient with thyroid eye disease.

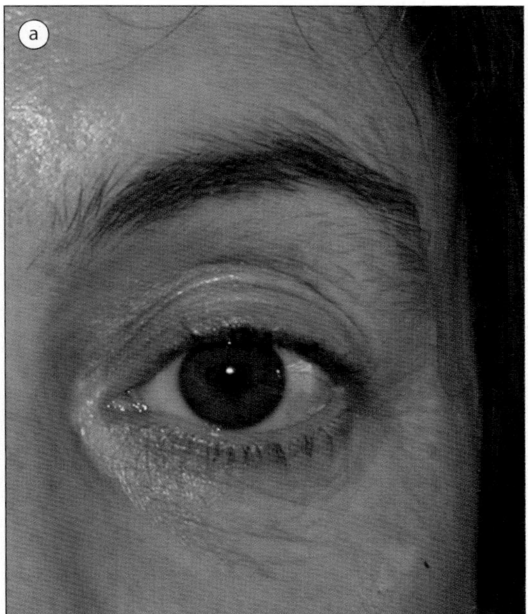

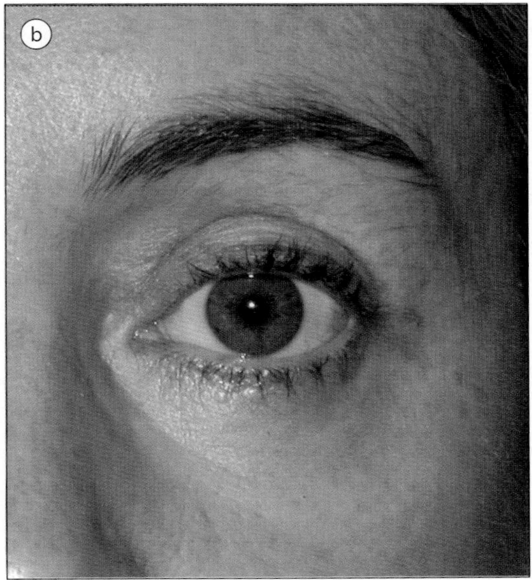

Fig 11.21 Transconjunctival lower lid blepharoplasty with CO_2 resurfacing (upper blepharoplasty also).

- **The patient may require lateral canthal tendon plications (tightening of the outer corner of the lids through fine incisions in the upper and lower corners) to prevent 'rounding' of the eye contour**

COMBINATION TREATMENTS

Some patients need botulinum toxin in combination with a filler, blepharoplasty and laser resurfacing to achieve the best result.

USER TIP

Do not give botulinum toxin injections at the same time as surgery. The effect may be altered by a local or general anesthetic and in the author's experience has been unpredictable. In contrast, fillers can be injected during surgery with good effect.

Lips

Figure 11.22a shows a patient who underwent laser resurfacing of her upper lip. Figure 11.22b shows the same patient post-operatively, with residual clefts between her orbicularis oris rhytids. Botulinum toxin had little effect on reducing the depth of these. Figure 11.22c demonstrates the lip immediately after an injection of Restylane.

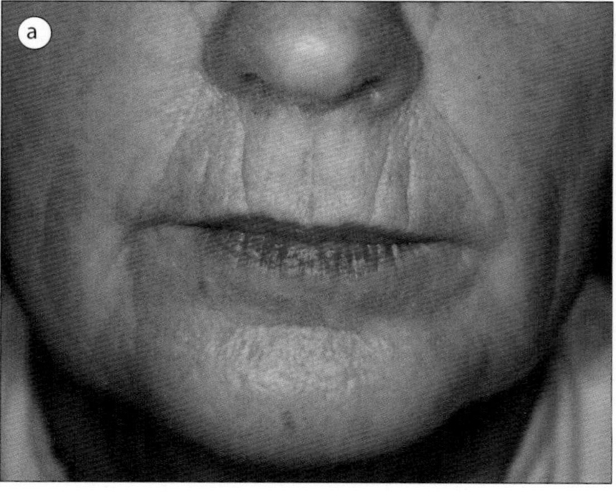

Fig 11.22 Before (a), after (b) CO_2 laser resurfacing to upper lip and (c), after Restylane® to vertical rhytides.

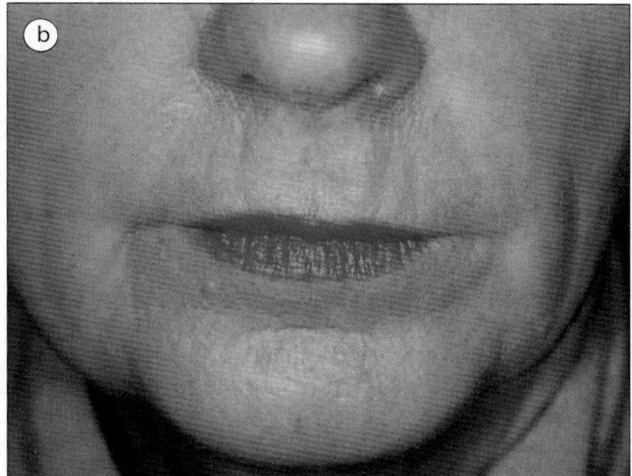

Fig 11.22 *Cont'd.*

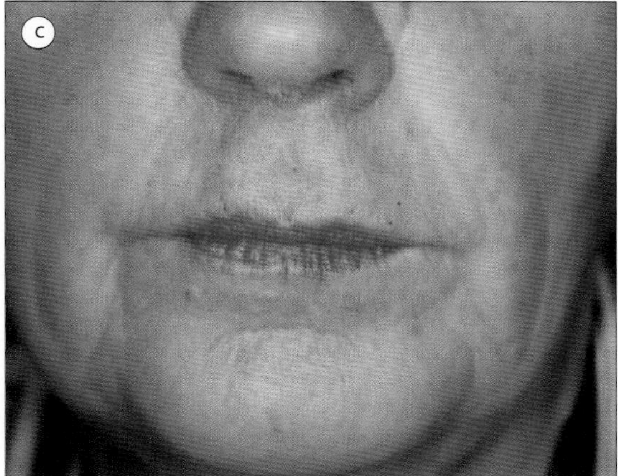

Frown

Botulinum toxin will reduce the size of hypertrophic frown muscles – the 'mountains' on either side of the valley of the frown. The skin will, however, remain wrinkled at the point of chronic compression. Figure 11.23ab shows a patient who had Botox® to her glabellar muscles, laser resurfacing of the sun damaged rhytid, and Restylane® to the base of the rhytid.

Figure 11.24ab shows a patient before, and three months after, laser resurfacing and Botox® to her glabella.

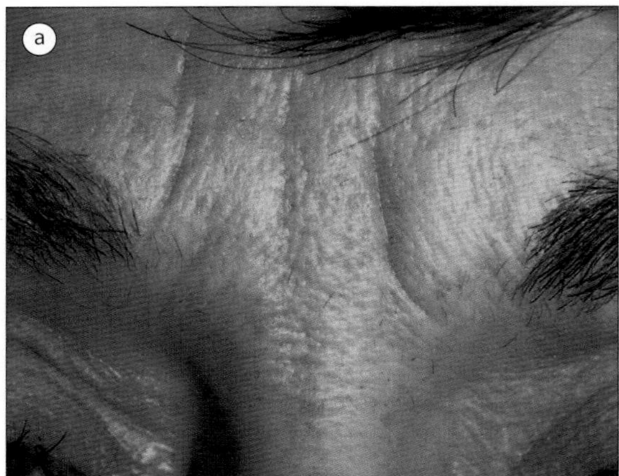

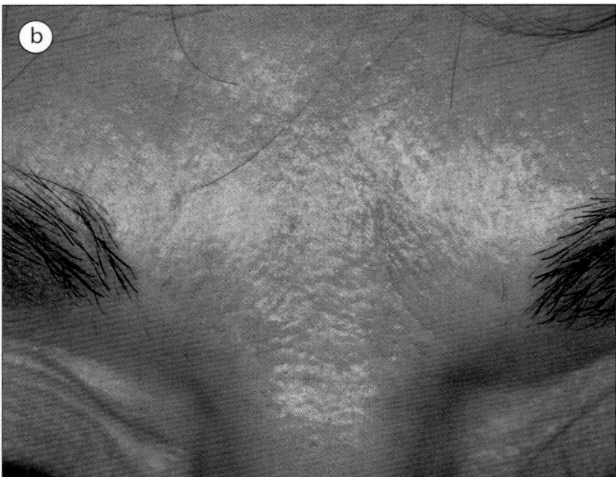

Fig 11.23 Before (a) and after (b) CO_2 resurfacing, Botox® and Restylane® to glabella.

Face

Figure 11.25ab shows a patient before and after full face CO_2 resurfacing including the upper lids, with Botox® to crow's feet and frown, and Restylane® to upper lip and perioral rhytids.

Rejuvenation of the skin

It is important when considering the management of crow's feet or frown lines to address the underlying causes. Inform patients that smokers have damaged 50% of the collagen in their skin at the age of 50 compared to non-smokers. Demonstrate their sun damage by comparing the skin on the inside of the upper arm with that on their face. Tell them that laser resurfacing might achieve

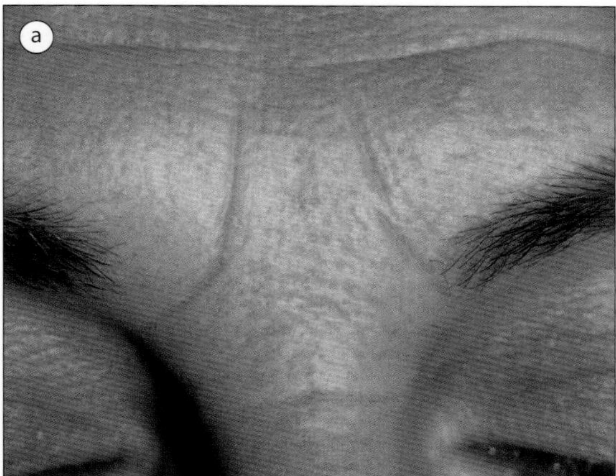

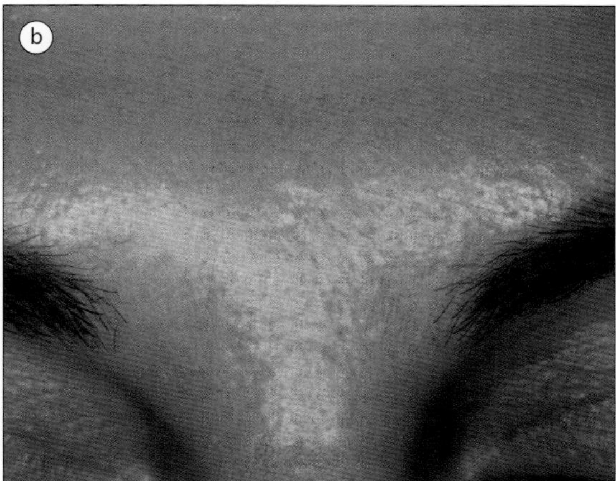

Fig 11.24 Before (a) and after (b) CO_2 resurfacing and Botox® to glabella.

the translucency of skin undamaged by the sun, but that this must then be blended in with the skin on their neck and the rest of their face.

An aesthetic nurse can spend time at the initial consultation explaining the effects of UVA and UVB on the skin, discussing different types of sun block, and giving suitable samples. Interested patients can be provided with an anti-ageing regime that includes vitamin C and E and alpha hydroxy acids. Retin-A® may be prescribed when appropriate. Such a regime, in combination with botulinum toxin alone, can provide dramatic results.

Patients who have booked laser resurfacing of their crow's feet with botulinum toxin are strongly recommended to have a course of intense pulsed light (IPL) and/or particle skin resurfacing to micro-dermabrade the damaged

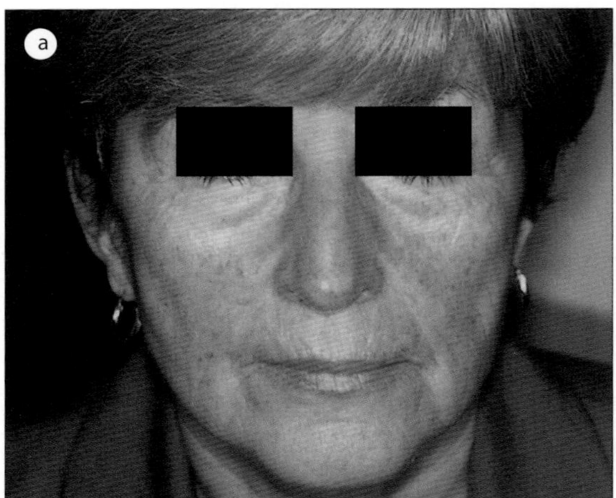

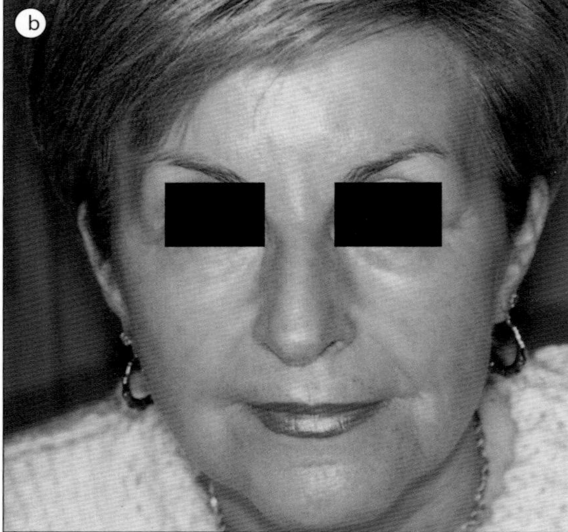

Fig 11.25 Before (a) and after (b) full face CO_2 resurfacing, Botox® and Restylane® to upper lip.

stratum corneum and to stimulate collagen production in the adjacent skin and neck.

NON-ABLATIVE COLLAGEN STIMULATION

Chemical peels and microdermabrasion stimulate collagen production. More recently, the results of stimulating collagen with light are emerging e.g. by the use of IPL®, N-Lite® and Cooltouch®. These systems offer a gradual stimulation of collagen production with no downtime but are currently associated with considerable discomfort. The results of further developments in this promising area are awaited.

Table 11.1. Indications for alternative treatments with or without botulinum toxin

Indication	Treatment
Crow's feet at rest	Laser resurfacing, coblation, hyaluronic acid
Lower lid bags	Laser blepharoplasty
Vertical frown with low lash brow distance	Endoscopic brow lift, hyaluronic acid
Frown with heavy upper lid skin	Upper lid blepharoplasties, brow repositioning, hyaluronic acid
Upper lip rhytids, mouth zone rhytids	Laser resurfacing, hyaluronic acid
Platysma bands, neck rhytids	Lower face lift, ligation of platysma, submental tuck.
Poor skin tone, sun damage	IPL microdermabrasion, chemical peels, Retin-A®, alphahydroxy acid skin regime, vitamin C and E serum, sun protection

12 Guide to good cosmetic practice

Many doctors who use botulinum toxin will already be involved in a cosmetic practice e.g. oculoplastics or plastic surgery; for others, however, its use will be the only aesthetic procedure offered in a busy medical clinic. This chapter offers the latter some suggestions on how to run a cosmetic practice.

LOCATION OF PRACTICE

Confidentiality is an important part of any medical practice: in a cosmetic practice this is mingled with a strong desire on the part of the patient for privacy. Many patients do not want to be seen approaching the clinic or, more particularly, leaving it. An ideal cosmetic clinic, therefore, would have a separate entrance in an inconspicuous part of the building, perhaps with a separate exit too, so that patients do not meet one another. A separate waiting room could be offered to each patient.

However most practitioners are not in a position to relocate when they start a cosmetic practice. The following considerations should then be taken into account:

Waiting room

In a general clinic, the real purpose of a patient's visit need not be apparent to others as, for example, a patient attending for a regular Botox® visit may equally well be keeping a routine appointment with another practitioner for a routine spectacle examination. In the same way, a waiting room shared with non-cosmetic practitioners also enables patients to remain inconspicuous, if the receptionist rather than the cosmetic practitioner calls the patients from the waiting room – preferably without using their full name.

Telephone

The receptionist should always avoid mentioning one patient's name in the presence of another, particularly when making appointments and confirming details. Members of the practice should never identify themselves to others when telephoning a patient unless that patient has given prior approval. Similarly, they should not leave a message on an answering machine that could be intercepted by someone other than the patient.

Account

Avoid dealing with one patient's account in the presence of another patient as this could reveal the extent and nature of the treatment. A receptionist should ideally meet patients in a private room to settle their accounts and to make follow-up appointments.

Exit

Some patients may be bruised after treatment. A private exit is invaluable for them, and can conveniently be used too as an entrance for patients with a high public profile.

PATIENT INFORMATION

Repeat visits for botulinum toxin take very little time, but the initial consultation can take up to 90 minutes. Patients must be fully informed about the risks and side effects of every chosen procedure. This information must be given verbally and in writing. It is important to ensure that the patient has 'heard' the information and understands it fully. It is also advisable to record that patients have received this information. Always remember that some patients smile in an understanding fashion but may not be capable of comprehending the information given to them.

It is useful to appoint a fully trained aesthetic nurse to counsel patients. Such a nurse can see patients before their medical consultations: if so, the practitioner must double check that they fully understand the information given by the nurse, and correct any misunderstandings or unrealistic expectations.

PATIENT COUNSELING

Counseling should include taking a detailed medical history (see Chapter 5 on patient selection). Written and verbal information about the treatment and its likely outcome should be given and the patient carefully photographed.

Table 12.1. Sample information checklist

Information	Yes	No	Comment
Family history of neuromuscular disorders			
Bleeding disorders			
Advised about bruising			
Advised that BTX lasts 12–14 weeks			
Advised that BTX may not work until 5–7 days			
Advised about allergies to protein etc.			
Warned that treatment is contraindicated in pregnancy			

Information may also be provided on alternative solutions and adjunctive treatments, such as blepharoplasty and microdermabrasion. Again, there should be documentation to show that this information has been given. The author's practice uses a customized software package with an auditable trace (no information entered can be altered without this being detected). It includes checklists, which the nurse fills in as each topic is covered with the patient (Table 12.1).

PHOTOGRAPHY

Photography before treatment is essential. Patients may telephone to say that the botulinum toxin has not worked, but are usually pleasantly surprised when shown their pre-treatment pictures. Many patients attend for repeat treatments, and regular photography is a useful record of facial changes and progress. Most of all, photography provides essential medical evidence that cannot be refuted.

A 35 mm camera has long been the traditional choice for medical photography. Its main drawbacks are a lack of immediate confirmation of the desired result, and the expense of films and their development. Advances in digital photography have now resulted in digital cameras of high resolution.

A Polaroid™ macro camera is very useful. The focusing system allows for repeated photography from exactly the same distances; this is ideal for an inexperienced photographer. Disadvantages include a limited ability to photograph both eyes simultaneously at a moderately high magnification, although an attachment is now available to help this. Color reproduction is also poor, with different batches of film giving different skin color tones. Film is expensive.

The digital cameras currently used in the author's practice are the Kodak™ 260 zoom and the Nikon Coolpix™. It is possible to select the degree of resolution desired. The important thing about digital photography is to have an auditable database for storing the photographs. They may be uploaded into a patient file with auditable software (e.g. Ocuco™) or moved to a non-reusable cd-rom for retrieval and storage. It must not be possible to alter either the image or the date on which it was taken, otherwise the record will not be acceptable legally.

The cameras mentioned above are easy to use but lighting and flash settings may have to be altered to maximize the recording of wrinkles and contours. An automatic focus setting is fine for most photographs but can create a problem in patients whose large nose attracts the automatic focal point instead of their nasolabial fold or eyelid. Practice makes perfect; and practice nurses perform all photography in the author's clinic.

Digital images eat up a computer's memory. It is often enough to select a lower resolution that requires less disc space. One full-face photograph and two side views suffice as most software packages allow adequate zoom to enlarge separate face zones from the one image. This also saves computer space.

A patient's written consent should always be obtained before displaying any photographs in practice albums or elsewhere.

A BASIC BOTULINUM TOXIN CLINIC

Botulinum toxin clinics are often run from general surgeries. The following requirements should then be considered.

Cold storage (see Chapter 4)

Reconstituted Botox®, Dysport® powder, and NeuroBloc® solution also have to be kept cold – try an insulated container such as a vaccination box (Fig. 12.1) or a wide thermos flask. Remember that reconstituted botulinum toxin should not be frozen. Take great care not to agitate vials of reconstituted solution during transportation. A small refrigerator (must operate at 2–8°C) and a freezer (must freeze to minus 5°C) can easily be purchased (Figs 12.2 and 12.3).

Basic botulinum toxin kit

- **Protective gloves**
- **Alcohol swabs**
- **1.0 ml or 0.50 ml syringes (e.g. insulin or tuberculin syringe)**
- **25-gauge and 32-gauge needles**
- **Vials of normal saline**

Fig 12.1 Insulated container for transport of botulinum toxin.

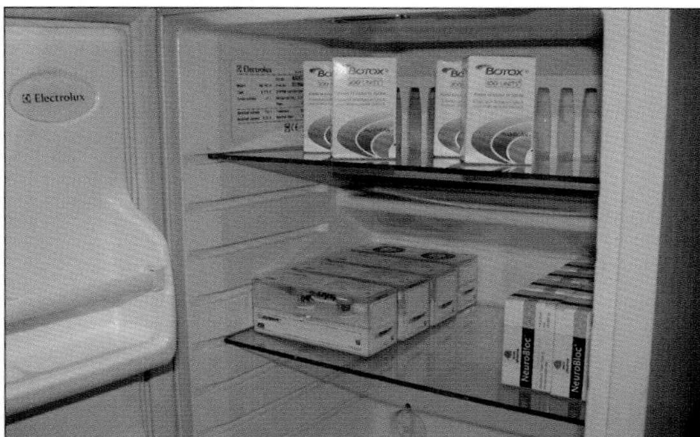

Fig 12.2 Small fridge full of botulinum toxin.

Fig 12.3 Small freezer unit for storage of frozen Botox®.

- **Gauze swabs or tissues (for pressure on injection sites to prevent bruising)**
- **Sealed sharps disposal unit (for sharps, toxic and blood contaminated materials)**
- **Cold storage as above**

The aesthetic nurse

Highly trained aesthetic nurses are an invaluable asset in any cosmetic practice. They can be trained to do the following:

- **Prepare patients for botulinum toxin**
- **Prepare patients for fillers**
- **Patient counseling**
- **Patient photography**
- **Rejuvenating skin care (chemical peels etc.)**
- **Microdermabrasion**
- **Preparation and storage of botulinum toxin**
- **Laser hair removal**

Non-ablative collagen stimulation

Patients may be offered a consultation with the aesthetic nurse while waiting for their medical appointment.

Botulinum toxin is highly effective when combined with skin rejuvenation. An aesthetic nurse examines and classifies the skin. A regime of care (in particular, sun protection) is advised and this may include alphahydroxy acids, bleaching agents, and a recommendation for a prescription of Retin-A®.

Rhytid management is discussed. Microdermabrasion, chemical peels and intense pulse light (IPL) can be discussed too, if indicated. Information on cosmetic surgery (see Chapter 11) is given, particularly if it involves treatment of the presenting complaint, for example eyelid bags.

Laser nurse

A nurse can also be trained to remove hair effectively using a laser. This is often requested by older patients who have attended for the treatment of upper lip rhytids.

Many patients with sun damaged skin want their facial telangiectasia and 'age spots' removed. In many countries, a qualified nurse can treat these under medical supervision.

In the author's clinic, a Gentlelase Alexandrite™ laser (Candela™) is used for hair removal, and a KTP Yag laser for telangectasia.

All patient should be examined by a doctor and treated with an initial test patch.

Laser safety

It goes without saying that safety is paramount. All staff involved in laser treatment should have attended a laser safety course – run by a suitably qualified professional body, a university or a laser company – and be aware of laser safety issues. The laser room must be adequate for its purpose, with signal lights above the door to show when the laser is in use, and non-reflective surfaces. Specific laser requirements must be adhered to. Information on laser safety guidelines and on compliance with health and safety legislation is available from national departments of health, and from laser companies.

Fillers

A skilled nurse can be trained to administer submucosal anesthesia before lip treatment. In the author's clinic, nurse practitioners are allowed to inject fillers and submucosal anesthesia (though not nerve blocks) and this has greatly improved the service to patients. All injections are given with a doctor on the premises.

Bibliography

Ascher B, Klap P, Marion M-H, et al. La toxine botulique dans le traitement de rides fronto-glabellaires et de la région orbitaire. [Botulinum toxin in the treatment of frontoglabellar and periorbital wrinkles. An initial study.] Ann Chir Plast Esthet 1995;40:67–76.

Black JD, Dolly JO. Interaction of 125I-labelled botulinum neurotoxins with nerve terminals. I. Ultrastructural autoradiographic localization and quantitation of distinct membrane acceptors for types A and B on motor nerves. J Cell Biol 1986;103:521–34.

Blitzer A, Binder WJ, Aviv JE, et al. The management of hyper-functional facial lines with botulinum toxin. Arch Otolaryngol Head Neck Surg 1997;123:389–92.

Blitzer A, Brin MF, Keen MF, et al. Botulinum toxin for the treatment of hyperfunctional lines of the face. Arch Otolaryngol Head Neck Surg 1993;119:1018–22.

Borodic GE, Cheney M, McKenna M. Contralateral injections of botulinum A toxin for the treatment of hemifacial spasm to achieve increased facial symmetry. Plast Reconstr Surg 1992;90:972–9.

Borodic GE, Cozzolino D. Blepharospasm and its treatment, with emphasis on the use of botulinum toxin. Plast Reconstr Surg 1989;83:546–54.

Borodic G, Johnson E, Goodnough M, Schantz E. Botulinum toxin therapy, immunologic resistance, and problems with available materials. Neurology 1996;46:26–9.

Borodic GE, Joseph M, Fay L, Cozzolino D, Ferrante RJ. Botulinum A toxin for the treatment of spasmodic torticollis: dysphagia and regional toxin spread. Head Neck 1990;12:392–99.

Brandt FS, Bellman B. Cosmetic use of botulinum A exotoxin for aging neck. Dermatol Surg. 1998;24:1232–4.

Bushara KO, Park DM, Jones JC, Schutta HS. Botulinum toxin – a possible new treatment for axillary hyperhidrosis. Clin Exp J Dermatol 1996;21:276–8.

Carruthers A, Carruthers J. The treatment of glabellar furrows with botulinum A exotoxin. J Dermatol Surg Oncol 1990;16:83.

Carruthers A, Carruthers JDA. The use of botulinum toxin to treat glabellar frown lines and other facial wrinkles. Cosmet Dermatol 1994;7:11–5.

Carruthers A, Carruthers J. Aesthetic indications for botulinum toxin injections. Plast Reconstr Surg 1995;95:427–8.

Carruthers A, Carruthers J. History of the cosmetic use of botulinum A exotoxin. Dermatol Surg 1998;24:1168–70.

Carruthers A, Carruthers J. Cosmetic uses of Botulinum A exotoxin. In: James WD, Cockerell CJ, Dzubow LM, et al, eds. Advances in Dermatology. Chicago: Mosby-Yearbook, 1997:325–48.

Carruthers A, Kiene K, Carruthers J. Botulinum A exotoxin use in clinical dermatology. J Am Acad Dermatol 1996;34:788–97.

Carruthers J, Carruthers A. Treatment of glabellar frown lines with C. Botulinum exotoxin. J Dermatol Surg Oncol 1992;18:17–21.

Carruthers J, Carruthers A. The adjunctive usage of botulinum toxin. Dermatol Surg 1998;24:1244–7.

Carruthers J, Carruthers JA. Botulinum toxin use for glabellar wrinkles. Presented at the annual meeting of the American Society for Dermatologic Surgery. Orlando Florida, March 13–17, 1991.

Carter SR, Seiff SR. Cosmetic botulinum toxin injections. Int Ophthalmol Clin 1997;37:69–79.

Drobik C, Laskawi R. Frey's syndrome: treatment with botulinum toxin. Acta Otolaryngol (Stockh) 1995;115:459–61.

Dutton JJ, Buckley EG. Long-term results and complications of botulinum A toxin in the treatment of blepharospasm. Ophthalmology 1988;95:1529–34.

Foster JA, Barnhorst D, Papay F, et al. The use of Botulinum A toxin to ameliorate facial kinetic frown lines. Ophthalmology 1996;103:618–22.

Foster JA, Wulc AE. Cosmetic use of botulinum toxin. Facial Plast Surg Clin North Am 1998;6:79–85.

Frueh BR, Felt DP, Wojno TH, Musch DC. Treatment of blepharospasm with botulinum toxin. A preliminary report. Arch Ophthalmol 1984;102:1464–8.

Garcia A, Fulton JE. Cosmetic denervation of the muscles of facial expression with botulinum toxin. Dermatol Surg 1996;22:39–43.

Gartland MG, Hoffman HT. Crystalline Preparation of botulinum toxin A (Botox®): degradation in potency with storage. Arch Otolaryngol Head Neck Surg 1993;108:135–40.

Glogau RG. Botulinum A neurotoxin for axillary hyperhidrosis: no sweat BOTOX®. Dermatol Surg 1998;24:817–9.

Guyuron B, Huddleston SW. Aesthetic indication for botulinum toxin injection. Plast Reconstr Surg 1994;93:913–8.

Hankins CL, Strimling R, Rogers GS. Botulinum A toxin for glabellar wrinkles: dose and response. Dermatol Surg 1998;24:1181–3.

Hartman JP. Second batch of Botox® may be more potent than the first. Skin Allergy News 1998;29:1–7.

Heckmann M, Schaller M, Ceballos-Baumann A, Plewig G. Botulinum beyond wrinkles. Dermatol Surg 1997;23:1221–2.

Huang W, Foster JA, Rogachefsky AS. Pharmacology of botulinum toxin. J Am Acad Dermatol 2000; 43: 249–50.

Huilgol SC, Carruthers A, Carruthers JD. Raising eyebrows with botulinum toxin. Dermatol Surg 1999;25:373–5.

Jankovic J, Brin MF. Therapeutic uses of botulinum toxin. N Engl J Med 1991;324:1186–93.

Jankovic J, Hallett M, eds. Therapy with Botulinum Toxin. New York: Marcel Dekker, 1994.

Kalra HK, Magoon EH. Side effects of the use of botulinum A toxin for treatment of benign essential blepharospasm and hemifacial spasm. Ophthalmic Surg 1990;21:335–8.

Keen M, Blitzer A, Aviv J, et al. Botulinum toxin A for hyperkinetic facial lines: results of a double-blind, placebo-controlled study. Plast Reconstr Surg 1994;94:94–9.

Keen M, Kopelman J, Aviv JE, Binder W, Brin M, Blitzer A. Botulinum toxin A: a novel method to remove periorbital wrinkles. Facial Plast Surg 1994;10:141–6.

Klein AW. Cosmetic therapy with botulinum toxin: anecdotal memoirs. Dermatol Surg 1996;22:757–9.

Klein AW, Wexler P, Carruthers A, Carruthers JDA. Treatment of facial furrows and rhytids. Analysis and treatment of the ageing face. Dermatol Clin 1997;15:595–607.

Lange DH, et al. Distal effects of locally injected botulinum toxin: incidences and effects. Adv Neurology 1988;50:609.

Lowe N. Botulinum toxin type A for facial rejuvenation: United States and United Kingdom perspectives. Dermatol Surg 1998;24:1216–8.

Lowe, NJ, Maxwell A, Harper H. Botulinum A exotoxin for glabellar folds: a double-blind, placebo-controlled study with an electromyographic injection technique. J Am Acad Dermatol 1996;35:569–72.

Lowe N, Wieder J. Botulinum toxin for hyperkinetic facial lines: a placebo-controlled study. Cosmetic Derm 1995;8:46–9.

Maoriello JA Jr. Blepharospasm Meige's syndrome and hemifacial spasm: treatment with botulinum toxin. Neurology 1985;35:1499.

Matarasso SL, Carruthers A. Botulinum toxin: treatment for glabellar furrows. J Geriat Dermatol 1997;5:13–4.

Matsudo PK. Botulinum toxin for correction of fronto-glabella wrinkles: preliminary evaluation. Aesth Plast Surg 1996;20:439–41.

Moore P, ed. Handbook of Botulinum Toxin Treatment. Oxford: Blackwell Science, Ltd., 1995:16–27.

Naumann M, Flachenecker P, Brocker EB, Toyka KV, Reiners K. Botulinum toxin for palmar hyperhidrosis. Lancet 1997;349:252.

Naumann M, Zellner M, Toyka KV, Reiners K. Treatment of gustatory sweating with botulinum toxin. Ann Neurol 1997;42:973–5.

Naumann M, Hofmann U, Bergman I, Hamm H, Toyka KV, Reiners K. Focal Hyperhidrosis. Effective treatment with intracutaneous botulinum toxin. Arch Dermatol 1998;134:301–4.

Pitanguy I. Indications for treatment of frontal and glabellar wrinkles in an analysis of 3,404 consecutive cases of rhytidectomy. Plast Reconstr Surg 1981;67:157–68.

Pribitkin EA, Greco TM, Goode RL, Keane WM. Patient selection in the treatment of glabellar wrinkles with botulinum toxin type A injection. Arch Otolaryngol Head Neck Surg 1997;123:321–6.

Schnider P, Binder M, Auff A, Kittler H, Berger T, Wolf K. Double-blind trial of botulinum A toxin for the treatment of focal hyperhidrosis of the palms. Br J Dermatol 1997;136:548–52.

Schnider P, Binder M, Kittler H, Steinhoff N, Auff E. Use of botulinum toxin. Lancet 1997;349:953.

Scott AB. Botulinum toxin injection into extraocular muscles as an alternative to strabismus surgery. Ophthalmology 1980;87:1044–9.

Scott AB, Rosenbaum A, Collins CC. Pharmacologic weakening of extraocular muscles. Invest Ophthalmol 1973;12:924–7.

Shelley WB, Talanin NY, Shelley ED. Botulinum toxin therapy for palmer hyperhidrosis. J Am Acad Dermatol 1998;38:227–9.

Shorr N, Seiff SR, Kopelman J. The use of botulinum toxin in blepharospasm. Am J Ophthalmol 1985;99:542–6.

Simpson LL. Kinetic studies on interaction between botulinum toxin type A and the cholinergic neuromuscular junction. J Pharmacol Exp Ther 1980;212:16–21.

Simpson LL. The origin, structure, and pharmacological activity of botulinum toxin. Pharmacol Rev 1981;33:155–88.

Simpson LL, Dasgupta BR. Botulinum neurotoxin type E: studies on mechanism of action and on structure–activity relationships. J Pharmacol Exp Ther 1983;224:135–40.

Strimling RB, Rogers GS. Correct toxin dose, multiple site injection: keys to erasing frown lines. Dermatol News 1997;18:8.

Tsoy EA, Buckley EG, Dutton JJ. Treatment of blepharospasm with botulinum toxin. Am J Ophthal 1985;99:176–9.

Wieder JM, Moy RL. Understanding botulinum toxin: surgical anatomy of the frown, forehead, and periocular region. Dermatol Surg 1998;24:1172–4.

Zide BM, Jelks GW. Surgical Anatomy of the Orbit. Philadelphia: Lippincott, Williams and Wilkins, 1985.

Index